ML
956.7044 M928 WITHDRAWN
Munson, Peter J., 1975-
Iraq in transition : the legacy of

IRAQ in Transition

RELATED TITLES FROM POTOMAC BOOKS

Losing the Golden Hour: An Insider's View of Iraq's Reconstruction
—James Stephenson

Iraq and the Evolution of American Strategy
—Steven Metz

After the Taliban: Nation-Building in Afghanistan
—Amb. James F. Dobbins

IRAQ in Transition

The Legacy of Dictatorship and the Prospects for Democracy

Peter J. Munson

Foreword by Steven Metz

Potomac Books, Inc.
Washington, D.C.

Copyright © 2009 by Peter J. Munson

Published in the United States by Potomac Books, Inc. All rights reserved. No part of this book may be reproduced in any manner whatsoever without written permission from the publisher, except in the case of brief quotations embodied in critical articles and reviews.

The views expressed herein are those of the author and do not reflect the official policy or position of the Marine Corps, the Department of Defense, or the U.S. government.

Library of Congress Cataloging-in-Publication Data
Munson, Peter J., 1975-
 Iraq in transition : the legacy of dictatorship and the prospects for democracy / Peter J. Munson ; foreword by Steven Metz. — 1st ed.
   p. cm.
 Includes bibliographical references and index.
 ISBN 978-1-59797-300-7 (hardcover : alk. paper)
 1. Iraq—Politics and government—2003- 2. Iraq—History—2003- 3. Islam and politics—Iraq. 4. Hussein, Saddam, 1937-2006—Influence. 5. Democratization—Iraq. 6. Insurgency—Iraq. 7. Postwar reconstruction—Iraq. 8. Iraq War, 2003- I. Title.
 DS79.769.M89 2009
 956.7044'3—dc22
                                        2008047623

Printed in the United States of America on acid-free paper that meets the American National Standards Institute Z39-48 Standard.

Potomac Books, Inc.
22841 Quicksilver Drive
Dulles, Virginia 20166

First Edition

10 9 8 7 6 5 4 3 2 1

I have not lived so long without having had the experience of many wars, and I see those among you of the same age as myself, who will not fall into the common misfortune of longing for war from inexperience or from a belief in its advantage and its safety. . . . Let us never be elated by the fatal hope of the war being quickly ended by the devastation of their lands. I fear rather that we may leave it as a legacy to our children.

—Archidamus, Spartan king, 432 BC

Kind-hearted people might of course think there was some ingenious way to disarm or defeat an enemy without too much bloodshed, and might imagine this is the true goal of the art of war. Pleasant as it sounds, it is a fallacy.

—Carl von Clausewitz, Prussian strategist, ca. 1830

The first lesson the student of international politics must learn and never forget is that the complexities of international affairs make simple solutions and trustworthy prophecies impossible.

—Hans Morgenthau, professor of international relations

Contents

Foreword *by Steven Metz*	ix
Acknowledgements	xiii
1. Introduction	1
2. A Crushing Legacy: The Roots of Chaos	11
Iraq's Modern History	16
The Seeds of Downfall	35
The Rise of the Tribes	42
Islam	46
The Threads of Transition	50
3. Iraq's Collapse and the Crisis of Governance	53
Collapse and Crisis	58
The Making of a Vacuum	62
Governance and Security	78
4. The Rise of Shi'a Power in Iraq	81
Shi'a Identity and Post-Invasion Organization	86
5. Setting the Stage for Insurgency:	
The Sunni Heartland and the Ba'ath Regime	109
The Regime's Preparation for War and Internal Defense	116
Themes of Sunni Discontent	125
6. The Widening Insurgencies: 2003–2007	135
The Power of Islam	138

Tying the Network Together: Funding and Support	150
Sunni Politics and the Way Ahead	156
7. Building a New Order	**161**
Staking Out the Official Political Process	170
Elections in the New Iraq: Obstacles and Outcomes	177
The Constitution	182
The December 2005 Election and Iraq's Permanent Government	190
The Official Political Process at Work	194
8. Iraq Looks into the Abyss of Civil War	**199**
The Rise of Communal Identity	201
Taking the Gloves Off	203
9. Prospects for Stability, Prospects for Democracy	**211**
The Awakening	214
Shi'a Maneuvering and Broader Political Developments	219
Development from the Bottom Up	235
10. Whither Transition?	**241**
The Lessons of Iraqi Transition	244
The Broader Lessons	248
Looking for the Future in Our Past	253
Selected Bibliography	257
Notes	261
Index	315
About the Author	321

Foreword

The American intervention in Iraq was burdened with ignorance. While we were flush with facts gathered by technical means, there were immense gaps in our understanding of how Iraq's political, economic, and social systems functioned (or did not function). We possessed the chimera of knowledge but not its reality. Had the goal simply been to defeat Saddam Hussein's armed forces, reaching it would not have been a problem. But the United States sought much more—to turn Iraq into a stable democracy— and this demanded exactly the sort of knowledge we lacked.

The damage came quickly. Within days of the invasion we realized that we knew little about Saddam Hussein's irregular forces or how the Iraqi population would respond to American troops. We later found that we were wrong about Hussein's weapons of mass destruction program (which had been an important rationale for removing him from power). But most deeply— and most damagingly—we were ignorant of how badly Hussein's rule had brutalized Iraqi society and how Iraqis had learned to survive and function in a pathological environment. Unfortunately, this information was vitally important for guiding Iraq toward democracy. The United States thus intervened with lofty strategic objectives but without the knowledge to attain them. We operated in a psychological and cultural darkness.

There is an ongoing and often rancorous debate over where the fault lies. Should regional experts in the military and the intelligence and diplomatic communities be blamed? Or did senior Bush administration officials ignore what professionals had told them (or decide to not ask in the first place, knowing that the answers could undercut support for the invasion)? Whoever is culpable, "mistakes were made." Even officials who shaped the invasion (including former President Bush) now admit that. Ultimately, though, assigning blame is less important than learning from mistakes. This is the value of *Iraq in Transition*, where Maj Peter Munson provides a powerful and erudite explanation of what he calls "the strange ways of Iraqi politics," illuminating what Americans have learned in six torturous years and suggesting what we should have known from the beginning.

As Major Munson demonstrates, Saddam Hussein's rule and a decade of U.N. sanctions left Iraq wounded. Sycophancy and corruption were not only pervasive, they were the only avenues for personal advancement. The state was parasitic, existing to benefit those who controlled it (and their cronies) rather than to promote the public good. Those who were excluded from its largesse, particularly Iraq's Shiite majority and various smaller minorities, looked to sectarian-based organizations, tribes, and extended families to promote group interests and provide protection. Once the old regime had fallen, most of these groups armed themselves. Hussein had thus left Iraq without the basic skills needed by a democracy: a willingness to compromise, tolerance for the rights of others, respect for the law, and the ability to organize around shared interests. After all, it is not the individual desire for freedom that fuels democracy. It is the willingness to accept the freedom of others.

The problems did not end there. Iraq also suffered a pervasive lack of initiative. Under Hussein, to demonstrate initiative was to attract the attention of state security forces and often to die a grisly death. When sycophancy was not an option (as for most Shiites), passivity and secrecy were the keys to survival. Having been the victims of regime propaganda and disinformation, Iraqis were ill equipped to separate fact from fiction or resist the siren calls of foreign extremists. Iraq was a barren ground for open government and the peaceful resolution of conflict. By all standards of political and economic development, it had regressed under Hussein's rule and was less hospitable to democracy than it had been a half a century earlier.

The Bush administration, probably lured by the successful democratic transitions in Eastern Europe, Latin America, Sub-Saharan Africa, and the Pacific Rim during the last quarter of the twentieth century, believed that simply decapitating the Ba'athist beast in Iraq would pave the way for open governance. Munson describes a grim reality at diametric odds to this notion, tracing how Iraq's social, economic, and political pathologies led inextricably to violence, whether ideological, sectarian, criminal, or personal. That alone would be a valuable service to scholars and strategists. But Major Munson does not stop there, instead suggesting that the misunderstanding that imbued the invasion of Iraq was not case specific or even limited to the Bush administration. Iraq is simply one devastating case study of what he calls "our American failure to understand many of the societies that inhabit the world." Since U.S. strategy seeks to assist states in the transition to stable democracy, this misunderstanding can be debilitating.

The key question is whether America's misunderstanding of other cultures is inherent or can be remediated. An argument can be made that because the United States itself has a bewilderingly complex culture, Americans downplay its importance and thus are incapable of grasping the complexities of other, different cultures. Moreover, if Americans think seriously about the difficulty of helping a different culture build democracy, they may decide that it is not worth the effort. Knowledge can impede action. Had Americans understood in 2003 how complex and costly Iraq's transition would be, the Bush administration would have been hard-pressed to mobilize political support for it. But would that be a bad thing? Might a United States with a better understanding of the complexities of democratic transition be more judicious in where it becomes involved?

Ultimately, Americans must decide whether the *concept* of a guided transition to democracy is flawed or was simply mismanaged in Iraq. Major Munson is guardedly optimistic, suggesting that the transformation of Germany and Japan after World War II demonstrates that the United States can do it if properly organized, determined, and, most importantly, equipped with a sophisticated understanding of the transitioning state and the complexities of the process. I hope he is correct but remain skeptical. While Iraq certainly is better off than under Hussein, I question its ability to sustain what Americans would consider democracy and rule of law. To me, Iraq shows America's limitations when guiding a radically different culture toward a democratic future. The glass is at least half empty, perhaps more. Still, Major Munson makes a powerful argument to support his point and provides important clues to an important strategic puzzle. As the debate over America's role in the world evolves, we should all be thankful for his contribution. Here's hoping that he is right and I am wrong.

STEVEN METZ
U.S. ARMY WAR COLLEGE STRATEGIC STUDIES INSTITUTE
AUTHOR OF *IRAQ AND THE EVOLUTION OF AMERICAN STRATEGY*

Acknowledgements

This book would not have been possible without the assistance, guidance, and encouragement of a great number of people. Foremost, it is meant to be useful to those who are called to serve in Iraq or in other places like it in the future and those who have a hand in deciding to send them there, from voters to policymakers. I thank my friends and colleagues who provided their firsthand insight and experiences and pushed me to continue working toward my goal, particularly David Jupiter, Brad Fultz, John Tempone, and Scott Koltick. Dr. Vali Nasr provided simple yet incisive comments that guided my work in the right direction. I thank Drs. Donald Abenheim and Ken Hagan and James Russell at the Naval Postgraduate School for their support and encouragement. I am indebted to my editor, Hilary Claggett, whose belief in my work made this book a reality in the end.

Most important, I thank my children, Riley and Lauren, for their patience and interest in Daddy's book, and my wife, Wendi, for her faith, willingness to listen, and ability to put up with the idea of writing a book in my "spare time."

This book is dedicated to my friend, Maj Michael D. Martino, USMC, who was killed in action in an AH-1W Super Cobra over Ar Ramadi, Iraq, while supporting Marine ground units on November 2, 2005. May his sacrifice, and the sacrifices of all those who served, bled, and died there, be honored some day by a stable and peaceful Iraq.

1
Introduction

Nothing is more important for the future of Iraq than a clearheaded understanding of its past.[1]

—Kanan Makiya, Iraqi exile author, 1993

Nothing in Iraq has been anything but hard.[2]

—GEN David H. Petraeus, Commander of Coalition Forces in Iraq, September 15, 2008

A small island of green, Firdaus Square is located in the heart of Baghdad, only a few blocks from the banks of the Tigris River and directly across from Saddam Hussein's infamous Republican Palace. The two tallest buildings in Baghdad, the storied Palestine Hotel and the Sheraton, overlook the square and the grand Fourteenth of Ramadan Mosque that sits beside it. The square was once home to Iraq's unknown soldier monument, erected in 1959, though Saddam[3] had the earlier monument demolished in 1982 to make way for a monument to his own tragic cult of personality. While poor Shi'a lived in squalor only miles away in what was then known as Saddam City, Saddam erected a massive statue of himself, surrounded by an arc of columns engraved with his initials.

Firdaus means paradise in Arabic. Though the square did not represent paradise during the years of the Ba'ath regime, it was a fitting scene for the symbolic end of Saddam's reign. On April 9, 2003, the world watched as a U.S. military vehicle pulled Saddam's statue off its pedestal. Eerily reminiscent of the triumphal dismantling of the Berlin Wall, the fall of Saddam's statue, many hoped, would signify the beginning of Iraq's road to recovery. Unfortunately, true calm has not returned to Baghdad. Since the statue's fall, the square has been the scene of bombings and demonstrations and is often closed off by razor wire and strewn with wreckage. The proud hotels on the west side of the square are virtually empty, despite early hopes of an influx of foreign investors and tourists. On the east side of the square, worshipers at the Fourteenth of Ramadan Mosque, seeking solace from the ongoing strife, have often been forced to pray at home, afraid to venture out and tempt the militias and death squads. When U.S. Marines tore down Saddam's statue in 2003, many hoped that a paradise would spring up from underneath its ruins. Instead, Saddam's fall exposed the roots of chaos that bloomed into insurgency and sectarian strife and brought the country to the brink of civil war.

While the fall of Saddam's statue symbolized the end of a ruthless dictatorial regime, it also yielded the first glance at the legacies left behind: a social and political landscape radically reshaped by years of violent and corrupt rule. The society was atomized and cowed into inaction. Potential unifying leadership had been removed, and no group possessed a well-developed ideology or political program, leaving opportunistic politicians returning from exile to draw on ethnic and sectarian identities to create new constituencies. This landscape fueled violent political conflict and confounded attempts to establish a capable unified government. The conflict forced the American military out of its comfort zone of fighting high-technology twentieth-century conventional battle and introduced it to a confused twenty-first-century war against an unfamiliar enemy.

American forces liberating Iraq from Saddam Hussein's rule were told by senior military and civilian officials to expect a heroes' welcome and a swift return to the United States. Architects of the war against Saddam anticipated that all but the highest levels of the government would remain in place, easing transition to a new Iraqi leadership within a few months of the regime's fall. Instead, U.S. military commanders found that they had inherited a country devoid of government institutions and working infrastructure. Saddam's regime collapsed and governance at all levels ceased well before the occupiers handed down any edicts. Although military practitioners were steeped in the art of war, they were not linguistically or culturally prepared to work and communicate with their new Iraqi partners. Combat commanders became city managers, improvising their new role with little planning or guidance. The Coalition groped in the dark to address this alien task in a foreign land.

American policymakers understood little about the Iraq that existed outside the palaces and military bases of Saddam Hussein. The picture painted for them by trusted Iraqi exiles was dangerously out of date. Few in America recognized names such as Sadr or Sistani. Even fewer could speak the language of Iraq. Thus, lessons about Iraq's true nature were hard-won; their cost often coming in the form of human life as Western troops grappled with the local and sectarian powers that vied for control of Iraq. Military formations built to strike hard and fast had neither the manpower nor the training to police and govern the vast country. Iraq entered a crisis of governance that was extended by years of Coalition and Iraqi government missteps.

While the Coalition was ill prepared to step into this role, other powers were willing and able to take advantage of the windfall. The fragmented groups left behind by Saddam's social manipulation thrived, leading Iraq down a dangerous path toward the brink of civil war. In the latter years of Saddam's rule, the costs of an epic war with Iran, the failed invasion of Kuwait, and the ensuing international sanctions took their toll. Unable to maintain his crushing centralized rule, Saddam turned to tribes, key businessmen, security officials, criminal gangs, and even religious leaders for legitimacy and control of Iraq's periphery. He traded patronage and power for their unwavering loyalty. The power of these societal groups grew within a mafia-like network of crime, corruption, and violence. When the regime fell, Saddam fled and the government collapsed; the network of societal power groups remained, however.

In the summer of 2003, these groups thrived in the chaos, growing in strength even as the worst collaborators with the old regime were murdered or chased away. Because of the government's collapse, there was no one to maintain order, pay salaries, or provide basic services to the Iraqi people. Many citizens pinned their loyalties to the first organization that could fill this yawning vacuum. When the Coalition failed to step into the breach, Iraq's contentious societal powers, often shaped by cooperation with or opposition to Saddam's rule, proved capable. These groups won the loyalty of many Iraqis and eagerly highlighted Coalition shortfalls at the same time.

Tribes, religious networks, and local gangs provided a semblance of security and order, and their members began to promote their visions for Iraq's future. The ability of these groups to organize and act in the absence of any overarching leadership was critical. Instead of lining up behind nationwide institutions, many Iraqis followed their local mosque, their tribe, or other regional leaders who had stemmed the chaos and provide services in the days after the invasion. These smaller institutions, however, had narrow goals in mind. Taking hold of various powers of state, they started a trend of decentralization and factionalization of Iraq that has yet to be reversed.

In the crisis of governance following Saddam's demise, these local and sectarian groups flourished. With no government and few Coalition forces to oppose them, opportunists moved quickly to expand their power and consolidate control over their domains. In the Sunni areas, these groups turned to armed resistance against the occupying Coalition, which threatened their way of life and placed Shi'a exiles in power in Baghdad. Military and security experts of the former regime gave these rising forces training, weapons, and other assistance. Tribal groups and criminal gangs also asserted their power and presented obstacles to the establishment of a new order in Iraq. In the scramble for power, it became apparent that Sunni Iraq was factionalized and leaderless. While this prevented a unified uprising, it also meant that no single approach would be sufficient to stop the violence. Beneath the surface of Sunni resistance to occupation, a conflict simmered between tribal peasants and sheikhs, Islamic extremists and nationalists, and rural and urban Sunnis. These splits would eventually turn the resistance against itself, leading to an uneasy calm in Anbar Province in 2007 and 2008.

The lay of the land in Shi'a Iraq was different. Collaborators with the former regime were ousted, and the power of Shi'a religious institutions was evident soon after Saddam's demise. The old regime had come down harshly on the traditional religious establishment because it was seen as a threat to Saddam, especially after the 1991 uprisings prompted by the Gulf War. While the clerical hierarchy was weakened, the local clerics presiding over Iraq's disenfranchised urban poor were strong and often radical. Therefore, when Shi'a clerics reasserted their power, it was not with one voice, but several. Although the Shi'a largely followed the counsel of their foremost religious leader, Ayatollah Ali al-Sistani, and avoided open conflict with the Coalition and the Sunnis, radical followers of Muqtada al-Sadr and others like him were not afraid of using violence and thuggery to pursue their goals. Other Shi'a groups, such as the powerful Supreme Council for the Islamic Revolution in Iraq (SCIRI), amassed powerful militias as well, guarding against the day when they would need to use them to have their way. Though the disunity of Shi'a factions was overshadowed early on by the desire to make good on their demographic power in forming the new government, as events grew increasingly violent, rifts widened among the various groups, spilling over into Shi'a-on-Shi'a battles.

Of all Iraq's groups, the Kurds emerged from Saddam's grasp with the greatest cohesion. Although two Kurdish factions warred in the past, a decade of autonomous rule created relatively strong leadership and institutions in the north, and Kurds set about preserving their special status. Although the Kurdish north was the least violent region after Saddam's fall, the thorny issues of Kirkuk and the borders of Kurdish territory in Iraq have yet to run their course.

In spite of the chaos, Iraqi leaders and their Coalition partners pushed forward an ambitious political process. The process resulted in a permanent constitution and a freely elected government, yet many flaws along the way fed sectarian and other divisions in Iraq. Initial political activity often played on the ethno-sectarian fault lines dividing Iraq's three major communities—the Shi'a, the Sunni, and the Kurds—to mobilize voters. Organization along sectarian lines would drive the deterioration of sectarian relations to the point of open violence. These major divides concealed further rifts within each group, all of which fostered a disunity that paralyzed governance and reconciliation attempts.

The diffusion of Iraq's state powers that occurred with the collapse of the old regime proved difficult to reverse. Furthermore, many political bosses had no desire to return these powers to the central government. As a result, the official political process has yet to solve many delicate issues and has failed to produce a government capable of rebuilding trust and effecting reconciliation. Political organization within and across sectarian lines must move beyond fragile, temporary coalitions and a few laws of questionable utility. Even though the progress made in 2007 and 2008 is remarkable, it has yet to grow real roots. Iraq is still inching back from a precipice that may give way at any moment.

In the five years after the lightning drive to Baghdad, the contours of the struggle changed several times, although violent conflict remained a daily occurrence even with a large occupation force in the country. Despite the initial belief of some American officials that setting Iraq back on its feet would be a cakewalk, the Coalition has been forced to come to grips with the often-changing nature of politics and violence. A Sunni insurgency rapidly bloomed and raged on for years. By 2006, the insurgency itself was overcome by the expanding ethno-sectarian conflict that threatened to bring Iraq into outright civil war. Appraisals of the situation in Iraq were almost universally grim, even, as was later disclosed, behind the closed doors of the White House.

Though catastrophe loomed, a number of events combined to produce a remarkable turnaround in 2007. New leadership, more troops, and a new strategy allowed the Coalition to blanket key cities with troops and begin to arrest the spiraling sectarian violence. The troop surge also gave much-needed breathing room to a Sunni tribal rising that had been building against the most extreme insurgent groups since 2005. This Awakening of the tribes, along with a concentrated American campaign in Anbar, dramatically lowered violence in the lawless west. Finally, faced with the threat of American troops on one side and clashes with other Shi'a powers on the other, Muqtada al-Sadr called for a series of truces that greatly defused the situation in Baghdad and the south.

By the fall of 2008, the Sunni insurgency had apparently been broken, Baghdad's shops were reopening, refugees were returning, and a small number of American troops were cautiously withdrawn. Iraqi and American voices alike began calling for greater troop withdrawals, based not on defeat, but on success, if not victory. Discussions turned to an endgame that did not invoke the images of America's ignominious evacuation of Saigon in 1975. The endgame in Iraq, though, is not an American game. All along, narratives in the West have pigeonholed Iraqis as bit players or legions of similarly costumed extras and focused almost exclusively on American officials, soldiers, and policies. At no time is this more dangerous than in the "endgame," when real security successes in Iraq must be parlayed into Iraqi political development and reconciliation. The endgame is an Iraqi game played by a cast of characters that do not fit easily into the roles classified by conventional wisdom. It will be a subtle game in which rules and logic will often be foreign to Americans. It may be a game that stabilizes Iraq. It may degenerate into a winner-takes-all catastrophe that wipes out the gains won in the past five years at the cost of countless Coalition and Iraqi lives. To understand the shapes this endgame may take, one must focus on the Iraq that emerged from decades of dictatorship in 2003.

Iraq sits atop an ancient confluence of civilizations whose accumulated legacies still give shape to modern life. Parts have been home to Arab, Persian, Turkic, and Kurdish civilizations. Iraq has been crossed by conquerors and absorbed by empires. It has seen periods of greatness, too. In the eighth century AD, the Caliph Abu Ja'far al-Mansur, sketched the design for his new capital, Baghdad, with a sword on the banks of the Tigris River. The city, known in Mansur's time as "Medina al-Salam" (the City of Peace) grew after a few decades to become second only to Constantinople, the capital of the Roman Empire.[4] Yet, Iraq also has many troubled legacies. While many of Iraq's pathologies result from the recent manipulations of Saddam's regime, other trends reach back to the Ottoman Empire and even the dawn of Islam nearly fourteen centuries ago. Iraq cannot be understood at a glance. Transition in Iraq, in fact, requires not more laws and votes, but change in society, realignment of loyalties, and rebuilding of trust. Iraq is undergoing an epochal realignment of social and political loyalties. Democratic and rational-legal concepts are vying with religious, familial, and tribal norms and organizations, causing no small degree of dislocation and upheaval. To understand this time of change, one must look back at the social, political, and economic landscape that preceded it.

The intent of this book is to describe how the legacies of Saddam Hussein's rule and the longer sweep of history in Iraq produced the conditions that fueled insurgency, sectarian warfare, and intra-sectarian political maneuvering and violence. The growing body of publications on Iraq has omitted a crucial part of the story of Iraq's transition from Ba'ath rule. Many have provided excellent narrative accounts of military actions, reconstruction efforts, insurgent groups, and foreign policy, yet these works have failed to provide a broader understanding of Iraq's complex reaction to transition.

A number of questions will guide the exploration of this Iraqi reaction. What was the social and political landscape in the Iraq of 2003 that provided the foundation for post-invasion Iraq? What led to the almost complete collapse of Iraqi governance in the wake of invasion, and what was its effect on the various social power groups? How did the appearance of armed groups, from militias to insurgents, fit into the context of the crisis of governance and the official political process? How did the official political process unfold and how did this process, along with the high levels of violence, contribute to the rise of sectarianism and other divisions between Iraqi groups? Most importantly, what is the current state of these factors, and what policies can guide Iraq toward the best of its many possible futures? These questions demand an investigation of the recent history and shape of Iraqi polity and society. The current events in Iraq are not a spontaneous accident, but are the product of motivations and organizations etched into Iraq by decades of harsh rule. This is not to say that events in Iraq were entirely predestined. The legacy of the old regime provided a set of conditions that interacted with policies and events since the invasion to produce the outcomes seen today. It is imperative that policymakers understand the givens in the situation, the legacies of former circumstances, so that they may design policies that will interact with these conditions to produce a desirable outcome.

Even though Iraq has a constitution and a democratically elected parliament, its transition to democracy will not be complete any time in the near future. The year 2009 holds several critical mile posts on the path to transition, with provincial elections held in January and the much more critical parliamentary elections scheduled later in the year. These will provide the first chance for a peaceful, democratic transfer of power at both the local and national level and could produce peaceful and meaningful political change, marking a major step toward true democracy in Iraq. Even so, a great deal of work will remain. The fact that Kurdish politicians were fearful of the central government's attempt to acquire F-16 aircraft in 2008 indicates the level of mistrust that is yet to be overcome. Alternatively, the elections could be marred by violence or rendered meaningless by illegal manipulations on the part of the country's power brokers. Such outcomes would jaundice the already fragile reputation of the political process.

In the long term, Iraq may build the trust, reconciliation, and social, civil, and legal institutions required to support democracy, yet there are countless points at which the process of transition could be derailed. While transition to democracy requires years of accumulated progress, only one short series of events could send Iraq down the path of illiberal majoritarian rule, dictatorship, civil war, or state collapse. Each of these outcomes has regional implications that must be considered before action is taken. Partition of the country, a move opposed by most Iraqis, leaves Sunnis with barren desert devoid of resources. Turkish officials, fearful that an independent Iraqi Kurdistan would encourage violent separatism in Turkey's Kurdish southwest, have strongly warned Iraqi Kurds against secession from Iraq. Shi'a majoritarian dominance has been decried by other Sunni governments who may provide material aid to Sunni insurgents should the United States pull out.

Such dire scenarios seem less likely in 2009 than they did only a year ago. Markers of progress abound. Indicators of violence dropped precipitously in 2008 to the lowest levels since the invasion. Parliamentary blocs have shown some fluidity and are beginning to align on issue over sect. Some key legislation has been passed, opening the way for elections. A degree of normality has returned to the streets and markets of Iraqi cities. Yet, problems and pitfalls loom. Despite the remarkable improvement in security, absolute levels of violence remain high by any measure and claim nearly five hundred civilian Iraqi lives a month in addition to a monthly toll of nearly one hundred Iraqi police and soldiers. Enemy-initiated attacks still approach two hundred per week. The Sons of Iraq, local groups paid by the United States to keep vigil over their neighborhoods, are in the process of being transferred to Iraqi government control. Although the fate of roughly 100,000 Sons, many of whom are former insurgents, is unclear, most will likely be cashiered back into unemployment in the coming months. While political development progresses, it has never been capable of moving at the pace hoped for in the West. Resolution of many thorny issues continues to be delayed as parliamentarians push constitutional reform, oil sector regulation, and a permanent solution for the contested city of Kirkuk into the future. All of these issues must be solved peacefully in order for Iraq to march toward democracy. Peaceful solutions are far from assured on any of these issues, but the power to solve—or bungle—is ever more concentrated in Iraqi hands.

America and its foreign-policy institution stand Janus-faced astride a new era. A part desires a return to the era of a bipolar world with concrete threats and conventional formations it may devastate with its peerless military. Another part realizes that the unconventional and poorly understood challenges of a multipolar world must be faced. No portion of America is more conflicted than a military trained for big-formation battles, but faced with irregular threats and complex security and stability operations. To be prepared for the challenges of this and future conflicts and to lead a world characterized by changing political organization, the United States must achieve a deeper understanding of socio-cultural, economic, and political forces.

Because no country can go from dictatorship to democracy overnight, especially not one subject to the sort of historical legacies found in Iraq, Iraq could very easily slip back into authoritarianism or even state failure over the short term. Democracy, if reached, is a distant prospect. It will take years to build the infrastructure, institutions, and trust required to sustain a peaceful democratic mechanism for the transfer of power in Iraq.

Iraq will not be the last case of transition to face the world. Policymakers will undoubtedly shy away from embarking on any ambitious project that remotely smells of Iraq in the near term, yet they may have no choice but to shepherd transition again. States will fail, regimes will collapse, and regions will break away. In many of these cases, regional or international powers will have no choice but to become involved in the complex dirty work that is nation-building. The military and political leaders and the officials responsible for the details of such missions will once again have to learn the minutiae of an alien culture, its social structure, and the political and economic drivers of human interaction.

Nation-building, which paves the way for transition, is much more complex than building roads, painting schools, and digging wells. Often, a country's entire infrastructure will have to be rebuilt, all the while having to defend against the opportunists who seek to perpetuate chaos. At the same time, the country's people must be taught to respect, maintain, and share resources and public goods. Laws must be written, yet without the ability to enforce them and the growth of respect for them, they mean little. Building the infrastructure and securing it takes time, surely, but the real challenge is in preparing a people to use it wisely, share it, and respect the rules that govern it. Without an understanding of the legacy of the past, such an incredibly hard endeavor is doomed to failure.

2
A Crushing Legacy: The Roots of Chaos

Thirty years of tyranny do terrible things to a people: It breeds a culture of dependency; it breaks the spirit of civic responsibility; it forces people to fall back upon tight-knit familial, ideological or sectarian groups for safety and support. . . . Freedom, democracy and rights are not magic words.[1]
—John Agresto, CPA Senior Advisor for Higher Education, November 17, 2003

My greatest fear is that the Iraqis can't put the past behind them. We liberated them from thirty-five years of tyranny. We can't liberate them from the fears and prejudices that grew up in the last thirty-five years. They have to do that themselves.[2]
—Gen. George Casey, Commander of Coalition Forces in Iraq, February 10, 2007

Though Saddam Hussein shaped much of the thirty-five years of Iraqi history prior to the 2003 invasion and his shadow will fall darkly over the next several decades, his execution came secretly in a clandestine location in Baghdad while most of his former subjects slept. Hussein met his ignominious end before dawn on December 30, 2006, when he was hanged until death, carrying out the sentence handed down by an Iraqi court for the murder of 148 Shi'a residents of the town of Dujail. Three and a half years earlier, American soldiers had placed the noose around the neck of Saddam's statue in Firdaus Square. Now, on the cold December morning, Saddam's executioners were Iraqi Shi'a.

In the early hours that Saturday, the former dictator was flown by helicopter from his cell in Camp Cropper, a Coalition facility for high-level detainees near Baghdad International Airport, to Camp Justice in the Khadhimiya area of northern Baghdad. The facility had formerly been a headquarters of the Istikhbarat, Saddam's feared intelligence organization. It was now the abode of the Facilities Protection Service, or, in the eyes of Iraq's Sunnis, the new warren of the Shi'a death squads.

Attired in a black coat against the chilly air of the Baghdad winter and with his hands bound behind his back by plastic cuffs, Saddam was led into a room adjacent to the gallows. The chief judge of the trial, Muneer Hadad, read out the judgment amid interruptions and shouts from Saddam; then the condemned was given time to pray with a Sunni religious leader before his demise. Saddam clung tightly to a green, leather-bound Koran, which he asked the chief prosecutor Munqath al-Fer'aoun to give to members of his family.

Just before Saddam was walked to the gallows, the representative of Ayatollah Ali al-Sistani asked him if he was afraid of his coming death. Saddam responded, "I am courageous and I am not afraid of death. I chose this way." He then shouted, "Long live the people of Iraq. Long live the *mujahidun* [holy warriors]. Long live the nation. Death to America and Iran." Saddam showed no remorse and requested no quarter. The convicted killer walked outside and climbed the steps to the gallows under his own power.

The execution itself was attended by fourteen government and political personalities, including Prime Minister Nouri al-Maliki, his security advisor Mowaffaq al-Rub'aie, Minister of Justice Hashim al-Shibli, chief prosecutor Munqath al-Fer'aoun, judge Muneer Hadad, Abd al-Aziz al-Hakim (leader of the Shi'a Supreme Council for the Islamic Revolution in Iraq), and a representative of Ayatollah Ali al-Sistani. The only non-Shi'a in attendance was an unnamed Kurdish representative. While a Sunni religious leader prayed with Saddam in an antechamber prior to the execution, no Sunni leader agreed to attend the execution. Likewise, Shi'a leader Muqtada al-Sadr refused to send a representative.

The proceedings were captured strangely on a cell phone video that quickly made its way around the world on the Internet. The moments leading up to his execution were a bizarre encapsulation of how the political order in Iraq had been turned upside down over the preceding three years. The Shi'a guards with their thick southern accents offered Saddam a black hood, which he refused. He chose instead to go to his death with his eyes open. Standing atop the scaffolding as the hooded executioners placed the noose around his neck, Saddam began a prayer. "Peace be upon Mohammed and his holy family." Chants arose, adding "supporting his son Muqtada, Muqtada, Muqtada." Saddam turned his head toward the voices in disbelief, "Muqtada?"

In a striking turn of fortunes, Iraq's former Sunni dictator was to be executed by supporters of the upstart Shi'a cleric, Muqtada al-Sadr, son of the cleric Mohammed Sadiq al-Sadr whose assassination Saddam is widely believed to have ordered. Then came the cry, "Long live Mohammed Baqir al-Sadr," Muqtada's uncle, a prominent Shi'a cleric whom Saddam's henchmen tortured and executed in 1980. Hussein and the men traded insults before a lone call for calm and dignity. As the room became quiet once again, Saddam began reciting the *shahada*: "There is no god but God and Mohammed is His messenger." The crash of the trapdoor interrupted a second recitation and Saddam dropped to his death. Amid the shouts and confusion, one can make out the proclamation: "The tyrant has fallen, may the curse of God be upon him." The witnesses filed out, leaving the lifeless body hanging in the noose for as many as ten minutes. When Saddam was lowered from the rope and taken through the hall where the witnesses were gathered, bystanders reportedly spit on his body.[3]

Although the sentence for his killing of 148 Iraqis had been carried out, history will judge Saddam as directly responsible for the deaths of thousands more. His reign over Iraq reshaped the country and its people and left a lasting legacy. Without an understanding of this legacy, it is impossible to understand Saddam's bizarre end and the significance of Iraqi reactions to the event, for all of these are products of Saddam's brutal rise to power and the violent stranglehold he maintained on the nation for more than twenty years.

As reports of Saddam's execution came in, expert commentary was accompanied by the replay of the fall of Saddam's statue in Firdaus Square. Watching it replayed three and a half years on, I noticed something in the video that I had missed before. As Saddam's image slowly fell to the ground with its arm oddly outstretched, the crowd's reaction was not uniform. The Iraqis nearest the statue rejoiced. They lifted their arms to the skies as they danced feverishly and jumped up and down on the dictator's bronzed body. Farther from the center, however, many of the Iraqi witnesses stood motionless. They showed no reaction, no emotion when the statue tumbled. They looked on with arms crossed over their chest as the others rejoiced. Not everyone reveled in Saddam's fall. Some Iraqis were beholden to the regime and the order that Saddam had established in Iraq. Others simply were skeptical that the American-led invasion would deliver all that it promised. Still others feared the unknown, the coming chaos, or the specter of a new Iraq that would head in a direction vastly different from what they wanted.

When Saddam was executed, it was reported that witnesses danced around his body, but again the reaction was mixed. Divisions between Iraqis had grown immensely in the years since the events in Firdaus Square. Though Shi'a towns reverberated with celebratory gunfire and joyous chants, the reaction in many Sunni areas was subdued and defenses of Saddam could be heard, and have been even years after his regime's demise. Bombings struck Shi'a neighborhoods and towns throughout that day, likely in response to what was seen by Sunnis as a sectarian execution. Although his rule had ended and the feared tyrant had been captured and executed in the pre-dawn hours of December 30, 2006, his crushing legacy has not yet been erased from Iraq. The roots of the chaos that has dominated Iraq since April 2003 sprung from the lasting effects of Saddam's tyrannical rule that reshaped Iraq and will haunt it for years to come.

Across the Tigris River from Saddam's infamous statue in Firdaus Square sat the Republican Palace. The imposing palace complex symbolized Saddam's reign and dominated the best real estate along the Tigris River. Throughout the country, Saddam's palaces sat as shining monuments that demonstrated the power of the regime and its ability to appropriate choice tracts of land for its use. The ever-growing number of palaces also reflected Saddam's growing fear of his own people. He rarely spent more than a night in the same palace. Once atop a wave of popular support, fueled by swelling oil revenues and gleaming new public works projects in the 1970s, the regime presided over misery in its later years.

Baghdadis once were able to walk the banks of the Tigris, stopping at popular restaurants on Abu Nawas Street where freshly caught fish could be picked live from special basins, then cooked and enjoyed in the comfortable evening air. They relaxed during weekend evenings in tents and modest resorts along the river in the city center. Saddam's regime, however, put a chill on Baghdad's nightlife, and many areas were closed to the public. Baghdadis hoped that their city would return to its full glory once the hated leader was deposed. Iraqis wanted the lofty palaces given back to them, along with their vast swathes of prime real estate. The palaces were not the only problem, however. Infrastructure was ruined. Great portions of the population were impoverished, some even radicalized. Divisions between the country's many ethnic and sectarian groups were barely hidden under the surface of the Iraqi national identity, ripe for political exploitation. State and society were clearly damaged, yet the pervasive nature of this damage was covered up by an opaque government, allowing optimists and exiles to predict a swift return to stability. The ruined and alien landscape would prove to be difficult terrain for the Coalition's plans of creating a new order in Iraq.

Following on the heels of the invasion, Coalition military and political leaders ensconced themselves in Iraq's palaces. These large, well-placed, and well-protected compounds made perfect sense for use as temporary headquarters that would be soon turned over to a new Iraqi government. In fact, the Coalition never planned for the Republican Palace to be its headquarters. After the idea of working from a hotel was rejected on security grounds, planners selected a smaller, less symbolic palace down the river from Saddam's grand Republican Palace. When they arrived in Baghdad, however, they found that the selected building had been destroyed during the aerial bombardment of regime targets. The Republican Palace, though, still stood tall and ready for the Coalition to move in.[4] Coalition leaders saw a perfect structure that could be controlled and isolated from the threat of regime fanatics fighting on sporadically in the days after Saddam's fall. What they did not see, however, was the viewpoint of the Iraqis who were hoping to walk freely through their cities once again. Many of these Iraqis would soon come to view the Coalition as a new authoritarian leadership, tucked safely away from the population and handing down edicts from afar.

The Coalition Provisional Authority (CPA) entrenched itself in the Republican Palace and, out of necessity, set up a heavily fortified area of exclusion that would come to be known as the Green Zone. Most Iraqis could not enter the Green Zone, just as most Americans could not exit because of the threats outside its walls. CPA staffers and military officers in the Green Zone could only see the tops of the Sheraton and Palestine Hotels over the high blast walls that protected them. Although they were only miles away, they would never see these buildings up close during their time in Iraq. From across the river on Saadoun Street near Firdaus Square, Iraqis sweltering without electricity in the early evening heat needed only to look across the waters of the Tigris to see that the Green Zone was awash in lights, reminding them of their continued plight.

Saddam's rule has left many legacies. Scars in Iraq run deep on both the infrastructure and the human material that makes up state and society. Many of these legacies were unknown to the liberating Coalition. Some were unwittingly exacerbated by Coalition actions, others by the rise of powers hidden under Saddam's iron-fisted rule. To understand the complex landscape that has faced the military intervention in Iraq, it is necessary to examine the legacies that Saddam's rule created.

Iraq's modern history feeds into three major threads of Iraqi transition. The collapse of Iraq's government in 2003 stemmed from a historical weakening of the Iraqi state in the latter decades of the twentieth century and set the new Iraq up for the endemic crisis of governance—the first theme of Iraqi transition. Amid this crisis, the Coalition and its Iraqi partners attempted to start a new official political process, marking the second thread of transition that will be followed throughout the book. This process was plagued by historical tensions and conflicting claims among Iraq's major ethno-sectarian communities.

The rise of narrow groups and their armed wings is the final important thread to be considered. Prior to the Baʻath Party's complete domination of the political sphere, Iraqi nationalists and pan-Arabists competed for dominance on the Iraqi political scene. Iraqi nationalists emphasized an inclusive Iraqi identity that embraced Sunni, Shiʻa, and Kurds, while pan-Arabists tied into the wave of Arab nationalism that was sweeping the Arab world, especially after Gamal ʻAbd al-Nasser's rise to power in Egypt in 1952. Although the Baʻath Party was a major proponent of Arab nationalism, the pan-Arab political strain in Iraq quickly assumed an air of Sunni exclusivism. Saddam Hussein greatly narrowed the scope of this political movement until it was reduced to a cult of personality based on him alone. With the collapse of the Baʻath Party and the ensuing crisis of governance, many hoped that a new, inclusive, and liberal Iraqi nationalism would rise triumphantly through a democratic political process. Yet, deep divisions cleaved Iraqi society. These went well beyond the now familiar ethno-sectarian camps and created a dense thicket of political groups, many of which were unafraid to use violence to consolidate their power into competing fiefdoms. Together, these three threads—a weak central government, the Coalition's problematic introduction of an official political process, and the rise of various power groups—interacted to produce a chaotic and unpredictable transition toward democracy based on the complex legacies of Iraq's modern history.

Iraq's Modern History

The modern history of Iraq is a story of repeated attempts to build an Iraqi nation-state punctuated by frequent violence and unrest. The state of Iraq was born from the upheaval of the collapse of the Ottoman Empire at the end of World War I. Three Ottoman provinces—Basra, Baghdad, and Mosul—were cobbled together by the British in the land grab following the war. While it seemed logical to lash these provinces together into a British protectorate in the colonial atmosphere of the times, Basra, Baghdad, and Mosul did not form "a geopolitical or economic unit," in the words of noted scholars Marion Farouk-Sluglett and Peter Sluglett. Each province had a different historical outlook, making formation of an Iraqi state difficult. Basra had historic ties to the Gulf States and India, Baghdad was central to important routes between Syria and Iran, and Mosul was oriented toward the northern reaches of what is now Syria and Turkey. Each of these areas used different weights, measures, and currencies. Even the price of common goods varied widely throughout the three provinces.[5] A true and enduring Iraqi identity grew out of collective political and social action over the course of a half-century between 1920 and 1968; however, the seams still show from Iraq's manufacture early in the twentieth century. Because the construction of an Iraqi nation was never completed, a complex set of sub-state loyalties continues to trump nationalism across the board.

Each of the three provinces had a distinct make-up. The Kurds resided predominately in what had been the Mosul province, located in northern Iraq, although a significant portion lived alongside Arab Sunnis in the province's southern reaches. The Kurds, an ethnic minority currently at 15 to 20 percent of Iraq's population, speak a different language, Kurdish, than the rest of Iraq and have a different ethnic origin. The other major communities in Iraq are both ethnically Arab, though they come from different sects of Islam: the Sunni and the Shi'a. Iraq's Shi'a are a majority of 60 to 65 percent. The Sunni make up about 20 percent of Iraq's current population. Their stronghold has long been the vast western desert in today's Anbar, Salah al-Din, and Ninawa Provinces. The Ottoman governorate of Basra was largely the domain of the Arab Shi'a, while the cosmopolitan center of Baghdad has been historically mixed, yet politically dominated by the Sunni minority.

Iraq's tripartite division is not as clear-cut as it seems, however. The post-2003 segregation of Iraqi politics into three large blocs along ethno-sectarian lines and the brush with ethno-sectarian civil war were a phenomenon driven by political opportunists more than an innate hatred, and many accounts invite oversimplification of Iraqi identity into three categories: Sunni, Shi'a, and Kurd. These are only segments of Iraqi identity, competing for dominance with other characteristics: Iraqi nationalism, Arab identity, Islamic identity, tribal and family allegiance, profession, urban or rural provenance, and socio-economic condition. These identity markers overlap significantly, which makes Iraqis' loyalties much more complex than a map of ethno-sectarian affiliation. Many of Iraq's groups, from political parties to insurgent networks, are described by their sectarian affiliation, though marauding Shi'a death squads, Sunni insurgents, and even many of the political parties do not represent the whole of their communities. Further, the broad ethno-sectarian blocs (political and social) are riven with other fault lines. Ethno-sectarian make-up, however, is a critical factor of political organization and violence in the new Iraq, and therefore, its basis must be explored.

Primary identity has long been an important factor in Iraqi politics and, indeed, across the broader Middle East. In the term "primary identity," I refer to the identity that creates what anthropologist Clifford Geertz called

> primordial loyalty . . . an attachment that stems from the subject's . . . sense of the givens of social existence—speaking a particular language, following a particular religion, being born into a particular family, emerging out of a particular history, living in a particular place; the basic facts, viewed again from the actor's perspective, of blood, speech, custom, faith, residence, history, physical appearance, and so on.

This is not to say that primary identity and primordial entities are ancient and unchanging, or that they are predispositions to hate between peoples.[6] Although primary identity changes over time, even within the span of a single lifetime, it is the most basic level of group identity and can engender strong feelings. These feelings are especially strong when primary identity is politicized and used to draw seemingly ancient distinctions between peoples, even though the distinctions may be imagined or recently concocted.

Despite the longstanding sectarian division of Islam, sectarian identities in Iraq are not old and immobile. Many of Iraq's Shi'a are relatively recent converts. As nomadic Arabs settled around the southern Shi'a cities of Iraq in the last century and a half, many converted from Sunni to Shi'a Islam. This relatively new identity thus coincided with geographic lines, but often clashed with other identities, such as tribe and family. More importantly, while sectarian distinctions are real, there is no deep-rooted predisposition to sectarian hatred in Iraq, and sectarian relations in the country have not been perpetually bloody. The coincidence of sectarian and political lines, however, has worked to bring Iraqis into conflict.[7]

Most Sunni and Shiʻa lived separate lives until the middle of the twentieth century. While there were areas of significant mixing, especially in the capital and along demographic borders, a great number of Iraqis lived in relatively homogenous areas. In the words of Hanna Batatu, a pre-eminent scholar of Iraq's social and political history, most Shiʻa and Sunni "seldom mixed" socially and "as a rule did not intermarry." Sunni Arabs were intimately tied into the Ottoman provincial ruling system while Shiʻa saw the Sunni caliphate as "usurpation" and caused them to reject government service and public schooling. Beyond these differences, Batatu noted that economic and other factors "tended to favor the growth of a strong spirit of localism"[8] that can often still be seen today.

The period of mandatory rule, when Britain supervised the Iraqi government under the 1920 League of Nations mandate, did not improve sectarian integration in the country. The colonial administrators chose the urban Sunnis who had staffed the local institutions of the Ottoman Empire as the preferred drivers of modernization, shunning Shiʻa clerics as impediments to progress. Likewise, the officer corps of the new Iraqi Army was also almost exclusively made up of former officers of the Ottoman Army, the vast majority of whom were Sunni. Sunni dominance in the Iraqi government was a fact established from the earliest days of its existence.[9]

Despite this Sunni dominance, a fragile Iraqi nationality began to grow under British occupation during World War I. When Britain was awarded a League of Nations mandate to rule Iraq in 1920, Shiʻa, Sunni, and Kurd alike resented the colonial administration. A string of British missteps inflamed the discontent and protest soon turned into revolt. While the rising was unsuccessful in ousting the British, it did help to cement an Iraqi identity or at least a sense of community in opposition to the foreign occupation. Though the British put the revolt down through superior force, they also attempted to address the roots of discontent by appointing a new Iraqi government consisting of representatives of the various regions and populations. In 1921, the British, with the help of this pliable government, named Faisal, the son of Hussain the Sharif of Mecca, to be the first King of Iraq, despite the fact that Faisal was not Iraqi and had never lived there. Thus began a long process of outlining the shape of state institutions, as the British were forced to find ways to expand Iraqi participation in government while attempting to maintain control of the state's policies. In 1924, this process resulted in the drafting of a constitution. When Iraq officially became a constitutional monarchy in 1925, Iraqis founded political parties with little regard for sectarian considerations and elected a national parliament, albeit under heavy manipulation at the hands of Iraqi elites and the British mandatory administrators. Iraqis continued to develop their political sphere as several parliamentary elections were held during the monarchical period. Iraq's freest election, held in June 1954, demonstrated that, under permissive conditions, the "politically active urban populace" could organize quickly and "engage in sophisticated political discourse and activities." Unfortunately, these permissive conditions were short-lived, as the deterioration of the monarchy's legitimacy and the resultant 1958 military coup snuffed out this political development. From the establishment of the Kingdom of Iraq in 1921 to the 1958 coup, political parties sought to outline Iraqi identity. Some sought to define it along Arab lines that excluded the Kurds of the north and often followed international Sunni trends to the detriment of Shi'a involvement. Explicitly Iraqi nationalist movements were more inclusive of the country's varied identity markers. Over time, ideological failings and other circumstances served to empower increasingly narrow and sectarian pan-Arab cliques to gain and abuse power.[10]

Even as political involvement narrowed, cross-sectarian social associations grew. Unions, guilds, student associations, newspapers and journals, and artistic and cultural clubs experienced marked growth starting in the 1930s and continuing even into the 1960s. Many of these publications, associations, and cultural movements were remarkably inclusive of Iraq's various communities, even if they did draw their membership from an urban, educated population. Sectarian relations into the 1960s were "if not ideal, at least amicable."[11] While many regions were relatively homogenous, the sects mixed peacefully in Iraq's major cities and intersectarian marriages were not unheard of.

During the same time period, women participated in the growth of publications and associations to make their voice heard. Although women's clubs and journals began to emerge in the 1930s, they were not given official recognition until after 1958 when the monarchy was overthrown by a military coup that established the Republic of Iraq. Naziha al-Dulaimi was the first Arab woman to become the head of a government ministry when she was appointed as the Minister of Municipalities in 1959. Dulaimi was a staunch feminist but her appointment did not mark a watershed in women's rights. Although membership in women's associations grew into the 1960s, the Ba'ath Regime severely restricted women's activism. Despite limitations, women in Iraq enjoyed a much higher status and many more job opportunities even in Ba'athist Iraq than in other Arab countries. Women attended school, worked, and drove cars, and there was no prescription of Islamic dress. Women were especially well represented in the teaching, dentistry, and pharmacy fields, with smaller but significant numbers working as physicians, although only 16 percent of government workers under the Baʻath were women. Laws passed in the 1970s also afforded women more freedom from patriarchal traditions with regard to marriage and financial and legal responsibility. These advances eroded, however, in the late 1980s and 1990s as Saddam turned to tribes and certain visions of conservative Islam to legitimate his rule and help to control the populace. In this atmosphere, women's rights were rolled back to a degree.[12] After the fall of the regime, the situation ironically worsened. Subject to patriarchal control of renewed tribes and the admonishments of backward clerics and roving morality patrols, many women faced more hardships in the first years of the new Iraq than they had in previous years. Even as Iraq's overall situation deteriorated greatly, provisions of the new Iraqi constitution would ensure that women were represented in proportionally greater numbers in the parliament than most countries in the world.

At a social level, Iraqi national identity continued to grow, overlaying other lines of division; however, at a political level, this identity was contested along sectarian lines. The first Iraqi nationality law of 1924 distinguished between those who held Ottoman citizenship prior to 1924 and those who held Iranian citizenship. Iranian citizenship was enticing for Shiʻa in the south, because it afforded an opportunity to avoid Ottoman taxes and military duties, even though many of these Shiʻa were ethnically Arab. Though the nationality law was not heavily enforced at the outset, the first Baʻath regime in 1963 and the ʻArif government in 1964 recognized the pre-1924 Ottoman citizens as *asliyyun*, or original Iraqis. All others were required to apply for citizenship, which provided an avenue for discrimination against both Shiʻa and non-Arab minorities. The pan-Arabists' preoccupation with authentic Arab origins undercut inclusive versions of Iraqi identity. Writing in the 1970s, Batatu observed, "the new national loyalty . . . is still hazy, uncertain of its direction . . . unacceptable of the Kurds, [and] poorly assimilative of the Shiʻis."[13]

Although three decades of Baʻath rule inflamed sectarian tensions, the Baʻath Party was not a solely Sunni entity. Before it came to power, the party had been a broadly multi-sectarian endeavor. Although Shiʻa made up more than half of Baʻath membership until 1963, several factors combined to skew the party toward Sunni dominance. After a 1964 split, many Shiʻa members followed a dissident, ʻAli Saleh al-Sʻadi, into obscurity when he formed a splinter group due to a row with one of the party's founders, Michel Aflaq. More significantly, while a crackdown following ʻAbd al-Salam ʻArif's 1963 coup targeted Baʻathists in general, the Sunni-dominated police were especially harsh in hunting down Shi'a Ba'athists, rather than the Sunnis that often came from their own town or tribe. This led to a considerable decline in Shi'a membership and a concomitant rise in Sunni and especially Tikriti power in the party. Thereafter, it became an increasingly Tikriti- and Saddam-centered body, but the calculation was borne more out of power than sectarian hatred.

The debate over nationality became strong enough during Ba'ath rule that some Shi'a writers began to term it *ta'ifiyya*, or sectarianism. Shi'a decried policies that favored the Sunni minority over the Shi'a majority for top government positions and military appointments in the officer corps. In the cultural arena, the Ba'athists resurrected earlier pseudo-academic tracts to question Shi'a loyalties. Written in the 1960s to support Arab nationalism over a more inclusive Iraqi nationalism, these works were brought back into print in the early 1980s. Shi'a were referred to as *al-'ajam* and *al-shu'ubiyun*, terms for the Arabized Persian bureaucrats who staffed the 'Abbasid caliphate that ruled in Baghdad from 750 to 1258 AD. This term became recurrent in Iraq during the 1950s pan-Arab movement to label Shi'a communists and other opposition figures as foreigners. These concepts were expanded greatly by the Ba'ath regime's supporters during the Iran-Iraq War to encompass an entire narrative about historical Iranian jealousy of Iraq's supposedly superior civilization. Under this narrative, Persians covet Iraq and are wont to take it over by any means, internal or external. Saddam even offered "pure Iraqis" married to those with Iranian backgrounds $2,500 to divorce.[14]

It is unclear how many mixed couples there were in Iraq. One Iraqi sociologist stated that nearly one-third of Iraqi married couples were Shi'a/Sunni unions. Former Iraqi minister Ali Allawi, however, stated, "The number of intersectarian marriage households was insignificant, never more than a few percentage points of all households." The mixing of the sects was widespread in some areas, but non-existent in others. Iraqis' perceptions of sectarian relations often depended greatly on whether they were from a mixed area or not. For those who grew up in the former, sectarian tensions seemed to be something introduced by the U.S. invasion, although the true roots lie deeper.[15]

Despite this history, the development of an overt political "sect consciousness" has been a recent phenomenon. Sectarianism emerged as a political movement among Iraqi Shi'a in the 1990s. Prior to this time, Shi'a political movements had been wrapped up with communism, Arab nationalism, and other ideologies. Conferences and academic discourse among the exile community in the decade before Saddam's demise brought Shi'a identity to the forefront of their political consciousness. A July 2002 statement titled "The Declaration of the Shi'a of Iraq" was the culmination of this trend. Authored by future National Security Advisor Mowwafaq al-Rubai'e, future Minister of Defense and Finance Ali Allawi, and activist Sahib al-Hakim, the document called for a "new Iraq based on the three principles of democracy, federalism, and community rights" in Allawi's summation.[16]

For many Sunni, the awakening of a Sunni political identity came even later. Since the Sunni were long at the pinnacle of power in Iraq, they never really had to come to terms with a sectarian political identity. They simply felt that Iraq was a country of Iraqi Arabs, which they controlled. Perhaps for this reason, researchers found solidarity and trust between Arab Sunnis to be the lowest of the three ethno-sectarian groups in Iraq, a fact that was made clear in the incoherence of Sunni politics after Saddam's fall.[17]

Sectarian identity and sectarianism is only one aspect of a broader trait of xenophobia and what sociologists term "in-group solidarity" in Iraq. These phenomena, which were greatly heightened by the Ba'ath regime's propaganda and manipulation of cultural and historical memory, mean that divisions between ethno-sectarian groups in Iraq are ripe for exploitation, yet Iraqis still hold more mutual trust between their groups than do separate nations in Europe. In a 2004 survey, researchers found that Iraqi Arabs were the most likely to emphasize group loyalty over individualism out of any population surveyed. Unsurprisingly, Iraq's ethno-sectarian groups showed strong loyalty within their own population: 96 percent of Kurds trust other Kurds a "great deal." Eighty-six percent of Shi'a and 68 percent of Sunni gave the same response. While this mindset can exacerbate tensions among groups within Iraq, it is overlaid by a strong Iraqi identity among Arabs. Eighty-six percent of Iraqi Arabs were "very proud" of their national identity. Only 34 percent of Kurds responded similarly. Thus, although only a third of Iraqis expressed a high level of trust for those outside of their ethno-sectarian group, this was nearly twice the figure for Europeans who labeled other European nationalities as "very trustworthy."[18] The worn adage of "me against my brother, my brother and I against my cousin" has been borne out by statistics in Iraq, and it is an important aspect of both the internal strife and the general refutation of a permanent partition of the country.

The father of Iraqi sociology, Ali al-Wardi, discussed the characteristics and divisions of Iraqi society in detail. His books are in increasing demand in the bookstores reopening in many cities as Iraqis make sense of the new era, even though those who disagree with him often dismiss his findings as unscientific. Like many students of Arab culture reaching back to the fourteenth-century Arab writer Ibn Khaldun, Wardi believed that Iraqi society was divided between urban (*hadari*) and nomadic (*bedawi* or Bedouin) groups and cultural values. Though general trends in Iraqi society have ebbed and flowed between these poles, Wardi asserted that the pendulum swings toward tribal values whenever the state and its urban centers become weak in Iraq. A prominent feature of tribal values in these times is their in-group solidarity (*asabiyyah*—a key topic of Ibn Khaldun's discourse as well), which runs directly counter to loyalty to the state. Whenever the state was weak and incapable of provision and protection, people resorted to the refuge of the tribe, because the tribe can be "equivalent to the state. The individual finds in his tribe the security and care he needs." The in-group solidarity ingrained by centuries of tribal life was not easily forgone once Iraqis migrated to the cities. Conflicts often broke out between rival groups, yet these groups would also unite against outside threats on their city. Wardi made much of the clash of tribal and urban values in modern cities and cited it as a source of cultural confusion and contradiction.[19] In the new Iraq, this clash underpinned a number of the competitions between rival armed groups and political factions.

Although sectarian tension is a reality in Iraq, it is not a defining characteristic. While extremist groups and their opportunistic leaders brought sectarian insecurities into open violence, many Iraqis saw beyond the rhetoric and realized that families similar to theirs existed on the other side of the divide, struggling to survive and hoping it would soon end. At an individual and social level, sectarianism did not and still does not define Iraq and sectarian hatred is not a general phenomenon, even though many armed groups are driven by an animosity that targets anyone in their way. At the political level, as will be explored later, sectarianism came to define Iraq's power groups almost exclusively. Yet, beneath these grand sectarian definitions, many other issues divided Iraq's groups, from tribal-urban conflict to class and the personal ambitions of manipulative leaders.

Lines of power and economic influence controlled by opportunistic leaders often underpin conflicts in Iraq. The prevalence of patronage and the establishment of powerful client-patron networks was a key development in Iraq. Tribal and local elites looked to the rulers in Baghdad for patronage and favorable government decisions on important matters. In turn, they supported the central power. Early on, governmental authorities primarily used land for "purchasing social order," and land grants helped to create or reinforce the powers of loyal tribal sheiks. Later, as oil revenues became more significant, they funded a higher level of patrimonial distribution. Because of conflicts with the foreign-run Iraq Petroleum Company, the Iraqi government issued Public Law 62 in June 1972 to nationalize the corporation. This decision, followed by soaring oil prices resulting from the 1973 Arab-Israeli War and the resultant OPEC oil embargo on supporters of Israel, placed an unprecedented amount of resources in the hands of the regime. Oil revenues in 1972 had totaled $575 million. This sum would soar to $1.8 billion in 1973, $5.7 billion in 1974, and $26 billion by 1980, once again placing unprecedented resources in the hands of the regime.[20] Though some of these funds paid for healthy programs of modernization, much more went to building massive military and security formations and funding increasing levels of patronage.

The oil wealth had other effects as well. While migration from Iraq's rural areas to urban centers was already a well-established trend by the 1970s, the influx of revenue after 1973 caused a boom in this movement. The increased funds meant new urban jobs, and Iraqis flocked in from the countryside to take advantage of the newfound prosperity. The majority Shi'a, especially, crammed into planned developments on the outskirts of Baghdad as they left their traditional rural homes in the south. The populations of these slums grew by a factor of ten. In comparison, Baghdad's general population had only grown by a factor of three from 1962 to 1975. As Iraq expert Phebe Marr expressed, this migration did not produce an effect of "urbanization as much as ruralization of the cities."[21] Even though this explosive population growth had serious consequences in political and religious organization, activism was strictly kept in check by the regime.

Since the foundation of the state, Iraq went through several forms of government, and the changes were almost exclusively accompanied by violence. Instead of seeking a wide social base and building up broad institutions, rulers used the government to dish out patronage to narrow groups of supporters. They turned to the armed and security forces to cow the rest of Iraq into obedience. Therefore, changes of government were almost always violent battles over the coercive and distributive instruments of state, often stemming from a perceived weakening of regime control. The rise of oil revenues in the 1970s gave the government unparalleled resources to fund both the networks of patronage and the coercive levers of state.[22]

These trends culminated with the brutal rule of the Ba'ath regime, which came to power through a coup on July 17, 1968. This regime received the windfall of the post-1973 oil profits directly through the newly nationalized Iraqi Petroleum Company, allowing them to centralize power and wield patronage and violence like never before.[23] Saddam Hussein, a favorite henchman of President Ahmed Hassan al-Bakr, played an important role in the consolidation of Ba'ath power through the use of the security services and the party militia.

Both Saddam and al-Bakr were sons of Tikrit, a rural Sunni town in what would become Salah al-Din (also written as Saladin or Salahuddin) Province north of Baghdad. They ousted the old urban Sunni elites and replaced them with loyal rural Sunnis. Saddam and al-Bakr played complementary roles in this campaign. Al-Bakr projected himself as a "father figure" and reassured the public about the increasingly unsettling events, while Saddam reveled in the behind-the-scenes dirty work that secured their position atop Iraq.[24]

After taking the reins of the National Security Bureau of the Revolutionary Command Council (RRC) of the Ba'ath Party and the General Security Service in 1969, Saddam built up his following in the security services and key social circles. Although he was assigned the title of general in 1976, Saddam was not a professional military officer. His route power rested in his tribal and Ba'ath Party connections, through which he gradually extended his reach across the key levers of government. By the late 1970s, his domination of the security services and the Ba'ath Party was complete. In 1977, he took sole control of Iraq's oil policy, further cementing his hold on the levers of power in Iraq. In July 1979, al-Bakr, who had ruled Iraq since the Ba'ath coup, announced his resignation and Saddam assumed office. Shortly thereafter, Saddam announced that he had discovered a coup plot, which he used as an opportunity to undertake a massive purge that placed him undisputedly at the pinnacle of Iraqi power.[25]

Saddam set about securing his new position atop the Ba'ath regime with a characteristic lack of remorse. After calling a meeting of the RRC in July 1979, Saddam watched silently as his pawns in the security service called out sixty-six senior members for treason. He calmly puffed on Cuban cigars as senior officials were escorted out of the room. The accused were tried in a secret court lasting less than two weeks. Twenty-two were sentenced to execution and the rest were imprisoned. Those sentenced to death were led back to the basement of the building where the original accusations had been made. Saddam gave each of the members of his RRC and his cabinet a handgun. He then had the highest-level officials of the regime execute those individuals they would replace. This sadistic twist was characteristic of Saddam. In one stroke he eliminated his opposition, made his new coterie complicit in his crimes, and provided a graphic reminder that he would brutally remove even the slightest threat to his rule. Saddam's foreign minister and close associate, Tariq Aziz, called the purge "the cruelest thing Saddam did that I know of." Once Saddam had completed his housecleaning, he surrounded himself with political and intellectual nonentities. In the words of a senior Iraqi leader, Saddam's appointments to key positions were "uneducated, untalented, and those who posed no threat to his leadership."[26]

Thus began a reign of terror that outdid even Iraq's long tradition of political violence. Under Saddam's rule, security services penetrated Iraqi society and reigned supreme through a combination of informant networks and ruthless physical intimidation and violence. Any competitor for power, whether real or imagined, was dispatched with brutal efficiency. Evidence of the breadth of this campaign of violence is still being uncovered. By the end of 2005, investigators had unearthed 286 mass graves from Saddam's era. In Hilla alone, a southern Shi'a town, fifteen thousand victims of the regime had been buried around the city.[27]

While waiting in the wings under al-Bakr for his chance to take power, Saddam began building the vast security apparatus he would later use against his own people. Key servants were mostly Sunni Arabs, chosen for their family, clan, and tribal ties to the ruling elites. As Saddam's reign continued, those in positions of power maintained their place only by their personal allegiance to the ruler and their willingness to be complicit in the regime's crimes. Those who remained in service gained impressive status and perks in contrast to the oppressed masses.[28]

Service in Iraqi security institutions was a personal venture more than a public one. Lacking any power or prestige apart from that given to them by Saddam, these cronies wholeheartedly identified with the status quo. Any threat to this status quo, such as the transition in 2003, threatened these violent servants with loss of power, criminal charges, or death at the hands of vigilante retribution. Members of Saddam's security services were the best trained, best connected, and most violent members of the old order. Unsurprisingly, many chose to fight the transition in 2003—to them, it was an affront to their twisted way of life.

Saddam divided his security force into a number of isolated and mutually distrustful security services. This move prevented them from forming a bloc capable of action against the regime, while also making their remnants cellular and difficult to root out after the regime's collapse. All of the security services reported directly to Saddam, further emphasizing the theme of personal loyalty to the leader, rather than to the state itself. Most of the security and intelligence services maintained regional offices throughout Iraq, which spread Baghdad's reach and the security network.[29] When the central element of the regime was removed from the picture, these security organizations melted away, leaving a network of small cells in key locations throughout Iraq.

The RCC was the central hub through which Saddam and his closest associates controlled the state, the network of security services, the military, and Ba'ath Party cells nationwide.[30] The members of the RCC were personally invested in Ba'ath rule and commanded the networks of patronage that ran from Saddam, through the RCC membership, to various state and social institutions. RCC members were the bosses of the state, each controlled a fiefdom and received its benefits, but all were beholden to Saddam for their power and their continued survival. Several RCC members would become key figures in the resistance, especially in funding and coordinating activities.[31] The numerous security organizations that existed below the RCC provided a network of cells of well-trained and loyal Iraqis that RCC members could fund to resist the new order in Iraq.

The Ba'ath Party was a classic revolutionary cellular organization and set up an ideal structure for the networking of resistance. The basic element of Ba'ath Party organization was the cell: a unit consisting of three to seven men that oversaw a neighborhood or a business. Two to seven cells constituted a division, which oversaw a greater residential area or a larger business or government establishment such as a factory, university, or government establishment. Two to five divisions made up a section that covered a large urban neighborhood or a large rural area. Two sections fell into a branch, responsible for an entire province. Every branch fell under the regional command, which in Ba'athist organization was responsible for all of Iraq (a national command was putatively responsible for the pan-Arab "nation"). This cellular organization was similar to that of the 1940s Iraqi Communist Party and successful insurgent forces such as the Algerian Front de Libération Nationale (FLN).[32] The Ba'ath Party structure provided a ready-made conduit for RCC members to fund and control fragments of Iraq's vast security organization after the invasion.

The members of the security services were generally well trained, equipped, and paid. Several of the services exchanged technology, expertise, and intelligence with the Soviet KGB intelligence organization. The services were competent enough to undertake high-profile missions abroad in the Middle East and reportedly as far afield as London and Detroit, Michigan. Iraq's agents also cultivated clandestine relationships with various activists at home and in other Arab countries. In all, Saddam's loyal security servants had access to a wide range of training and equipment, as well as experience in covert and guerrilla operations and contacts throughout Iraq and the greater Middle East.[33]

For many of Saddam's security servants, separating themselves from their former role as henchmen of the Ba'ath regime would have proven nearly impossible. Cultivation of loyalty to the regime was a long process that started with programs for school-age children and culminated in a portfolio of incentives and threats that maintained compliance. This lifelong process produced a hard core of supporters of the status quo who identified with the old regime personally and ideologically. For many, resistance to a new order that disabused them of their power was virtually a foregone conclusion.

The indoctrination of selected Iraqis into the Ba'ath structure began in grade school with an organization called the Pioneers (*Ruwad*). Older youths could join the Vanguards (*Tala'i'*) at ten. This organization was said to have consisted of more than a million students in the mid-1980s. These Ba'athist students were singled out as class leaders and praised for their loyalty at the direction of the Ba'ath Party supervisors in the school system. Thus began a lifetime of special treatment. The *Shabab* group was the final youth organization, for seventeen- to twenty-one-year-old Iraqis and had 72,000 members. Youth organizations fed into a party structure that conferred many perks to eager young men and promised a bright future in a society where many important jobs were open only to Ba'athists. Aspiring members received preferred jobs in the public sector and fast-track promotions in return for new recruits and information on "disloyal" Iraqis.[34]

The Ba'ath made it nearly impossible to rise to any position of even local prominence in Iraq outside of the party system. In the latter half of the 1970s, Ba'athists rewrote the regulations of Iraq's trade unions and other organizations so that only Ba'athists could hold leadership positions. Further, the Ba'ath made many union figures full-time party apparatchiks or even members of the security services so that they could surveil the workplace. Across Iraq, businessmen, doctors, university professors, and technicians were compelled to join the Ba'ath in order to advance. Though the Coalition barred the highest level of Ba'athists from involvement in the new Iraqi government, rank in the party structure was an imprecise way of judging loyalty. Technocrats who excelled in their positions were often offered promotions into the higher reaches of the party.

These promotions were not subject to refusal, unless the technocrat was ready to risk being fired or imprisoned for opposition to the regime. Even schoolteachers were found in the higher levels. The CPA fired ten to fifteen thousand teachers, because they were within the four highest levels of the Baʿath Party.[35]

Some of the most ambitious and adventurous Iraqis were drawn to the security services. State security officers had tremendous power over those they surveilled, detained, and often tortured. Because of this power, security officers were regarded with fear and deference, which set them up for perks such as protection, money, elite treatment, and even easy access to women. Such power is not easy to give up, especially when one faces the prospect of a trial or revenge killing for atrocities committed under the old regime. The regime ensured that security officials were complicit in the regime's crimes and unable to return to a normal life outside of the regime. For instance, Saddam's personal bodyguards reportedly had to murder a member of their own tribe, in addition to someone from another tribe. This event not only branded them as guilty in the regime's brutality, it also placed them at the mercy of tribal vendettas if they ever tried to leave the regime. Saddam explained his logic to King Fahd of Saudi Arabia. "They are very loyal to me because every one of them, his hand is bloody. Every one of them knows that when I die . . . I'll be cut to pieces, and if that happens to me, they're all finished."[36] This sort of bloody-hands insurance policy is used by many criminal organizations and gangs to hedge against members "going clean" or informing on them. Saddam understood that this was the best way to intertwine his fate with that of his ruling class.

Leaders within the security services were further conditioned through a combination of patronage and coercion. Perks and bonuses were accompanied by the fear of being the subject of an informant's revelation of a transgression, real or imagined. In this "system of spying on spies," no one was immune from the grips of fear.[37] The effect was a dependence on the regime for continued personal success and survival.

In many Sunni areas, regime employment was simply the primary way of life. In one town, the local police commander explained that "just about every family had someone working in security or the army or some government job . . . it was normal to join the Baʿath Party—it was like a rule." In the same town, a fifty-seven-year-old former regime security officer struggled to understand how the job he had once been so proud of now caused him to be treated poorly. "Was serving the country some sort of crime? . . . We were on top of the system. We had dreams. . . . Now we are the losers. We lost our positions, our status, the security of our families, stability. Curse on the Americans." Prior to the Ba'ath regime's rise to power, Sunni towns in Anbar and near Tikrit had been rural backwaters with little access to government jobs or money. The Sunni town of al-Dur, roughly ten miles north of Tikrit, was hardscrabble farmland until Saddam came to power. Once he opened the doors of the military colleges and other national service to his rural cousins, it became a center of regime manpower.[38] These Sunnis lost the only way of life they knew with the fall of the regime. While most Iraqis were happy to be free of the yoke of Ba'ath oppression, some Sunnis feared their loss of position and privilege with Saddam's demise and guarded the symbols of their old way of life. These Sunnis would present the biggest challenge to the Coalition's project.

The most dedicated Ba'athists were complicit in Saddam's crimes and responsible for maintaining the delicate balance of patronage and violence that safeguarded the Ba'ath Party's hegemony over Iraq. The sheer size of this support mechanism defied expectations of a surgical regime change and provided many advantages for those who wanted to resist the coming of a new order. Many important members of Saddam's regime can still be found at the core of Iraq's current problems of violence and corruption.

Iraq's military was a different story, however. Even though the military was involved in some of Saddam's egregious acts of ruthlessness against his own population, the bulk of the army consisted of conscripts from across Iraq's ethnic and sectarian groups. The military was a source of national pride, yet in the later years of Saddam's rule, it became increasingly incapable of conducting operations. Saddam's constant manipulations removed any leaders with talent or initiative and bred a fear of mistakes that often led to inaction. Military planning and execution was highly compartmentalized and lines of command were "stove-piped" directly to the highest levels of the regime. Making matters worse, according to a senior Iraqi officer, the military experienced an "unchecked spread of administrative corruption and bribery, especially in the last few years."[39]

A bloated Sunni-dominated officer corps led the Iraqi armed forces. In 1968, Saddam and al-Bakr began reforming the Iraqi Army in the first of a series of purges that removed potentially threatening leaders and replaced them with safer alternatives. By 1970, they had appointed three thousand new officers, many of whom were loyal and subservient followers of al-Bakr, Saddam, and their entourage. These indoctrinated commissars, controlled by the Directorate of Political Guidance, were instructed to carry out critical orders only with party approval, which provided a secondary means of stopping a renegade officer.

These commissars would be augmented in later years by civilian minders from the Special Security Service. Although they had no military experience, they entered into every decision and reported every detail back to Saddam's son Qusay and ultimately to Saddam. Although professional officers reviled these individuals because of their lack of military training, there was no way of circumventing regime meddling.[40]

The Special Republican Guard (SRG), or *al-Haris al-Jamhuri al-Khas*, was the elite core of the military, consisting of twelve to fifteen thousand active-duty troops and a similar number of reserves. The main function of this unit was to protect the regime in and around Baghdad.[41] It was the most loyal, well-trained, and well-equipped military unit and, therefore, the most likely to resist regime change. The SRG was networked with many of the security services when it came to defense of the capital. For example, a building in the 'Amil district of Baghdad housed a communications center, "One-One," where Special Intelligence, Special Security, and the SRG coordinated operations. This center was responsible for security of the airport highway from the Republican Palace to Baghdad International Airport. The center was also located next to the Umm al-Tubul Mosque.[42] Both the airport highway and the Umm al-Tubul Mosque (renamed Ibn Taymiya after the fall of the regime) became hotbeds of insurgent activity.

Though men of the military and security services did not single-handedly create the insurgency, they were an extremely dangerous tool used by resistance groups of many different types. As one expert commented, the former regime members "know each other, have combat skills, understand discipline, have experienced commanders, and share the same provenance." It should be of no surprise that military and security members were a source of trained muscle for the resistance. Scholars who have noted and warned against this problem observed past cases of attempted democratic transition. For this reason, transition scholars advised that such groups must be rehabilitated from their former roles under the old order and shielded from the politics of the transition period.[43] The Iraqi military and security services, however, were disbanded in the invasion's aftermath and left to their own devices.

Dangerous and anonymous, many of these men were well trained in the ambush and ordnance skills that fueled the insurgency. They were tied in to a military network, yet also retained strong ties to their hometowns, which made them an indispensable link between local resistance groups and national military knowledge. Most countries' militaries are billeted within a few hours of a hometown in which their extended family has lived for generations. While U.S. soldiers spend their weekends and off-times with friends from their units near their bases, Arab bases become ghost towns as the soldiers return home to friends and family. After spending a couple days in Jordan riding around back roads in grimy old cars with Jordanian Special Forces officers, an American colleague and I witnessed how such operators could easily disappear into their hometowns and wreak havoc.

In contrast to American soldiers who often do all they can to stand out as a society of their own, most Arab soldiers are still rooted in the family and local society from which they came. They can easily slip into a *dishdasha*, roll unnoticed through a checkpoint, and disappear into houses of friends and family. When events do not go in a favorable direction, it is no stretch for Arab soldiers to join friends and family in resistance, whether that resistance be tribal, Islamic, or tied to other former regime members.

As a result of Iraq's extensive network of security services and special military units, trust and social cohesion shrunk to ever-smaller circles. Iraqis never knew who might be an informant. Even overeager teachers coaxed children into revealing their parents' transgressions. Iraqis had no refuge from the prying eyes of the government.[44] The former regime's cultivation of paranoia and secrecy was a legacy that assisted insurgents in maintaining their cover, while at the same time helping them to terrorize the population and discourage assistance of the Coalition. Their erosion of trust and social cohesion meant that social and political movements in the new Iraq would often be based on narrow categories of identity. Reconciliation and unified action would prove to be difficult.

More than 500,000 Iraqis were part-time informants for state security institutions. Some were volunteers, but many more were coerced. The broad net cast by state-run informers shut down the normal discourse of the people and allowed the regime to float "fantastic lies" that, in the absence of any open criticism, tended to stick.[45] In particular, Saddam attributed nearly every public failure to an elaborate conspiracy against the Iraqi people. In the summer of 2003, focus group research found that Iraqis still believed a great deal of the propaganda he had pushed over the years and had a propensity for buying into rumors of conspiracy.[46] The logic imbued by decades of such stories is a difficult legacy to overcome as paranoia and conspiracy theories are often better received than facts to this day, even among highly educated professionals who have spent decades in the West. There is no way to undermine confidence in such stories, as a simple "that's what they want you to think" is the only defense needed to blunt the most logical attack.

Not even private family discussions were safe from surveillance. At school, children were encouraged to talk about what their parents said behind closed doors. Therefore, few parents dared to talk openly about the regime, even at home. Further, Saddam emphasized the importance of using children as vanguards against their parents' backwardness and breeding a deep distrust of foreigners in Iraqi youth. The resulting generation of children knew only Saddam's propaganda, reinforced by parents' feigned loyalty. On the day of the regime's fall, a 12-year-old lamented, "I'm sad. The Americans have stolen freedom," whereas her father explained, "Until now, I haven't been able to speak my feelings about him."[47] Many observers, both Iraqi and foreign, have noted the difference in ideology between those who were born before the Ba'ath reign and those who experienced only its terror.

By the end of the 1990s, 56 percent of the Iraqi population was under the age of nineteen, having lived their entire lives under Saddam's reign, his wars, and economic crises. During these times, their education was severely lacking. Schools were under supplied and in poor material condition. Faced with fixed salaries and spiraling inflation, teachers were forced to find second jobs or quit. Student enrollment concurrently dropped. In 1995 alone, 150,000 students dropped out of classes, forced to stay at home or find work to help their families. Falling standards of living, increasingly expensive school supplies, and the newly required school tuition all contributed to plummeting enrollment. Literacy rates dropped from 67 percent in 1980 to roughly 57 percent in 2001.[48] Young Iraqis were poorly prepared for the challenges of building a democratic state in the wake of the 2003 invasion.

Even as Iraqi schools were failing, the regime was rewriting the nation's history to serve its ends. According to scholar Eric Davis, the regime's attempts to manipulate historical memory were a critical part of its campaign to control society. The Ba'ath sought to replace fear-induced obedience with the much more pervasive control that arises from self-compliance. By manipulating history and culture, Saddam sought to provide Iraqis with a frame of reference that justified his rule and their obedience to it.[49]

Oil revenues funded rewriting of textbooks—historical "research" to dredge up convenient new facts—and a gamut of cultural and historical products that attempted to create a reality that supported Saddam's rule. The sense of identity that the Ba'ath promoted was "insular and xenophobic" and warned society against the constant threats outsiders presented to the regime. The result was a sense that the state was constantly under siege from Jews, Persians, and Westerners. These threats, in turn, were used to legitimize the state's draconian security measures in the eyes of the political elite and the Ba'ath Party's base of support. Iraqis became one of the most xenophobic societies on the planet: recent research found that Iraqis exhibit a level of distrust of foreigners much higher than found in nearly any other country. At the same time, they showed an intense level of solidarity with their own ethno-sectarian group.[50] However, Saddam's foreign policies were what would sow the seeds of his downfall.

The Seeds of Downfall

The worst violence in Iraq's history came in the last two decades of Saddam's rule. The collapse of the Ba'ath regime in 2003 really began on September 22, 1980, when Iraq invaded Iran with the aim of wresting control of several disputed pieces of land and the Shatt al-Arab waterway. The surprise invasion gave way to a protracted and costly war. The massive human and economic toll of Iraq's war with Iran pushed Saddam to grasp at ever more desperate measures to maintain his position atop Iraq. Eventually, the disastrous series of events would lead to the Coalition invasion of 2003 and the complete collapse of Iraq's rotten shell of government.

Saddam's attack against Iran led to eight years of all-out war between the two countries, including horrific human wave attacks and the first major use of chemical weapons in seventy years. The level of casualties relative to the two countries' populations rivaled that of the European combatants of World War I (at least 680,000 soldiers and civilians died in the war, on the order of 1 percent of the total population killed), exhausting both society and economy. Iraq's southern regions, especially Basra, were the hardest hit. Bitter fighting destroyed the area's industrial infrastructure and agricultural production.[51] It must be noted that although the Shi'a south bore the brunt of the destruction in a war against their Persian co-religionists, there were never any major defections, discipline problems, or mutinies by the overwhelming majority of Shi'a conscripts that composed Saddam's army. As noted above, Iraqi nationalism is a strong element of identity. In the end, Saddam failed to gain anything through the eight years of war, and the borders returned to the status quo.

At the end of the war, Saddam was faced with difficult economic and political decisions. The war left behind a massive and costly million-man military, yet paradoxically Saddam was unwilling to reduce its size. Discharging soldiers into the weakened economy would be cashiering them into unemployment, a dangerous situation for a man fearing unrest. The regime attempted to assuage potential unrest by proposing an ambitious set of public works projects, but the execution of these plans fell far short of the state's grand visions. To make matters worse, Iraq's oil sector was working well under capacity. Though funds were needed to upgrade infrastructure and replace war-ravaged equipment, the regime was unable to provide the investments required.

Saddam still longed for a triumphant leap to a more prominent leadership position in the Arab world. The post-war situation, however, was hemming him in. By the end of the war, Saddam owed between $40 and $50 billion to non-Arab lenders and another $30 to $40 billion to Arab countries, specifically Saudi Arabia and Kuwait. Faced with massive military and rebuilding costs and unable to repay loans from its Arab neighbors who had partially bankrolled Saddam's battle with Iran, the regime chose to gamble once again, "robbing the bank to the south" with an invasion of Kuwait in 1990.[52] This disaster ended in the U.S.-led 1991 Gulf War that ejected Iraqi troops from Kuwait.

Sweeping air strikes on Iraq's infrastructure accompanied the expulsion from Kuwait. The war was followed up by more than a decade of economic sanctions and military containment. In this decade, Iraq changed greatly. The damage resulting from Saddam's disastrous decisions in the 1990s left Iraq weakened and dysfunctional.

With a number of Iraqis emboldened by Saddam's resounding defeat, dual rebellions broke out in March 1991. In the Shi'a south, uprisings occurred in several large Shi'a cities. While Islamist opposition parties such as Hizb al-Da'wa and the Supreme Council for the Islamic Revolution in Iraq (these parties will be discussed more thoroughly later) aided the uprisings to some extent, the general tenor of the unrest was local and spontaneous. As such, there was little organization or leadership, and critically, the rural and tribal Shi'a did not join their urban compatriots. Republican Guard units soon rallied to the areas of urban unrest, and the revolt was quickly and brutally repressed.[53] At the same time, a Kurdish revolt sprang up in the north, progressing as far as the capture of Kirkuk. These early successes were turned back once Saddam's troops shifted their attention from the crushed uprising in the south, and the regime retook Kirkuk and other areas, causing a massive exodus of Kurds into Turkey and Iran. The fear of Saddam's brutal repression loomed large.[54]

These twin revolts resulted in a massive death toll. Over a hundred thousand Iraqis were killed. Additionally, more than two million Kurds were displaced within Iraq, fifty thousand Shi'a fled across the border into Saudi Arabia, and as earlier mentioned, several hundred thousand Kurds sought refuge in Turkey or Iran. There was a sectarian element to the violence, as highlighted by Republican Guard tanks sporting such anti-Shi'a graffiti as "No more Shi'a after today," but sectarianism was not a driving consideration to either side.[55] The Shi'a wanted an end to Saddam's tyranny, and the regime wanted to remain in power. Even though it was a political fight, it did contribute to fears and antipathy between the sects that would rise to the surface in the new Iraq.

In addition to rising sectarian tension, the weakening economy drove Saddam to seek alternative methods for controlling Iraq, which further exacerbated the divisions and pathologies of Iraqi society. Severe international sanctions followed Iraq's defeat in Kuwait and the Ba'ath regime's subsequent refusal to comply with UN resolutions regarding reparations and verification of the destruction of its weapons of mass destruction capabilities. The sanctions prevented Iraq from trading its oil, thereby crippling its economy. Economic woes combined with the Ba'ath oppression deeply scarred Iraqi society.

Economic indicators show the depth of Iraq's troubles. The average per capita income plummeted from $8,161 in 1979 to $2,108 by 1989, largely due to Iraq's disastrous decision to war with Iran. The 1991 Gulf War and the ensuing UN sanctions compounded the damage. Per capita income dropped to $609 in 1992 and hovered around $500 by 1995.[56] Gross domestic product stood at $47.56 billion in 1980 and fell to an estimated $15.35 billion by 1997 before settling at $26.117 billion by 2002. At the same time, Iraq's population grew from 13 million in 1980 to 23.3 million in 2000.[57]

Regime policies only intensified the crisis. The government simply printed more money to cover its expenditures, causing catastrophic inflation that reached a mind-boggling annual rate of 100,000 percent by 2002. Transactions were literally carried out with bags of cash. Combined with approximately 50 percent unemployment, Iraq was in an economic disaster. For those who were employed, their fixed wages became virtually worthless as inflation soared.[58] Iraq's public sector workers were among the hardest hit. The CPA estimated that, at the time of the 2003 invasion, as many as 1.5 million Iraqis were civil servants on the state payroll, not including the large pool of pensioners. Others estimated that more than 40 percent of Iraqis were directly dependent on the state payroll for their living. These government employees were severely affected by hyperinflation. For example, in 1995, a mid-level government employee earned 5,000 Iraqi dinar (ID) per month, but one kilogram of chicken cost ID 2,500. In

1991, however, the average government wage was about ID 100–200, but the kilo of chicken cost only ID 3. In order to feed their families, employees turned to corrupt practices and kickbacks to supplement their paltry salary. Many also turned to the informal sector for employment. This "shadow economy" ran the gamut from unofficial businesses to rampant economic and organized crime. It is estimated that Iraq's black market made up approximately 30 percent of the gross domestic product in 2000. Nearly 70 percent of Iraq's labor force was involved in this informal economy, a symptom of severe economic dysfunction.[59]

Much of this dysfunction can be attributed to the twisted logic of Iraq's socialist economic programs. The state promoted failing industries, pouring good money after bad despite their inability to succeed. The government then forced these factories to buy substandard materials above the world market price from other Iraqi ventures. Thus, the range of products was of inferior quality and priced higher than their foreign competitors. Because of these and other extreme inefficiencies, Iraq was filled with failing, deeply indebted industries. The CPA's director for management and budget, David Oliver, found that the majority of Iraq's state-owned businesses were losing enterprises and costs the bankrupt Iraqi government roughly a billion dollars yearly. These foundering industries would either have to be continued on life support or allowed to fail, adding to the already endemic unemployment. Throughout the Iraqi economy, poor policy and massive subsidies promoted inefficient business practices, robbed the country of capital and labor productivity, and gave incentive for massive smuggling and corruption.[60]

Perverse economic incentives contributed to informal and black-market ventures as well. Corrupt officials and restrictive laws made it difficult for legitimate business to survive. Owners who registered their businesses legally, after paying bribes to each regime functionary involved in the process, were only opening themselves to further shakedowns, as various government officials used registry rolls to guide them on bribe-seeking rounds. A mere threat of investigation or an accusation of disloyalty and most of these businessmen would fork over the requested bribe rather than risk the alternative. In contrast, businessmen who kept a low profile might only have to bribe one or two officials who happened across their shop.[61]

Iraqi society was crushed by the deepening economic crisis. Diseases of poverty and malnutrition rose sharply, especially among children, and social ties were severed by the costs of transportation, hospitality, and the like. In this environment, the 1990s witnessed a precipitous decline in the norms and morals of Iraqi society, which contributed to a rise in crime and a willingness to excuse bad behavior as a product of hard times. Oil smuggling and other illegal enterprises became endemic in the later years of Saddam's rule through a "widespread, globally networked criminal operation."[62]

During the 1990s, the kingpins of business, smuggling, and organized crime became known as "the cats of the embargo." Despite the sanctions, these ruthless opportunists made fortunes through contracting and import/export trade. Construction contractors were generally linked to the regime and profited from the Baʿathists' ongoing development projects while the rest of the population sunk further into poverty. Import/export traders also benefited from the large disparity in commodity prices between Iraq and its neighbors caused by the embargo, rationing, and subsidies. Smart traders could manipulate the prices and the laws to turn huge profits, especially through smuggling. Importation of luxury goods from Jordan also proved lucrative.[63]

The regime ignored, if not sanctioned, smuggling, foreign currency trading, and criminal enterprises that supplied elite Iraqis with cash and commodities. Regime elites controlled large portions of this embargo economy and sometimes came into open rivalry over the spoils. Saddam's son Uday Hussein and Saddam's half-brother Barzan al-Takriti were reportedly the most prominent of these kingpins and sparked a deadly rivalry that resulted in a multiple killing of Iraqi businessmen in Amman, Jordan, in 1998. One Iraqi observed that, under embargo, the rich could do virtually anything except "say bad things about Saddam or compete with his family. . . . In Baghdad there is no law. You can kill, steal, do whatever you want."[64]

Many of this mafia's foot soldiers were combat veterans of Saddam's wars and were linked to powerful rural tribes in both the Sunni and Shiʿa areas. Discharged into a jobless economy at the end of the 1991 Gulf War, these soldiers now turned to crime as a way of life, working for the new kingpins or tribal chiefs as the muscle behind the new black-market economy. This connection between former soldiers, criminals, and tribal elements was a precursor to the pattern that would dominate many areas after the fall of the regime and the disbanding of the Iraqi security apparatus. During the 1990s, these men made heavy use of historic smuggling routes through the al-Qaim, al-Rutbah, and Qusaybah areas—routes that later proved useful for infiltrating foreign fighters into the country to take part in the insurgency. Qusaybah's transition from a pre-war smuggling hub to an insurgent infiltration center led U.S. military forces to call it "the *jihad* Super Bowl."[65]

In addition to the creation of a thriving sector of ruthless opportunists ("rent seekers" in economic parlance), the economic hardship of the 1990s devastated Iraq's professionals and the large middle class. Sanctions forced up to 63 percent of professionals to find employment as laborers. The cats of the embargo moved into their affluent, middle-class neighborhoods as they moved out. These rags-to-riches Iraqis were seen as profiteers and criminals by the middle-class professionals whose neighborhoods they had taken over. The professional middle class was gutted and replaced by a poorly educated, ruthless class of opportunists.[66]

The hope for a new, democratic Iraq was largely based on the conjecture that an enlightened, secular elite and middle class would re-emerge intact in the country. Ali Allawi scoffed at such notions, asserting, "The middle classes were fragile, and their precarious hold on prosperity was seriously challenged in the 1990s." Hanna Batatu, writing much earlier, also noted that the "incohesiveness" of the middle class left the field of politics open to increasingly narrow groups of strongmen, as evinced by the progression of regimes since 1958. The fragility and "incohesiveness" only worsened with time. Many of the potentially moderate and secular members of the middle class were either impoverished by the decades leading up to the invasion, or had fled the country.[67] The one sector that many hoped would unify Iraq had been all but destroyed.

In the hard times and shifting social environment of the 1990s, tensions were high. One Baghdadi related that his city had become "an angry place" owing to the stress of severe economic hardship. "So many people are on edge, and can easily break into a fight at any moment."[68] This highly-charged atmosphere would fuel chaos in the wake of invasion. The Baʻath regime was successful in keeping a lid on the increasingly troubled society; however, once this lid was removed, years of pent up frustrations and anxiety exploded into an orgy of looting and violence. The chaos of post-invasion Iraq was building for years, as were the tribal and religious groups that would exploit the coming vacuum.

The economic decline of the 1990s weakened the regime as well. Saddam was no longer able to rule the country with an iron fist from central Baghdad and was forced to rely on social powers such as tribes and clerics to maintain order in the periphery. Saddam was profoundly spooked by the events following the 1991 Gulf War. A series of popular uprisings and the discovery of high-level coup plots from within his Sunni coterie highlighted his precarious position and resulted in a new emphasis on internal control through unconventional means. Saddam bolstered his failing base of support by creating new militias of fanatical supporters and turning to the traditional institutions of Islam and the tribes as the power of the Ba'ath Party and its ideology waned.[69] In exchange for their support, Saddam granted cooperative tribal and religious leaders local power and relative autonomy.

Despite growing confrontation with the West, Saddam remained fixated on the most immediate internal threats. Saddam fielded new forces, such as the *Fedayeen*, the al-Quds Army,[70] and the Ba'ath militia, to provide dedicated local forces capable of quickly and brutally putting down internal uprisings. The most prominent of these forces, the Fedayeen (literally "those who sacrifice themselves"), consisted primarily of young Tikritis trained by the Republican Guard. Created in 1994, the force may have consisted of up to 100,000men. The Fedayeen were involved in some of the fiercest guerrilla actions during Operation Iraqi Freedom and gave the Coalition its first look at the unconventional and fanatical tactics that would plague it for years to come. Fedayeen training involved the use of silenced weapons, communications equipment, shaped explosives, and special timers. Many of the Fedayeen fought on after the collapse of the regime, which planted the critical seed for continued resistance, and much of their knowledge would later be passed down to Iraq's growing network of insurgents.[71]

The Fedayeen were far from completely loyal servants of the regime, however. Captured documents detail a large number of criminal investigations connected to Fedayeen members.[72] Crime was a major source of funding for insurgent activities, and the well-established criminal enterprises of the Fedayeen probably went on to bankroll the resistance.

The Fedayeen also had important links to foreign fighters. According to captured documents and the accounts of Marines and soldiers who encountered Fedayeen during the initial push to Baghdad, Fedayeen were involved in training foreign volunteers. For example, in the town of Hayy in southern Iraq, villagers informed Marines that the fanatical Fedayeen fighters they were encountering were mostly foreigners. This information was corroborated by Syrian passports found on some bodies. In the passports were entry stamps from al-Qaim on the Syrian border dated during the first week of the invasion. The purpose of visit was listed as Jihad.

Other units found evidence of Syrian, Jordanian, Egyptian, Sudanese, and Yemeni fighters. In one area of Baghdad, army units were engaged by foreigners almost exclusively, with a total strength of roughly three hundred. Following these engagements, twenty-eight of thirty detainees held Syrian passports. An intelligence officer who helped debrief the prisoners found that the leaders were generally older and bearded, and many had experience in *Hizb Allah* or *Hamas* militias.[73] These leaders were respected for their age, piety, and experience and may have been a key factor in leadership and training during the early days of the insurgency.

Saddam's military and security forces were not solely Sunni, nor would the members be limited to fighting for the insurgency once the regime fell. Many of these groups simply melted back into society. Others became Iraq's new army and police forces. Critically, however, some former members of Saddam's massive security and military apparatus provided muscle, leadership, and tactical expertise to Iraq's various armed groups that sprung up in the wake of the regime's collapse. Sunni regime loyalists made the biggest initial impact in turning to armed insurgency, although Shi'a men had also served in the army and even the Ba'ath militia and the Fedayeen. Many of these experienced fighters would soon be part of militias such as the Mahdi Army, the Badr Corps, and other local groups, biding their time for action.[74]

Despite Saddam's myriad of armed supporters, he could not rely on them alone to maintain his grip on power. No matter how brutal it became, the regime simply could not erase Iraq's traditional social structures. Rather than eradicating religious, tribal, and family structures, Saddam co-opted them.

The Rise of the Tribes

Tribes and tribal identity have long been powerful in Iraq. Collective social organizations based on kinship ties, tribes ruled Arabia prior to the rise of the modern state and are still quite powerful in most Arab countries. Historically, because of this mode of familial organization, lineage is crucial and gives rise to both the patronymic naming system used by Arabs (in full this is a five-generation family tree) and the tradition of marriage within the tribe, if not within the clan or family. Ruled by sheikhs, many Iraqi tribes are large and extend across the Arabian Peninsula without regard to the recently drawn political borders. Tribes can further organize themselves into tribal confederations, such as the Dulaim of western Iraq. Even though tribes are nominally based on geneology, tribal identity can be constructed and is always changing. According to one expert in the region, "sometimes they just invent these things. Sometimes families get associated with a tribe and convince themselves that they, too, are descended" from the original ancestor to which that tribe's founding is credited.[75]

Tribes maintained a semblance of balance and order through a system of tribal hierarchy and norms of solidarity and vengeance that discouraged random crime and violence in their lands. Between tribes, status and prestige was accorded to the tribe's mode of living and its historical performance in raids and conflict. Nomadic camel-herding and raiding tribes stood on the top tier, with status descending through pastoral tribes to tribes that traditionally were craftsmen and petty traders.[76] This hierarchy remained, even as tribes settled into a more sedentary lifestyle, although tribal control tended to wane in urban areas as new forms of standing and allegiance took over. Political manipulations, however, kept the tribes alive into the twenty-first century.

From the earliest days of Iraq as a state, after the end of World War I, British officials worked within the existing tribal hierarchy, allowing sheikhs to settle disputes and collect taxes for the central government. This measure was expedient for an occupying force that was under severe manpower and budgetary restraints in the 1920s. This system was codified into the *Tribal Criminal and Civil Disputes Regulation* written in 1916 and included in the 1925 constitution.[77] These laws would surface again almost in their entirety when Saddam revitalized the tribes in 1996.

While the urbanization of Iraq and the increasingly sedentary nature of the tribes should have weakened tribal power, events of the early twentieth century gave them a new lease on life. As tribes turned to agriculture, sheikhs became the landowners of vast swathes controlled and tended by their tribe. The British and the Iraqi monarchy also turned to sheikhs to control the outlying areas. The British, in particular, encouraged the transformation of the sheikhs into feudal landlords, whose tribesmen, or tenants, farmed commercially for the growing urban areas, which, in effect, changed the tribal dynamic. Thus, the tribes escaped the fate that modernization might otherwise have dealt them. This change, along with government manipulations, made sheikhs more autocratic in their dealings with the tribes.[78] From this position of economic advantage, many sheikhs became increasingly ambitious in their projects as they came to manage major business rings, both legal and illegal.

When the Ba'ath Party gained power by coup in 1968, the small Sunni inner-circle set about securing their precarious position by stocking the regime's military and security services with Iraqis of the same tribal provenance. Tribal ties extended the regime's base in society, provided loyal recruits for its coercive structures, and helped to create cohesion and trust among members of the regime center.[79] Saddam's Al Bu Nasir tribe and its allies, approximately fifty thousand in number, formed the core of the regime's patrimonial distribution networks. The core of regime elites came from a smaller group, the Beijat subclans. Tribes that supported the regime, most prominently al-Dulaim, al-Duri, al-Jubur, and al-Shammar, benefited handsomely from the arrangement in the form of influential positions and lucrative government contracts, creating newly rich and powerful individuals in what had previously been poor, although regionally powerful, tribes. Later, as coup plots spooked Saddam, he installed members of less important tribes in organizations such as the Special Republican Guard.[80] Since these smaller tribes did not have a large power base, they were more reliant on Saddam's patronage and, therefore, more likely to remain loyal. Throughout the rural Sunni west, tribesmen owed their new wealth and position to the Ba'ath regime.

Even as Saddam cultivated his tribal power base, the weakening of the central state in the regime's latter years gave tribal power a life of its own. As government control weakened and services to the public declined, the tribes filled the gap in terms of protection, administration, and charities. The regime recognized and co-opted this phenomenon to ensure that it did not lose its grasp on the periphery of the country. The return to tribalism was not unique to the Sunni west. Shi'a tribes grew in power as well. Where no tribal leaders remained or where the existing leadership refused to be co-opted, the government created new ones, derisively called "Taiwan sheikhs" by fellow Iraqis due to their lack of authenticity.[81] Despite these cases, it is crucial to understand that the autonomy and power that the tribes gained in the last decade of Saddam's rule was not solely a regime-driven phenomenon that would die with the Ba'ath Party.

The new relationship between tribes and the government was formalized in 1996 when the regime revived the tribal laws of the British mandatory period. Sheikhs became intermediaries between the government and the tribes, with the authority to handle matters of local law and order and mediate disputes between tribes. Some tribes went so far under this arrangement as to standardize "blood money" paid for violent crimes and murders. Sheikhs were responsible for tax collection and were also given control of a portion of the government's development budget to spend on local initiatives in their area. These roles provided tribes with revenue and rising power within the state.[82]

Leaders of compliant tribes were given reduced military enlistment quotas they could fill as they saw fit, rather than direct conscription by the central government. In turn, Saddam armed neighborhood and tribal militias with small arms, rocket-propelled grenades, mortars, and even howitzers, primarily as a guard against local uprisings. These tribal militias were activated to protect important locations in several cities in November and December 1998 due to heightened tensions with the United States.⁸³ In all, rising tribal power robbed the state of a key source of legitimacy: the ability to provide for and protect its citizens.

The tribes showed their unruly nature even before Saddam's demise. Tribal justice began to rival Iraq's police forces and courts, even in cases of murder. Bureaucrats without tribal affiliation complained of being powerless in the face of tribally backed opponents. Confrontation between state bureaucracies and tribes became increasingly common, leading in some cases to tribal assassination of regime functionaries such as policemen and judges who were adversely involved in tribal affairs. Tribal organization also spawned gangs that undertook an alarming amount of criminal activity, including looting and kidnapping. In this atmosphere, urban Iraqis who had become disconnected from the tribal system and its protections were compelled to invent new tribes of their own or attempt to integrate with an existing tribe in order to find a form of security from exploitation under the emerging system.⁸⁴

In one example of tribes' rising power, Saddam gave tribes in the Fallujah area "virtual autonomy" prior to his demise. As a result, clerics and tribal sheikhs were in sole control of the city prior to the arrival of Coalition troops. Tribes protected buildings, ran needed institutions, and backed clerics' attempts to establish law and order.⁸⁵ These forces had no interest in cooperating with the Coalition and giving up their powers to a new government. The dispute over control of the city was a major factor in the subsequent events that led to one of the biggest battles of the occupation.

Saddam's tribal policies were to have important implications in the new Iraq. First, a segment of Sunni society came to link its identity with political power due to the prevalence of tribalism within the regime. Second, the rise of tribalism in the periphery created tribal leaders who held state-like powers and were in no mood to relinquish them to the Coalition or a new Iraqi government. Finally, emphasis on tribes and tribal honor produced an impetus for vengeance and a mechanism for enforcement against collaboration with the Coalition, stoking the violence of insurgency and counter-insurgency in Iraq.

The considerable powers attained by tribes near the end of Saddam's rule would not be easily forsaken. Heavily armed tribes provided a fertile ground for resistance cells. The role of tribes in the new era was not as straightforward as might be thought, however. Tribes, tribal identity, and tribally associated business and crime remained strong. Many tribal leaders, tainted by collaboration with Saddam's regime, did not remain so. Soon after the regime's collapse, some "Taiwan sheikhs" found themselves ridiculed by graffiti or even chased out of the country to Syria or Jordan. The shake-up in the tribal hierarchy invited power struggles that simmered violently behind the headlines of the Sunni insurgency, until a new generation of young sheikhs began to ally with the Coalition to expel extremists and reclaim their families' power over the tribes.[86]

Islam

Tribes could provide protection and order for their members, yet not the sort of solace found only in religion. Iraq's mosques afforded a place of assembly, a network of charitable assistance, and an alternative ideology to the Baʻath reign of terror. While no statistics are available on the subject, journalists, scholars, and Iraqis all note that religious devotion increased markedly in these difficult times. Unfortunately, radical clerics used this growing religious devotion to spread intolerant fundamentalist messages. In many areas during the last two decades of Saddam's rule, Islam was increasingly sectarian in outlook[87] and fueled Iraq's political troubles in transition. The charged religious atmosphere resulting from the Islamic resurgence of the 1990s would stimulate Sunni insurgent groups and clerically backed Shiʻa parties after the invasion and bring the country to the brink of civil war.

The power of religion in Iraq did not owe itself wholly to any particular message of Islam, but rather to the organizational and ideological power of religion in such a chaotic environment. Religious institutions have long been centers of charitable and social services, filling gaps in state provision. For example, churches were central in the creation of a free African-American community in the Reconstruction following the American Civil War. Religious groups continue to provide social and charitable services today in America, where the state is strong and free and other forms of social organization are unfettered. In repressive countries, there are few outlets for people to assemble and act collectively. Unions, clubs, all manner of social organizations are highly regulated, if not banned completely. In such states, the last bastion of relatively free space is often found in religious institutions. Furthermore, the conditions of chaos, violence, and corruption found in a state such as Iraq drive people to seek solace and familiarity. Religion often becomes the touchstone.[88] In such a situation, people may cling strongly to religion, which gives religious leaders great power. Not all use this power for peaceful and harmonious ends.

Growing numbers of Iraqis turned to religion in the later years of Saddam's rule and after the occupation due to the debilitating environment of corruption, crime, and chaos. Some found radicalizing influences in the powerful language of militant political Islam and were among the earliest activists in organizing armed militias and resistance to foreign occupation.[89] Sunni religious rhetoric and the involvement of clerics proved important to the resistance. The various factions of the Iraqi Shiʿa religious establishment played a pivotal role in the organization of political and militia activity for their followers as well.

In the face of the crises of the 1980s and 1990s, religion became a tool for Saddam's regime when he adopted a policy of re-Islamization to stabilize and legitimize the state. As confrontation with the West grew, Saddam allowed anti-Western political rhetoric in the sermons of Sunni clerics and emphasized the image of a foreign assault on Islam, going so far as to call his confrontations with the United States and Britain a jihad.[90] Despite Saddam's shallow motivations, politicization of Islam found a receptive audience in some circles.

In addition to rhetoric, the state distributed several million copies of the Koran, instituted mandatory religious courses, and opened new mosques and the Saddam University for Islamic Studies. Archaic Islamic punishments, such as amputation, were implemented starting in 1994, along with a crackdown on alcohol and prostitution. The regime was forced to resort to evermore draconian measures to stem the endemic criminal activity that grew as a result of the tough economic times. Using Islam as a cover for these measures proved convenient to justify the increasingly harsh penalties.[91]

Regime rhetoric and the hardships of life under sanctions spurred attendance at mosques, which was said to have doubled in the five years before the 2003 war. Reporting from Baghdad in 1999, Jason Burke expressed, "Attendance at mosques has rocketed in the past two years, more young women wear the veil, enrollment in religious schools is rising fast and the rhetoric of the preachers is getting harsher and harsher."[92] Mosques, along with the tribes, were the last spaces where Iraqis not interested in the Baʿath Party could assemble. As Baʿath ideology waned, youths turned increasingly to an insular form of Islam.[93] While many Islamic activists quietly disdained the Saddam regime, their distaste for the West was equally powerful. Ayyash al-Kubaysi, a representative of Iraq's Muslim Ulema Council, stated that the Iraqi mujahideen who appeared soon after the 2003 invasion were "reared in the mosque. The mosque embraced them." He went on to claim that *ulema* (Islamic scholars) secretly educated the youth under the Saddam regime. In his words, "the fruits of this secret education were seen once the lid was removed" by the 2003 invasion.[94]

Although some mosques went on to fuel the most virulent groups in Iraq, the mosques' influence in general exceeded the radical fringe. They became a focus of political activism with no small bearing on the rise of sectarian politics in Iraq. Lacking any other forum for activism, even avowed secularists found themselves obliged to draw on a religious base for votes. In the most striking condemnation of politicians' opportunism, Sunni national security advisor Mowaffaq al-Ruba'ie stated that even former Ba'ath Party officials were now using mosques as their political headquarters.[95] Because of the old regime's destruction of all political space, mosques became the main centers for political activism. It is critical to understand, though, that political parties used sectarian institutions and definitions more than sectarianism drove political organization. While there was little difference in the violent results, the future implications are critical.

Saddam used Islam in a gambit for legitimacy and control, but the Islamist activism that grew out of it was a political ideology in opposition to the Ba'athist program. Islamism, also known as activist or political Islam, is an ideology holding that Islam provides a complete program of political guidance that is the only proper basis for government. In this view, the government of a Muslim country should be founded on Islamic laws and principles, rather than secular constructs. While the other two Abrahamic religions, Judaism and Christianity, were founded in a milieu of minorities oppressed by a strong government, Islam quickly became the religion of a powerful and expanding empire. Thus, there is a well-developed body of Islamic jurisprudence regarding proper Islamic government. Islamist viewpoints of how an Islamic government should look vary widely from those who believe Islam prescribes a tolerant, liberal democracy to those, including the Taliban and al Qaeda, who would establish a radical, intolerant religious dictatorship under clerical control. Even though Iraqi Islamists of all stripes were opposed to Saddam's ruthless and secular rule, few dared to stand up against him in a move that would bring a certain and painful death.

Iraqi Islamist activity operated within a larger regional context. Despite regime censorship, Iraqis were not completely isolated from outside Islamist influences. Publications and audio tapes were smuggled in across porous borders. Though these influences did not motivate Iraqis to resist Saddam's government, a campaign certain to fail, they were probably instrumental in preparing Iraqis for Islamist resistance to occupation. Iraqi Islamist Mohammed Ahmad al-Rashid's books were among those secretly imported from Egypt to a receptive audience. His readers were introduced to theories of jihad but were warned to wait for the proper time of action.[96]

Several themes of regional Sunni Islamism resonated with the situation inside Iraq. Sunni identity and anti-Shi'a violence were common themes of Sunni Islamic militancy across the region, however. These messages were well received by Sunnis facing domination by their historical subjects, the Shi'a. The perception that the Coalition placed a heretical Shi'a power at the helm of Iraq instead of the extreme version of Sunni Islam preached by the extremists may contribute as "proof of 'sinister' U.S. intentions toward Islam," fueling anti-American violence as well.[97] Conversely, the rise of Shi'a religious activism further activated Sunni fears of Shi'a religious domination.

A regional influence that shaped the most extreme resistance groups is the Salafi movement. These Salafists are a splinter from the Wahhabi strain of fundamentalist Islam promoted by Saudi Arabia. The small, yet powerful Salafi movement strictly adheres to a narrow and violent interpretation of the Koran and the acts and sayings of the Prophet Muhammad and his followers. The oneness of God (*tawhid*) is central to its members' beliefs, as is the rejection of any role for "human reason, logic, and desire." The resultant interpretation rejects any possibility of Islamic pluralism and specifically denounces the Shi'a.[98] After battling the Soviet Union in Afghanistan with U.S. and Saudi backing, Salafi jihadists brought their radical and violent campaign back to their homelands and eventually to the West. The uncompromising nature of Salafi beliefs and the militancy of the jihadists are important to understanding the polar and unyielding nature of the most radical Islamist groups in Iraq, especially al Qaeda. The virulence of the Salafi feelings about Westerners and Shi'a in the Middle East fed some of the most inflammatory and divisive attacks in post-invasion Iraq.

Islamists outside Iraq were affected by the situation there as well. Iraq was a focal point of regional Islamist activism during the sanctions of the 1990s. The impact of sanctions on the Iraqi people was well publicized in the region, emphasizing the suffering of fellow Arabs. Islamist mosques, especially in Jordan, were centers of charitable activism for Iraq.[99] Such activism provided a venue through which regional Islamists were drawn into the Iraqi cause. Some radicals activated by this topic were well positioned to embrace the transition to resistance in 2003. Furthermore, the availability of inexpensive weapons in Iraq led to a smuggling trade between Iraqi cab drivers and foreign Islamists on the Jordanian border. Some of these weapons were stockpiled in Jordan, while others found their way to Saudi Arabia and Palestine.[100] These transactions created a network of contacts between Iraqis and Islamist militants in Jordan and throughout the region that would later facilitate movement of ideology, funds, and Islamist recruits into Iraq.

The Threads of Iraqi Transition

By the time the Baʿath regime fell, Iraq's modern history had left behind a deeply fractionalized population. Ethno-sectarian divisions were quite real, while universal sectarian hatred was not. The severe sectarian violence that came later was not a given. Although an Iraqi national identity overlaid these divisions, many contested its outlines. Within the three major ethno-sectarian blocs, there were numerous divisions among parties, tribes, and local power groups. Because of three decades of single-party rule, there was no institutional or ideological framework within which Iraqis could quickly reorganize their political sphere. The divided nature of Iraqi society and the lack of unifying political leadership created huge challenges for reconciliation and progress. While the events of Iraqi transition were far from inevitable, Iraq's history provided the field on which they would play out.

Three key threads characterized Iraq's attempt at transition from dictatorship to a more representative form of government and stemmed from the legacies left behind by decades of harsh rule. The first theme was the pervasive crisis of governance, which set extremely difficult conditions for transition in Iraq. From the earliest point, political transition existed in an unstable environment. Government institutions, infrastructure, and the economy were weakened by regime mismanagement and the multiple crises since the 1980 Gulf War. In addition, Saddam gradually gave away powers to supporters in the society, including revenue collection and the use of armed force, which further weakened the legitimacy and importance of the central state. Because of these legacies, the entire Iraqi government collapsed in 2003.

In the wake of this collapse, sub-state power groups proliferated, creating a confused collection of political blocs and another major thread in Iraqi transition. In the chaos following Saddam's fall, narrow powers quickly stepped into the breach and provided services and protection to their supporters that the Coalition could not. These sub-state powers had grown strong in the later years of Saddam's rule and would dominate the landscape of the new Iraq. From these sub-state groupings, a Sunni resistance quickly arose amid an atomized population, ensuring a violent and conflict-plagued transition. The Shiʿa population was also highly armed, and armed militias openly supported several key factions. This thread stemmed from and reinforced the crisis of governance and had significant interaction with the next thread as well.

The final major thread was the official political process that resulted in a constitution and an elected government. This thread offered hope for a better future in Iraq, yet the crisis of governance and the power of local and sectarian groups led to flawed constitutional and electoral processes. The powers formerly held by the central government in Iraq dispersed to the local groups upon the collapse of the regime. These local and sectarian groups have since dominated the official political process and guaranteed that the new government would not threaten their interests. Faced with the gridlock of the political process, the country drifted along for several years before the sectarian bloc system began to give way to a more fluid set of alliances that may yet produce political progress and reconciliation. These three threads are intertwined, each affecting and being affected by the others. These threads will be carried throughout the book. Only through informed policy in these three areas can the path of Iraqi transition be altered.

Iraqis have had difficulty coming to terms with the new order. In the words of one Iraqi, "people aren't ready to jump to democracy. Over the last thirty-five years, all sorts of authoritarian ideas were imposed on us. They established dictatorship even in the primary schools, where one child would be singled out as the leader of the class. So we feel the superiority of our leaders."[101] An Iraqi returned from exile put it more succinctly: "When you tell them [the Iraqi people] they have such a great opportunity to express their opinion, they don't give a damn. It means nothing to them, they don't have anything to express, they have no opinion."[102]

Mark Etherington observed the results of this legacy during his tenure as CPA governor in Wasit Province. The "curious absence of the majority from political debate allowed all factions to claim its tacit support in turn; and this very absence precluded public refutation."[103] Iraq would not witness an explosion of civic organization or national unity. Many Iraqis simply kept their heads down in the days after the invasion and the fall of the statue in Baghdad, although a critical minority, often those radicalized and empowered in the latter days of the weakened Ba'ath regime, quickly acted to step into the breach. These Iraqis, shaped by the legacies of the old regime, would come to dominate the scene in Iraq in the years after the invasion with dramatic consequences.

3
Iraq's Collapse and the Crisis of Governance

We must not disguise from ourselves that we go to found a city among strangers and enemies, and that he who undertakes such an enterprise should be prepared to become master of the country the first day he lands, or failing in this to find everything hostile to him.[1]
—Nicias, Athenian statesman, 415 BC

Security may be 10 percent of the problem, or it may be 90 percent, but whichever it is, it's the first 10 percent or the first 90 percent. Without security, nothing else we do will last.[2]
—LTC John Paul Vann, Advisor for Military Assistance Command Vietnam, 1962

From the beginning in planning for a post-Saddam Iraq, we failed to seize a window of opportunity to get military, political, economic, and informational effects harmonized to bring order to a chaotic situation. While the Ba'athist hardliners would have opposed the coalition under any circumstances I believe the insurgency's mosaic of affiliations was not a preordained event.[3]
—LTG David McKiernan, commander of land forces in Iraq

From the moment Saddam's statue fell in Baghdad on April 9, 2003, the clock on Iraqis' patience and support for the Coalition began ticking loudly. While American troops expected a heroic greeting, they soon found that they had inherited a rotten state. The police had vanished. No ambulances were running. The power grid had failed, and in many areas, sewage flowed in the streets. Damage from battle and looting added to the toll of years of neglect and mismanagement. Even in these early days, before the military and security services were cashiered and the Baʿathists rooted out from the police and the ministries, the government as a whole had disappeared. Though the shooting had mostly stopped for the time being, the battle had only just begun.

Unable to turn matters over to local officials and redeploy to the United States, combat-weary units were faced with the vast and, for most, unprecedented tasks of municipal governance. Iraqis came to Coalition troops for mundane tasks of daily governance that Americans take for granted. Emergency services, trash collection, water, sewer, and electrical services, government salaries, mediating disputes—these became the domain of American warriors. Virtually every service and every decision had been undertaken for the Iraqi people by the Baʿath regime, all in the name of control. When the regime collapsed, so too did the vestiges of governance, services, and controls on the population. Faced with a wide range of unexpected tasks, the Coalition forces realized that time and a great deal of trial-and-error would be necessary to sorting out their new role and provide results to the Iraqi population. Unfortunately, competing powers were already acting in Iraqi towns as the race for popular support got off to a lopsided start.

Coalition troops were at a severe deficit in their capacity for the most basic of tasks facing an occupying force: the ability to understand and communicate with the local citizens. Troops and civilian administrators alike were almost universally unable to speak Arabic, and few Iraqis spoke English fluently. Critical communications went through a handful of military specialists and other government employees who could speak Arabic or, more often, through locally hired Iraqi translators whose loyalties and command of the English language varied widely. Mutual understanding was extremely hard to come by.

Communication and language consist of more than a simple transfer of code from one format to another. The most basic translators, and even computers, can transform words and phrases for troops and administrators, yet the meaning is often lost. If the computer or translator involved does not understand the intent of the language, the translated product is likely to be garbage. Thus, officers and officials trying to effect complex agreements, draft new laws, or facilitate negotiations between disputing parties were at a severe disadvantage. Even though they had the assistance of translators, no one could vet the quality of translation and shape the other side's understanding of Coalition intent.

At a deeper level, language carries many meanings and historical connotations that are important to a native speaker's understanding, but are often missed by all but the best linguists with extensive experience in the culture and history of the target audience. In Iraq, words that sum up the simplest premises of the Coalition presence in Iraq carry the most baggage in translation. For example, the Arabic translation for "occupation," *ihtilal*, is straightforward; however, the cultural and historical connotations this word carries are anything but. Western officials discussing occupation conjure thoughts of international law or perhaps the successful occupations of Japan and Germany at the end of World War II that culminated in the return of both countries to prominent positions in the international system. Invariably, the first images an Arab speaker will associate with ihtilal are humiliating scenes of Palestinians under the foot of the Israeli occupying authorities. Arab press dispatches from Palestinian towns come under datelines such as "Occupied Ramallah" and are filled with references to the occupying forces and their offenses against Palestinians. Ihtilal brings to mind the plight of the Palestinians, which, to Arabs, means injustice. This miscommunication played no small part in the negative turn in perception of the Coalition from liberating force to occupying power in the summer of 2003.

In contrast to the connotation of ihtilal is *muqawama*, "resistance." The Arab resistance to occupation, whether in Palestine, Algeria, or Lebanon, is legendary. Songs made famous by Arab singers such as the Lebanese sensation Feyrouz celebrate intense pride for the resistance. Resistance stories, a mixture of fact, embellishment, and pure legend, as are found in any culture (e.g., folk tales of the American Revolution such as the one of Paul Revere), have spread throughout the Arab world. For Iraqis, their resistance carries on this legacy. Muqawama comes from the root *qama*, to stand up. Resistance fighters are seen as nobly standing up for their rights, their culture, and their religion against an oppressive outsider: the occupier. While the most virulent foreign terrorists have been unable to claim this mantle, local Iraqis attacking Coalition troops are known as muqawama rather than *irhab* (terrorist) or *mutamarid* (rebel or insurgent). To many Iraqis, these local resisters are the minutemen, not terrorists.

Terms for the chaos facing Iraq also have loaded connotations in Arab and Islamic history. While chaos can be known as *foudha*, which also connotes anarchy and misrule, a more apt term for the strife between the different groups battling for the new Iraq is *fitna*. Fitna has several meanings, including riot and sedition. In another sense, the word connotes a calamity, disaster, or severe trial. In sum, for an Arab, the meanings hearken back to the discord that split the early Islamic community and allowed non-Islamic empires to roll back the early successes of the Muslims. By extension, the difficult conditions Muslims face to this day arguably emerged out of this strife. In Iraq, conflict between communities is seen as fitna, a severe trial and an internecine discord that is robbing Iraqis of the freedom, stability, and prosperity they deserve. Some acknowledge that this fitna is a problem between the Iraqi people; others accuse the West of sowing seeds of dissension to cheat Iraq of its future.

We in the West like to think that we deal in objective truths when we communicate and that our intentions should speak for themselves. It is important to remember that our words and our actions often have a different meaning when translated into a different language, a different cultural context, and a viewpoint radically different from ours. We must realize that what many in the West see as legitimate security operations, others see as illegal occupation. What we call terrorists, others see as valiant nationalist resistance figures. There are no truths to be had in this discussion, for people have differing aims and values, and these viewpoints create differing perceptions of truth. Once we realize this inevitability, we can begin to come to an understanding of each other's values and perceptions and then translate our words, actions, and goals into a message understandable in the context of other societies' languages, cultures, and histories. Such mutual understanding was absent in 2003.

As Saddam and the American-led Coalition faced off in the spring of 2003, both sides failed to recognize the nature of the struggle they were about to enter. For his part, Saddam refused to believe that the United States would carry through on its threats to unseat him. He instead prepared to counter the internal uprisings he believed would follow Coalition air strikes or limited ground incursions.

Although Saddam recognized the fragile nature of his state, the Coalition, focusing on Saddam's belligerent leadership and his potential weapons of mass destruction, failed to imagine the fallout of the Iraqi government's collapse. Some Coalition policymakers seem to have fully believed that once the heavy lifting of destroying Saddam's military and ousting the Ba'ath Party was complete, regime change would be a simple matter of replacing the old leadership with a new group of friendly exiles. Iraq's government was expected to stay in place, its infrastructure to remain largely intact, and its people to jubilantly welcome the liberating troops. Within months, a new Iraqi government would be established, Iraqi oil sales would begin providing revenue for reconstruction, and most American troops would be on their way home. Reality quickly outpaced these expectations as Iraq's weakened government and infrastructure folded before the Coalition's eyes. Afterward, policymakers struggled to keep up with events. The Coalition expected a simple liberation and regime change. Instead, it became the shepherd of an extensive process of transition.

Success in any endeavor requires a proper definition of the task at hand. No matter how high the quality of planning and execution, any military or diplomatic action is doomed to failure if it is based on a fundamental misunderstanding of the situation. When American policymakers defined the operation in Iraq as a simple, surgical regime change, they committed the most basic error. The complex and massive tasks of assisting a society in its transition to a new democratic form of rule were obscured behind a deceptively simple definition of regime change. In the years since the invasion, much has been made of American domestic politics and the ideological biases of the administration. Unfortunately, the majority of the criticism has been inwardly focused; it has challenged U.S. policy, but failed to search for a better definition and understanding of the problems faced in Iraq.

The essence of democratic transition, the move from a non-democratic form of rule toward a democratic one, is the confrontation between historical legacies and the establishment of a new order. History has shown that this confrontation is often lengthy and complex,[4] yet many assumed that transition in Iraq would be a simple matter of installing a new government, consisting largely of exiles, amid the cheers of a population happy to be freed from the horrors of Saddam's rule. Unfortunately in Iraq, many layers of damaged social, economic, and political institutions defied such a solution.

Taken at face value, Sunni resistance groups, Shi'a militias, rampant crime, decrepit infrastructure, and a chaotic electoral and constitutional process seem to be a set of topics lacking any connection. Indeed, many of these problems are addressed independently. Military, political, and economic agencies and experts tackle each issue with the specialized tools they possess, but often lack an overarching frame of reference. When viewing Iraq through a lens of transition, however, the relationship between these problems becomes visible.

When we realize that the military, social, economic, and political problems facing Iraq are all part and parcel of one overarching theme, the connections between issues and the requirements for integrated solutions emerge. The theme linking these issues is transition: the period of chaos and conflict between old legacies and new realities as the old form of rule gives way to a new order. The problems that Iraq has faced did not spring accidentally to life, but were products of the entrenched historical factors laid out in chapter 2. The way in which the problems manifested themselves was not predetermined, but resulted from the clash between historical legacies and new actions, events, and policies. To craft policies and reach solutions for these complex problems successfully, policymakers must address the historical legacies and their more recent complications.

The mistaken definition of the task at hand in Iraq, regime change rather than transition, led to the belief that Iraq could be turned over to a new democratic government in a matter of months. In April 2003, Secretary of Defense Donald Rumsfeld's spokesman, Larry Di Rita, boldly stated, "We're going to stand up an interim Iraqi government, hand power over to them, and get out of there in three to four months. All but twenty-five thousand soldiers will be out by the beginning of September [2003]."[5] Such thinking was the basis for the most controversial aspects of the tragically termed "post-conflict" portion of Operation Iraqi Freedom, including the low force levels and lack of rigorous planning for security and stability operations. Rosy assumptions based on the paradigm of regime change ignored the past cases of unpredictable transitions.

Unfortunately, these strongly held assumptions were not easily adjusted. Many military leaders and observers dismissed the forces behind growing unrest in Iraq. Rumsfeld termed them "dead-enders . . . those remnants of the defeated regimes who'll go on fighting long after their cause is lost."[6] Before long, insurgencies were clearly a much more complex mix of groups and motivations. Further, the resistance is only one facet of the treacherous landscape of Iraqi transition. The early focus on the Sunni insurgency in Iraq contributed to the U.S. government's over reliance on military methods and robbed policymakers of a broader perspective that could suggest more effective, integrated solutions. In Iraq, the complicated nature of factions in the tumult of creating a new political and social order requires a different frame of reference. The insurgency cannot be considered in isolation from the collapse of governance in Iraq, the official political process that would begin by the fall of 2003, or the other powerful sub-state groups in the country. These areas are interconnected and require an all-encompassing viewpoint to understand and combat the forces that promote disorder in Iraq. Success in Iraq's transition will only come from integrated measures meant to address problems in a systematic and interconnected way. The most basic of these problems is Iraq's crisis of governance.

Collapse and Crisis

In more than one conflict in the Middle East, the people caught in the carnage have expressed their simple wish to be able to leave their homes for the mosque, the church, or the store and expect to return alive. For the faithful, the minimum measure of successful governance lies in their ability to travel to mosque in safety. In Iraq, many of the faithful had been forced to pray at home by 2006. In addition to the most fundamental requirement of security, Iraq remains deficient in nearly every other category of governmental provision as well. The state is too weak and wracked by corruption to provide for its people. In the simplest evaluation of government as a vessel for provision of the common good, the Iraqi government has failed in the short term.[7]

Iraq's fledgling government must first provide real and stable security for its citizens in order to begin its climb out of the abyss. Events in 2007, including the "surge" of additional U.S. combat forces, Muqtada al-Sadr's truce with the government and the Coalition, and the rise of Sunni tribal forces against al Qaeda, constituted a tentative step in the right direction. Each of these moves was a temporary remedy to the violent symptoms of Iraq's underlying condition, however. Although the security situation improved in 2007 and into 2008, the gains could be erased in a matter of days or weeks. Beyond security, other fields of governance must be cleared to convince the people that the state can once again provide the common good. Until this happens, Iraqis will continue to place their trust in tribal and sectarian leaders, rather than the national government.

Most regions in Iraq saw little fighting during the initial invasion. An uneasy calm initially prevailed in these areas as Iraqis warily sized up the troops that moved in after Saddam's fall. The euphoria of liberation seen in several quarters of the big cities quickly gave way to chaos, however, as government institutions disappeared and widespread looting occurred. The looting was the beginning of a crisis of governance that has haunted Iraq until today.

Historian and CPA staffer Drew Erdmann described the collapse simply: "The state disappeared. Either the people melted away or the institutions were melted down by them."[8] As the Coalition forces fought in the capital, the regime center gave way. Without this essential element, Saddam's house of cards crumbled. Hardcore Ba'athists fled the country or went to ground. Some were afraid for their lives, while others were planning a fight to the death. More mundane servants retreated to their homes in anonymity. Everything in Iraq came to a halt. Without the threat of Ba'ath retribution, the police had no power, even if they did remain at their posts. In the resulting vacuum, the society released all of its pent-up feelings in an orgy of looting and destruction. Many Iraqis watching this spectacle could feel a cold wave of dread wash over them. They feared the spread of this unchecked freedom.

The Coalition was completely unprepared for these events. Without plans or orders to safeguard infrastructure or rules of engagement for stopping the looting, troops could only stand idly by as Iraqis gutted the state's infrastructure. Infamously, the only building protected by the Coalition was that of the Oil Ministry, which fueled many conspiracy theories in the days to come. While some commentators tried to pass off the unrest as little more than a boisterous welcome to newfound freedom, the truth was more sinister. The looting took a massive toll on Iraq in terms of economic loss, arms proliferation, reconstruction time and cost and, most importantly, public confidence in the occupiers. Though these events may have been unexpected to many, they were not unprecedented. During the Shi'a uprising following the 1991 Gulf War, rampant pillaging had been a problem as well, hinting at the instability that lay under Saddam's iron rule.[9]

Iraq's decrepit state infrastructure severely complicated the task of transition in Iraq. In June 2003, Peter McPherson, the CPA's top economic advisor, assessed the challenges.

> The electricity system is marginal and erratic; the supply of water in one of the most fertile areas of the world is unreliable; the health system is a disgrace; and the communications and transportation system is of fourth-world quality. Overall the quality of the infrastructure of Iraq is much worse than that in the other countries that have successfully managed transition.[10]

Iraq and the Coalition faced an incredible mission: rebuilding a state while attempting to reconcile major differences among three ethno-sectarian communities in what had been one of the most violent and corrupt states in recent times. As the enormity of the work that lay ahead became clear and the CPA was stood up, the Coalition quickly shifted from a minimalist approach to a vast, idealistic vision of Jeffersonian democracy and free market economy. Soon soaring violence and Iraqi demands for sovereignty changed the timeline once again, scuttling idealistic CPA staffers' plans for a grand new Iraq.[11]

Prior to the war, planners believed that military action could neatly remove the top level of the regime without disturbing the functions of the state at-large. This assumption missed the incredibly weakened nature of Iraq's state institutions and the role that the highly personalized Ba'ath leadership played in maintaining these rotten structures. Once the leaders were removed, the institutions crumbled. Without any indigenous institutions, the U.S. military forces, which were tailored for a lightning strike and not a massive, long-term security presence, were unable to step into the breach. The transition between "major combat operations" and the more mundane tasks of security, stability, and reconstruction was rough and caused the Coalition to lose precious time in stabilizing Iraq. The rotation of personnel, from combat units to the highest level of leadership—including the departure of GEN Tommy Franks (commander of U.S. Central Command) and the turnover from Jay Garner and the Office for Reconstruction and Humanitarian Aid (ORHA) to L. Paul Bremer III and the Coalition Provisional Authority (CPA)—contributed to a significant loss of momentum in the early stages of building a new Iraq and prolonged the crisis of governance.[12]

This breakdown damaged Iraq in a number of ways. First, it left a vacuum in which sub-state power groups armed and established themselves as local quasi-governments. Some groups had been armed by the regime prior to the war, and others made off with vast caches of weapons found throughout the country to become resistance groups or local militias. Since Coalition troops were absent from many areas following the invasion, these militias were the only form of law and order in sight. Iraq has suffered from this profusion of arms, armed groups, and insecurity ever since. The monopoly on weapons and armed force was lost in the early days of the occupation and has yet to be regained, as local militias still reign throughout most of the country.

Second, the crisis of governance had severe economic effects. Endemic looting resulted in an estimated direct loss of $12 billion, adding greatly to the costs and timeline for reconstruction.[13] Additionally, the collapse of the government resulted in the unemployment of countless former regime members with critical skills and knowledge. Some of these found lucrative pay assisting the armed groups, rather than helping rebuild Iraq. The loss of revenue, knowledge, and infrastructure greatly complicated the sparse Coalition reconstruction plans, which were predicated on relatively healthy facilities and continued oil revenues to pay the costs of getting Iraq back on its feet. However, this economic toll was slight compared to more intangible factors.

The crisis turned many Iraqis' perceptions of the Coalition from liberating heroes to inept occupiers. As weeks stretched on without competent local government, critical services, or government employment and subsidies, Iraqis were dumbfounded. Again and again, people stated their disbelief at how the Western powers could topple Saddam in a matter of weeks, but could not institute solid governmental structures. This was often explained in conspiratorial terms: the lack of reconstruction progress was cited as evidence of Western designs to destroy Iraq. This conviction opened the way for sub-state groups to establish themselves as quasi-governments across Iraq.

In the words of a Baghdad bus driver on April 10, 2003, "if they want to change the regime, they have to put another government in its place. Liberty like this is not good."[14] Iraq has come a long way since 2003, though many Iraqis still live in daily fear with no help from the government. Until the crisis of governance is permanently stemmed across Iraq, there will be no peace.

The Making of a Vacuum

With most attention on Iraq's leadership, its military formations, and its potential weapons of mass destruction, planners had little information on Iraq's mundane governmental institutions. Assumptions about the course of the "post-conflict" turnover of power to the Iraqis were wildly optimistic. GEN Franks told commanders to expect a functioning Iraqi government in thirty to sixty days after the fall of the regime. Plans called for initial combat forces to be withdrawn in sixty days and replaced by follow-on forces that anticipated leaving Iraq within 120 days. This guidance was passed down from the combatant commander even before many regions had seen a major American force. Under these plans, many areas would be virtually unoccupied.[15]

According to a high-level officer, the war plans in October 2002 called for an additional division of troops to control the restive Anbar Province, yet by January 2003, the division was dropped and Anbar was considered to be an "'economy of force' area." Only a cavalry squadron would be allocated to this area that was to become the stronghold of the resistance. Later in 2003, as the troubles lurking in Anbar became more evident, more troops were deployed; yet the task was still monumental. One regiment of 4,400 troops was responsible for security, stability, and governance of a territory consisting of more than six hundred square miles and over a million Iraqis, a massive task by any measure. The critical Sunni region was to have one of the smallest occupying contingents.[16]

The misconceptions about requirements for stability and security operations were not solely a failure of military imagination. Condoleezza Rice, then the President's national security advisor, stated in an interview, "The concept was that we would defeat the army, but the institutions would hold, everything from the ministries to police forces. . . . You would be able to bring new leadership but we were going to keep the body in place."[17]

Douglas Feith, head of the Pentagon's Office for Special Plans (OSP), was betting on Iraqi exile Ahmed Chalabi to provide this new leadership. Unfortunately, Chalabi was a poor man's version of Hamid Karzai, the Afghani statesman who quickly stood up a post-Taliban government. Chalabi had lived outside Iraq since 1958, when he was only thirteen years old. His experience included running a failed bank and escaping from a twenty-year sentence for embezzlement charges in Amman, Jordan.[18] Chalabi was long on promises of a quick return to stability, but short on credibility (outside Feith's office) and recent knowledge of the real state of Iraq. Neither Chalabi nor the other returnees from exile were able to rally Iraqis to unity or to swiftly reconstitute the government.

With no local governance and insufficient occupying troops to take up the task, Iraq's sub-state power groups offered their services. According to George Packer, a journalist who was in the country at the time, "those who reacted first and fastest were the country's long-oppressed Shiite clerics: They filled the vacuum with energy and organization, taking over hospitals and schools, providing social services to the poor, and imposing their Islamic code on daily life." On a more local level, Sunni religious and tribal leaders also attempted to establish order and provide services.[19] Narrow, local groups became the first actors to show their power in the new Iraq. This turn of events would greatly hamper the establishment of broad, unifying political associations as transition in Iraq progressed. Meanwhile, Coalition military officials were in a quandary over how to deal with their new responsibility.

Many in the U.S. military were counting on a rapid and significant contribution from Iraqi forces to aid the departure of Coalition troops. Despite the apparent melting away of the Iraqi military, there were high hopes for quick re-establishment of military formations. Coalition forces waged a major psychological campaign aimed at convincing Iraqi soldiers not to resist the invasion. They were urged instead to return to their homes and await instructions. Many soldiers did, including one Sunni lieutenant colonel who exclaimed to a reporter, only days before Ambassador Bremer's dramatic arrival in Iraq, "We're waiting for our orders. We are ready to help our country."[20] At a minimum, these Iraqi soldiers were to have been armed after the invasion with shovels, paintbrushes, and trucks to help in the vast task of rebuilding the nation.

A few senior Iraqi officers came forward early on to offer to aid in the reconstruction. The commander of Coalition ground forces, LTG David McKiernan, hoped to create a new Iraqi general staff from willing remnants of the old military.

He met with Faris Naima, the former commander of al-Bakr Military College, who offered a plan to reconstitute three Iraqi divisions and provide a company to augment police in each major town. Naima claimed that he could bring officers who had not been committed Ba'athists to restore the force. He also pointed out the need to compensate military, police, and government employees in order to avoid unrest. Other officers approached U.S. troops inquiring about their pay and indicating a willingness to cooperate with the Coalition. Garner, the ORHA head, confirmed that there seemed to be potentially obliging officers and units. "We sent out feelers, and by the first week in May we were getting a lot of responses back. We had a couple of Iraqi officers come to me any say, 'We could bring this division back, that division.' We began to have dialogues and negotiations." According to LTG Ricardo Sanchez, GEN John Abizaid, CENTCOM commander, also received "extraordinarily positive" feedback from Iraqi generals he sat down with in Baghdad to discuss the possibility of reforming units.[21]

These negotiations would come to naught as Garner's ORHA gave way to Ambassador Bremer's CPA in May 2003. One of the first actions of the new CPA was to officially disband Iraq's security and military services. As with most decisions regarding Iraq, the move to disband the army has been pointed to as inevitable by one side and as a completely unnecessary disaster by the other. The complex landscape of Iraq requires a more nuanced understanding of the factors behind the decision, demonstrating to partisans on both sides that nothing in Iraq is as simple as it seems.

While some military officials thought it would be feasible to recall entire units of the former Iraqi Army, Ambassador Bremer and Senior Advisor for Defense and Security Affairs Walter Slocombe felt that recalling the army would create major political repercussions. Slocombe, a former defense official in the Clinton administrat, believed that Shi'a conscripts would not return to service if recalled. If only Sunni conscripts returned and were under the authority of the overwhelmingly Sunni officer corps, this situation would present the potential of restoring Sunnis to a position of military power over their Shi'a and Kurdish country mates. The Shi'a or the Kurds would not accept such an outcome. Even had the army been recalled, thousands of Sunnis from the incredibly bloated officer corps would still have been cashiered and available to forces opposing the new order. Problems with readying the army for service extended beyond manpower. Looting had stripped old barracks and bases of plumbing and wiring. Even the brick walls had been taken apart. Added to that, there were no intact facilities or equipment stores for the army to use. For these reasons, Ambassador Bremer and the CPA elected to disband the military and security services.[22]

Memoirs and interviews in the years after the edict was issued demonstrated that the decision was not made by consensus. According to the well-researched account of Michael Gordon and Bernard Trainor, it was discussed only with advisor Walter Slocombe, Secretary of Defense Rumsfeld, and most likely President Bush or Vice President Cheney. Military leaders in Iraq were largely blindsided by the decision, as was National Security Advisor Condoleezza Rice. Indeed, Bremer's plan was not announced to the National Security Council until May 22, 2003, the day before it was officially issued. Further, high-level on-the-record interviews conducted by Gordon in 2008 demonstrate that the decision—which reversed earlier presidentially approved policies to use the military in securing and rebuilding the country—was made "without thorough consultations within government, and without the counsel of the secretary of state [Colin Powell, who was in Paris at the time] or the senior American commander in Iraq," LTG McKiernan.[23] In reality, another major motive behind the edict was Bremer's desire to decisively enter into Iraq as the head of the CPA, which would signal his control of the situation and determination to take Iraq in a new direction. An internal memo penned by Bremer stated, "It is desirable that my arrival in Iraq be marked by clear, public and decisive steps."[24]

On May 23, 2003, Coalition Provisional Authority Order Number 2 announced the dissolution of the Iraqi armed forces and security services, leaving half a million men with military training jobless. Bremer considered the choice to disband the Iraqi Army and security forces as the most popular during his tenure in Iraq. Perhaps it was, but a senior advisor offered a critical qualification. "The people it was popular with were already on our side. . . . If you want to come in and restore things, you want to come in with malice toward none and charity toward all. . . . Our whole approach was wrong."[25] Slocombe defended the move, claiming, "We didn't disband the army. The army disbanded itself." Conversely, Marine MajGen James Mattis stated, "We were working with the army when we were told to disband them."[26]

In a March 12, 2003, National Security Council meeting, Feith briefed the president on the plan to retain the Iraqi Army. Saddam's Republican Guard would be cashiered, yet the rest of the military would be kept in service. Three to five divisions were to have formed the new core of the army, while other soldiers would have been employed in reconstruction roles.[27] In the long run, such a plan to keep Iraqi soldiers in service of the state, even if it was only a partial recall of willing troops, would have made much more sense than the bold proclamation issued from an occupying power.

Regardless of the rationale behind Order Number 2, the edict certainly disenfranchised many Iraqis with military training. Whether the problems cited by Ambassador Bremer in recalling the Iraqi army could have been rectified will never be known, the bottom line is that the dissolution of the Iraqi army and the destruction of its infrastructure were severe blows to American transition plans and a boon to those who wished to resist the transition with force. Recalling the Iraqi army certainly would not have been a cure-all. Many soldiers would not have returned, among them the most committed insurgents. For those who did, a great deal of retraining and reconstruction of facilities would have been required. Despite these setbacks, the occupier would not have made what was seen as an arrogant edict to disband the national army and throw its soldiers out on the streets. Furthermore, the CPA would have had at least some workers to assist it in the gargantuan task of rebuilding.

The reality of the situation is far too complex to lay blame at the feet of any one person, agency, or decision. For many reasons, there was a severe lack of manpower for the reestablishment of security and governance in Iraq. These factors are simplified by Gordon and Trainor: "Rumsfeld limited the number of American troops in Iraq, and Bremer limited the number of Iraqi forces that were immediately available. The two decisions combined to produce a much larger security vacuum." A U.S. officer operating in Baghdad put it more succinctly: "When Bremer did that, the insurgency went crazy. May was the turning point. . . . When they disbanded the military, and announced we were occupiers—that was it. Every moderate, every person that had leaned toward us, was furious."[28]

The CPA's reasoning for its move was never explained to what might have been the most receptive audience: the Kurds and the Shi'a. One Kurd lamented, "Fifty percent of Iraqis are out of jobs—especially the former armed forces personnel. Bremer put them out of work, but the Iraqi army did not commit crimes. They were trying to defend Iraq and not Saddam." On this and other issue areas, the CPA's public information campaign was either insufficient or non-existent. This incompetence or absence contributed to the rapid spending of good will and it ceded ground to the other groups in Iraq who were eager to detail the CPA's shortcomings.[29]

Stripped of its military and security services, Iraq lacked trained police to contribute to the effort of securing the new Iraq. The officers of this once sixty-thousand-man force were "thuggish, uneducated, and largely untrained." The brutal and corrupt force was not highly regarded by Iraq's citizens. Since the police did not have an active patrolling presence before the fall of the regime, it was no surprise that the force disappeared amid the chaos of April 2003. Later that year, in August, the CPA's police advisor, former New York City police commissioner Bernie Kerik, briefed Ambassador Bremer that Iraq required one policeman for every three hundred residents. In Iraq, this requirement translated to at least sixty-five thousand police. At that point, Iraq had no more than thirty-two thousand police officers, many of whom were poorly trained and equipped. Kerik estimated that training an additional forty thousand police would take up to six years.[30] This estimate was disturbing to many Coalition members, especially military officials who were counting on Iraqi forces and police officers to replace American troops.

A critical requirement for permanently stemming the chaos in Iraq is the establishment of competent security forces with loyalty, above all, to the national government. One reason why the Coalition went in "light" was due to the assumption that Iraqi security forces would continue to maintain order. When this expectation was dashed, there was little or no fallback planning on how to re-establish these forces. Precious time was lost as the Coalition foundered for months before turning seriously to the task of training Iraqi police and troops. Even once the Coalition committed, the training was often poor and the trainees less than fully dedicated to their new job.[31] These factors contributed to Iraqi forces with reduced capabilities, which prolonged the crisis of governance.

The Department of Justice ran a comprehensive training program for Iraqi police officers in Amman, Jordan. Aimed at producing professional community police, this program was relatively thorough, yet still paled in comparison to earlier post-conflict training efforts in terms of length and depth of instruction. Because the Coalition quickly needed to stand up police units, put an Iraqi face on security and counterinsurgency efforts, and provide relief to U.S. troops, the Amman program consisted of only ten weeks of classroom instruction and no field training. A similar program in Kosovo had consisted of five months in the classroom and twelve weeks of field training.[32]

Police-training programs run by the U.S. military were generally much less intensive than even the short program in Amman and often relied on recruiting personnel with previous training. Unfortunately, many of these recruits' loyalties lay with tribal, religious, or local groups, rather than the national government. What is more, recruits were often the targets of insurgent attacks, which scared off potential police officers and thinned the ranks of trained personnel. The Iraqi government, therefore, was unable to provide the good community policing required to protect its citizens from insurgency and crime.[33]

The dilemmas with police and Interior Ministry forces continued into 2006, even as Iraqi and Coalition officials attempted to improve the situation. A fingerprinting campaign among members of the Ministry of Interior's police forces uncovered that 1,228 police officers and other employees had been convicted of violent crimes including rape and murder under the old regime. A Western diplomat commented, "The impression I got is that there are a lot more out there."[34]

For policing to lead to the restoration of the rule of law, arrests must be backed by an efficient, fair, and trusted judicial process. Coalition and Iraqi tactics combined with the paucity of institutional development in Iraq quickly developed into an overburdened judicial system that did little to restore Iraqis' faith in their courts. First, the huge number of detainees netted by Coalition and Iraqi sweeps represented a massive caseload for investigators, attorneys, and the courts. Detainees were kept for lengthy periods of time, and little or no information was given to family members simply because the systems in place were incapable of processing the cases and determining which individuals were worthy of further intelligence collection and criminal prosecution and which were in the wrong place at the wrong time.[35]

In the wake of an ambush or improvised explosive device (IED) attack, it was extremely difficult to sort out the good from the bad. Early on, any suspicious persons were held for further questioning, yet the backlog meant an indefinite wait in detention. Furthermore, Iraqi and Coalition troops rarely collected evidence in the midst of combat operations until several years into the insurgency. Even once troops began to pay attention to such details, the security situation in many areas made evidence collection an unacceptable risk.

Still, if the suspects are detained, processed, and indicted, true justice is hard to come by in the face of high caseloads and an under-resourced judicial system. Defense attorneys are underpaid, overworked, and often uninterested in providing much assistance to their clients. According to a 2006 Department of Defense report, most courts in Iraq refused to investigate and prosecute "insurgent- and terrorism-related cases" due to the risk of retribution, instead transferring the responsibility to the highly overworked Central Criminal Court in Baghdad. Into 2008 the courts were still swamped by the caseload, though the capacity and quality of the system was improving as hundreds of new investigators and judges were hired and trained.[36]

The court system suffered not only from a lack of capacity, but also from a culture inexperienced with due process and institutions of justice. High-level officials frequently presume guilt, even in public statements, and trials can be startlingly cursory. One Central Criminal Court trial in 2006 for a man accused of possessing explosives for insurgent activities lasted only fifteen minutes. Beyond saying that BGEN ʿAbd al-Karim Khalaf was innocent, the lawyer, who had not spoken to his client previously, did not challenge the evidence provided or support Khalaf's insistence that his nephew was the man the authorities actually wanted. After four minutes of deliberation, a three-judge panel handed down a guilty verdict and a thirty-year sentence.[37]

The overburdened system lends itself to lengthy detentions of innocent men, the release of guilty insurgents and criminals, and lack of trust for the rule of law in Iraq. As men disappeared into Iraq's prisons and its often arbitrary court system, citizens unsurprisingly compared the judicial system to Saddam's rule. The reasons were not tyranny, but rather institutional incapacity. The Coalition and its Iraqi partners, who worked diligently to improve the system, recognized these shortcomings. However, building a judicial system under the strains of massive caseloads and violent threats against officials was an uphill battle.[38]

Faced with the collapse of their government and the disappearance of their police forces, Iraqis required an extensive amount of foreign assistance. Seeing that the Coalition was desperate for international partners, the burgeoning insurgency quickly targeted potential supporters. On August 19, 2003, a massive truck bomb destroyed much of the United Nations' Baghdad headquarters and killed Sérgio Vieira de Mello, the charismatic rising star from Brazil who headed the UN Assistance Mission in Iraq. This blow came on the heels of the August 7 bombing of the Jordanian Embassy in Baghdad. A few short months later, on October 27, 2003, a string of strategically targeted bombings shook Baghdad, striking the headquarters of the International Committee of the Red Cross and a number of police stations. Iraq and the beleaguered Coalition were increasingly cut off from the world. A taxi driver in Baghdad viewing the carnage on October 27 remarked, "There was a man bringing discipline and now he's disappeared. No one fired even a bullet in Saddam's time."[39]

Finding little hope of rescue from the outside world, the people of Iraq sought out whatever help they could find in the chaotic vacuum. CPA staffer Drew Erdmann observed, "People in a desperate situation need help . . . if you're not giving them help, they're going to go somewhere else." A Shiʿa woman from

Sadr City explained to interviewers in July 2003 that such help was not available. "There is no place to go, no one responsible—there are no police, no one to take your problems to."[40] With a collapsed Iraqi government and an invading force incapable of providing pervasive security and other governmental functions, the existing structures of Iraq's sub-state organizations took over.

Iraq's tribes, mosques, and other local institutions began providing what the occupiers and the central government could not. These groups were well prepared to act decisively, because their powers had already begun to grow under Saddam's weakening rule. Once the central government vanished, they flourished like weeds and have proven extremely difficult to root out. Even with the formation of a permanent Iraqi government, tribes, mosques, and other local groups have continued to act in many areas where the government simply is unable.

Mosques became primary providers of services in sectors where the government failed, including education and health care. Adel Hizad, a worker at a mosque-run charity, stated that the network she is affiliated with provides assistance to more than 25,000 Iraqi families. The benefits, however, came with baggage. A father of three explained that

> [t]here are not enough of these organizations, and they have a limited budget, and normally they work under a political party or [religious] organization, so they are not moderate. But with a government that can do nothing, I think they are very important, at least until the government can stand up again and provide all these services.[41]

The "services" offered by some groups were quite cynical. For instance, the lack of police presence allowed criminal and insurgent groups to set up protection rackets. In areas of Anbar Province, resistance groups guaranteed safe passage to Iraqi aid workers based on an "insurance fee" and confirmation that they were not "supplying the enemy" Iraqi and Coalition forces.[42] These groups not only robbed the government of control, but they also profited off of the vacuum and used these gains to strengthen their power. The ongoing crisis of governance factored significantly into the rapid evaporation of good will toward the occupying forces. Another main element in inflaming resistance and undercutting support for the Coalition was the occurrence of early missteps at both the tactical and strategic levels. Some of the good will that was generated by throwing off the oppressive dictator was lost as troops and administrators came into early conflict with the Iraqi public.

While negative perceptions may have been countered by slick public information campaigns explaining the Coalition's intentions, the CPA was at a serious disadvantage in its efforts to counter years of suspicion and pessimism. Saddam's legacy of propaganda and conspiracy stories created an unreceptive audience in Iraq for Coalition information. Iraqis were often misinformed or uninformed on Coalition policies. A Shi'a man explained a more basic obstacle in the summer of 2003. "Bremer is appearing every Saturday and announcing problems, but unfortunately, there is no central channel so we don't hear what he says."[43] The Coalition's attempts at information operations, or simply publicizing good news and clarifying bad, were hampered by a distrust of American motives and governmental honesty in general. At a more fundamental level though, the television products broadcasted by the Coalition were simply not well received by the Iraqi people.

The CPA paid little attention to the re-establishment of *al-Iraqiya*, Iraq's national TV channel, and the reconstruction contractors were wasteful, if not criminally negligent, in the way they prioritized their expenditures. Since the station's programming was often stale and irrelevant, Iraqis tuned to other regional stations like al-Jazeera for their news. When a massive truck bomb shook Baghdad in August 2003, destroying the UN headquarters, Iraqis turning to al-Iraqiya for news of the event found an Egyptian cooking show still broadcasting. When they turned to al-Jazeera, they found live on-the-scene coverage. The accompanying commentary denounced the illegal American occupation and was sympathetic to the Sunni insurgents.[44]

A State Department study in late 2003 found that 63 percent of Iraqi satellite-TV viewers watched the international Arabic channels al-Jazeera or al-Arabiya for the news, while only 12 percent tuned in to al-Iraqiya or affiliated radio stations. A producer from Science Applications International Corporation (SAIC) lamented that within six months of the invasion, the SAIC-run media network "had become an irrelevant mouthpiece for Coalition Provisional Authority propaganda, managed news, and mediocre programs.... We have already lost the first round" in the battle for ideas. This handicap continued with the permanent Iraqi government, to the extent that one Iraqi official proposed reforming the much-maligned Ministry of Information to manage the government's message.[45] Although good news stories are important to disseminate, if officials refuse to acknowledge bad news stories, these stories will be covered in a much less sympathetic venue with no counterpoint.

Even had information operations been better, more fundamental problems would have plagued the Coalition. Shortfalls in the most basic services rapidly wasted good will toward the occupiers. Lack of electricity was the most cited complaint plaguing the reconstruction. In the sweltering heat of Baghdad's summer, the lack of electricity for air conditioning and evening lighting was an ongoing annoyance. It also disrupted economic re-growth as businesses were unable to run equipment for large parts of the workday or were forced to buy and operate costly generators to keep their shops open.

Much of the blame for the electrical system's initial problems must be assigned to the former regime. The Coalition avoided attacking critical infrastructure during the 2003 campaign, yet Iraq's electric grid was a shambles before the war. In the 1991 Gulf War, American aircraft targeted power stations to cripple the regime and its communications, command, and control systems. Though Iraqi engineers brought the system back on-line in roughly four months using ad-hoc repairs, the result was a weakened grid running on a shoestring. The network was working at no more than 40 percent of full capacity in 2000, resulting in frequent blackouts throughout the country well before the invasion. Officials from the UN Development Program found Iraq's electricity system to be "technically and economically obsolete" in a 2002 report and noted that there was a nationwide shortage of 2,500 megawatts, a huge amount when considering that Iraq's total demand was around 6,200 megawatts and that 1 megawatt could power around 1,500 homes. An American pre-war study likewise found that the system was in dire need of repairs, and the dearth of cultural lighting in nighttime satellite photos pointed to frequent blackouts in many of Iraq's cities.[46]

Fearing a repeat of Gulf War tactics that used weapons designed to short out power lines, many Iraqi engineers shut down their fragile grids preemptively as the war started in 2003. Others used blackouts as a warning signal when American aircraft flew over. The infrastructure was in such delicate shape that the surges caused by closing and opening the circuits blew out equipment and permanently incapacitated the grids. In Baghdad, fighting felled one section of lines and the imbalance knocked out the entire grid in the capital region. In addition, post-war looting gutted many control stations. Even power lines were stripped from utility poles for the valuable metal that could be sold on the black market.[47]

More fundamentally, Iraq's infrastructure was not meant to serve the entire country reliably, according to Eric Bauer, a CPA staffer. While business districts, elite neighborhoods, and Baʻath Party warrens were sure to have reliable services, many homes in places such as Saddam (later Sadr) City had no electricity or other services. One faucet might serve forty families, and raw sewage ran through the streets. When these targeted services were widened to encompass the whole country after the fall of the regime, there was naturally a shortage of available power, water, and other capacity. Bauer noted that the man paying a bribe under Baʻathist rule for his electricity or water may have been miffed by the outage, yet this was to be expected.[48] Unfortunately, the man who used to pay a bribe for a higher standard of living might also be willing to pay into the coffers of the insurgency.

Once the electricity did return, there was no incentive to conserve power. Since electricity had been provided for free by the Baʻath regime, there was no system for metering and charging for electricity once the Coalition restored services. With no economic incentive to conserve electricity, demand for power far exceeded the capacity of the weakened infrastructure and the load continued to damage equipment and lines. A November 2006 Department of Defense report noted that establishing a fee for electrical services would be "a crucial step toward solving the supply gap problem," because it would "encourage conservation and reduce the effects of corruption." An electricity rationing scheme that limited a family's draw to ten amperes through a circuit breaker began to come on line in Baghdad in 2007, though in the absence of fees or surveillance the system was subject to corruption and numerous work-arounds.[49]

The long hours of blackouts in the sweltering summer heat reminded many Iraqis of the Coalition's shortfalls. A Marine reconnaissance platoon leader was one of many Coalition officers who encountered pointed questions on the subject during patrols through western Iraq's neighborhoods. "We have failed a lot of people in al-Anbar with undelivered promises. The question I used to get was, 'How can America take Iraq in three weeks and not get the lights on in years?'"

Iraq's electricity output has yet to rise consistently above pre-war levels, despite a massive rise in demand. The estimated peak demand in late summer of 2005 was in the vicinity of 170,000 megawatt-hours (MWh), although the supply available varied between 70,000 and 110,000 MWh in the same period. Even in 2008, averages hovered near 100,000 MWh for most of the year. Operating hours dipped as low as four hours a day in the capital in May 2006, before climbing through 2007 to a high of nine hours a day in November. The nationwide average exceeded twelve hours a day only twice between the beginning of 2006 and summer of 2008.[50]

Much of the blame for Iraq's electrical woes, as with many other problems, falls on the shoulders of both Iraqi leaders and the groups that attempt to sabotage every one of the government's moves. By the end of the summer of 2007, Iraq's electrical grid had progressed little. In fact, it stood at the brink of collapse. Rising demand in the summer heat, sabotage at the hands of insurgents and criminals, and infighting among the provinces over the distribution system had brought Iraq's electrical system to ruin. There were four nationwide blackouts in a two-day period in August 2007, and Baghdad was receiving only a few hours of electricity a day in the hottest month of summer. Many provinces had taken their power plants off the national grid, husbanding their resources, while others kept their cities on the grid after they had used up their allotted share of the power, drawing down the national supply. The lack of national unity showed even in electrical distribution. The severe power shortages caused huge problems in the form of sewage backups and the inability to supply water to the citizens. To top it off, a national fuel shortage drove gas prices through the roof, preventing Iraqis from running the ubiquitous generators that had helped them avoid blackouts in the past. Despite improved security in 2008, a drought impacted hydroelectric generation capacity and continued rises in demand from residential and industrial growth overtaxed the system, with several areas of Baghdad receiving as little as one hour of electricity a day. By December 2008, most areas of the country were finally receiving over fourteen hours of electricity, but were still far short of a full day of power.[51]

There is more to reconstruction than building or renovating infrastructure. Lack of maintenance and proper management often ruined what did work in Iraq. U.S. government audits found that successfully completed projects in areas quickly fell into disrepair due to misuse or improper maintenance. In a hospital, employees could not find the key for a costly and unused incinerator, leaving medical waste to contaminate water supplies. In other projects, electrical components had been looted or were inoperative because of a complete lack of upkeep. Poor initial construction also contributed to problems in the facilities surveyed.[52] Reconstruction plans must take into account not only the rebuilding itself, but also plans, funds, and training for use and preservation of infrastructure.

Iraq's oil infrastructure was also significantly degraded by years of neglect, in addition to the post-invasion looting. U.S. officials estimated that $20–25 billion of yearly oil revenues would boost reconstruction efforts shortly after Saddam's fall; however, such profits were slow to come. From the fall of the Iraqi government in April 2003 until the end of that year, only $5.09 billion in oil revenues was realized. That figure climbed to $17.18 billion in 2004, still well short of the planning figures, despite the unexpectedly high price of oil. Only in

2005 did oil revenues climb above $20 billion a year. The total from April 2003 to December 2006 was only $77.3 billion, falling short of U.S. expectations. Deputy Secretary of Defense Paul Wolfowitz, for instance, testified to Congress in 2003, "The oil revenues of that country could bring between $50 billion and $100 billion over the course of the next two or three years." It was not until 2006 and 2007 that revenues began to meet expectations, climbing over $30 billion each year. High oil prices and increased stability in 2008 finally allowed Iraq to begin seeing significant increases in oil revenue.[53]

Sabotage of Iraq's oil pipelines was a particularly detrimental problem that contributed to the shortfall in oil revenues. Although cases of pure sabotage occurred, the damage was more often the side effect of crude theft and smuggling enterprises. These operations funded criminal and insurgent groups, while at the same time requiring costly repairs and robbing the government of up to a billion dollars of revenue each year. The problem consisted of "a mix of insurgents, organized criminal groups and scores of independent operators . . . working together in some loose network to keep their grip on the system and turn enormous profits." The criminals and insurgents were so well interconnected and informed that saboteurs often waited until refineries were full of oil before blowing the pipelines that would carry excess oil to neighboring countries for sale. Thus, the refineries were able to produce fuel for smugglers and the oil had to be shipped by truck, which created opportunities for profit and graft for those who could move it across the border. The effects of this sabotage were softened in late 2007 as redundancy and hardening of pipelines was increased.[54]

Fuel subsidies established by the old regime encouraged black marketeering by artificially keeping fuel prices in Iraq much lower than those in Syria and Turkey, although fuel was often hard to come by for average citizens in Iraq. This encouraged smugglers to buy cheap fuel in Iraq and sell it at higher prices across the border. The smugglers returned with a truck full of foreign gas and sold it at a profit on the Iraqi black market as well. The subsidies have endured until today, and so has the smuggling problem.[55]

Despite the fact that looters and smugglers caused massive injury to Iraq's infrastructure and economy, the Coalition took the blame for shortfalls. In Saddam's Iraq, there was no such thing as civic responsibility. The government was the provider of subsidized fuel, food, electricity, and many other necessities. The people were not welcome to craft improvements or take up projects on their own. In the new Iraq, a degree of civic responsibility is required. People must understand the effects of their actions, yet years of keeping their heads down have had a lasting impression. All that happens or fails to happen is considered to be the fault of the central power, despite an overwhelming lack of involvement on the part of the citizens.

Saddam's legacy of fear also had dramatic impact on bureaucratic structures in Iraq. Even as reconstruction money was allocated to various projects throughout Iraq, the funds never arrived in a timely manner. Bureaucrats who learned under Saddam that a mistake could be fatal were slow to decide and sought as many second opinions as possible before committing to a course of action. For this reason, the Iraqi bureaucracy continues to move slowly. Ministries were unaccustomed to dealing with major funds and projects, because most large undertakings were tightly controlled by Ba'athists outside normal bureaucratic structures. The CPA found that only around 8 percent of the budget went through the Ministry of Finance. According to CPA economic advisor David Oliver, "the vast majority of government spending was controlled directly by various offices attached to the presidency . . . and Saddam's hand-picked party cronies. And under Saddam the budget was a state secret."[56] These factors greatly complicated the task of reconstruction in Iraq.

Further complicating matters, Iraq's government employees under Saddam's reign began to look out for their own interests before worrying about the good of the institution, an extension of the personalization of governance and the legacy of patronage issue. Mark Etherington, the CPA governor of Wasit Province, gave a tragic example. "A child playing was killed by falling masonry in late 2003; yet I never met a head-master who did not vigorously insist that his own office should be refurbished before any other work was done."[57] Beyond individual greed, there are larger social and cultural issues behind this mindset.

The culture of patronage and graft entrenched during Saddam's rule is difficult to overcome in the new Iraq. Etherington aptly described Iraq's "essentially feudal system" of patronage and loyalty to identity group. "Economic, social and local considerations, rather than national ones, governed their analysis. . . . Writ small, this meant that the vast majority of Iraqis whom the Coalition employed saw their task as being to promote the cause of their own clans." A tribesman who did not earn for his tribe risked being shamed or completely shunned by his tribe, thereby losing his entire social support network.[58] In the absence of an impartial national government capable of providing public goods for the citizens, narrower social groups developed ways of taking care of themselves at the expense of the broader good and the rule of law.

What Americans see as unacceptable graft, Iraqis see as the normal mode of doing business. When Americans think of corruption, a corporate or government official ensconced in a comfortable office with a comfortable life lining his or her pockets for the sake of extravagance is envisioned. In Iraq, most people are scraping to make ends meet. Many Iraqis take a cut simply to provide a decent meal to their families. Corruption abounds at the higher levels of society where the extra income becomes a luxury rather than a need, yet the idea of skimming an extra percentage for the family or the broader clan or tribal unit is seen as taking care of those close to you, not as a reprehensible crime. It is a different culture with a different set of norms. This culture works against building new, rule-bound institutions and saps the funds of a government trying to establish itself and rebuild the country's infrastructure. MG Michael Diamond observed in June 2006, "There has been a lot of progress in the governance area, but corruption is eroding a lot of what is taking place." One senior Iraqi official estimated in 2006 that corruption, in all its forms, cost the country $5 to $7 billion per year.[59]

One high-profile case of embezzlement demonstrated how corruption not only weakened the state, but often directly aided the insurgency. Meshan al-Juburi, a Sunni member of Iraq's National Assembly, was charged in February 2006 with embezzlement of millions of dollars of U.S. funds slated for protection of Iraq's oil pipelines. Instead of launching the force, al-Juburi collected salaries for a list of ghost soldiers and then fled to comfortable accommodations in Syria when charges were brought against him. As if this slick getaway was not enough, al-Juburi reportedly channeled large amounts of the embezzled American funds to insurgents and turned his satellite TV channel, *al-Zawra*, into a mouthpiece of the insurgency, broadcasting gruesome videos of attacks on Coalition and Iraqi troops and vitriolic statements against the occupation and Iraq's Shi'a-led government.[60]

Graft also had detrimental effects on Iraq's new military. Iraqi officers were often found to be skimming a cut from the pay of their soldiers at almost every juncture from the Ministry of Defense in Baghdad down to the company level. The result is that the average soldier often went months without pay. Further, American advisors in cases were hard pressed to account for significant portions of the soldiers on the rolls of Iraqi units, although these soldiers' pay was taken every month. The many ghost soldiers on these units' rolls were another symptom of the endemic corruption that plagued Iraq since Saddam's rule. Some of these problems have been corrected, but others are more systematic.

The lack of a widespread and trustworthy banking system also depletes the army's ranks. Lacking a reliable banking system, Iraqi soldiers were given up to ten days of leave a month to return home to their families to deliver their pay. The trip was often harrowing, as Iraq's new soldiers were prime targets of insurgent attacks, and the monthly leave periods meant that up to one-third of Iraq's army was absent on leave at any time.

Iraq is in dire need of improvements in state infrastructure, capacity, and capability in order to end the crisis of governance and begin to provide for its citizens. Until Iraqis see their government benefiting them, the state will have no legitimacy and little support. While Iraq must strive to produce a "government of laws and not men,"[61] building such a government has proven all but impossible in the violent environment dominated by sectarian and tribal interests. Therefore, governance and security are Iraq's most precious commodities.

Governance and Security

The initial collapse of order in April 2003 brought about several reactions. On a local level, sub-state powers supplied security and services, but this came at a high price. These groups took on governmental powers that they would not readily sacrifice to the Coalition or the new Iraqi government. Sub-state groups and militias gained a degree of popular legitimacy and support from early actions to protect and provide for local populations. Additionally, many local resistance groups sprung up. These groups added to the pervasive insecurity and made even the simplest tasks of governance and reconstruction dangerous and difficult.

The CPA came into this environment with a grand vision for a bold new Iraq, though many of its well-intentioned efforts faltered because basic governance and security were sorely lacking. A senior aide of Bremer admitted shortly before the return of sovereignty to Iraq's government, "We were so busy trying to build a Jeffersonian democracy and a capitalist economy that we neglected the big picture. We squandered an enormous opportunity, and we didn't realize it until everything blew up in our faces." CPA staffers hoped to reshape Iraq in America's image, undertaking sweeping projects to rewrite laws, reinvent markets and institutions, and restructure government and economy. Although these projects were noble in conception, the Coalition did not have the capacity or the time to complete them. Moreover, the grandiose initiatives failed to account for the disastrous state of Iraq's institutions and address the most immediate and crushing problems.[62]

The most crippling blow to these plans was the November 15th Agreement, which provided a timeline for handing sovereignty back to an Iraqi government before June 30, 2004, as will be discussed in detail below. Journalist Rajiv Chandrasekaran wrote, "The November 15 Agreement was the writing on the wall for the neoconservative experiment in Iraq." With only seven months remaining on their mandate, CPA staffers had to jettison their grand plans and turn to short-term measures. Months had been wasted on these grand visions, never to be completed. Because of these now-wasted projects, officials had eschewed the sort of stopgap measures needed to make short-term improvements. A senior American general confided that the CPA's misguided plans and mistakes "cost us one very valuable year."[63]

Even six years on, the Iraqi government has only just begun its campaign to wrest responsibility, authority, and legitimacy for local governance and security back from sub-state powers. In such an environment, governance and security is hard to come by. The only way to proceed is by reclaiming the government's monopoly on violence. Secretary of State Condoleezza Rice explained the dilemma during a visit to Baghdad. "You can't have in a democracy various groups with arms. You have to have the state with a monopoly on power and that will be represented by the Ministry of Defense for the army and the Ministry of Interior for the police." Secretary Rice then implicated militias as a major obstacle to this monopoly. Conversely, the power of militias stemmed from the government's inability to provide security. The Department of Defense acknowledged in a May 2006 report to Congress that militias "provide protection for people and religious sites where the Iraqi police are perceived to be unable to provide adequate support."[64] This sort of catch-22 is exceedingly difficult to unravel. On one hand, a monopoly on arms is required to establish security. On the other hand, people do not want to relinquish their arms or stop supporting the local militia until the government has established security.

In a telling observation, journalist Megan Stack remarked in 2006, "Iraq may be the only country in the world where militia members and anti-government insurgents walk the streets with bare faces while government workers, soldiers and cops cower behind masks."[a] Police and government workers are working at a deficit for two reasons. First, in many places, sub-state forces are simply more powerful than the government and enjoy support as locals. Second, governmental forces are held, at least nominally, to a standard of rule-bound conduct, yet the sub-state forces have no such restrictions. Police forces are often inefficient at finding and detaining insurgents and militia members. By their nature, it is difficult to identify and track down these shadowy fighters. Even once captured, many are released shortly thereafter. In contrast, insurgents can easily identify police officers and other government workers and kill not only them, but also their families. Little by little, this deficit is being overcome by increased military and police strength and proficiency, as well as greater public trust and support, though insurgents and militias still have the upper hand over Iraqi police in many areas.

Even as Iraqis tire of the violence, they are often powerless in the face of the well-entrenched insurgent and militia groups. While local groups were successful in chasing extremist insurgents out of Anbar Province in 2007, the future of these groups is questionable. Many of their members are former insurgents, and the movement has done nothing to increase loyalty to the state or reclaim the state's monopoly on violence. These local groups, while a short-term solution, may only be a part of a longer-term problem.

As will become clear in the following chapters, the leaders of the Iraqi communities that stepped into the light of the new Iraq had few intentions of placing national interests and central government power ahead of their own. As a result, the political process created a weakened and corrupt central government that did little to win back the population's confidence.

4
The Rise of Shiʿa Power in Iraq

> We order the people to obey us. When we say stand up, they stand up. When we say sit down, they sit down. With the collapse of Saddam, the people have turned to the clergy.[1]
>
> —Ali Shawki, Shiʿa Cleric, Sadr City, 2004

Coalition troops entering Baghdad in 2003 were amazed by the squalor they found only a few miles across the Tigris from the Republican Palace. In a densely packed northeast Baghdad neighborhood, two million Shiʿa lived in a community designed for less than half of its current population. This crowded and confusing warren of haphazard buildings, low-strung electric wires, and narrow streets overflowing with trash and sewage was built in the early 1960s as Revolution City. In 1982, it was renamed Saddam City. From April 2003 on, it would be known as Sadr City after its one-time champion, Grand Ayatollah Mohammed Sadiq al-Sadr. Al-Sadr, a populist Shiʿa cleric renowned for his links to Baghdad's Shiʿa underclass, was assassinated by the regime for his political activism. His legacy lives on through his son, Muqtada, and a strong network of radical clerics. As confusing as the city's layout was, the Shiʿa social, political, and religious landscape was more byzantine. The troops on the ground knew little about Iraq's important Shiʿa majority. The upper reaches of the Coalition focused on important Shiʿa exiles, including the clerics Mohammed Baqir al-Hakim and Abd al-Majid al-Kho'i and the politically secular Ahmed Chalabi and Ayad Allawi. These exiles, however, had no influence in places such as Sadr City.

Iraq's Shi'a clerics draw on two different demographic power bases. Traditional clerics tend to be allied with the established middle class of merchants and businessmen. Rival preachers have created a separate power base by offering services and incitements to the masses of urban dwellers, many of whom live in the slums of Baghdad and the cities of the Shi'a south, notably Basra and Najaf. These masses can be mobilized for elections, protests, or riots, and angry youths provide the muscle for various militias. Many of these poor city dwellers are relatively new arrivals from the rural areas of the south, forced by economic hardship, government relocation, and Saddam's draining of the vast southern marshlands in the 1990s to leave behind their traditional homes and tribal structures for packed urban areas.

This trend peaked in the 1970s as the country's new oil wealth drew record numbers away from the rural south to Basra and Baghdad. Migrants crowded into planned developments on the outskirts of the city, rapidly overwhelming its capacity. Social and class differences between the established city dwellers and the new rural arrivals kept the two communities from integrating. The established Shi'a elite were successful merchants; their rural cousins were poor and uneducated. Further, the latter brought with them a bewildering web of tribal allegiances, tended by more than three hundred tribal leaders in Sadr City alone. Likewise, these Shi'a did not assimilate fully into the traditional Shi'a religious structures, practicing instead a rural form of Islam infused with folk and tribal influences. The new city dwellers' social status, religious beliefs, and lack of integration into the existing urban society all played into the increasing popularity of communism's promises of equality.[2] This initial brush with politics prepared many for the populist forms of Islamist activism that became increasingly vocal in the following decades.

Shi'a clerics, fearing that they would lose followers to godless communism, began to practice a new, populist, and politically active form of ministry. Clerics became more heavily involved in providing social services and promoting political activity in the slums. This phenomenon has adapted over the intervening decades until blossoming into the chaotic conditions that followed Saddam's fall. Radical young Shi'a clerics are the champions of areas such as Sadr City. The government neglected such areas for years, the tribal structure was broken by migration to the cities, and even the familial structure has been destroyed in many cases by the tragedies of the past decades, leaving many families widowed, disconnected, and in dire need of charity, security, and spiritual solace. The Shi'a clerics supply it, drawing a strong following. Along with these services come powerful, populist, often radical messages. When clerics decided that the Coalition was not delivering on its promises, that message became a call to arms.

Instead of well-practiced political maneuvering between Coalition officials and urbane Iraqi elites, Coalition troops and radical Shi'a clerics waged a cutthroat battle for the support of the Shi'a masses. Although officials and pundits dismissed firebrand clerics in Sadr City as inconsequential rabble-rousers, they competed directly with Coalition troops and the Iraqi government by providing security, stability, and services to their constituents. While the Shi'a would largely steer Iraqi politics, they were by no means a unified bloc.

America's only real insight into this community came from exiles, many of whom had been out of Iraq for years. Iraq's Shi'a had been affected by Saddam's long rule, reshaping the community and bringing relatively unknown leaders to prominence. U.S. officials were enamored with Shi'a exiles who had spent years in London, Europe, and America. Journalist George Packer went so far as to say that "Shi'ite power was the key to the whole neoconservative vision for Iraq."[3] There were new Shi'a power brokers, however, who had suffered in anonymity under Saddam's brutal reign and proved much more difficult to mold than the exiled Shi'a leaders with whom the Coalition hoped to work. The Coalition was unable to engage these new elites and their loyal followers. The two most emblematic faces of the Shi'a community in this dawning era were relatively unknown to the West prior to the 2003 invasion.

On one side, Ayatollah Ali al-Husseini al Sistani was situated atop Iraq's traditional Shi'a clerisy. Al-Sistani, although of Iranian origin, represented Iraq's traditional conservative clerical establishment and sought Shi'a majoritarian dominance of Iraqi democracy. He aimed to ensure that Iraq's Shi'a stood unified so as to never again fall into the position of repressed majority. He saw the new political system of Iraq, which he had a large, if indirect, part in forming, as the best method for attaining that goal.

On the other side of the Shi'a community stood the enigmatic Muqtada al-Sadr. Al-Sadr was the antithesis of the stoic, learned, and patient al-Sistani. Although the son of a revered cleric, al-Sadr had virtually no legitimacy within the traditional clerical hierarchy. This fact caused many observers to dismiss him as a small-time troublemaker in the early days of the new Iraq. Nothing could have been further from the truth. Al-Sadr rode on a wave of social upheaval within the community and especially within the religious establishment. His lack of standing within the traditional Shi'a clerisy did not harm the credibility he held with his disenfranchised power base. In fact, it may have helped him.

Al-Sadr represented Iraq's poor and dispossessed with populist zeal. While al-Sistani worked within the political system, al-Sadr was an opportunist, remaining free to use violence and riots when necessary, but also coming into the political fold in time for his followers to gain a large number of seats in the National Assembly and four major ministries in government.

Neither al-Sistani nor al-Sadr were deemed winners by Coalition policy-makers who threw in their lot with several seemingly influential secular politicians and moderate clerics. These exiles returned to an Iraq that had changed greatly during their absence. They expected to be welcomed back with open arms; however, skepticism, distrust, and subterfuge awaited them. Shiʻa have lined up behind several visions for the new Iraq. These range from al-Sadr's angry populist rhetoric to al-Sistani's calm calls for political engagement and defense of the Shiʻa majority vote. Other strains of Shiʻa activism exist—some hoping for an Iranian-style religious republic and others for a vibrant modern democracy. All too many politicians espouse one of these lines, yet act only to secure narrow power interests. The Shiʻa are divided, leaving the field open for radicals and opportunists to steer events through violence and mob politics.[4] Beneath the seeming consensus of the Shiʻa votes in 2005, conflicting interests abounded.

Although inter-sectarian violence tended to obscure intra-sectarian differences, the lack of Shiʻa unity presented a major problem for halting this violence. Some insurgent groups purposely targeted the Shiʻa with horrific mass-casualty attacks meant to inflame sectarian tensions. These groups hoped to spark a civil war, or at least cause enough chaos that the Shiʻa would be unable to realize their demographic majority in a stable democracy. Until 2006, Shiʻa leaders were largely successful in convincing their followers to refrain from tit-for-tat reprisals, but after the February 2006 bombing of Samarra's golden domed al-Askariyya Mosque, violence ratcheted upward. Although al-Sistani and others continued their calls for peace, many factions of the Shiʻa community had ceased listening. Political parties splintered over how they should react and the dissimilarities boiled over into violence, political gridlock, and high-profile walkouts from the National Assembly; both local and national governments were adrift through 2007. Shiʻa politics also derailed any hopes for a unity government of moderates, leaving reconciliation attempts toothless. Even as sectarian violence decreased sharply, Shiʻa infighting over the way ahead grew. To understand Iraqi politics, one must understand the Shiʻa and their factions, which often fall along lines of age and economic status.

The split between Shi'a and Sunni arose in the mid-seventh century from a dispute over the rightful successor to the Prophet Mohammed as leader of the faithful. Some believed that Mohammed's successor should come from within his family and that he had designated his cousin, Ali, as his representative. Others believed that succession was a matter that should be determined by a council of Mohammed's followers. In the end, Abu Bakr (not a close relative, but an early follower of Mohammed) was chosen to take leadership of the Muslims after Mohammed's death. While Ali became the fourth caliph after Mohammed's death, Ali and the house of the Prophet would be subject to poor treatment and intrigue at every turn, concluding in his martyrdom and that of his two sons.

This early divide widened over the course of many years and subsequent political struggles to produce two main sects in Islam, the Sunni and the Shi'a. Around 90 percent of the Islamic community worldwide is Sunni. Most of the remaining 10 percent are Shi'a. Resulting from the resolution to follow community consensus and choose a worldly ruler, the Sunni do not have a rigid clerical system and their clerics are not seen as having extraordinary voice in religious affairs. In contrast, Shi'a believe that there is an infallible Imam, or leader, in direct descent from Ali who proffers spiritual guidance and interpretation for the faithful. According to the main Shi'a sect, this line of Imams stopped when the twelfth Imam went into hiding or occultation. In his stead, Shi'a must select a learned cleric as an "object of emulation" (*marja' al-taqlid*, collectively the *marji'iya*) and follow his interpretations and rulings regarding the religion as it relates to every facet of life. As a result, the Shi'a clerisy is hierarchical, with clerics advancing through several levels of scholarly achievement to attain knowledge requisite for the highest rankings, often referred to as Ayatollah (sign of God) and Grand Ayatollah. Because of this system, Shi'a clerics are much more central to life and activism than their Sunni counterparts.

Throughout history, the Shi'a have generally been a dispossessed minority. This standing is a major influence on Shi'a worldview and political activity. The Shi'a have a long tradition of persecution and martyrdom, emphasized in their religious imagery and rites. After becoming the fourth caliph, Ali was assassinated from within his following, because he preferred to arbitrate a power struggle with a rival for the caliphate named Mu'awiya, rather than press a military advantage in battle. Soon thereafter, Ali's son, Hasan, abdicated the throne of the caliphate and, according to the Shi'a, was fatally poisoned as a result. Wishing to avoid threats from the line of Ali, Yazid, the son of Mu'awiya, marched against the seventy-two-man force of Ali's other son, Husain. Yazid cut Husain's band off from the waters of the Euphrates for several days and brought battle in Karbala on the tenth day of the month of Muharram (a month when fighting is proscribed for Muslims) in 680 AD. Husain's companions were slaughtered and Husain was martyred, his head carried to Damascus. Only Husain's young son survived the slaughter. Husain's martyrdom is reenacted annually on ʿAshura (literally ten, for the tenth day of the Islamic month).

This tradition of treachery and martyrdom is vital to Shiʿa ritual and thought. In the words of scholar Reza Aslan, Shi'ism is "a religion founded on the ideal of the righteous believer who, following in the footsteps of the martyrs at Karbala, willingly sacrifices himself in the struggle for justice against oppression."[5] Certainly, the Shiʿa of Iraq experienced more than their share of oppression under the old regime. More recent sectarian attacks also raise the specter of persecution and play into Shiʿa religious stories and symbolism.

Shiʿa Identity and Post-Invasion Organization

When Iraq emerged from the collapse of the Sunni-ruled Ottoman Empire following World War I, British officials gerrymandering the region appointed King Faisal I as the country's monarch. Faisal was a Sunni and not even Iraqi. He was the son of the Grand Sherif of Mecca, born in Taʿif (now in Saudi Arabia) into the Hashemite clan, of which Mohammed was a member. Even though Iraqis—Sunni, Shiʿa, and Kurd alike—revolted against the British imposition, the uprising was brutally repressed and the majority of Shiʿa soon found themselves marginalized by the regime and its colonial minders. For many Shiʿa leaders, the bitter memories of the 1920 uprising and subsequent revolts served as a key factor in the early restraint shown by the Shiʿa in the face of post-2003 Sunni attacks. In the words of one scholar, "the ballot box and its promise of majority rule represent a golden opportunity finally and peacefully to throw off decades . . . of oppression and second-class treatment."[6]

Shiʿa leaders hedged their bets on democracy, though. They retained powerful armed groups and used religious trump cards to guarantee a firm grasp over the political arena. Most importantly, they manipulated Shiʿa identity to mobilize the population in their support. The narrative of Iraqi Shiʿa as a disabused majority provided a shared "sense of grievance" that helped cement a common identity, even among secular Shiʿa, and mobilize voters behind a single Shiʿa bloc, despite varied political programs.[7]

The Shiʿa clergy in Iraq have long been a center of power unto themselves. Whereas Sunni clergy were often tied to the government in a number of ways,

Shiʻa clerics obtained financial support and legitimacy from their followers, allowing them a greater degree of independence.[8] Shiʻa faithful are obliged to follow the edicts of a cleric of their choosing on subjects ranging from religious practices to intimate personal issues. These followers are also beholden to give a percentage of their income and holdings to the cleric in the form of a religious tithe, which the cleric then uses to fund religious programs and charities. Key clerics also control important Shiʻa shrines, gaining international stature and donations from the pilgrims who come to pay tribute.

Fearful of this independence, the Baʻath government assumed control of Shiʻa religious funds and shrines in March 1980 in an attempt to deprive the Shiʻa clergy of its sources of power.[9] This and other regime persecution weakened the power of the traditional clerical establishment. Events at the close of the 1991 Gulf War further gutted the system. Sensing a moment of weakness after Saddam's defeat in the Gulf War, many Iraqis rose up against his rule in April 1991. During this uprising, Shiʻa religious leaders were looked to for guidance and leadership. While the United States had called for the Iraqi people to throw off the dictator, it had more of a palace coup in mind. A general revolt was viewed to be too messy and unpredictable, therefore, key Shiʻa leaders' calls for U.S. assistance were denied and the Baʻath successfully and brutally quashed the revolt. The housecleaning that ensued severely damaged the Shiʻa religious leadership. More than two hundred prominent clerics were dispatched by the regime. Many others fled to exile. Even Ayatollah al-Sistani was attacked in his home in 1996. As a result, the Shiʻa seminaries' throughput of students was significantly reduced and the Shiʻa religious leadership was drastically destabilized.[10]

Despite its weakened status, the Shiʻa clerisy became a powerful, if disunified, force after the invasion. Because of the diminishing of the traditional clerical center, Shiʻa clerics empowered by the collapse operated much more independently than they otherwise would have. In addition, there were no governmental structures or services to rival the clerisy. The religious charities and services were the only show in town and radicals had free reign once out from under the thumb of the government and the strong clerical organization. Religious leaders were in a position of great power due to the rising religiosity of Iraqis in trying and uncertain times and the lack of alternative national leaders. Renewed travel, trade, and pilgrimage after Saddam's fall provided flows of cash, people, and other resources that rejuvenated Iraq's Shiʻa structures.[11] As the chaos worsened due to the crisis of governance in post-invasion Iraq, Shiʻa religious leaders stepped into the breach, dramatically impacting the course of Iraqi transition.

This situation was not unprecedented. Similar conditions existed in the Iranian Revolution two decades earlier. The pre-existing political institutions of each country were shaped around the personality of one man, Saddam in Iraq and the Shah in Iran. Neither country had a real, internal opposition party structure to speak of and the population was greatly divided over its vision for the future. In both countries, the Shi'a religious establishment retained critical sources of power in its institutions, clerics, and the people's support for Islam. When the despot was removed, the government buckled and the clerics filled the vacuum.[12] The contrast in the two cases is that Ayatollah al-Khomeini and his supporters in Iran ruthlessly pursued their revolutionary vision, while in Iraq Ayatollah al-Sistani was much more circumspect in his leadership role, seeking only to retain the various Shi'a groups headed in a vaguely similar direction, toward majoritarian domination of the new Iraq.

Though Shi'a did not constitute a unified bloc after the invasion, they held a shared interest in avoiding disorganized violent resistance. They pursued policies that would allow them to capitalize on their demographic power to shape the future of a new nation. Ayatollah al-Sistani was central to promoting Shi'a unity and involvement in the political process, shunning violent reprisals against the Sunni. Shi'a religious leaders rapidly mobilized in the turmoil following the invasion to control and stabilize the public and ensure that disorganization would not jeopardize Shi'a chances for realizing political power in the new Iraq. While most had these broad goals in mind, the means and details were contested and a significant power struggle occurred within the Shi'a religious community. This struggle pitted the traditional Shi'a clerical establishment represented by the likes of Ayatollah al-Sistani against new, radicalized elements of the Shi'a underclass with Muqtada al-Sadr and similar clerics as their lions. The rise of a new Shi'a Islamist political element would have significant echoes in the country's political future.

In his travels in the Shi'a areas shortly after the invasion, CPA advisor and democracy expert Larry Diamond discovered that "the Islamist parties and militias formed a confusing patchwork of shifting loyalties and alliances." In Basra alone, the CPA estimated that there were approximately one hundred and fifty militias and political groups by March 2004. The bulk of these were criminal gangs or local Islamist militias. Several larger groups, however, established their credibility by doling out social services lacking in the frenzied environment of post-invasion Iraq.¹³ The groups best positioned to provide these services were based on existing religious structures.

Four major Shiʿa political forces vied for power in the new Iraq, all Islamist to differing extents. The direct followers of the traditionalist Ayatollah al-Sistani were generally the most moderate of the religious Shiʿa. *Hizb al-Daʿwa al-Islamiyya* (The Islamic Call Party) and the Supreme Council for the Islamic Revolution in Iraq (SCIRI, which changed its name to the Islamic Supreme Council of Iraq, ISCI, in May 2007)¹⁴ were more activist, as will be detailed below. Specifically, SCIRI had at its side the Badr Organization, the largest Shiʿa militia, capable of as much brutality, both sectarian and intra-Shiʿa, as any force in Iraq. Finally, the Sadrist movement and its Mahdi Army was the most radical and populist major Shiʿa movement and the first Shiʿa force to rear its head in the invasion's aftermath.

Initially, many religious establishments advised their followers to prepare for an unknown future, stop the looting and violence, and cooperate with the Coalition. Rapidly formed Shiʿa militias even came to U.S. checkpoints armed and clad in black, thinking they would be welcomed to help maintain order. There were great expectations that the invading forces would soon provide both the freedom and the security many Iraqis craved, but the honeymoon period was short. In the words of Iraq expert Ahmed Hashim, "The Shiʿa were prepared to challenge the authority and legitimacy of the Coalition if the gap between its promises and its achievements was too great."¹⁵ The clock ticked most rapidly in the slums of Baghdad and other southern cities where a new, radical force had risen owing largely to the former regime's gutting of the clerical institutions.

Muqtada al-Sadr, born in Najaf on August 12, 1973, to a noted clerical family, was the Shiʿa leader that stood most ready to confront the Coalition and take advantage of the new order in Iraq. He represented the unpredictability of the Shiʿa world in a microcosm. Although al-Sadr's rise was unexpected by many, it was emblematic of the shifting landscape created by the legacies of the old regime and the crisis of governance. Al-Sadr's power base lay among the disenfranchised poor Shiʿa in such slums as Sadr City. His control over the movement was exercised through a network of young clerics who were well positioned to harness the anger of the vast hoards of young, unemployed men in the cities.¹⁶ An upstart such as al-Sadr would not have succeeded amid a stronger clerical establishment, yet the weakening of the Shiʿa hierarchy by Saddam's persecution, combined with the post-invasion vacuum, unveiled a critical opportunity.

Muqtada's father, Ayatollah Mohammed Sadiq al-Sadr, championed the poor and dispossessed urban Shi'a in the later years of Saddam's regime. Al-Sadr's popularity grew from the provision of social services to his followers in the 1990s during the height of the sanctions. From this charitable base, he built a loyal network of followers, gaining the allegiance not only of the underprivileged masses, but also their tribal leadership. He went to great lengths to reconcile tribal practices and Islam, even authoring a book titled *Fiqh al-'Asha'ir*, (*Tribal Jurisprudence*). Al-Sadr brought to Iraq an unprecedented type of Shi'a religious activism, which concentrated on building a link between the clerical establishment and the poor and needy. Working off of the strong tribal ties maintained by the new migrants to the cities and the growing importance of tribalism across Iraq, he established a "jurisprudence for the tribes" that merged Islamic and tribal customs, thus gaining the support of tribal networks. He also eschewed the traditional quietist stance, which he blamed for the plight of Iraq's Shi'a, choosing instead a more politically vocal and activist posture. The elder Sadr contrasted between the "silent jurisprudent" and the "speaking jurisprudent," arguing that top Shi'a clerics were ethically required to denounce injustice.[17] His support swelled as he established grassroots networks of schools and charities that focused on assisting the most impoverished Baghdadis.

Becoming ever more political, in 1997 al-Sadr began to sermonize to his followers in Friday prayers. Because most Shi'a clerics viewed these sermons as inherently political, this practice was frowned on. Friday sermons, however, became a powerful venue for al-Sadr's leadership, placing him in a position threatening to both the regime and the traditional clerical establishment. His activism quickly became too much for Saddam to tolerate. On February 19, 1999, al-Sadr and two of his sons, Mustafa and Muammal, were assassinated when unknown gunmen sprayed their car with machinegun fire in Najaf. The driver and al-Sadr's sons died immediately, though al-Sadr did not succumb to his severe wounds at the scene. The cleric was taken, along with the bodies of his sons, to a nearby hospital that was soon inundated with regime security men. As guards held back a growing crowd at the hospital's gates, Saddam's henchmen barred doctors from the room in which al-Sadr bled to death. Al-Sadr's followers filled the streets in grief and protest, but the Republican Guard quickly put down any hope of a general uprising.[18]

Mohammed Sadiq al-Sadr's activism widened a divide between the Shi'a classes that would continue to grow in the new Iraq. While the urban commercial classes maintained close ties to the traditional clerics, the rural poor and their kin who had migrated to the cities' slums largely followed al-Sadr's legacy. This split was deepened by rivalry between al-Sadr's supporters and SCIRI members and their exiled leader, Ayatollah Baqir al-Hakim. The SCIRI camp in Iran accused al-Sadr of being a regime collaborator. Coming shortly before al-Sadr's death, these accusations seemed especially egregious in retrospect, to the extent that, during a ceremony mourning al-Sadr's death in Qom, Iran, Sadr supporters chanted that the Hakims were traitors and chased Baqir away from the mosque in a hail of shoes. The legacy of bad blood between the groups spilled over into the new era[19] and paved the way for the rise of a popular cleric, albeit one unqualified by traditional terms.

Though the Sadr offices were closed after al-Sadr's martyrdom, his powerful network of followers lived on, including both the original tribal leadership brought by migrants from the south and new religious and professional leadership cultivated in the city. Some sources maintain that a number of young clerics quietly tended the network that Mohammed Sadiq al-Sadr had built. Muqtada was constantly watched by the regime after his father's death. Any misstep would have resulted in his ignominious end. His survival suggests a level of political shrewdness for which few gave him credit. Sadr surprised his rivals and critics when he used his political acumen and capitalized on the post-invasion opportunity to become one of the most powerful men in the new Iraq. In his words, "I found a vacuum, and no one filled that vacuum."[20]

Muqtada resurfaced shortly before the fall of the regime. In the early days of April 2003, Shi'a militias expelled regime forces from Saddam City and renamed it Sadr City, in honor of the martyred Ayatollah and the larger family legacy, not after Muqtada himself. Mohammed Sadiq Al-Sadr's martyrdom profoundly affected his following, which was a main component of the movement's success in the new Iraq. One young man explained, "We believed Sadr II [Mohammed Sadiq al-Sadr] was like the Prophet Mohammed because he did so many things for our community. We, his followers, had a sense of failure and guilt that we had not been able to stop him being killed, so we felt it our duty to support his son and complete his work."[21]

Muqtada, who became an experienced organizer under his father and had been responsible for Sadr City, quickly organized forces to secure key facilities in the city and began caching weapons abandoned by fleeing regime supporters. Muqtada reportedly stayed in contact with twelve to fifteen clerics in Sadr City after his father's murder. This base soon spread to a network of ninety young clerics, through which Sadr's supporters gained control of the area. In the ensuing days and weeks, Sadr's followers brought order to the area by stemming the looting, demanding the return of goods, and even acting as a relief organization "providing food and medical aid to poor neighborhoods."[22]

Interviewed by journalist Anthony Shadid shortly after the fall of the regime, Muqtada recounted the ways his network had reacted to the collapse of government in various areas. Militiamen protected hospitals and government buildings, set up security checkpoints to curb the rampant looting, guarded the workers on U.S.-funded projects, and even organized lines at gas stations and stopped price gouging. His followers from dozens of mosques around Sadr City distributed fuel and flour for cooking, paid salaries, and even returned stolen cars.[23] Such early efforts were critical in the battle for hearts and minds. In addition to these services, Sadr's local offices provided an easily accessible outlet for addressing grievances and resolving problems. If there were problems in the area, residents could "complain to the Sadr office," explained a 42-year-old resident of Sadr City. "How do we complain to the Americans? Whom do we complain to?" Another local resident confessed that people would rather go to Sadr's offices for help than to the police station, "which does nothing." Sadr's "Arbitration Committee is well organized. It summons the relevant people, and the matter is adjudicated after the various parties have been heard." Moving through the cities in heavily armed convoys or quick-moving foot patrols, Coalition troops were not as accessible as the indigenous powers. Muqtada's network of services quickly expanded as he capitalized on his successes and established similar administrative offices in other key Shi'a areas.[24] These efforts won the loyalty of many, as the first face of order seen by many residents was a Sadr supporter, while discontent with the Coalition and the Iraqi government only grew.

Many of the early analyses and news reports were dismissive of the young al-Sadr. He was described as young, impetuous, and lacking clerical credentials and support among Iraq's Shi'a elite. These characterizations were true, yet all missed the point. Muqtada's power base did not arise from these traditional factors, but rather from his populist message to the angry, poor masses in Iraq's slums. Disenfranchised from the traditional elitist clergy and their more commercial and educated followers, the deprived Shi'a of many troubled neighborhoods were drawn to Muqtada's underdog status, his lack of education, his stance against the establishment, and most importantly to the services he and his network provided to them.

Despite expectations, then, Muqtada al-Sadr became a major force in Shi'a politics. There is still debate over whether Muqtada was a rising force of his own, or whether Coalition actions in 2004 catapulted an otherwise small-time figure to fame and prominence. The Coalition hardly referred to him in its press briefings until March and April 2004, when Muqtada's increasing bellicosity precipitated a series of moves against him. These moves included the arrest of a key Sadr lieutenant, Mustafa al-Yacoubi, on charges resulting from the murder of a major Shiʻa cleric, Abd al-Majid Khoʼi, in April 2003 (discussed below). At the same time, the Coalition ordered the closure of Sadr's newspaper for sixty days for inciting violence. These moves gave rise to a standoff between the Coalition and Muqtada's forces. Ultimately, the Coalition backed down from the confrontation to avoid a collapse of the interim government and the process that would result in transfer of sovereignty a few short months later. These events may have widened Muqtada's audience and burnished his anti-Coalition credentials, but his power stemmed more significantly from his ability to exploit the divided nature of the Shiʻa political field through crafty use of his radical network of followers and his growing popularity among the disenfranchised Shiʻa.

Muqtada did not progress far in the traditional Shiʻa religious education system. He lacks the credentials to officially administer many of the functions expected of leading clerics, yet he has found various ways around this problem. Muqtada's father designated Ayatollah Kadhim al-Ha'iri as his successor, though al-Ha'iri stayed in exile in Iran and was in no rush to return to the chaos in post-Saddam Iraq. Al-Ha'iri, probably considering Muqtada to be no threat to his future return, allowed Muqtada to perform in his name many duties reserved for senior clerics. Al-Haʻiri's backing gave Muqtada a modicum of legitimacy, even though this temporary transfer of power may not have made much difference to his followers. Even Sadr's more educated disciples were often dropouts from the religious schools who "preferred street politics to pious education." His popularity among the mass of young Shiʻa who emerged from the economic disasters of Baʻath regime was unaffected by his lack of official credentials. What many observers perceived as a weakness was actually a strength that propelled Sadr to notoriety. Still, Muqtada was careful not to issue *fatwas* and he clearly stated on numerous occasions that he was not a pretender to high clerical status, advising his followers to refer to proper clerical authorities on religious questions.[25]

Ultimately, radical Shiʻa leaders such as Muqtada and his lieutenants did not have to win over the whole population. They simply had to secure a cadre of staunch supporters and thugs who would cow the rest of the population into staying out of the way. Observing the path of Shiʻa politics from Wasit Province,

CPA governor Mark Etherington remarked, the "passive majority had been intimidated by a minority."[26] Muqtada's power with the angry Shi'a poor was enough to propel him into a vital position in Iraqi politics.

In a Friday sermon in April 2003, Muqtada declared his position with respect to the Coalition. "They declared that they are occupiers of this country, Iraq, and they are not liberators. We will not allow this. We want them to leave soon. This country has many men who can rule and administer it." His followers had already demonstrated their ability to manage their warrens and did not wish for outside interference. As with many of the other sub-state powers in Iraq, they were not tolerant. He urged his followers to form local vigilante committees to patrol the streets, keeping order and enforcing their vision of Islamic morality.[27] Strict religious adherence was imposed by violence and thuggish "virtue patrols" were virtually the only authority in town.

The committees that initially undertook Sadr's missions were cellular structures of ten to fifteen men, many of who reportedly had operated together for the last ten years of Saddam's rule.[28] The effect of Saddam's repression on Shi'a religious structures was an insular and radicalized network of these tightly-bound activists. Many of the cells had been active under intense pressure and surveillance, keeping the networks of the Sadr movement quietly alive. They were well prepared for action when the vacuum presented itself and provided the muscle behind Sadr's movement: the Mahdi Army. The name of the militia is a reference to the Shi'a version of the Messiah, the Twelfth Imam descended from the line of Ali. Twelver Shi'a (the largest of several subdivisions of the Shi'a sect) believe that this imam went into hiding or occultation over a thousand years ago and that he will return as the Mahdi in the end times. Those fighting under his name are waging holy war to hasten his coming.

Political and military analysts initially scoffed at this rag-tag band of militia cells, yet these cells are a dangerous force for a number of reasons. First, Muqtada's command of the Mahdi Army invested him with a veto power over political and reconstruction projects early on during the Coalition's tenure in Iraq. The ability to push mobs out into the streets, undertake violent operations against the Coalition, and occupy key religious sites by force allowed him to catapult himself into prominence and stifle political developments that he did not agree with. Second, the Mahdi Army's involvement in sectarian violence both destabilized Iraq and increased Muqtada's standing in areas. As violence worsened, many Shi'a Iraqis turned to the Mahdi Army as their sole protector, succeeding in their eyes where the government and the U.S. troops failed. This reinforced the Sadrists' influence at the expense of the Iraqi government and made disarming his militia virtually impossible without major battle. Finally, the most hazardous aspect of the Mahdi Army was its decentralized control. Many of the cells consisted of ruffians who used the Mahdi name to legitimize their own criminal enterprises. These cells were essentially leaderless, making them difficult to rein in.[29] The radical fringe would cause trouble for Muqtada even as his authority became more and more entrenched.

Though funding for Muqtada's network was initially paltry, it expanded rapidly with his rising power. While his money paled in comparison to the resources commanded by Ayatollah al-Sistani, he had access to many more organizational and financial resources than did any potential non-religious competitor. As the following spread and integrated into the Iraqi government, the network siphoned off government assets and augmented its income through essentially criminal acts. As will be discussed more fully later, Sadrists became a powerful force within the official political process, gaining 23 of 275 seats in the January 2005 elections for the transitional assembly. Their take rose to thirty-two seats in the December 2005 elections for the permanent National Assembly, giving Muqtada a bloc large enough to heavily influence the actions of the leading Shiʿa coalition. His shrewd political strategies within the government also added to his clout. He guided his followers to accept control only over social or service ministries. The benefits were two-fold. First, Muqtada avoided thankless high-profile posts such as defense or interior ministries. Second, under this strategy, Sadr's followers became the smiling face of government services extended to the people. These services were doled out by the six Sadrist ministries: health, agriculture, transportation, provincial matters, tourism, and civil society matters. Thus, Sadrists increased their popularity while opponents sullied themselves toiling in other unappreciated jobs.[30]

Sadrist clerics did not sit in ministry positions, but were commanding behind-the-scenes advisors to the technocrats appointed in their stead. Interviews conducted by the International Crisis Group (ICG) disclosed the strategy behind these moves. Sadrists chose weak appointees so that their backers could easily manipulate them. A ministry employee stated, "Every Sadrist minister is controlled by an imam who has been dispatched by Muqtada. The minister cannot do anything his adviser opposes." More specifically, another explained, "In truth, the health minister doesn't have a minister's stature. He merely was a doctor in a Sadr City hospital. . . . He is a puppet."[31] Shrewd populist politics catapulted Muqtada from the role of rabble-rouser to kingmaker in Iraq, although he operated in a crowded field of Shiʿa leaders.

The Sadr legacy was large enough to encompass more than Muqtada's movement. Sheikh Muhammad al-Yaqoubi, a student of the elder Sadr, split with Muqtada's followers to found *Hizb al-Fadhila al-Islamiyya*, or the Islamic Virtue Party, in 2003. Al-Fadhila followed the Sadrist line of Islamic political activism, but followed al-Yaqoubi's clerical leadership. Al-Yaqoubi studied under Muqtada's father, Mohammed Sadiq al-Sadr, as well as the revered Ayatollah Kho'i. In 2005, he received the backing of Ayatollah Ha'iri, al-Sadr's chosen successor. Partly for these reasons, al-Fadhila has been described as the "educated [or cultured] Sadr Party."[32] The Fadhila Party gained a bloc of fifteen seats in the December 2005 elections, enhancing the power of the greater Sadr movement, and eventually proving itself to be an influential and independent voice amongst the Shi'a parties. Muqtada was not the only religious leader poised to gain large blocs of support.

Shi'a cleric 'Abd al-Majid Kho'i was a favorite of the U.S. administration. Kho'i was the son of one of the most revered Shi'a clerics who had been the mentor of Ayatollah al-Sistani. The United States backed Kho'i's return to Iraq from exile in London, where he ran one of the Shi'a world's largest charitable foundations. The relatively moderate Kho'i was a religious authority in his own right and was seen by the United States as a critical intermediary to the Shi'a community. However, by many Shi'a inside Iraq, especially supporters of Sadr, he was seen as an unwelcome interloper. On April 10, 2003, Kho'i made his attempt to return to prominence in Iraq. Kho'i, accompanied by the caretaker of the Imam Ali Mosque in Najaf, tried to enter the sanctuary and reassert his prominence over the religious scene in the city. The problem for Kho'i was that the caretaker, Haidar al-Rufaie al-Killidar, was a parliamentarian in Saddam's hated regime; he had even appeared with Saddam on television. Crowds shouting Sadrist slogans surrounded the party, trapping them inside al-Killidar's office. The mob became violent and demanded that Kho'i turn al-Killidar over. When a cleric accompanying Kho'i fired his AK-47 into the air in a fruitless attempt to disperse them, a lengthy firefight ensued, in which a cleric in the party was mortally wounded and Kho'i was injured by a grenade. Surrounded, out of ammunition, and with Kho'i wounded, the party forced its way out into the mob. Al-Killidar was brutally murdered with swords and knives. Kho'i was stabbed repeatedly, yet managed to escape the throng and stumbled to Muqtada al-Sadr's nearby office for refuge.

Kho'i collapsed at Muqtada's doorstep, but Muqtada reportedly refused to open the door. Several of the clerics dragged Kho'i into a nearby shop; the mob, however, forced their way in and heaved Kho'i into the street where he was fatally shot. His lifeless body lay there for hours.³³ After an investigation was conducted at the request of the United States, an Iraqi judge issued an arrest warrant for Muqtadas involvement in the killing; it was never served, though. It was the day after the fall of the regime and intrigue and violence had already begun in the quest for dominance of Shi'a politics.

Perhaps emboldened by the taste of blood, Sadrist crowds soon surrounded the homes of the traditional clerical powers, Grand Ayatollah al-Sistani and Ayatollah Mohammed Baqir al-Hakim, giving them forty-eight hours to leave Najaf in Muqtada's hands. Had he succeeded in chasing the clerics from the holy city of Najaf, he would have been in possession of some of the most important territory in the Shi'a world. Known as *al-Hawza al-'Ilmiya*, literally the Territory of Learning, Najaf's establishment of seminaries is a prime center of clerical power. The Sadrists' early attempt to wrest control of Najaf failed when city leaders mustered tribal forces to dispel the mob on April 14, although Muqtada would clearly continue to present difficulties for Iraq and the Coalition, in one way or another.³⁴

Ayatollah Mohammed Baqir al-Hakim was another noted cleric who had fled Saddam's regime to exile in London. He was the clerical head of SCIRI, the Islamist group that had operated in exile in Iran during Saddam's reign. Like Kho'i, al-Hakim also reportedly returned to Iraq with U.S. funding and support. Many, though, did not welcome his return. Young Sadrist cleric Sheikh Kadhim al-Ebadi al-Nasseri complained, "He is acting as if he is the most important leader in the Iraqi religious opposition. . . . All those who claim to be opposition figures were traitors who left Iraq and left us suffering here."³⁵

While many in Washington were enamored of the Iraqi exile community, which seemed to promise the world for Iraq's future, there was a major disconnect between the exiles who had been safely in the West, or even in Iran, during most of Saddam's reign of terror and those who had suffered inside the state. In April 2003, when exiled politicians first convened in Nasiriya with those who had remained in Saddam's Iraq, the two groups sat at separate tables.³⁶ Though not all Iraqis deemed these exiles traitors, many preferred leaders who had shared in the last decade of suffering with them. Albeit from an Iranian perspective, Reza Aslan eloquently expressed the relationship between exiles and those who have suffered in the troubled state. Twenty years after the Iranian Revolution and his family's exile, Aslan returned to Iran to visit. Upon arriving in Iran, he handed over his passport to the customs agent. When he informed the agent that his point of origin was the United States, a subtle but poignant exchange ensued.

> He stiffens and looks up at my face. I can tell we are the same age, though his tired eyes and his unshaven jowl make him appear much older. He is a child of the revolution; I am a fugitive—an apostate. He has spent his life surviving a history that I have spent my life studying from afar. All at once I feel overwhelmed. I can barely look at him when he asks, "Where have you been?" as all passport agents are required to do. I cannot help but sense the accusation in his voice.[37]

Many of Iraq's exiles returned with none of the humility expressed by Aslan, which was a major barrier to their success among those who had suffered through the worst of Saddam's terrors. Not all exiles were judged the same, however. Although some Shi'a may have been opposed to al-Hakim, he and SCIRI commanded significant support across the broader Shi'a population, especially for their continued resistance to the regime from exile. Al-Hakim's greatest threat lay not in Shi'a squabbling, but in the increasingly deadly Sunni resistance and the extremist tactics of groups seeking to foment civil war.

On August 29, 2003, al-Hakim led Friday prayers in Najaf's Imam Ali Mosque. Shortly after the prayers concluded, a massive car bomb outside detonated, killing more than eighty Shi'a faithful. Hours passed as residents dug through the rubble in search of loved ones and the revered cleric. Throughout the day, people traded nervous rumors about al-Hakim's fate. Some related stories of his miraculous survival, as others whispered about personal effects of the Ayatollah that had supposedly been found in the rubble. At eight o'clock that evening, the sound of a muezzin's voice from loudspeakers tore through any veil of remaining hope. "*Inuna li-Allah wa ilayhe muraja'un*. We are of God and to God we return." Confirmation of the Ayatollah's death was met with despair, both for the martyred al-Hakim and for the severe trials that surely lay ahead for Iraq's Shi'a.[38] Although al-Hakim's brother carried on to lead SCIRI, the loss of the cleric was a great blow to SCIRI and the Coalition. Two of Iraq's most eminent clerics and leaders had been killed within months of Saddam's fall.

The bomb that killed al-Hakim was the work of Sunni insurgents. The driver of the car bomb was Yassin Jarad, a native of Zarqaa, Jordan, and Abu Musab al-Zarqawi's father-in-law. While al-Hakim's martyrdom did not provoke the sectarian reprisals that the extremists probably hoped it would, it did strike a significant blow to American efforts to shape events in the new Iraq.

Journalist Anthony Shadid argued that with al-Hakim's death "U.S. officials lost perhaps their most important link with the [Shi'a] community at a time that they acknowledged as delicate." The radical Sadr was both unacceptable to the United States and openly opposed to the Coalition. Grand Ayatollah al-Sistani remained at arm's length from the United States as well. Al-Hakim had been the Coalition's best hope for an influential intermediary. In addition, the removal of another key cleric, especially in such a manner, could only strengthen Muqtada by providing him new, angry followers.[39]

Al-Hakim was the scion of Iraq's oldest line of Shi'a Islamist activism, arising from the party known as al-Da'wa. *Hizb al-Da'wa al-Islamiyya* (the Party of the Islamic Call) originated in 1958 in response to the waning power of the Shi'a clerisy and the weakening religiosity of the Shi'a population, due in part to the rising popularity of Arab nationalism and communism as secularizing forces. From these roots, al-Da'wa worked with several other Islamist groups to oppose the Ba'athist regime. Although undertaken by another group, the Islamic Action Organization, an attempted assassination on Iraq's deputy prime minister, Tariq Aziz, in 1980 resulted in the execution or exile of most key al-Da'wa activists. Some clandestine cells remained within Iraq and carried out further assassination attempts, most notably against Saddam in 1982 and 1987 and the nearly successful 1996 attempt against Saddam's son Uday. Al-Da'wa activism became primarily an exile movement, however, and had offices in Damascus and Kuwait. Many Iraqis hold al-Da'wa in considerable esteem because of its continued resistance against Saddam's regime.[40]

Although al-Da'wa rhetoric in the 1980s indicated that the party would not accept a democratic form of rule if it were not Islamist, more recent statements suggest that, while the ultimate goal remains an Islamic regime, the party will accept whatever choice of the people. A senior party member remarked, "If [the people] do not choose Islam, this means they are not prepared for it. If Islam is imposed, it will become an Islamic dictatorship and this would alienate the public."[41] This comment fits in well with a thread of Islamist thinking that Islamic rule is the ultimate goal, but the will for Islamic rule must arise from the bottom up—from the people. The reasoning is that an Islamic republic is not created through imposition, but by working to make the individuals and the society thoroughly Islamic. A society Islamicized from the grassroots will eventually opt freely for Islamic rule.

A major leader and example of al-Da'wa's strategy was Ibrahim al-Jafari, who was a member of the Interim Governing Council and became Iraq's first prime minister under the transitional government. Al-Jafari fled Iraq in 1980, settling first in Iran, then in London as al-Da'wa's spokesman there. The fact that al-Da'wa advanced al-Jafari, who is not a cleric but a physician, signified the party's desire to promote a technocratic, non-clerical leadership, despite their overall commitment to an Islamic state.[42]

Despite al-Da'wa's long lineage, it faced serious encroachments on several fronts. A splinter group emerged from al-Da'wa, calling itself "The Iraqi Organization" of the al-Da'wa Party. Although this faction followed a similar political program, it diluted the power of al-Da'wa proper in the alliance system of Iraq's new political process. The new Sadr movement robbed it of much of its traditional base in the poor urban Shi'a population. The more powerful SCIRI movement also vied with al-Da'wa for the core of the Islamist population's support.[43]

SCIRI was an influential offshoot of the older al-Da'wa party established by Mohammed Baqir al-Hakim on November 17, 1982, during the Iran-Iraq War. The success of Ayatollah Khomeini's Islamic Revolution in Iran prompted the more activist members of al-Da'wa to align with Iran and its Islamist ideology, particularly the concept of "rule of the jurist-consult" championed by al-Khomeini, by which the most learned Shi'a cleric is best equipped to rule in the absence of the Imam in occultation. As these activists fled over the border into Iran, they coalesced into an organization that came to be known as the Supreme Council for the Islamic Revolution in Iraq by November 1982. Shortly thereafter, Saddam's henchmen rounded up eighty members of al-Hakim's extended family that remained in Iraq and executed six of them in May 1983, three of whom were al-Hakim's brothers. Ten more of al-Hakim's family members were executed in 1985 and another was assassinated in Sudan in 1988. SCIRI's close association with Tehran and the fact that its ranks were heavily peppered with deserters from the bitter Iran-Iraq War led many Iraqis to label it as a movement of traitors. Although the "Council" was, at first, a forum that held adherents to al-Khomeini, al-Da'wa Party members, and independents, al-Da'wa followers and the independents soon divorced themselves from SCIRI. Deprived of Iranian support and safe haven, al-Da'wa withered as SCIRI grew increasingly well organized, which would later enable SCIRI to dominate Shi'a politics in the new Iraq.[44]

SCIRI expanded in size and sophistication during its exile in Iran. Defectors from the Iraqi Army during the deadly Iran-Iraq War provided SCIRI with the manpower to create the Badr Corps, its military wing, in 1983, under the supervision of the Iranian Islamic Revolutionary Guard Corps (IIRGC). Although SCIRI and the Badr Corps attempted to use their muscle during the Shiʻa uprising following the 1991 Gulf War, local Iraqis rejected their efforts to lead the revolt, distrusting them as Iranian agents with only their own interests in mind. After its failure to capitalize on the 1991 uprisings, the Badr Corps executed small-scale infiltration and guerrilla attacks against the Baʻath regime up until the 2003 collapse, though it was never capable of directly confronting the Iraqi Army. The Badr Corps grew to between four thousand and eight thousand members in the late 1990s. Renamed the Badr Organization after the invasion, its leaders claimed in 2005 that they could muster fifteen thousand men. Regardless of the actual strength, the Badr Organization was detested by many Sunnis and suspected of carrying out sectarian executions. The Sunni group al Qaeda in Iraq even created a wing named the Omar Brigade (a caliph revered by Sunnis and reviled by Shiʻa) specifically to target Badr Organization fighters.[45]

As with al-Daʻwa, SCIRI had to adjust to its political stance in the new Iraq. There was a generational split in SCIRI. On the one hand, older members followed a more traditional clerical core and supported the idea of a Khomeini-like clerical rule. After al-Khomeini came to power in Iran, he called on Iraqi Shiʻa to throw off the "non-Muslim Baʻath" rule in their country. Prior to SCIRI's split from al-Daʻwa, one of the party's most prominent members, Ayatollah Mohammed Baqir al-Sadr, telegraphed al-Khomeini in reply to congratulate him and to observe that "other tyrants have yet to see their day of reckoning."[46] This tradition of direct support of al-Khomeini's Islamic teachings died out from the mainstream of these parties, yet strong supporters of Islamic rule remained. This history also inflamed Sunni mistrust and accusations of Iranian control over SCIRI and al-Daʻwa.

Conversely, the younger members were more interested in an activist Islam, like that of the elder Sadr, which linked Islamic structures to the people rather than concentrating on clerical rule from atop. The move away from the Iranian model was expressed in a conference held in May 2007, when SCIRI decided that it was time for a name change to suit the new political realities in Iraq. The group became known as the Islamic Supreme Council of Iraq (ISCI, *al-Majlis al-Aʻala al-Islami al-'Araqi*), dropping the reference to the Islamic Revolution to reflect its position as a dominant force in mainstream Iraqi politics.

SCIRI's return to Iraq was less than triumphant, though. There was little reaction, however, to Mohammed Baqir al-Hakim's attempt at a homecoming tour. Attitudes of many Iraqis still in Iraq were soured by SCIRI's tainted record.

Already accused of being Iranian puppets, SCIRI members were now seen as riding the U.S.-led invasion back to political distinction. Despite this deficit, shrewd political maneuvering brought them to prominence in the new Iraq. They played all sides, divorcing themselves from Iran and rule of the jurist-consult and at least rhetorically embracing democracy. They stayed close to the United States and the official political process, all the while denouncing the United States in public statements. Once in government, they strengthened their power by aligning themselves with the Kurds in an attempt to create a Shi'a super-region that they could control.[47] The tactics served them well, bringing them great power in the new political system. Yet, many of their political actions have been divisive, not only between sects, but within their own political bloc, as will be discussed below.

Regardless of the political parties, the greatest power in the Shi'a sphere rested in one man who, in contrast to the impetuous Muqtada al-Sadr, was widely respected and followed as the pre-eminent Shi'a Islamic scholar. Born in 1930 in Mashhad, Iran, Grand Ayatollah Ali al-Husseini al-Sistani was raised in a well-known religious family. His name, al-Sistani, refers to the Sistan region of Iran and, along with his birthplace, brought on many accusations of close ties between his followers and the religious regime in Iran.

These accusations were chiefly unfounded as al-Sistani distanced himself from the Iranian "guardianship of the jurist-consult" pioneered by al-Khomeini. As aforementioned, al-Khomeini believed that in the absence of the Imam the cleric rules the state in a theocracy. Al-Sistani held no such pretensions. His support for a Shi'a majoritarian democracy was more of a threat to Iran than most other Shi'a platforms in the new Iraq, because it afforded an attractive alternative to the stranglehold that the clerics have held over Iranian politics since the revolution.

Al-Sistani's position on the cleric's role in political affairs was much more nuanced than the traditional division between "quietist" and "activist" leaders, as Shi'a politician Ali Allawi pointed out. Further, Westerners' and Iraqi secularists' view of al-Sistani as a quietist and the Shi'a clerisy, or *marji'iya*, as inherently democratic was "wishful thinking" in Allawi's words. Al-Sistani's position was developed well prior to the 2003 invasion and was the product of a lifetime of academic study.[48]

He commanded the most prevalent network of religious and social service organizations in Iraq. According to annual polls of Shi'a pilgrims traveling to

Mecca conducted by Iran, al-Sistani has the largest following of any Shi'a cleric in the world. One source accumulated data suggesting that up to 80 percent of Shi'a faithful look to al-Sistani for religious guidance. His foundation has offices throughout southern Iraq and branches abroad in Syria, Lebanon, Iran, Afghanistan, Pakistan, India, Georgia, Africa, Britain, and the United States. Through these offices, al-Sistani was able to draw considerable donations from worshippers and friendly Muslim countries, funding for example $5 million worth of students' and teachers' stipends. As pilgrimages to Shi'a holy sites multiplied, so did the finances at Sistani's command. Estimates in 2006 placed the Sistani network's annual income at $500 to $700 million, with assets in excess of $3 billion. The other major Shi'a parties' cooperation with al-Sistani, specifically that of SCIRI and al-Da'wa, further strengthened his preeminent position in Iraq.[49]

Al-Sistani was the guardian of the traditionalist Shi'a school of thought, centered on the *Hawza al-Ilmiyya* that Muqtada al-Sadr had tried to snatch in the early days of the new Iraq. The Hawza generally refers to the religious educational center in Najaf that represents the traditional, relatively quietist sector of the Shi'a clerisy. Although al-Sistani's influence on political affairs was massive in the formative stages of the new Iraq, he did not become actively involved in the daily workings of government and shunned any role for clerics in the fledgling government. Both SCIRI and al-Da'wa advocated a leading political role for the clerisy in their past programs and struggled to reconcile differing views over technocratic or clerical rule in the new Iraq.[50]

Although al-Sistani's council was a moderating influence welcomed by many in the West, his advice was also shrewdly calculated to avoid any tripwires in the way of Shi'a majoritarian dominance. There are few real insights into al-Sistani's ideology beyond the carefully worded fatwas issued by his office. One glimpse into an audience that the reclusive cleric granted to an Islamic scholar suggests that al-Sistani may not have been the democrat some hoped him to be. In 1998, Abdulaziz Sachedina, an academic specializing in Islam, had an audience with Ayatollah al-Sistani in Najaf in 1998 regarding the theological propriety of his lectures. From Sachedina's account, the audience seemed to have been quite one-sided and turned hostile when it appeared that he would not bend easily to al-Sistani's will. Al-Sistani's harangues included criticism of Iranian President Mohammed Khatami's liberal views, and he upbraided Sachedina for his love of the "idea of coexistence and pluralism." He asked, "What is this nonsense about Abrahamic religions?" When it was clear that al-Sistani's arguments were failing to produce their desired effect, he offered to pay Sachedina half of his yearly salary if he resigned from his teaching position, essentially offering to bribe him.[51]

Al-Sistani's voice was a commanding factor in Shi'a involvement in the new Iraq. His demand for a constitution written by an elected body and his subsequent close supervision of the drafting process through his loyal intermediaries left a lasting impression on Iraqi politics. The success of the Iraq's largest political bloc, the United Iraqi Alliance, in remaining cohesive and attaining a great number of seats in the National Assembly also owed significantly to al-Sistani's influence and calming effect. Throughout, al-Sistani remained at arm's length from the Coalition and from direct political activity. According to Shi'a representative Hussein Shahristani, "He refuses even to meet with the alliance now. He says, 'You were elected, so it's up to you now. Don't drag me into it.'"[52]

Despite al-Sistani's distance from official political power, his counsel was authoritative. Specifically, three of his positions were critical to the success of a democratic Iraq. First, according to Shahristani, "He rejects any role for the clerics in the governance or administration of the country." This position prevented Iraq from lapsing into an illiberal theocracy in the short term. Second, al-Sistani strongly opposed sectarian violence. When influential Shi'a politician Mohammed Bahr al-Aloum demanded permission from Sistani to take up arms in response to sectarian killings, the quiet response was, "Please don't do this. Please be civilized. We don't want to start a civil war. This is the most important point." As violence soared in July 2006, al-Sistani once again was a lone voice of reason. In a July 20th statement, he called for peace, imploring Iraqis to "comprehend the scope of the danger that threatens the future of their country, stand united in their rejection of hatred and violence, and replace them with love and peaceful dialogue."[53] Finally, al-Sistani's order for Shi'a unity resulted in electoral successes for the Shi'a majority, had significant impacts on the constitution, and defined politics under the new government.

It is impossible to determine the reclusive cleric's exact intentions, though it seems likely that al-Sistani's greatest fear was a division of Shi'a powers. Such a division, even in the name of isolating extremists and finding common ground between the sects in Iraq, threatened to dilute the 60 percent Shi'a majority and cheat them of the chance to rule Iraq. Al-Sistani certainly feared such an outcome, much as he must have feared that any plan to break up the Shi'a bloc would be a path leading back to Sunni domination. Under his guidance, virtually all Shi'a parties of note ran as a bloc in Iraq's elections for the permanent

National Assembly under the United Iraqi Alliance list. The outcome of this election ensured that the Shi'a would dominate the freely elected government. While Shi'a unity was al-Sistani's preeminent concern, continued adherence to a majoritarian line blocked hopes for a moderate government of national unity from across the ethno-sectarian landscape.

The Shi'a bloc was unified in name only, however. Internecine struggles deadlocked political progress. Even with the stabilizing influence of al-Sistani's power and restraint, the many divisions among the Shi'a population complicated the task of controlling the violence. While calls for calm may have affected a majority of the populace, small radical forces continued their rampages. The various Shi'a political currents guaranteed that, though Iraq's largest bloc had many shared goals, the Shi'a were far from being monolithic. This became increasingly clear in 2006 and 2007 at both the national political level and on the streets of many Shi'a cities, as will be discussed below.

Iraq's Shi'a emerged from Ba'ath rule with some leadership and organization and a general goal of finally turning their demographic majority into political power. This objective was a main driver behind their general restraint from open conflict with the occupying Coalition or the Sunni insurgency. Most Shi'a groups chose to work within the political system. Beyond this common consensus, however, Shi'a unity was difficult to find.

Iraq's major Shi'a factions were at great variance regarding how their majority rule in an Iraqi democracy should play out. These visions were the subject of difficult negotiations as Iraq's permanent constitution was drafted. Overall, the lack of Shi'a consensus contributed to the localization of politics and power in Iraq. As groups vied for position in the new government, districts and ministries became pawns in a game of power and patronage. Instead of becoming an arena of national unity, political activity of the different factions became a contest with ever-higher stakes. By 2007 and 2008, the main players in this game were SCIRI (by then ISCI) and the Sadrists, fighting an asymmetric battle. ISCI's chosen strategy was to seize and hold power within the government, building its might from the top down. In contrast, Muqtada's approach was to continue with the grassroots campaign that his father had initiated, playing to and controlling the crowds as a primary goal and working from that power base to influence politics.[54] This contest would turn deadly, but the asymmetry of the groups' preferred strategies meant that the moral distinction between putatively government forces and militias were not always as clear as they seemed.

The collapse of the old regime and the crisis of governance in Iraq transferred the powers formerly held by a central Iraqi national government to these localized, sectarian groups. The return of these powers to the central government, even a Shi'a-dominated one, has not occurred to date. Therefore, the major Shi'a factions became increasingly potent in localized geographic areas, at the expense of national and even Shi'a unity. The growing authority of the central government as oil revenues rose and violence declined in 2008 intensified the competition between localized groups even more, deepening the enmity between Shi'a politicians.

Iraq's position in the midst of larger Shi'a upheaval also contributed to instability, fueled sectarian fears, and weakened Shi'a unity within the country. Ties between Iraq's Shi'a, the Iranians, and Lebanese *Hizb Allah* (Party of God) were the subject of many of Sunni Iraq's worst fears. These ties also concerned U.S. military leaders. In 2006, GEN George Casey stated that Iran has provided Shi'a groups with training and materiel. Iranian special operations forces and the Lebanese Hizb Allah organization provided weapons to Iraqi groups and were behind a rise in deadly shaped-charge explosives and explosively formed penetrators, a more dangerous form of improvised explosive device capable of punching through U.S. armor.[55]

By 2008, the Iraqi government and even Shi'a militia members were articulating similar accusations. Mahdi Army members charged Iran with funding splinter groups, which came to be known as "special groups" to the U.S. military. These groups were trained and armed by the Iranians, according to both U.S. reports and government of Iraq statements. Muqtada al-Sadr's position was typically elusive. He adopted a nationalist line early on, and his supporters denounced the Iranian-supported Badr Organization; in 2008, however, al-Sadr curbed his rhetoric toward Iran significantly. His moderation likely stemmed from the pressure of the U.S. troop surge and the emboldened Iraqi government, which forced him to seek refuge in Iran. His opponents alleged that the Mahdi Army was now receiving large-scale assistance from Iran, though Sadrists denied this. Many blamed intra-Shi'a fighting, which flared in 2007 and 2008, on Iranian influences as well.[56]

Iraqi and Coalition troops found caches of Iranian weapons after the 2008 assault on Basra, some recently manufactured, and detainees told of training received from the Iranian Islamic Revolutionary Guard Corps—Quds Force. Even as overall violence levels declined in the spring of 2008, the number of rocket attacks involving Iranian weapons rose and the number of explosively formed penetrator attacks were the highest on record in April 2008.[57]

Iran undoubtedly trained and funded some Iraqi groups and fighters, but with the situation as fluid and unstable as it was, the Iranians were too shrewd to back any one horse. While they kept their options and channels of communication open, dabbling a little, they preserved their capacity to inflict more chaos on Iraq should it become strategically necessary. Evidence found in the form of weapons caches was incontrovertible, yet statements of militia members must be taken with a grain of salt due to their penchant for blaming all ills on outsiders and discrediting opponents by linking them to a cast of foreign characters.

Iraq's Shi'a behemoth was not a singular community, but a dangerous mix that was too weak to govern effectively or to control its own radical fringes. While the Sunni insurgents grabbed headlines, Shi'a politicians and the kingmakers behind them reached for government power. Though power brokers in Iraq had different goals and chose different methods for achieving them, few scruples stood in the way of the raw power calculations that drove them all.

5
Setting the Stage for Insurgency: The Sunni Heartland and the Baʿath Regime

> Although the regular armies were destroyed or scattered, there were no signs that the will to resist of the people had been even substantially weakened. Popular patriotism, religious fanaticism and an almost hysterical hatred for [the occupiers] remained as strong as ever, and over the next five years the world was to see the development of a new type of ruthless war waged by guerillas who refused to come into the open . . . and defied all efforts to destroy them, in the meantime causing a heavy toll of casualties.[1]
> —DAVID G. CHANDLER, BRITISH HISTORIAN WRITING ABOUT THE 1808–1814 SPANISH GUERILLA CAMPAIGN AGAINST NAPOLEON'S ARMY

The Sunni heartland of Iraq lies in the vast desert of Anbar Province. This expansive western swath is the largest province in Iraq, stretching from Baghdad Province to Iraq's borders with Jordan and Syria. Home to more than a million Iraqis, mostly Sunni, the land is sparsely populated and virtually devoid of resources, yet critical to a peaceful Iraq.

During the initial invasion, Anbar saw little combat and even fewer American forces. Signs of tension quickly appeared, however, as Coalition troops moved into the Sunni cities of Ramadi and Fallujah. Mosque sermons turned from cautious to inflammatory, and confrontations with Coalition troops became deadly. The insurgency in Anbar Province simmered in 2003, then exploded with the March 2004 attack on a small band of American security contractors and the subsequent siege of Fallujah. That standoff would fester until Fallujah was cleared, block-by-block, in a massive Marine assault in November 2004.

Heavy fighting dragged on for three more years before tapering off in 2007, as the tribes turned against violent extremists.

Unsurprisingly, this wild-west Sunni stronghold defied most American attempts at engagement and understanding. Those best able to comprehend the thicket of connections and allegiances in Anbar did so by likening its logic to that of the Sopranos or the Corleones of mafia lore.[2] The interests of pious or thuggish foot soldiers, opportunistic gang-leaders, and don-like imams and sheikhs were layered and complex. Nationalism and Islamism competed with political and economic interest, driving an intricate game in which allegiances were fleeting and aims were fluid. American troops were at a great disadvantage as they tried to play this new game by much different rules than the Sunnis who had played their entire lives.

Anbar is a poor, rural region, its residents much different than Iraq's urban masses. Most Anbar residents have never been uprooted from the region's dominant age-old family and tribal structure, which has worked for them for ages and adapted well to life under the old regime. Social structures in Anbar are deeply, maddeningly rooted, unlike those of recent migrants to Iraqi cities. A thick set of overlapping loyalties stymies nearly all attempts at engagement by outsiders. Immediate family, clan, tribe, village, and religious affiliations take precedence over any national loyalties and certainly trump any devotion to foreigners, no matter their aims. It is not only foreigners who fall outside the circle of trust, however. Suspicion is quick to arise in relationships beyond members of immediate family.

To understand the importance of the family and the tribe to Iraqi Sunnis, one must first consider their living conditions. These Iraqis live in a world of real and constant danger—a world of self-reliance. No government agencies or watchdog groups guard them or provide the public good. No statutes regulate safety or protect the environment. There is essentially no law. Rural Sunnis rely completely on their family, their clan, their tribe, and their tribal confederation. Within these associations, members work together to provide collectively, maintain order, and protect one another from the many dangers of a lawless world.

Tribal Arabs follow a patronymic naming system, by which each name after the given name is the father, the grandfather, and so on five levels down the genealogical tree. If two Arabs have a common ancestor within the five names, or *khams*, then they can expect to demand certain rights of solidarity and assistance from one another. In a strictly Bedouin sense, receiving assistance from a relative within the circle of the five names is not a rule of thumb, but an inalienable right.

Since the state gives Iraqi Sunnis next to nothing, their loyalties naturally lie in their tribal and familial associations. Even under Saddam, provision generally went through the tribal leaders, not through any governmental representative. Because tribes deliver, they draw loyalty. Social groupings from the immediate family through the tribal confederation afford Iraqis many social services that Americans take for granted. Their collective efforts provide a safety net that includes the equivalent of life insurance, unemployment coverage, health coverage, dispute resolution, protection against attack, and even banking services. None of these items are available to the average Iraqi commercially or through the government. To be cast out from a family or tribal unit is to forfeit your security. Likewise, a family or tribe that loses a member or honor is weakened in the cutthroat world of survival on very limited resources. Little has changed since 1910 when an Ottoman official wrote, "To depend on the tribe is a thousand times safer than depending on the government, for whereas the latter defers or neglects repression, the tribe, no matter how feeble it may be, as soon as it learns that an injustice has been committed against one of its members readies itself to exact vengeance on his behalf."[3]

For these reasons, Coalition troops faced a dense and bewildering tangle of competing loyalties when they attempted to cooperate with the Sunnis of Anbar. As noted above, the Sunnis must align with their fellow tribal members, insurgent or not, because the tribe is their only lifeline and the tribe will be there long after American troops have withdrawn. They must guard the honor and the prestige of their family and their tribe at all costs because showing weakness there is like blood in the water to others who covet their resources. Therefore, honor assumes a wildly different cast than Westerners are used to. Denying knowledge of insurgent activities, refusing to acknowledge wrongdoing, and adamantly refusing to own up to one's own missteps are not lies or violations of a personal moral code. In the minds of these Iraqis, they are noble defenses of personal, familial, and tribal honor, which is not an abstract concept, but a visceral measure of the strength of the social institution that prevents exploitation by others.

In this environment, Coalition troops had great difficulty breaking into the circle of trust. For tribesmen, to stand together is to survive. To act against tribal unity is to invite disaster. Tribal insurgents could easily gain support from, or at least avoid disclosure by, family members, tribesmen, or fellow villagers. Coalition troops were mistrusted outsiders from the beginning and, thereby, hard pressed to obtain useful information.

Even though groups such as al Qaeda operated outside this tribal circle, their ruthlessness initially worked against collaboration with the Coalition or the Iraqi government. The logic was clear for any Iraqi weighing the consequences of defying insurgent groups. Running afoul of the Coalition meant lengthy detention. Iraqi government forces sometimes tortured their victims. Yet these consequences paled in comparison to the certain and painful death promised by insurgent groups for any suspected traitors. An Iraqi captain explained the logic to Americans hoping to run an informant in an al Qaeda cell. "He'll never become an informant. Al Qaeda will know he's been captured. He'll go back to them and say, 'The Americans wanted me to be an informer, but I will be loyal to you.' He will be more afraid of al Qaeda guys than of the Americans."[4] It was better to risk detention by the Coalition than the certain death meted out by the extremists, belying an American notion that Sunni fence sitters could be pushed toward the Coalition by the threat of tough measures. Even when intelligence reached the Coalition, the insurgents' social support networks dulled the impact. Troops gauged the importance of a detained insurgent by the number of calls pouring in from tribal or government officials for his release. Such calls were often heeded in the name of broader political interests.

Coalition troops in Anbar spent years wading their way through this difficult tribal landscape. This social fabric was the medium through which the Iraqi insurgency collaborated, communicated, lived, and grew. Shamed or angered tribesmen were connected through this network to criminals, financiers, military experts from the former regime, and other sorts of facilitators and fixers that lubricated the operation and interaction of insurgent groups. Several forces operated within this network, each fighting for its own reasons, but each loosely connected to the same Iraqi Sunni social fabric.

Iraq's Sunni insurgency stoked the chaos following the 2003 invasion. The insurgency was an amorphous collection of malcontents that deepened the crisis of governance and heightened sectarian tensions to the breaking point. The ultimate goals of these groups ranged from the ejection of the occupying Coalition and the redress of Sunni grievances, to the re-establishment of Sunni dominance in Iraqi politics, to the beginning of a new Sunni Islamic Caliphate in Iraq. The near-term goal of many of these groups was causing the maximum amount of pandemonium possible in order to hasten the Coalition's withdrawal, weaken the Shi'a-controlled government, and foil the formation of a Shi'a super-region in southern Iraq. While early attacks were aimed at foreign assistance to

Iraq, many groups later found that the best targets for inciting turmoil lay along the sectarian fault lines that plagued the country. The excesses of some groups, however, eventually created a backlash that brought the tribes out against the violent extremists.

Many insurgent groups deliberately targeted the Shi'a in hopes of fomenting a civil war in Iraq. These insurgents believed that chaos would accelerate the occupying Coalition's withdrawal and disrupt the movement of Shi'a toward democratic dominance. The most important effects of the Sunni insurgencies were not the attacks on U.S. forces, which grabbed news headlines, but rather the sectarian tension and the narrow political groupings that grew amid the violence. Though the Sunni insurgency dominated accounts of Iraq following the 2003 invasion, until late 2006, soldiers, politicians, and journalists tended to focus on the military aspects of insurgency and counterinsurgency, missing the broader context of the Sunni resistance entirely. The majority of the Sunni violence was political, based on the political, social, and economic legacies of the former regime and their confrontation with new realities.

The tendency to paint the enemy as a monolithic bloc of insurgents was, for years, a significant failure of military thought in Iraq. In the words of a junior staff officer who was involved in daily operations at the Coalition's Combined/Joint Task Force 7 (CJTF-7) Headquarters, such differentiation was not generally discussed in the Joint Operations Center. "We used broad terms like AIF—Anti-Iraqi Forces. Looking back that was most likely part of the problem: not clearly defining who these anti-Iraqi forces were. Had we better defined the enemy in late 2003 and early 2004, we definitely could have done a better job of fighting them."

These "anti-Iraqi forces" were largely Iraqis themselves. Foreign jihadists were a minority. Nor were the fighters solely remnants of the old regime. The resistance encountered by the Coalition was a blend of groups with varied motives, structures, and backgrounds. Some of these fighters would have resisted occupation under any condition, others joined in response to Coalition blunders, insurgent propaganda, and the general crisis of governance. Motives ranged from rabid religious fervor, to intense nationalism, to revenge for the death of a family member, to financial incentives offered by the attack. The eventual split in the insurgency, in which tribal groups expelled the extremists from Anbar, viscerally demonstrated the vastly differing agendas among the Sunni groups. They require further explanation to clarify how they arose from the legacy of Saddam's rule and the crisis of governance, how and why the insurgencies were reinforced with new manpower and support, and why they eventually turned on one another.

Sunni violence had several lasting impacts on transition in Iraq. Progress in reconstruction, stabilization, and security was incredibly hard to achieve in the face of a ruthless, Sunni-dominated insurgency. Sunni resistance to the transition also greatly affected the official political process in Iraq, disrupting it and contributing to a localization of politics that resulted partially from the difficulties politicians found in moving about in Iraq. Hoping that the insurgency would derail the political process and generally rejecting the reality of Shi'a power, Sunnis boycotted the political process until after the constitution was drafted. This contributed to its majoritarian design and the subsequent weak central government favored by many Shi'a and Kurdish politicians. These developments, in turn, ensured that Sunnis would overwhelmingly reject the document. Finally, the violence brought Iraq to the brink of civil war.

The widening sectarian violence born out of inflammatory extremist attacks caused many Sunnis to feel that they must align with their more violent kin in order to protect themselves from the reprisals of militias and rogue government forces. Tribes in Anbar allied against the immediate threat of the al Qaeda extremists in 2007, though they still feared the threat of marauding Shi'a police and militias. Despite progress in the security situation, healing wounds could easily reopen.

When the regime collapsed in 2003, the Kurds had an existing leadership and the Shi'a relied on indigenous and exiled figures, but the Sunni had no figures of stature outside the former regime. Removing the hub from the Ba'athist network left a constellation of isolated cells from the party, security apparatus, and other regime supporters scattered throughout the country. Some cells consisted of local security service offices or military units. Others were supportive tribes or religious groups. These elements were connected through personal and professional ties that allowed them to coordinate as a loose network. Without the central power and guidance of the regime, cells were free to pursue their own interests in a frenzied and fragmented environment. For those who wished to resist the new order, this dispersed network was the perfect organization to maximize chaos while minimizing vulnerability to attack.

There are several key aspects to the shape of the Sunni resistance. First, the Sunni resistance did not have a unified, long-term political goal, strategic vision, or leadership. The goals of former members of the regime, Sunni nationalists, and Islamic extremists were often mutually exclusive. Thus, the resistance was not a single, unified insurgency. Writ large, the Sunni-Arab population as a whole lacked the overarching leadership to provide any semblance of guidance and unity on par with an Ayatollah Sistani or the two Kurdish leaders, Barzani and Talabani. Ever since Iraq's Sunni figureheads vanished with the old regime, the society has been atomized and conflicted.

Second, the disparate groups of the insurgency initially shared an interest in instability and ejection of Coalition troops as short-term goals. They all rejected the Shi'a-dominated trajectory of the transition. To pursue these immediate objectives, some groups set aside their differences in long-term goals and collaborated to carry out specific operations. Such partnership largely ended when it became clear that their overarching aims were not compatible.

Third, the majority of the resistance to the Coalition and the Iraqi government through 2007 consisted of Iraqi Sunnis. While Shi'a groups figured prominently in sectarian violence and slightly in resistance to American forces since 2006, Sunnis continued to compose the bulk of the active insurgency and the vast majority of detainees (80 percent in late 2007). Throughout, the largely Iraqi-Sunni face of the resistance overshadowed the foreign component.[5]

Many of the earliest combatants were remnants of the former regime, tied into other Sunni structures by kinship or tribal identity, religion, and Sunni nationalism. Sunni nationalists, radical Islamists, tribal forces, and criminals soon followed the vanguard of former regime elements (FREs) and *Fedayeen* (fanatic paramilitary fighters) into the bedlam of violent resistance. Not all of these forces were admirers of the former regime, yet many held links to former regime staffers and most possessed some motivations in common with the FREs, which included the rejection of foreign occupation and a fear of Shi'a dominance over the former Sunni ruling minority. Instead of being dead-enders, as suggested by U.S. officials, the FREs became the center around which a network of insurgent groups formed.

The rapid development of the resistance indicates that it was based on pre-existing structures. The resilience of resistance activity despite the removal of numerous high-level figures suggests that the resistance was a broad network of cells rather than a traditional, centrally directed effort. Its ability to expand in scope and membership implies that the resisters served as a cadre, attracting more fighters by exploiting dissatisfaction with the occupation, the pace of reconstruction, and the new leadership of Iraq. Despite these strengths, it lacked the singular political goals and strategy characteristic of a classic insurgency.

Motivated by a wish to maintain Sunni dominance and a fear of the majority Shi'a's power, rejectionist groups rapidly filled the vacuum formed by the regime's collapse. Some of these groups strived to provide local order, yet in a manner decidedly opposed to the official process of Coalition-led transition in Iraq. With increasing intensity, Sunni groups attacked the Coalition and its Iraqi supporters. It was only when cracks began to form between the various groups that the Coalition was able to play on their differences and bring some over to its side.

The Regime's Preparation for War and Internal Defense

A number of commentators view the quick emergence of resistance as evidence of a prepared "stay-behind operation" to oppose occupation; this resistance, however, was more a product of Saddam's legacy and his plans for unconventional and internal defense than any grand, centralized plan for a guerilla war. U.S. military commanders pointed to the caches of weapons and money that fuel the resistance as proof of prior planning, which they describe as "a concept of operations" to be implemented under decentralized control, rather than a centralized campaign plan.[6] Though these preparations were not an indication of a regime-centric insurgency campaign, they did benefit the former regime elements wishing to defy the Coalition. Sunni members of the regime were the core of resistance and their connection to the strong social fabric of tribalism supplied them with a ready-made network for spreading their fight.

Under Saddam's rule, paramilitary forces and foreign fighters were given training and equipment to augment the regime's conventional defense with guerilla tactics. These groups were primarily aimed at the many internal threats to the regime's authority, yet their training, equipment, and structure were well prepared to continue resistance after its downfall. According to a U.S. military intelligence report, Saddam sent a thousand officers for two months of guerrilla training at Salman Pak and Bismayah in the fall of 2002. These officers were selected from several intelligence services and were reportedly instructed to await orders in the event of regime collapse. A senior officer from the Presidential Palace also ordered the training of a group of one hundred Saudis, Afghans, and other foreigners under supervision of senior Fedayeen officers at al-Nahrawan and Salman Pak. These individuals were subsequently dispersed to fight against U.S. forces.[7]

According to captured documents briefed to Jay Garner, head of the Office of Reconstruction and Humanitarian Assistance (ORHA), and several months later to Amb. L. Paul Bremer, the *Mukhabarat* (Iraqi intelligence) was likewise instructed to wage an unconventional defense. An order issued January 23, 2003, instructed Mukhabarat agents to burn their offices, form covert cells, and train insurgents in the case of invasion. They were to undertake ambush and sniper operations as well as "sabotage and looting." Bremer quotes the document as calling for the Mukhabarat to "scatter agents to every town. Destroy electric power stations and water conduits. Infiltrate the mosques, the Shiite holy places."[8] It is impossible to know what impact these instructions had, albeit some of Saddam's most committed disciples likely carried out the intent.

A former Iraqi intelligence operative who became a leader in the Fedayeen in Fallujah stated, "We have been preparing for this kind of guerrilla war for a long time. We know each other and we have ways of communicating with one another. The Americans made a big mistake by thinking that we all disappeared after the war." Another resistance leader in Baghdad, reportedly an Iraqi general under the old regime, admitted, "Six months before the occupation, we started training and exercising resisting the American army in small groups."[9]

These reports must be understood within the context of evidence raised by the *Iraqi Perspectives Project*, which extensively debriefed high-level regime staffers to provide the Iraqi view of Saddam's preparations for and conduct of the war. Saddam never grasped the seriousness of the Coalition threat. He assumed that the invasion would stop well short of the heart of the regime, so his preparations focused more on the internal and Iranian threats than that of the Coalition. Since he did not believe the Coalition would topple him, there was no reason for him to plan a stay-behind defense. Instead, Saddam dispersed fanatics to augment the conventional defenses and, more importantly, counter internal uprisings that may have threatened the regime had the Coalition followed a limited campaign plan along the lines of the 1991 Gulf War.[10]

Some experts also deem that the regime distributed and cached weapons around the country to enable resistance in the wake of regime collapse, although less conspiratorial explanations exist. "The Americans . . . almost gave us the weapons," explained Mohammed, an insurgent from Fallujah. "They thought we were thieves. . . . They thought we were destroying the Iraqi army." In reality, some looters were collecting impressive arsenals for resistance. Tribal groups also stockpiled weapons that they would later use or sell. Tribal gangs were selling SA-7 shoulder-fired surface-to-air missiles at $325 each in 2005.[11]

FREs were not the only Iraqis with access to weapons, however. Many citizens stockpiled arms and ammunition from Baghdad gun stores in the days preceding the war. These purchases were motivated by the fear of anarchy in the event of the government's demise. The black market for armaments soared after the invasion, with supply and demand increasing. The Coalition issued weaponry to soldiers and police, which were then stolen or sold to the burgeoning black-market dealers. Glock and Walther 9-millimeter pistols, issued by the United States to Iraqi forces, fetched between $1100 and $1800 by the end of 2006, triple their price in the West and a huge sum in the Iraqi economy. Other weapons, such as AK-47s, sniper rifles, even police cars were available illegally. Between the enormous stockpiles of abandoned weapons and the ubiquitous nature of small arms in Iraq, the insurgents easily armed themselves after Saddam's fall.[12]

The wide variety of insurgent groups and motives that sprang up within the first year after the regime's collapse meant that any centrally directed efforts were largely irrelevant. With the fall of the Ba'ath regime, many Sunni elites lost a comfortable and prominent position in Iraq. As one scholar clarifies, they "lost power, they lost position, they lost influence, and no jobs program or provision of electricity can compensate for that."[13] Adding injury to insult, as their world came crashing down, many of these elites faced retribution or prosecution under the new order.

Unconventional resistance began with the battles of the Fedayeen and foreign fighters against the invasion force prior to the government's downfall. Attacks escalated within a week of the regime's collapse and carried on throughout the summer at a relatively low level of ten to twenty attacks per week.[14] At this early stage, the Coalition was slow to recognize the growing severity of the crisis, which was dismissed as the last gasps of the dying regime. By the fall of 2003, however, a string of high-profile attacks, deadly accurate in their strategic effect, had targeted the Coalition's external support and highlighted the gravity of the conflict. In October 2003, the combat deaths of seventy U.S. troops exceeded the monthly toll for the initial invasion. As violence continued to rise, the events of the spring of 2004 and the first battle for Fallujah clearly showed that the problem had grown beyond any dead-end resistance.

The CPA's first move regarding members of the former regime was Order Number 1, an edict on de-Ba'athification under which the top four levels of Ba'ath Party leaders were barred from public positions in the new Iraq. Many in the Coalition and Iraq's other major communities regarded this measure as an absolute necessity to dispense with the Ba'ath terror once and for all. The order was received enthusiastically by the majority of the Shi'a and the Kurds who feared and hated the Ba'athists, yet Sunnis declared it to be discriminatory.

One Sunni technocrat who had been a high-level party member warned, "If the party members are treated in a normal manner and they are given their rights, there will be no more party. If not, the Ba'ath Party will rise again." While the CPA estimated that the edict affected only a small percentage of Ba'ath Party members, the CIA station chief in Baghdad warned CPA proconsul Bremer that this figure consisted of some of the most well-connected and well-informed Iraqis in terms of operating the country and its infrastructure. "By nightfall, you'll have driven 30,000 to 50,000 Ba'athists underground. And in six months, you'll really regret this." The decision had already been handed down, however, and the de-Ba'athification order went ahead. De-Ba'athification would continue to be problematic when it was turned over to Iraqi politicians. A number of Shi'a politicians used the policy as a tool to weed out opponents and replace Sunnis with Shi'a in government. The sectarian nature of these actions was evidenced by the fact that Shi'a Ba'athists were often given a chance at rehabilitation while Sunnis were almost universally cashiered.[15] Many of these elites aggressively resisted being excluded from the country they had controlled for so long.

It was not only the Ba'athist elites who were thrust aside, however. The CPA next moved to disband Iraq's security and military forces, touching off angry demonstrations in May 2003. Troubles with former members of the military continued in June when Iraqi soldiers again protested, this time because a promised monthly stipend had not been delivered. In the resulting tensions, two former Iraqi soldiers were killed. Efforts of senior regime loyalists to draw unemployed soldiers into the fight against the Americans found increasing sympathy as patience wore thin due to broken promises. Both a former Iraqi general who became a resistance leader and U.S. MG James Marks, head of intelligence for Coalition ground forces at the time, believe that the decision to dissolve the Iraqi army factored significantly into the propagation of the resistance.[16]

Although many of these Ba'athists and soldiers were among the first sweep of fighters to rally against the new order that had tossed them into the dustbin of history, they were not alone for long. The insurgency was not solely a movement of FREs. A U.S. military estimate of the resistance in the fall of 2004 pinned its strength between eleven and twenty thousand members. Of this number, up to three thousand were thought to be "hard-core" FREs, with as many as ten thousand "part-time" supporters.[17] Though any distinction of FRE loyalty to the old regime soon dissipated into a broader, Sunni nationalist theme, the early impact of FREs in leading the fight and training others was unmistakable. Many of the hard-core FREs would have opposed the Coalition and the new Iraqi government regardless of whether or not the CPA had disbanded the Iraqi security forces and issued the de-Ba'athification edict. These higher-level and fanatical FREs provided much of the financial, intelligence, and other forms of support that enabled resistance operations across the country.

CPA orders primarily affected the mid- and lower-level soldiers and security officers. They were the technical and tactical experts of the old regime who would later dispense lower-level leadership, training, and facilitation for all types of insurgent groups in Iraq. Many of these soldiers and security servants may have been convinced to stay in the new Iraqi military had events progressed differently at the Coalition-policy level, yet the CPA did not cause the insurgency —it would have happened anyway. CPA decisions provided the insurgency with a greater field of trained military experts, however. While the extent of the effects of CPA Orders Number 1 and 2 will never be fully known, the impact of FRE assistance to the insurgent groups is relatively clear.

The significant role of former regime elements in training, financing, and other support was more critical to continued resistance than any numerical figure. A Defense Intelligence Agency report from late 2003 acknowledged "FREs' prewar operating and support structure, access to resources, and training and capabilities make them the greatest threat of all anti-coalition groups in the near term." These men had immediate access to rockets, mortars, and man-portable surface-to-air missiles. Most critically, the former officers and NCOs of the Iraqi military and security services had been trained to act as a cadre, leading, instructing, and employing volunteers from all walks of life to create a much deadlier insurgent network than would have otherwise formed. FREs also had connections to precise information regarding infrastructure that was critical to pinpoint attacks against targets such as Baghdad's oil supply lines. These attacks struck precisely at points of infrastructure that were the most difficult to repair.[18]

Iraqis with military training were undoubtedly behind several high-profile attacks soon after the fall of the old regime. In one instance on October 2, 2003, Coalition military intelligence intercepted communications coordinating an ambush on Ambassador Bremer's convoy as he exited a meeting in Baghdad. One member of the assassination team watched Ambassador Bremer's party as it boarded the vehicles, passing the details over radio to the ambush cell. Fortunately, the ambush cell was trapped in traffic and a third cell never answered calls for back up. Military intelligence analysts stated that the cells were communicating in "military-jargon Iraqi Arabic," indicating that the teams probably were former members of Saddam's military or security forces.[19]

These former regime elements held ties to key elements of the Baʿath Party who had escaped to Syria. In May 2003 in Baghdad, Izzat Ibrahim al-Duri, the highest-level member of the Baʿath regime still at large as of early 2009, held a meeting with four other high-level officials in a car where they agreed to support the resis-tance. Al-Duri was formerly vice president and a member of the Revolutionary Command Council (RCC), as well as commander of the Baʿath Party Regional Command under Saddam's rule (the regional level is the highest level in Iraq, owing to the Baʿath's origins as a pan-Arab movement in which the "national" level would consist of all Arab lands). Al-Duri's name has been associated with financing and direction of the insurgencies from Syria since that meeting.[20]

The exiled Baʿath Party organization was refined at a summit convened in al-Hasaka, Syria, in the spring of 2004. There, those tainted by contact with the Coalition or the Iraqi Governing Council were purged. After this reorganization, Baʿath activity resurged. GEN George W. Casey, U.S. commander in Iraq at the time, stated that high-level Baʿathists, renamed the New Regional Command, operated in 2004 "out of Syria with impunity . . . providing direction and financing for the insurgency."[21] This sanctuary made defeating the support mechanisms for the insurgent groups much more difficult.

Baʿath Party meetings quietly returned to a number of Iraqi cities where mid-level officials of the former regime chaired sessions aimed at collecting funds for insurgent groups. After the exodus of higher-level officials to Jordan and Syria, more anonymous functionaries reportedly returned to carry out these efforts. According to Iraqi journalists, there was a trend of Sunni employees of the new Iraqi government frequenting such meetings; evidence that the insurgents were trying to infiltrate the new government.[22]

Some Iraqi officials pointed to the resurgent Baʿath Party as helping to strengthen the insurgency. Key Baʿathists, including Saddam's half-brother Sabawi Ibrahim al-Hassan, former vice president al-Duri, and former aide Mohamed Yunis al-Ahmed, were thought to be financial backers of the resistance, operating through connections to former military officials.[23] These officials had maintained contacts among the ranks of former regime elements, as well as the network of support and operatives that Saddam's security services cultivated outside Iraq, and had access to funds within and outside of Iraq. For instance, a December 2003 raid on a Samarra safe house associated with al-Duri netted $1.94 million in cash, demonstrating the kind of resources that were at the disposal of these FREs.[24] Drawn from the various power centers of pre-invasion Iraq, these officials represented one means for networking the vast number of unemployed soldiers and security officers and the numerous insurgent groups to which they belonged.

The Arab press retained an interest in the Baʻath Party, even into 2007. A February 2007 special report in the Arabic daily *Asharq Alawsat* asked, "Will the Baʻath Return?" Four years after the regime's demise, Iraqi analysts expressed to the paper that the Baʻath Party, owing to its decades as the only political force in Iraq, remained the most powerful and unified party inside Iraq. They added that the armed wing of the Baʻath Party was still a prominent aspect of the armed resistance. Other Arabic reporting detailed the Baʻath's regrowth and organizational efforts throughout Iraq.[25] Despite this analysis, some Iraqis in the United States pointed out that the party had ceased to be a real political power under the old regime, as it was Saddam and not the institution that held the real power.

The insurgents were not solely former regime members, however. Many outside the regime had motivations for fighting the new order. Tribes, religious leaders, criminals, and businessmen were all able to capitalize on Sunni dominance in Iraq. While wars and sanctions had devastated Iraq's economy, not all Iraqis suffered equally. Supporters of the regime and "rentseekers" were able to exploit the conditions of the 1990s to make an opulent living off of corruption and smuggling. Many of those who had thrived under the lawlessness of the last decade were from the Sunni areas. Stately homes that line the Euphrates on the outskirts of Fallujah and in places such as Husaybah reflect the lucrative positions held by some Sunnis under the old order. These Sunnis who flourished in the conditions of the old Iraq had the funds and the means to resist any changes that threatened their position.

Even those Sunnis outside the elite feared that Shiʻa dominance would be forced on them. One young Iraqi in a Baghdad suburb stated, "The Shiites have a secret fifty-year plan to turn Iraq into an Islamic state like Iran. . . . There will be very few Sunnis left in Iraq, and they will not be able to resist."[26] Desires for power, fear of retribution and marginalization, and paranoid conspiracy theories all had their part in Sunni motives for resistance.

Though they resisted the new order, few Sunnis wanted a return to Baʻathist rule. In fact, many wished for an outcome that would vindicate the hell they lived through under Saddam, as a young Baghdadi explained. "The thing that really pisses me off—we've been under sanctions for thirteen years, everything we underwent for thirteen years . . . For nothing. For nothing. It was all a big joke."²⁷ This sentiment may have had been related to the eventual decision of many Sunnis to stand up against the tyranny of the extremist groups. Sunnis were searching for a best-case outcome in which they remained prosperous, and in control of their destiny. No one provided these Sunnis with a compelling political vision as to how to achieve their aims without violence, leaving the field open to the insurgents. The insurgents and their supporters believed that the Coalition and its Iraqi partners stood in the way of these goals and that the only means to their ends was through bloodshed. For a number of reasons, and through a variety of channels, the parameters of the Sunni insurgencies soon widened beyond the FRE hard core, with crippling effects on reconstruction and stability in the new Iraq.

Accounting for the different Sunni resistance groups will be complicated until the declassification of detailed intelligence reporting. More than thirty-five different Sunni-Iraqi groups issued public announcements regarding their activities, and many more small cells were active. An early analysis from the Baghdad weekly *al-Zawra* stated that many of the cells "do not know their leadership, the sources of their financing, or who provides them with weapons." Captured insurgents described their organization for journalist Zaki Chehab as small cells of three to five members. Some of these insurgents were fighting for a cause while others simply fought for the cash they could make per attack. According to U.S. government reports and Arab newspaper analyses, major nationalist resistance groups included the 1920 Revolution Brigades, the Army of Mohammed, the National Front for the Liberation of Iraq, the Secret Republican Army, and the Iraqi Resistance Islamic Front (hard-core Islamist groups will be discussed below).²⁸ It is difficult to assess the true nature of these groups due to frequent name changes, misleading statements, and the clandestine nature of these resistance groups.

Several groups have appeared to have sizeable FRE contingents. Col. Muayed Yassin 'Aziz 'Abd al-Razaq al-Nasseri confessed to becoming commander of the Army of Mohammed, one such FRE-heavy group, after two other leaders were captured. He alleged that it was "founded by Saddam Hussein after the fall of the regime on April 9, 2003." U.S. intelligence reports also implicate Saddam in creating this group, along with other resistance organizations. Moreover, journalist Mohammed Bazzi interviewed an insurgent leader who had a stack of Army of Mohammed leaflets in Fallujah on July 9, 2003, confirming the early date for the group's conception. The Army of Mohammed, according to Nasseri, has collaborated with the resurgent Ba'ath Party since April 2004.

Nasseri described the group as "a military armed one, which operated according to a principle of non-centralized command." The connections held by this group included the Ba'ath Party, the Syrian Ba'ath Party, and Fawzi al-Rawi, a financier whose name has surfaced in connection with numerous resistance groups. These different channels demonstrate the network that linked nearly all the resistance groups together, through varying degrees of separation.[29]

By the end of 2007, it appeared that the profusion of insurgent groups may have been whittled down to two main organizations, although a number of other small, independent cells remained active. Al Qaeda in Iraq, once led by Abu Musab al-Zarqawi, remained a major force in the insurgency into 2007, even as its extreme violence provoked a backlash from Sunni tribes. While al Qaeda continued to have an Islamic extremist, and often foreign, membership, the Islamic Army in Iraq seemed to be "homegrown" and comprise former Ba'athists.[30] Despite the power of FREs in these insurgent groups, without support, assistance, and new recruits, FRE resistance alone would have hit a dead-end under the onslaught of Coalition attrition. The all-important social network of Sunni Iraq provided the nourishment needed to widen the insurgencies.

It would have been much simpler if the insurgencies in Iraq had been limited to remnants of the Ba'athist regime. When Secretary of Defense Donald Rumsfeld referred to the budding insurgency as a group of dead-enders in the summer of 2003, he specifically invoked the example of the Nazi resistance that lived furtively on in the days after Hitler's fall.[31] Unfortunately, for Iraq and its Coalition partners, opposition to the new order was not limited to former Ba'athists. Iraq's thick social networks offered many avenues for resisters to collaborate and expand their numbers, a phenomenon not found in Nazi Germany.

In World War II's later stages when the Nazi resistance (known as the Werewolves) became active, German people readily pointed out Nazi agents to the occupiers. Exhausted by an epic war and terrified of reprisals, especially at the hands of the Soviets, the majority of Germans simply had no interest in further bloodshed. People considered the Werewolves an invitation for trouble they did not wish for, thus the Werewolves had little support from the populace and often found themselves hounded not only by the Allied forces, but also by the German people themselves.[32]

Coalition officers in Iraq, believing that they were in fact fighting a similar enemy, thought they were nearing victory in the summer of 2003. Officers at CENTCOM headquarters and in the field in Iraq expressed hopes that they were "over the hump" or "turn[ing] the corner" with regard to operations against the former regime elements.³³ In retrospect, of course, these predictions were tragically optimistic, though one can see the strategic mindset that caused such assessments. Had the Coalition been fighting an isolated, discredited, and desperate handful of staunch Ba'athists, the back of the resistance would have possibly been broken at that time. The truth was much more dangerous: the network of resistance was expanding quickly. New insurgents were popping up much more quickly than Coalition forces were killing them, and the cancer was metastasizing along the Sunni social fabric in western Iraq.

The Iraqi resistance proved to exist in much different circumstances than the Werewolves. Even though Saddam's rule devastated Iraq's economy, the level of exhaustion in Iraq was not comparable to that in Germany. Moreover, the Germans were soundly defeated as a nation in an epic conflict. The Iraqi military was surely dismantled by an impressive campaign, yet the waffling of the regime in Iraq did not leave the same impact that years of war had in Germany. In fact, many of the most troubled areas in Iraq were relatively untouched by conventional military conflict. Further, the occupation in Iraq is not as pervasive as it was in Germany, nor is the fear of reprisals from the Coalition similar to the fear of Soviet occupation. Thus, while the Nazi resistance of the Werewolves sputtered out, the Iraqi insurgency extended and threatened to engulf the country in a civil war.

Themes of Sunni Discontent

It was initially hard for many Americans to understand why Sunnis outside the regime would target Coalition troops after the hated dictator was deposed. Saddam and the former regime caused much suffering, yet many Iraqis viewed the West, specifically the United States and Britain, to be complicit in both Saddam's long reign and the crushing sanctions of the 1990s.³⁴ Several common themes explain this perception. First, many Iraqis remember contacts between the U.S. government and Saddam in the 1970s and 1980s as diplomats attempted to strengthen Iraq as a bulwark against communism and later to counter the menace of Iran after its Islamic revolution. Iraqi and U.S. officials signed an economic and technical assistance agreement in August 1987, and several Western governments secretly provided arms to Iraqi forces.³⁵ The grainy photos of smiling American diplomats shaking hands with Saddam are proof to many Iraqis that Saddam ruled at the pleasure of the United States and that America did nothing to stop his brutality until American interests were at stake.

Second, many Iraqis hold the United States directly culpable for the hardships of the 1990s. After 1991, Iraq was subject to a sanctions regime most vocally supported by the United States. During the same period, the country came under U.S. and British bombardment at regular intervals. Although Saddam's obstinacy and bellicosity were prime causes of these actions, some Iraqis felt they were under attack from the West despite being uninvolved in any of the regime's crimes. Additionally, the Iraqi people bore the brunt of the suffering caused by the sanctions, while Saddam and his coterie continued to live in luxury. Many Iraqis viewed America at fault for a policy that punished them, but not their recalcitrant leader.

Combined with these feelings against America was a strong sense of Iraqi or Arab-Islamic nationalism that motivated many insurgents. These themes resonated with a long-standing hatred toward foreign, especially non-Muslim, occupation in the Arab world.[36] The ongoing Israeli-Palestinian struggle kept this nerve raw in many Iraqis and other Arabs as well. Due to unwavering U.S. support for Israel, many Arabs associated America with Zionism and an assault on Islam. Disdain for the West was promoted by Saddam during his rule. The confluence of nationalism with self-preservation, self-interest, and rejection of the outsider provided a potent and mutually reinforcing mix of resistance motivations.

This mix of motivations was inflamed by the inevitable acrimony resulting from military operations in Sunni areas. Many Sunnis perceived that Coalition forces were at "war against the Sunnis themselves," which became a self-fulfilling prophecy. This impression was probably created in the early days of the occupation, when killings at checkpoints and through collateral damage by U.S. troops in the Sunni towns of Fallujah, Hit, Tikrit, and Samarra led to Sunni ambushes in retaliation. This started a cycle of self-perpetuating violence, exacerbated by the tribal imperative that the death of one of their number must be avenged. For these reasons, "the cycle, once started, was almost impossible to stop."[37]

Incidents in which troops damaged property or inadvertently killed civilians often played on tribal norms of honor and retribution that are vital for keeping order in a society with little to no rule of law. A slight gone unpunished in a tribe may signal to other tribes that it is weak and open to abuse or exploitation. For this reason, the wrongful death of tribal members must be answered by revenge or the payment of "blood money."[38] In the absence of a strong justice system, these norms create order by using tribal systems to prevent and police violence. This practice, emphasized in the later years of Saddam's rule, had a role in escalating the violence in regions as tribal militias sought revenge by attacking Coalition troops, drawing further military attention to the area.

Early on, several U.S. units refused or were unable to pay "blood money" to the families of Iraqis inadvertently killed by their troops. This tribal custom is a mechanism of maintaining order and avoiding costly feuds: the tribe of the deceased may accept blood money as compensation for the death in lieu of retribution. Coalition military leaders often did not understand the importance of this system. In Fallujah, for example, it was not until Marine units arrived in 2004 that the U.S. government offered blood money to the families of those killed in the early 2003 confrontations that helped to spark resistance. By this late date, half the families refused it.[39] Many planned on seeking justice in another way.

In practice, these compensations, known as *solatia* payments in military legal terminology, were difficult to disburse. Truly gauging their results is near impossible. According to military publications, the idea behind solatia payments is to provide virtually instant compensation for accidents before going through the process of investigation that determines fault. These immediate payments are meant to maintain good will between U.S. forces and the local populace. The maximum amount that was allowed to be disbursed was $2,500 per deadly incident. U.S. forces paid over $20 million in condolence payments in 2005 alone.[40] In Iraq, these payments avoided the double insult of killing and then ignoring the culture of paying compensation, but it is doubtful that good will was actually produced or preserved by them. They were more of a way of preventing a bad situation from getting worse.

A Marine finance officer involved in delivering solatia payments described one of his journeys. Wary of the very real possibility of a suicide attack, Marines manning a checkpoint in western Iraq had opened fire after a car ignored a series of signals to stop. In the incident, the driver was seriously wounded, his car destroyed, and his daughter killed. The unit's commander decided to offer a condolence payment to the wounded man, so the finance officer and a senior officer from his unit set off to track down the Iraqi man. Arriving at the local hospital, the two officers trekked through its corridors, asking anyone they could find about the whereabouts of the man. After what seemed like hours of climbing up and down the stairs in the stifling summer heat chasing down false leads, they found someone who instructed them to check in the hospital compound's guard shack.

The Marines discovered the man sitting with who appeared to be tribal leaders in the shade of the guard shack and began the negotiation process with the help of their translator. With condolence payments involving a death, the first offer is invariably refused, but after a lengthy discussion, the money is usually accepted. For condolence payments involving material damage, the first offer is taken, though more money will always be demanded. This is culturally how the process works. In this case, the man was offered payments for his daughter's death, the destruction of his car, and for his own injuries. After his initial refusal, the man did accept the condolence money offered, yet the other men's body language and the mutterings that the translator overheard caused the finance officer to wonder if, once the Americans departed, the grieved man would retain any of the money or if it would all go to the tribal leaders who were coaching him. Since there was nothing the Marines could do to ensure he kept the money, they headed back to their base, unsure if they had done any good that day. On the return trip, they narrowly avoided disaster as they spotted an IED lying on the side of the road and called for specialists to blow the deadly trap. The finance officer observed wryly, "That day was pretty much Iraq in a nutshell."[41]

Tribal norms also worked against those who collaborated with the Coalition. In one such case, a member of one tribe informed on another tribe, leading to a Coalition raid and subsequent confrontation where a villager was shot and killed by U.S. troops. Although masked when walking among the detained villagers and pointing out individuals for further questioning, the informant was identifiable by his deformed thumb. Tribal elders seeking vengeance clearly expressed that if the informant's tribe did not take action, they would take matters into their own hands. In order to avoid further violence, the offending tribe resolved the matter. The execution was carried out not by veiled insurgents, but by the informant's father and brother who reluctantly killed him face-to-face with AK-47s.[42]

Some Coalition tactics reminded Iraqis of bygone times. One Iraqi lamented, "They arrest people, they don't give information to families—like the Ba'ath. The past and the present—there's no difference. There should be a difference."[43] Coalition sweeps often netted large numbers of individuals, because troops had no way of discerning between a fighter who had quickly dropped his weapon and an innocent man in the house next door. As a result, these Iraqis were detained by troops with no information provided to family members on their fates. Many were determined to be of no intelligence value and freed hours or weeks later. While these actions were part and parcel of the difficulties of fighting an unconventional enemy, many Iraqis cited it as evidence of American oppressiveness.

Cultural gaffes were often interpreted as troops' arrogance or disdain for Iraqis, Arab culture, and Islam. Some of these missteps were simply limitations of the military system and a lack of experience in Iraq's daily operations. Early on, there were often no female soldiers available in front-line units to search female Iraqis. Iraqis viewed searches of women conducted by foreign men as a great shame to their honor. Another common complaint was U.S. soldiers' habit of placing their feet or knees on Iraqis' backs when the soldiers ordered these Iraqis to lie down during house searches. Although for U.S. troops this was, in part, a hard-learned lesson from incidents of uncooperative detainees and meant as a way to maintain control of the Iraqis' movements, Iraqis viewed it as a calculated insult, especially when a foot was placed on them. Culturally, Arabs consider the sole of the foot to be dirty, and merely showing it can be offensive. As a result, Iraqis see being stepped on as an unforgivable assault on their honor and culture. Americans simply underestimated the depth of the feelings that such acts would cause.

Cultural nuances aside, being treated like a criminal in your home by a foreign soldier is an event likely to embitter all but the most stoic in any country in the world. Coalition troops, unable to discern between friend and foe, have to protect themselves as well. It is a delicate situation where a middle ground that suits the needs of the searcher without angering the searched is almost impossible to find. At the root, the lack of basic cultural knowledge and rudimentary language skills forces U.S. troops to treat all Iraqis as possible insurgents simply because there is no communication or understanding to be gained during a search situation.

Some Coalition tactics, such as mass detentions in the course of military sweeps, have exacerbated these themes. Villages that are pegged by intelligence to have resistance activity are cordoned off and searched by Coalition troops. In such operations, a military unit encircles the targeted area and then goes house to house, searching for weapons and other indications of resistance activity. These operations are one of the best methods the U.S. military has for finding weapons caches and disrupting insurgent activity. Unfortunately, this method often results in innocent citizens being detained along with any insurgents who have not managed to slip away. Indiscriminate units may detain virtually all the military-age men in a village for days while they sort the good from the bad.

One such operation in the village of Thulayah resulted in the detention of roughly four hundred male residents, where all but fifty of these detainees were released after a few days. This event infuriated both the residents, because the detentions smacked to them of collective punishment, and those detained, because they were treated disrespectfully while being held.[44] Coalition troops must walk a fine line between using tactics that net an elusive enemy able to melt into the civilian populace and avoiding those tactics that disenfranchise normal citizens and result in further support for the resistance. The largest part of the problem with regard to mass detentions and coarse search tactics is that Western troops without a great deal of time in Iraq are virtually blind when it comes to differentiating between a potential insurgent and an innocent citizen. For these reasons, Coalition troops, especially early on in the war in Iraq, treated every villager as a suspect and searched every house thoroughly, often angering the residents in the process.

In contrast, some military members have remarked after working with Iraqi units that the local soldiers often know precisely which houses to search, what parts of the house to search, and what people to detain. Iraqi soldiers are cognizant of the minute details of what is and is not normal in Iraqi culture and daily life. They understand the language, unlike most Coalition soldiers, and detect details of inflection, body language, and the like that even a fluent Western linguist is likely to miss. They are better able to exploit on-the-spot intelligence from other village citizens. All of these factors lead to more precise searches and less discontent, if the Iraqi unit is professional and not out to settle old scores. Although these benefits were not initially available, they are increasingly helpful as more Iraqi units come on line. The sectarian tension between largely Shiʻa units and Sunni residents is often counterproductive, however. Even though the Iraqi Army is held in higher esteem than the militia-infested national police forces, many Sunnis see these units more as potential death squads than trustworthy guardians.

Beyond the clear difficulties of combating a ruthless enemy operating amid a civilian population, some Coalition troops harbor a disdain for Iraqis, which can create serious consequences. One U.S. soldier in an advisory role with Iraqi security forces summed up his feelings by saying, "I don't build bonds. I don't build friendships. I don't have contacts, with none of them." In turn, his Iraqi counterpart observed, "We are the police and they don't respect us. How is it possible for them to respect the Iraqi people?" This frustrated Iraqi officer quit his post.[45] Conversely, it is difficult to force troops to maintain cultural awareness and a cordial attitude when it seems to them that a majority of Iraqis would be happy to see them dead.

Many soldiers attempted to put forward the best possible image, respecting the culture as best they knew how, using simple Arabic greetings, and treating people with kindness. The efforts of hundreds of soldiers, however, could be wiped out by only one frustrated, scared, or boorish American yelling, cussing, and bullying Iraqis at checkpoints, in house searches, or on patrols.[46] The combination of adrenaline, animosity, and the language barrier has led troops to communicate through steadily increasing volume, thicker profanity, and more and more physical directions. It is imperative that military leaders recognize the seriousness of poor morale and discipline and rein in overly aggressive troops, because such behavior could influence the young Iraqi man to either assist the Coalition or the growing insurgency. Aggressiveness is good in a firefight, but outright hostility in many other situations is counterproductive to the mission and actually leads to more American deaths.

Nir Rosen, an Arabic-speaking journalist who traveled widely in Iraq, relates the story of a raid conducted by U.S. troops, clarifying the sorts of rough treatment that inflame ill will. Troops burst into what they believed to be the home of a Sunni insurgent. Understandably, they had few kind words for the residents whom they thought were out to kill them. A soldier forced one injured middle-aged Iraqi man to walk barefoot across rocks outside the home, barking at him, "You'll fucking learn how to walk." When none of the males detained at the first house matched the name of the raid's target, a detainee showed the Americans the house of a local military officer. There, they captured former Maj. Gen. Abed Hamed Mowhoush, a high-value target. The raid on the area continued, as did the soldiers' callous treatment. A pair of workers were stopped, their breakfast tossed onto the ground, and they were cuffed and commanded to "shut the fuck up." By the time the raid was complete, the troops had detained sixteen of the thirty-four Iraqi suspects on their target list, but they also rounded up another fifty-four neighbors and bystanders.[47]

When innocent men are cursed and belittled in front of their families, this is a huge blow to Iraqi honor, or the honor of any people for that matter. While one cannot expect troops to have compassion for the insurgents who are out to kill them, the imprecision of the intelligence process and the targeting of such raids means that troops very often inflame the passions of those who have not yet decided to openly oppose the Coalition. Each poorly aimed raid, each arrogant act creates more animosity toward the Coalition and fans the flames of resistance.

Many officials expressed exasperation at the double standard where Coalition missteps were jumped on while insurgents carried out bloody attacks that injured and killed scores of innocents. For example, the admittedly reprehensible acts at Abu Ghraib were extremely mild in comparison to the daily brutality that

Iraqis meted out on other Iraqis, yet the acts of the outsiders brought far more condemnation. This is the nature of insurgency and asymmetric warfare. In unconventional wars, such as the one in Iraq, public support is a major center of gravity. U.S. military doctrine defines a center of gravity as "those characteristics, capabilities, or sources of power from which a military force derives its freedom of action, physical strength, or will to fight." Coalition forces required positive public support both at home and in Iraq. With the waning of support at home, calls grew louder for troops to be redeployed. In Iraq, when Iraqis did not support the Coalition and Iraqi troops in their battle, the task of rooting out the insurgent groups was nearly impossible.

On the contrary, the resisters were already home and tied into family and friends who supported their fight. All that they required was a majority of the population that was too afraid to speak out or provide information against them, which places Coalition troops at a disadvantage in terms of public support and information operations that affect this support. Many military and civilian leaders refuse to recognize the importance of this information battle and the negative impacts of Coalition blunders and policies, as well as the ham-handed justifications offered for them. The phenomenon is not a new aspect of twenty-first-century warfare, either.

Writing about France's experience in Algeria in the 1950s and '60s, Alf Heggoy distilled the problems facing counterinsurgent forces. Counter-insurgency forces generally represent "another race, certainly another people and culture" than the insurgents, who are generally of the same race and culture as the population. The insurgents' excesses are often forgotten, while the counter-insurgency forces "must appear to be angels while fighting a dirty war."[48] This may be hard to understand from afar, but the reality is that foreign imposition is almost universally reviled, whether the intentions are good or evil.

Many Americans who grew up in the 1980s remember the Cold War resistance movie, *Red Dawn*, starring Patrick Swayze and Charlie Sheen as patriotic American teenage insurgents battling Soviet invaders. Americans cheered these youths as they ambushed and bombed Soviet soldiers. In one of the more troubling scenes of the movie, the teens find that the Soviets have bugged one of their comrades with a tracking device. Patrick Swayze's character executes the surviving, bound Russian commando. When Swayze's character cannot bring himself to shoot his bugged friend, another character steps in to finish off the liability. While the scene is delivered in a morally ambiguous way that neither condones nor condemns the actions, the back story certainly provides reasons to at least empathize with the executioners.

When trying to understand how the insurgents were seen within Sunni Iraq, Americans should remember this movie. Extremist outsiders like al Qaeda lost public support fairly quickly, yet many Sunni Iraqi nationalist insurgents became the "Sons of Iraq" with little irony. They were seen as defending Sunni Iraq against the foreign invaders, then against the foreign and homegrown extremists who had become a greater threat. For those questioning the equivalence of *Red Dawn's* "Wolverines" and the Iraqi insurgents, perhaps another approach will help. I have discussed the topic at length with several decorated and unfailingly patriotic combat veterans who fought some of the bitterest battles with the Iraqi insurgents in Anbar. More than one has told me that if he had been an Iraqi Sunni, he would have been an insurgent. Even though U.S. troops devoted blood, sweat, tears, and years of their lives to improving Iraq, many recognized the reasons why Sunnis fought them as outsiders.

The tribal culture and insecurity of Iraqis who have been through so much turmoil made local and tribal bonds much stronger than any dedication to the state. In this environment, local Iraqi police working with Coalition troops were cast as traitors to their own town. In the many areas of Iraq where local social institutions were stronger than the state, the dominance of local and tribal allegiances was natural. Tribesmen motivated by Coalition missteps were introduced through tribal connections to other disaffected Iraqis, including former regime members and Islamic jihadists. One young Sunni Baghdadi described a progression followed by many insurgents. "The idea of jihad came step by step as I watched what the Americans were doing to our country. In the beginning, we were only cousins and friends, and later other people came to join us, people who were presented to us by the sheikhs."[49]

As instability in Iraq dragged on, the themes of disempowerment, unemployment, and Sunni identity were reinforced as resistance motivations and transmitted along family lines. The confluence of motivations for Sunni resistance was well expressed by Gen. Mohamed Abdullah Shahwani, a former Iraqi national intelligence chief. "People are fed up after two years without improvement. People are fed up with no security, no electricity, people feel they have to do something. The army was hundreds of thousands. You'd expect some veterans would join with their relatives, each one has sons and brothers."[50]

6
The Widening Insurgencies: 2003-2007

> "If someone would have told you that we would have killed ten thousand, wounded ten thousand and imprisoned thirty-two thousand, you would have thought we would have won."[1]
> —U.S. MILITARY OFFICIAL COMMENTING ON THE INSURGENCY, 2005

In a region as ancient as Mesopotamia, very little is entirely new. Nearly everything is built on well-worn patterns. Religious devotees worship where the histories of their creeds were written. Many people live in areas that have been occupied by their tribe, clan, or family for centuries. Battles take place on ground bloodied since the earliest reaches of recorded time, and commerce still flows over ancient routes. On the eastern outskirts of Fallujah is situated a modern cloverleaf linking Iraq's highways. The ribbons of concrete overlie a crossroads that linked trade routes traveled by caravans moving from the heart of Arab Bedouin territory in what is now Saudi Arabia to the trading city of Aleppo in modern Syria. It connected the magnificent halls of Baghdad to the coastal cities of the Mediterranean.

While Fallujah is somewhat of a backwater, it has continued to sit astride an important road between Baghdad and the greater Sunni-Arab world. Traffic flowing through the major border crossings from Jordan and southern Syria must pass through Fallujah to reach the Iraqi capital. Fallujah likewise links the Sunni cities of Iraq's west, including Ramadi and Tikrit, and is the gateway to Anbar's Euphrates River towns. Not all the crossroads in Fallujah are plain to see, however. Back roads are abundant, yet often no more than dusty tracks in the desert, discernable only to those who had lived there all their lives. One visitor noted, "As a city built on smuggling, everyone knew how to sneak around . . . the main road is ignored by those who know."[2] For this reason, Fallujah was a key trade and smuggling hub under the UN sanctions of the 1990s. Relations between Ba'ath regime members from Fallujah and their tribesmen in the area were critical to the smuggling that allowed Saddam's henchmen to work around the stiff international sanctions.

Although regime members, specifically security service members, were heavily involved in illegal activities, the Fallujah tribes were essential in working with their confederates across Iraq's borders with Jordan and Syria to complete the smuggling ring. As the regime increasingly relied on illicit trade to fund its opulent lifestyle, tribal sheikhs and other businessmen prospered on the flow of goods and people through the crossroads.[3] The commercial and personal relationships that linked criminals, tribes, and former regime members provided both the motive and the means to resist a new authority in Iraq that posed a threat to their profitable arrangement. This was only one of many aspects that combined to fan the flames of resistance in 2003 and beyond.

In 2004, Fallujah was the epicenter of Iraq's varied Sunni resistance movements. Homegrown tribal guerrillas and religious zealots joined forces with foreign terrorists, criminals, and Ba'athist cadres to convert Fallujah into a hotbed of insurgent activity by the spring of that year. Akin to the road network, the alliances of convenience that constituted the insurgent network there were based on old and complex social relationships that have made up the area's power structure for ages. In 1920, the British attempted to open a dialogue to quell unrest around Fallujah. The officer representing the Empire, however, was killed in a confrontation with a local sheikh named Suleiman al-Dhari, kicking off a bloody rebellion. More than eighty years later, Coalition troops found themselves negotiating with al-Dhari's grandson over the same patch of restive land. They, too, found dialogue to be fruitless in clearing Fallujah of insurgents.[4]

Over the last two decades, Fallujah provided young men for the military and security services of Saddam's rural Sunni regime. These men were tied into the Sunni tribal structure, which has in turn been connected through ages of travel, commerce, migration, and marriage to a Sunni tribal society that spreads from Saudi Arabia, through Iraq and Jordan, and into Syria. Overlying these age-old social networks were new ties born of modern activism and communications and based on smuggling or religious fervor. Westerners are equipped, both technically and culturally, to look for the latest forms of association: terrorist or criminal networks using high-tech means of communication to coordinate their nefarious activities. Although a few foreign fighters were drawn into Iraq using these networks, the vast majority were recruited by friends, relatives, fellow Muslims, and other face-to-face means.[5]

In Fallujah, like much of Iraq and the Middle East, personal relationships are often much more important than in the West. Westerners used to power meetings and drive-thru windows have a hard time understanding that one of the most important men in Bedouin tribes in Iraq was traditionally the *qahwaji*. Literally the coffee-maker, the qahwaji was much more. He was the keeper of the reception house, where guests were feted and deals were worked out over coffee and dates.[6] While Iraqi culture has changed since those times, Iraq is a land where coffee and dates are still central to the face-to-face meetings. Coordination is often passed by word of mouth from brother to cousin to tribesman to longstanding trading partner along the ancient lines of communication that intersect in places such as Fallujah. It is along these lines that the insurgencies in Iraq joined forces, organized, and grew, far from the prying eyes of Coalition intelligence-gathering.

The confluence of fighters in Fallujah was methodically destroyed by U.S. troops in 2004. Following the ambush and infamous desecration of the bodies of a four-man team of Blackwater Security Company contractors, commanders at the highest levels decided that action must be taken against the scourge growing there. The city was cordoned and an assault began in March 2004, only to be postponed as Iraq's interim government came to the brink of collapse under the pressure of dueling crises in Fallujah and southern Iraq with the forces of Muqtada al-Sadr. In November 2004, the Marines were given the green light to reduce the city. They fought house-to-house to rid Fallujah of the insurgents that had overrun the City of Mosques. In all, 151 Americans were killed and over a thousand wounded in the battles for Fallujah, yet because the enemy was able to regenerate himself through his Iraqi and Sunni connections, the destruction of the insurgents in Fallujah did not break the back of the insurgency as many predicted it would.[7]

The resistance thrived on a changed political environment. The Ba'ath regime had ridden to power on the pan-Arab ideology, with its somewhat-secularized vision of an Arab-Islamic Golden Age. By the time the regime fell, however, Saddam had reduced the Ba'ath program to a twisted cult of personality, which opened the field for a new, Sunni-Islamist political ideology. The Islamist fervor that had grown in popularity across the Arab world with the demise of the pan-Arab dream played on many of the same themes as earlier pan-Arab discourse, especially the idea of the Arab-Islamic Golden Age. The program of Islamist groups ranged from imbuing relatively secular governments with Islamic principles to the creation of a global Islamic caliphate through means of *jihad*. Even though only the most extreme groups in Iraq were devoted to global jihad, for most Iraqis, a combination of nationalism and Islam was a fitting replacement for the political void left by the Ba'ath Party. Also, the adherence of most Shi'a to the sectarian Islamist United Iraqi Alliance left Sunni with few options in the political arena beyond the rapidly formed Sunni-Islamist parties.[8]

Driven by a mix of Islamist and nationalist ideology to one extent or another, several strands of violent resistance raged on in Anbar Province for four years. Resisters had widely varying levels of piety, ranging from nearly secular Iraqi nationalists to devotees to a global caliphate, but Islam provided language and symbols understood and embraced by all. At first, fighters all along the ideological spectrum set aside their differences to fight against the occupiers. Several years into the campaign, however, the extremists' radical plans were clearly tearing Sunni Iraq apart. It was not until the Sunni social fabric itself rejected the extremists and turned the local resisters against them, that the insurgency finally began to abate.

The Power of Islam

Faced with chaos and violence, as well as disgust with crime and corruption, Iraqis looked to the spiritual and ideological solace of religion. A Baghdad merchant explained, "During the U.S. invasion, I saw so much chaos and death that I turned to God. Now there is so much corruption and violence that we need an Islamic government according to *shari'a*. That would stop a lot of the suffering we have now." The trend, which had been growing in Saddam's later years, took off in the uncertainty of the new Iraq. In this environment, Islam was an utterly powerful influence used by many insurgent groups.[9]

Journalist Anthony Shadid saw "the first signs of a resurgent religion" among Sunnis in the summer of 2003 as it guided believers through the mayhem and provided a renewed Sunni-Iraqi identity in the changing and confusing times. Religious institutions were also able to offer stability in the cities where disarray reigned after the fall of Baghdad,[10] placing Islamic networks in a position of power and prestige in Iraq, from which they could fill the ideological void created by the Ba'ath's collapse with a narrow, Sunni-Islamist agenda.

Religion provided an unparalleled motivational tool for insurgents for a number of reasons. Foremost among these motivations was the belief that those fighting on the side of God could not be defeated in the long run. This line of reasoning sustained activism long after more worldly-minded participants would have given up. Ayyash al-Kubaysi, a representative of Iraq's Association of Muslim Scholars, explained the logic: "God is greater than the United States. God is with us. We are therefore stronger than the United States."[11]

Religion was also called upon to frame activism as a duty that true believers are required to perform. Numerous clerics invoked the concept of duty in promoting jihad against U.S. forces. High-profile Islamic scholars propagated such messages throughout the region on satellite channels and Internet pages. For instance, Muhammad Sayyed Tantawi, Sheikh of Al-Azhar University in Cairo, stated on April 5, 2003, that the U.S. invasion was against Islamic law, labeling jihad as an "obligation for every Muslim." Similar sentiments were expressed by other influential Islamic figures.[12]

The Association of Muslim Scholars, a group of hardline Sunni-Iraqi clerics, most fully developed this logic by generating detailed Islamic rulings regarding the resistance. Their *fiqh al-muqawama* or "jurisprudence of resistance" not only justified the insurgency, but labeled it as an obligatory duty (*fardh 'ayn*) for believers. The concept of jihad as religious duty found a receptive audience, judging from the proclamations of captured insurgents. Both Iraqi and foreign mujahideen referred to the sermons of Islamic clerics as motivations or justifications for their activities. The statements of extremist insurgent leaders, such as al-Zarqawi, were also laden with references to the "right path" and "missions of *al-da'wa*," the Islamic call to religious duty.[13]

Religion rationalized self-sacrifice in suicide bombings and helped to assuage fears in facing a heavily armed and well-trained Coalition forces. Viewing jihad as a religious act, sacred in and of itself was an important factor in legitimizing these missions of self-sacrifice.[14] Martyrdom can be actively sought to serve as an example for others, as evidenced by the statement of one group that undertook a brazen attack against Coalition forces that was certain to lead to their deaths.

> As we write this testament, our hearts ache over the fate of the Iraqi people. To all our brothers, friends, and beloved ones: Today, we call on you to join the jihad, to move, not to stay still in silence in the face of this oppression and anarchy. Today, we have sacrificed ourselves to defend our honor and

pride. . . . We have sacrificed our souls for the sake of Islam, sacrificed ourselves to get rid of the monkeys, pigs, Jews, and Christians. To all our brothers and sisters, we urge you to be joyful with us, we the ones who sacrificed ourselves for the sake of righteousness and Islam. We want you not to mourn us, but to remember us at all times.[15]

The concepts surrounding martyrdom in Islam also transformed the grim reality of violent death. Bodies of martyrs were described in idyllic terms by Sunni mujahideen: "When they become *shaheed* [martyred], it is a beautiful smell and their color stays fresh. And friends see this and they want to die."[16] In the same vein, a Shi'a fighter in the Mahdi Army described a "large bird with a loud voice" whose wings brushed away falling American bombs. Others recounted the protection of angels and shadows that immobilized tanks and prevented ordnance from exploding.[17] Such delusional statements hid the traumatic actuality of modern warfare and gave solace to those facing combat.

In addition to the motivational power of religion, religious institutions, particularly mosques, were one of the last relatively open spaces for people to congregate under Saddam's reign. Religious leaders were rising influences in the society as well, due to their prominent social position and their distance from corruption that surrounded the regime.[18] These institutions were the only major Iraqi social structures, apart from the tribes, standing after the regime collapsed. It was only natural that religious institutions would remain powerful in the new era.

Religious parties and religious leaders were prominent in the days after the regime's fall. As in the Shi'a areas, Sunni religious groups provided order and relief to citizens. In Fallujah, clerics and sheikhs worked together to appoint a new city council before Coalition troops ever arrived. Tribes protected municipal buildings while religious leaders called for law and order. According to Nir Rosen, "many Sunni clerics had become active leaders of the resistance" by the summer of 2003.[19]

Religious institutions also acted as organizational resources for insurgents, offering the perfect venue for drawing recruits into high-risk activism. Individuals willing to undertake this kind of activity are often found in supportive networks of other like-minded individuals. In many cases, they are already indoctrinated with an ideology that can be turned toward violent resistance. Many of the most motivated members of religious groups have performed some form of activism in the name of the religion, whether charity work, protests, or simple organizational activities. This eases the transition to higher levels of activism, even those that include the danger of death. Many mosques also created a means for potential resisters to speak with like-minded Muslims and perhaps form or join a bloc. Both inside and outside Iraq, mosques were successful recruiting arenas for convincing the faithful to join the fight.[20] The radical character of some mosques seems to be especially effective in attracting activists eager to up the ante of their involvement in Islamic struggle.

The religious groups recruiting from these mosques tend to provide activists with a rigor and support structure that increases adherence to the group and prevents defections, even as conditions grow harsh. The material and dietary sacrifices that religious groups such as Hamas and Hizb Allah require of their adherents, along with the support services they offer their members and their families, combine to make their fighters deadlier and less likely to quit under adverse conditions.[21] In all, many groups within Iraq and their recruiters around the world used the power of religion to draw in and employ highly devoted Islamic fighters.

The account of Peter Cherif, a young French citizen of North African ethnicity who was drawn into the fight in Iraq, demonstrates the power of religious groups to recruit from all parts of the world. After an injury disqualified him from his dream of serving in the French Marines, Cherif began visiting the Rue de Tanger mosque in Paris's Nineteenth Arrondissement. The mosque catered to North Africans under the spell of a young French Algerian "imam" by the name of Farid Benyettou. Only twenty-seven in 2008 when he was sentenced to prison for his activities, the imam was adept at attracting vulnerable young Muslims. Working with Boubakeur el-Hakim, a facilitator in Damascus, he sent as many as a dozen of these Muslims to Iraq, where several died in suicide attacks.[22]

Benyettou gradually isolated Cherif from the outside world, convincing him to cut off physical, phone, and Internet contact with his girlfriend in the name of piety. Cherif gradually became more radical in his beliefs and traveled to Damascus to study. His mother could sense that he was slipping into a more tightly controlled environment before she lost contact with her son in July 2004, when he said to her that he was going to a village without Internet connection. The last time she heard from him was a November phone call, but Cherif would not disclose where he was. His mother later learned that the call came from Iraq. On December 2, 2004, Cherif was detained by the Coalition in Fallujah and subsequently sentenced to fifteen years in prison by an Iraqi court for his involvement in the insurgency.[23]

Those less inclined to march into battle into Iraq could still participate by funding their Muslim brethren. Mosques acted as a conduit, through which outside donations were collected and then shipped to Iraq for distribution to resisters.[24] The role of mosques in alms-giving and other charitable networks provided resisters with access to ready-made funding channels that were hard to police, as any interference in religious matters provided additional propaganda against the Coalition.

While religion was a common language for most resisters, a small minority interpreted religious duty to the extreme. Radical *Salafi* groups were small contributors to the violence in Iraq, yet as the director of the Defense Intelligence Agency testified in 2005, they had a "disproportionate impact" due to "the strategic and symbolic nature of their attacks, combined with effective information operations."[25] Radical Islamists undertook influential and divisive attacks in Iraq, specifically those attacks aimed at isolating the Coalition from international support, such as the bombings of the UN and Red Cross headquarters and the Jordanian Embassy. Most significantly for Iraq's long-term stability, the Salafi extremists were at the heart of inter-sectarian violence. Because of their extreme interpretation of Islam, they viewed even pious Shi'a as apostates and believed that the chaos of a civil war stoked by sectarian killings would further their cause of creating a radical new order in Iraq. In the end, though, the extreme nature of their religious views and their violent tactics would be their undoing.

While foreign fighters were most prevalent in the Islamic extremist groups, owing to the power of Islamist networks and the call to jihad, the size of this element should not be overstated. In way of comparison, although the swell of Arab support for the Afghan jihad against the Soviet Union is legendary, the Arab contribution to that cause in terms of combatants was quite small. According to Milton Bearden, CIA station chief in Pakistan during the 1980s, up to 25,000 Arabs passed through Pakistan and Afghanistan over the war's ten-year duration. In contrast, between 150,000 and 250,000 Afghan mujahideen were active at a given time. Some sources assert that a total of only a few hundred Arabs engaged in combat operations. The vast majority of Arab support for the Afghans was in the form of finance, organization, and other support activities, largely coming out of Pakistan.[26] Similarly, despite the bulk of the insurgents in Iraq being Iraqis, they received support of many kinds from foreign activists.

Foreign fighters were estimated to constitute anywhere from 4 to 15 percent of combatants in Iraq, though their effects were disproportionate to their number, because they used tactics of extreme violence calculated to provoke civil war in Iraq. Several factors played into this violence. First, as foreigners and radicals, these fighters had fewer qualms about inciting widespread violence than Iraqi fighters whose families lived in the country. Second, many foreigners recruited and mobilized to come to Iraq had more absolute ends in mind than the often part-time Iraqi resisters. In a collection of the entry records for more than six hundred foreign fighters found in 2007, over half were listed as suicide bombers or "martyrdom seekers" (*'istishadi*) versus fighters. American military sources asserted that foreigners constitute 90 percent of suicide bombers in Iraq for reasons explained by an Iraqi handler who set up such attacks. "Iraqis are fighting for their country's future, so they have something to live for" while foreign volunteers "come a long way from their countries. . . . They don't want to gradually earn their entry to paradise by participating in operations against the Americans. They want martyrdom immediately."[27]

Despite this handler's assertions, the harrowing tale of a young Saudi man shows that not all foreigners arrive desiring immediate martyrdom, and they sometimes receive more than they bargain for. Ahmad al-Shayeʿ traveled to Iraq in 2005, following exhortations from a radical imam. Once he entered Iraq, insurgents took his money and Saudi passport, giving him a forged Iraqi ID. They asked Ahmad if he wanted to undertake a suicide operation, which he did not. He was set on participating in armed combat against the occupiers. His fate was now in the hands of the insurgents, however, with no money and no way to cross back into Saudi Arabia. After about a month and a half, he was given his first mission to move a gasoline tanker about a kilometer. He had no idea that his handlers were choosing martyrdom for him. When he was about 100 meters from where he had been ordered to park the truck, it was detonated. Although he was severely burned, he survived and returned to Saudi Arabia.[28]

The available statistical evidence suggests that foreign fighters were small in number throughout the conflict. Even during the height of the Sunni uprising, foreign fighters detained in Iraq were a minority, numbering only in the hundreds. The fighters hailed mostly from Arab countries, with Egyptians, Syrians, Sudanese, and Saudis being the most numerous respectively. From a high of more than four hundred in 2006, the number of Arab foreign fighters in detention in Iraq had dwindled to slightly over two hundred by the spring of 2008, in small part owing to fighters' transfers back to their home countries. The largest groups among those still held in Iraq were Syrian, Egyptian, and Saudi, each constituting just under 20 percent of the total. By the spring of 2008, the

251 foreigners confined in the Coalition's two main facilities in Baghdad made up only 1 percent of all detainees.[29]

There was little information on foreign fighters beyond detention until the fall of 2007 when Coalition troops discovered a cache of documents that sketched the biographies of more than six hundred foreign fighters smuggled into Iraq after August 2006. The Sinjar smuggling cell is thought to have been a main source of foreign fighters for the insurgency. Saudis were the largest group at 244 fighters or 41 percent of the total of records with nationality listed. Of these Saudis, 51 fighters hailed from the country's capital, Riyadh, alone. Libyans were the second largest group, with 112 or 18 percent of the list. Syria supplied 49 fighters, Yemen 48, Algeria 43, Morocco 36, and Jordan 11. Two fighters came from France and one each from Bosnia, Belgium, England, Iraq, Kuwait, Lebanon, Mauritania, Oman, Sudan, and Sweden. On average, these fighters were in their mid-twenties. Fighters were being smuggled into Iraq at a rate of 80 to 110 per month in the beginning of 2007, falling through the summer to a low of around 40 in October.[30]

These foreign fighters were unable to operate in Iraq without local support. Outsiders, even Arabs, stand out to native Iraqis due to their different looks, accents, and dialects. These foreigners relied on Iraqi facilitators for the support, protection, and intelligence required for their missions. This point was clarified by the complaints of Abu Anas al-Shami, a lieutenant of al-Zarqawi: "After one year of *jihad*... none of us could find a piece of land to use as a shelter or a place to retire to safety amongst some members of [his] group.... We would hide at daylight and sneak like a cat at night."[31] These foreigners were able to find Iraqis who had been conditioned by the regional Islamic context and were willing to harbor them in such places as the Kurdish north and Fallujah.

Many mujahideen entered Iraq prior to the invasion through the autonomous Kurdish north, where there were several significant outposts for Islamists prior to 2003. In the 1990s, Kurdish fighters returning from the jihad in Afghanistan set up two new Islamist groups, Kurdish *Hamas* and *Tawhid*. These groups' radical ideology was supported by Saudi-funded mosques and educational programs. In September 2001, the groups united as *Jund al-Islam* (Soldiers of Islam) before coming to be known as *Ansar al-Islam* (the Supporters of Islam, or AI).[32]

Ansar-controlled territories around Hallabja were a stronghold where Kurdish Islamism converged with the "Arab Afghans." These Arab Afghans were Arab mujahideen who had traveled to join the Afghani jihad against the Soviets and then stayed on in training camps in the mountains of Afghanistan once the war was over. Many fled to Kurdistan after the U.S. assault on their mountain abodes in 2001 and 2002 and turned to training local Islamists. AI, therefore, spawned some of the highest-profile Islamic insurgent groups, including *Ansar al-Sunna* (AS), a combination AI members and Iraqi-Sunni Islamists. AS was an important part of the insurgent network, taking part in high-profile attacks and keeping ties to the well-connected Arab Afghans who sought refuge in Kurdistan in 2001 and 2002. One of these Arab Afghans is thought to have been Abu Musab al-Zarqawi.[33]

Until his death in June 2006, al-Zarqawi was the jihadist leader with the highest profile in Iraq. A Jordanian of the Bani Hassan tribe, al-Zarqawi formally established his resistance group in April 2004, yet was active well prior to this date. Early major attacks attributed to al-Zarqawi's followers include the bombing of the Jordanian Embassy in Baghdad and the catastrophic attack on the UN headquarters in Baghdad, both in late summer of 2003. According to a Jordanian intelligence official, these strikes catapulted al-Zarqawi to fame, gaining "a lot of support for him—with the tribes, with Saddam's army and other remnants of his regime. They made al-Zarqawi the *symbol* of the resistance in Iraq, but not the leader. And he never has been." Al-Zarqawi's role in the insurgency was vital, but sometimes overstated. In fact, al-Zarqawi's prominence has even been linked to a U.S. campaign to play up his importance in an attempt to turn Iraqis against him.[34]

Al-Zarqawi's background is emblematic of regional extremism. He was born in 1966 as Ahmad Fadhil Nazzal al-Khalayla in a poor section of al-Zarqaa, Jordan (hence the name, Zarqawi). As part of a transition from "extreme depravity to extreme Islamism," he traveled to Afghanistan in 1989, arriving too late to take part in the jihad. Then al-Zarqawi, along with several other mujahideen, returned to agitate a Salafi movement in al-Zarqaa. Al-Zarqawi was jailed in the Jordanian al-Sawwaqa prison from 1994 to 1999, where he gained a sizable following. Unlike many of the jihadi prisoners, al-Zarqawi was a native Jordanian of a strong tribe. Despite many claims to the contrary, he was not a Palestinian. His tribal status and his experience as a former street tough enabled him to be a powerful leader in prison. Upon his release, he led many of his followers to Peshawar, Pakistan. After a tense meeting with Osama Bin Laden in the Afghan city of Kandahar, al-Zarqawi was given $5,000 to set up a camp in Herat, Afghanistan, where he later amassed a large following, mostly from Syria and neighboring countries. He was wounded by a U.S. air strike in 2001 and escaped into Iran.[35]

Over the next year, al-Zarqawi bounced between Iran and Kurdistan, where he was protected by Ansar al-Islam, and built up his army and a network of contacts. He frequented Syria and the Ain al-Halwa Palestinian refugee camp in southern Lebanon, his prime recruiting ground. Al-Zarqawi also reportedly spent a great deal of time establishing contacts in the Arab-Sunni west of Iraq. Shortly after the invasion in 2003, al-Zarqawi split from AI to create *Tawhid wa Jihad* (Monotheism and Jihad), a rabidly anti-American and anti-Shi'a group. In October 2004, he pledged his allegiance to Osama bin Laden and his group was renamed *Tanzim al-Qa'eda lil-Jihad fi Bilad al-Rafidayn* (The al Qaeda Organization for Jihad in the Land of the Two Rivers), which became infamously known as al Qaeda in Iraq (AQI). Association with bin Laden elevated al-Zarqawi's status over other insurgent leaders in Iraq, allowing him wider access to funding, recruits, and support, both regionally and worldwide. At the same time, al-Zarqawi proved able to harness the power of religion to draw former military and security members from within Iraq into his group.[36]

Hoping to increase support for its campaign within Iraq, AQI greatly lowered the profile of its foreign leadership, simultaneously emphasizing the Iraqi roots of new leadership in 2005 and 2006. The group chose a new spokesman, Abu Masara al-Iraqi, and its military commander at the time was reportedly Iraqi as well. In addition, the organization distributed an organizational chart in 2005, demonstrating a number of leaders with blatantly Iraqi names. Beyond these public-relations moves, AQI created a council of collaboration with other local groups in January 2006 and elected as its emir Abdallah al-Baghdadi, an Iraqi and a "hero of the second Falluja siege," according to one account.[37]

These moves certainly lessened the impact of al-lZarqawi's death on the al Qaeda organization. On the evening of June 7, 2006, a U.S. air strike destroyed a safe house in the village of Hibhib, where local residents had tipped off the Coalition to al-Zarqawi's presence. Early the next morning, Coalition and Iraqi authorities announced that the strike had killed al-Zarqawi. Although his death may have led to a weakening of AQI, it undoubtedly did not portend an end to the insurgency.[38] The real center of gravity of the insurgencies was not the AQI organization, but the local Sunni-Iraqi groups that ultimately decide the path of the Sunni community in Iraq.

The desired end state of AQI was the imposition of an Islamic state governed according to the harsh Salafi interpretation of Islam. It attempted to enforce this vision through terror in Sunni areas under the title of the Islamic State of Iraq. That goal proved to be unattainable, especially as the Sunni tribes began to turn against the extremists in 2007; the extremists, however, were successful in creating small enclaves. Fallujah, for one, was known as an "Islamic Republic" before it was cleared by U.S. Marines in 2004. Likewise, AQI imposed its severe version of Islamic law on certain districts in Baghdad. In western Baghdad's Amariya, Sunni clerics aligned with al-Qaeda-imposed rules that allegedly resulted in killing men for wearing knee-length shorts, expelling Shiʻa residents, banning Iranian products, and prohibiting women from working or attending school. Similarly, in early 2007, residents of Samarra fled what they deemed an "Islamic Emirate," escaping AQI's draconian vision of Islamic rule, that they said was beginning to resemble Kabul or Kandahar under the Taliban.[39] The ability of radical Islamists to control areas of the capital underlined their continuing strength despite the efforts of the Coalition, the Iraqi government, and the Shiʻa militias to root them out. In pushing the country to the brink of outright civil war, AQI also alienated the Sunni tribes and many more moderate insurgent groups, as will be discussed below.

Islamist and FRE insurgents became increasingly intermixed, with the FREs supplying funding, weapons, and logistics for the Islamists, who, in turn, provided motivated foot soldiers. This cooperation, despite radically different long-term goals, was lubricated by the common short-term goal of ejecting the occupiers and forestalling the development of a Shiʻa-dominated new order. For some, these objectives were driven by religious zealotry. For others, the main force was Sunni nationalism. Either way, cooperation helped them to achieve their goals in the short-term. The more secular forces needed the fanatical fighters, especially suicide bombers, which the Islamist groups could deliver. Conversely, the Islamists needed the funding, support, and expertise that FREs had access to through the Baʻath legacy.[40]

Beyond the small and extreme world of the Salafis, a blend of nationalism and Islamism fueled many small cells of disaffected Iraqi Sunnis. These cells were neither radical Salafis, nor former regime supporters. Anthony Shadid noted that for "the most disenchanted and disillusioned Sunnis in Iraq," the "simplicity of a struggle against the infidels, the veneration of death in sacred battle, and the empowerment that violence sometimes provides" was a direct result of the power of religion.[41]

Disgruntled Iraqi Sunnis, often poor and unemployed, were among the most receptive audiences of clerics' calls for jihad against the American occupation. These messages were readily available in local mosque sermons and recordings of radical preachers from other states in the region. These groups were not fighting with regional Islamic goals in mind, nor were they trying to reestablish the Ba'ath regime. They were motivated by a deep-rooted mistrust of the United States and a blend of religious and nationalist sentiments. A leaflet handed out at a Sunni mosque in late 2003 gives an example: "The goal of the infidels, after stealing our wealth, is to remove us from our religion by force and all other means, so that we become a lost nation without principle, making it easier for the Jews and Christians to humiliate us."[42] In this case, the motivation was a program for the defense of nation and religion, not the installation of an Islamic state.

These themes resonated strongly in tribal areas. Canadian journalist Patrick Graham called the resistance in Fallujah "a tribal uprising, controlled by religious leaders." Mohammed, a resister in the Sunni Triangle, explained that his motivations for involvement were a mix of revenge for civilian deaths caused by Coalition troops, religious duty, and the fear of Shi'a hegemony and reprisals for the abuses of Sunni rule. He stressed that his fight had nothing to do with Saddam. "The world must know that this is an honorable resistance and has nothing to do with the old regime," he stated. "We take our power from our history, not from one person." Although the Sunni tradesmen and professionals of Mohammed's group had no prior links and no loyalty to Saddam's regime, former Iraqi army officers became their trainers.[43]

Former regime members moved away from Ba'athist roots and moved toward the religious-nationalist middle ground as they turned to religion in increasing numbers due to their prolonged struggle against the Coalition. In the fall of 2003, one former rocket specialist of the Fedayeen stated that he was hoping for a return of the Ba'athist regime, but by the summer of 2004 he was fighting for an Islamic state.[44] The prolonged struggle and the frequent collaboration and contact between groups worked to spread the influence of Islam throughout all sectors of the insurgency. No matter what the religion, alignment of military resistance with religious duty and legitimacy, rather than worldly political ambitions, created greater motive to keep up the fight.

Religiosity was also catalyzed by stints in Coalition prisons. According to interviews of insurgents, prisons such as Abu Ghraib were venues where Islamic extremists educated former regime resistance members. One former Iraqi military officer detained at Abu Ghraib recounted, "We studied hard every day and often into the night" under the tutelage of Salafi detainees in cellblock 'mini-madrasahs.'" The nine-month detention of one former Republican Guard officer, "Abu Qaqa al-Tamimi," deepened his religious beliefs and provided him with extremist contacts, enabling him to become a handler of suicide bombers for several insurgent groups after his release, including both Iraqi nationalists and Islamic extremists. MG John Gardner, the commander of detainee operations in Iraq, admitted the problem of radicalism spreading through prisons in 2006: "We know that inside the compounds, individuals are trying to recruit and promote a fundamentalist network, and we are trying to mitigate that by fighting a small counterinsurgency."[45]

The role of detention centers in religious indoctrination is not new. Israeli prisons, for one, played a significant role in the education and mixing of secular and Islamist Palestinian fighters during the *Intifada* uprising of the late 1980s. The release of hundreds of detainees in Iraq in the summer of 2004 may have similarly contributed to increased interoperability of resistance groups through connections cemented in detention. Further, Iraqi resisters who had expanded their contacts in prison were more likely to cooperate with foreign extremists, at least until the extremist violence in Anbar reached a breaking point in 2007. In an example of such cooperation, the Battalions of Islamic Jihad (*Kata'ib al-Jihad al-Islamiya*), a FRE group, became a part of the Zarqawi network. In turn, the Battalion incorporated foreign fighters into its cells.[46]

This connection between FRE military experience and foreign mujahideen under AQI appears to have been behind one of the most significant attacks since 2003. In February 2006, the bombing of the al-Askariyya Mosque in Samarra was a disaster that nearly threw Iraq into sectarian civil war. Insurgents dressed as Iraqi security forces placed two bombs in the mosque overnight and detonated the explosives at dawn, destroying the beautiful golden dome. Although it caused no casualties, the event precipitated a major wave of sectarian violence. The Iraqi investigation found that a seven-man cell from AQI carried out the attack under the leadership of Haitham al-Badri. Al-Badri was a Sunni-Arab Iraqi, born in Samarra of a largely Sunni tribe, and had been a warrant officer in the Special Republican Guard. After the invasion, he worked with the group *Ansar al-Sunna* before joining AQI. Besides Badri, the cell consisted of one Iraqi, four Saudis, and a Tunisian who was captured in a late-June attack on an Iraqi military checkpoint. The details of the cell and its attack came from interrogation of the Tunisian Yasri al-Trigui (known as Abu Qadama), who had operated in Iraq since November 2003.[47] Consisting of foreign Islamists and Iraqi former regime members under the virulent AQI organization's flag, this cell demonstrated the powerful nexus between the different sectors of the insurgency.

Mowwafiq al-Rub'aie, Iraq's national security advisor, provided a succinct summary of the power of religion in the insurgency. "There's a tendency to religion-ize the insurgency. Religion is a strong motive. You're not going to find someone who's going to die for the Ba'athists. But Salafists have a very strong message. If you use the Koran selectively, it could be a weapon of mass destruction."[48]

Tying the Network Together: Funding and Support

While the lack of a central leadership authority made widely concerted insurgent action difficult, it also yielded an adaptive and survivable structure. The resistance in Iraq was such a network of cells, a common feature of many insurgencies, yet proved capable of bringing disparate actors together to collaborate on operations despite severe ideological differences. This collaboration can best be explained through the concept of "netwar," in which combatants organize in the form of loose networks rather than traditional hierarchical structures.

A horizontal network is a structure of multiple cells that are roughly equal in power. Various channels connect these cells to create a network. This concept can best be understood in contrast to a traditional hierarchical structure, in which structures are linked in a clear chain of superior-subordinate power relationships, such as a traditional military or bureaucracy. A traditional hierarchical adversary has clearly defined nodes of leadership and control. The removal of such nodes breaks the structure of a hierarchical organization. This removes the adversary's unity of purpose and fragments the unit into smaller, isolated cells, which can then be targeted.

In a networked structure, the removal of any leader or node may create a hole in the web; however, it does not significantly degrade the network because of the multiple power centers and means of contact between the nodes. For example, while the killing of high-profile terrorists, such as Abu Musab al-Zarqawi, is certainly a blow to morale, the network is able to survive intact, because there are so many interconnected cells and nodes of leadership. These cells are able to continue their fight, relying on alternate nodes in the network for leadership and support.

The Sunni insurgencies that arose from the legacies of Ba'ath rule were flexible and opportunistic. In the words of one expert, "movements 'franchise' to create individual cells and independent units, creating diverse mixes of enemies that are difficult to attack." Many groups consisted of small cells of two to three men. Others were dispersed formations that could combine in groups as sizeable as thirty to fifty for specific operations. Early on, groups formed temporary alliances and informal networks despite differences in long-term aspirations. Criminals were also exploited to attack infrastructure and fund the resistance.[49] Further complicating the picture, many groups changed names and affiliations, and announcements likely used dummy names to throw off Coalition intelligence. Without access to the detailed intelligence that will one day become declassified, it is impossible to come up with a complete insurgent "order of battle," but understanding the basic structure of the resistance can give insight into the strengths and weaknesses of the network.

In contrast to classic insurgencies, the resistance in Iraq consisted of a web of groups with different and often mutually exclusive goals; therefore, any grand strategy aimed at countering a monolithic insurgency was likely to fail. Moreover, the resistance in Iraq did not have a central figure or group with the capability to establish administrative structures above the city level. Unlike classic insurgent forces such as the North Vietnamese-supported Viet Cong or the Algerian FLN, the Iraqi resistance comprised "small, scattered, disparate groups" without "an explicit set of war aims."[50]

Aside from cleaving large numbers of nodes from the network, the only way to combat the network as a whole is to find and remove common sources of support or coordination. Two common sources, in particular, tied together the various groups of the insurgency and acted as the webs of support that they all needed. The first source, or web of support, consisted of "handlers" from the old regime who provided the support, intelligence, and organization for attacks. Intelligence indicates that connections between Islamist radicals and former regime members began at a very early date. Ambassador Bremer cited intelligence from the summer of 2003 indicating that radicals infiltrating from Saudi Arabia were attempting to link up with FREs, often through meetings in mosques. COL David Teeples, commander of the 3rd armored cavalry regiment, deployed to western Iraq in 2004, observed that

> the best network for anyone coming from outside to fight would be to contact former regime loyalists. Those were the people who knew who to call, where to find safe houses, where to get their hands on money, weapons, transportation. They had intelligence on where the coalition troops were [operating and] where mortars could be set up.[51]

Along similar lines, journalist Alexis Debat, referring to U.S. military and intelligence sources, suggested that a Mukhabarat section charged with monitoring subversive groups in Iraq and neighboring states supplied officers who served as contacts between FREs and Islamic extremists. Mukhabarat officers were also implicated in early recruitment of foreign fighters, mostly Palestinian refugees in Jordanian, Lebanese, and Syrian camps, before and during the war. According to a later report, a handful of these Palestinian fighters splintered from the Sunni resistance group, the 1920 Revolution Brigades, in 2007, and created their own faction under the name Hamas.[52]

One handler, a former Republican Guard officer, organized attacks for several groups, from Islamic extremists to Iraqi nationalists. He built a wide-ranging network of connections to varied groups, boasting, "Many people in the insurgency know me, even if they have never met me."[53] The networking function of this trained military officer shows how FRE hard-cores served as enablers for the varied groups of resistance.

The second and most important source was funding. The sophisticated attacks against Coalition targets were costly. The urban character of the insurgency brought several requirements such as rent for safe houses (for example, one handler had a number in Baghdad and throughout the Sunni triangle), payment of salaries, transportation costs, and the like. As the conflict wore on, this funding became even more important, as many of the vigilantes grew tired of the struggle. However, this system also presented a common vulnerability of the insurgent groups. This is a concept that was eventually seized upon by American planners. "We're killing a bunch of insurgents and capturing a bunch of insurgents, but we weren't really cutting the head off the snake," explained COL Stephen Twitty. "We said: How can we better conduct operations to cut the head off the snake? So we looked at finances. And we went after them hard."[54]

Many of the attacks in Iraq were on a for-pay basis. The bounty for successful attacks increased from around $500 shortly after the invasion to $3,000, to $5,000 by the end of 2003. Payment for attacks was a powerful lure when unemployment in Iraq at times topped 50 percent. A Baghdad police captain clarified, "There are people giving them money to prepare the bombs against the Americans, maybe the police or even other Iraqis. They are young, they have no work, so they deal in danger. Everything that is forbidden is lucrative." Several insurgents mentioned that they earned the title "emir" and a $1,500 monthly salary from Islamic insurgent groups by killing ten people. Pay also provided a powerful incentive for unemployed men offered $100 to $300 per roadside bomb. Official employment in Iraq was nowhere near as profitable. In 2004, civil servants earned between $72 and $380 a month, soldiers and police between $360 and $750, and laborers as little as $10 a day.[55]

According to American officials, militant groups were funded in the beginning by "'unlimited money' from an underground financial network run by former Ba'ath Party leaders and Saddam Hussein's relatives." Saddam had funneled cash into emergency funds outside the country for years, starting in earnest when he adopted the oil portfolio in 1977. In the days before the invasion, the regime sped up the process dramatically, transferring and trucking huge amounts of cash out of the country. Contributions from outside sympathizers augmented this windfall. For at least the first year or two, the Iraqis organizing the major financing of the resistance were believed to be a small group, drawn mostly from families with close ties to Saddam. Most sympathizers operated in Syria to organize the smuggling of cash, fighters, and weapons into Iraq.[56]

Several high-level FREs provided links between nationalist and more extremist groups. For example, Izz al-Din al-Majid was a high-level FRE and a key al-Zarqawi financier who was arrested in Fallujah in December 2004. A cousin and former bodyguard of Saddam Hussein, al-Majid had more than $35 million in his bank accounts and reportedly access to "$2 to $7 billion of former regime assets stolen from Iraqi government accounts." Under interrogation, al-Majid stated that his goal was to unite the groups *Ansar al-Sunna*, the Army of Mohammed, and the Islamic Resistance Army. Another tie between Islamists and the FRE-heavy Army of Mohammed was Maj. Gen. Abd Daoud Suleiman, who was arrested in early 2005. Suleiman was a founder of the Army of Mohammed and was also identified as a military advisor to al-Zarqawi. The U.S. government has also identified other al-Zarqawi financiers in Kuwait, Jordan, and Syria.[57]

Most of the money coming in from outside Iraq was carried by cash couriers on historic smuggling routes that were heavily used in the latter days of the old regime. These funds were augmented by influential Iraqi businessmen in Anbar Province. Some of these wealthy Sunnis funded resistance groups for commercial reasons. New foreign-investment laws and the influx of foreign goods severely hurt a number of Iraqi businesses. Increasing the violence reduced the competition from foreign businesses wary of investment and operation in an unstable Iraq.[58] Iraq's newly rich ruthless opportunists had no qualms about stoking violence to protect their businesses.

Saudi Arabia was a major foreign source of funds, deriving from Islamic charities and donations at mosques. Despite the Saudi government's measures to crack down on this flow, they were not completely successful. Cash was often carried over the border by truck and bus drivers, sometimes under coercion, as well as under the cover of religious pilgrimage traffic to and from Saudi Arabia.

Iraqi officials alleged that one such transaction in 2006 placed $25 million of Saudi cash in the hands of a prominent Iraqi-Sunni cleric and funded the purchase of weapons for the insurgency, including SA-7 anti-aircraft missiles.

Even within Iraq, lucrative trucking and smuggling businesses contributed funds, either directly or indirectly, to resistance groups. Even those criminals who did not pay directly into insurgents' coffers paid protection money to local gangs and insurgent groups to pass unmolested. A former Iraqi director of the State Oil Marketing Organization stated that the protection racket became relatively standardized in the lawless Iraq after the invasion, with prices around $500 for a tanker truck to pass safely through an area of Sunni insurgent activity. He also acknowledged that this money was "used to finance terrorism."[59]

Crime was another common source of income for the resistance. "'Industrial scale' criminal gangs" were well established in many urban areas in Iraq, which provided a strong potential ally for any resistance movement. In terrorist and criminal networks without strong central leadership, lower-level cell leaders have fewer reservations about opportunistic cooperation between "off-limits" groups. While a high-level leader may prohibit some activities as harmful to the long-term goals of the organization, lower-level leaders are more likely to focus on short-term cooperation to accomplish their goals. In an example from *The Godfather*, without Vito Corleone there is no one to tell mafia crews not to cooperate with drug dealers to profit in the short-term.[60]

Significantly, the tribal system provided a nexus between Islamic activists, regime members, and criminals. Even under the old regime, Islamic activists were "protected by the tribe and their relatively close ties to prominent members of the security apparatus of the regime." Further, the smuggling and criminal activities of the tribes, encouraged by the regime as a way of circumventing the sanctions of the 1990s, donated money and support to resistance groups. Former Fedayeen members also provided connections between FREs and the criminal world. Captured documents show that the Fedayeen were the source of a large amount of crime. As early as 2001, members were involved in weapons smuggling and shakedown checkpoints on Iraq's roads.[61] These crimes continued after the invasion, often funding the insurgency. As earlier mentioned, Sunnis in Saudi Arabia too contributed because of their tribal ties to Sunnis in Iraq's desert west.[62] The age-old movement of people along the region's historic trading routes left strong ties between Sunnis in the area and distributed tribes across newer political boundaries.

The various sources of income for the Sunni insurgency grew to such an extent that a November 2006 report acknowledged that insurgents' financial network was not only self-sustaining, but potentially had created such a surplus that it may have been able to fund terrorist groups outside of Iraq. The report estimated that the insurgents raised $70 million to $200 million a year from oil-related crime, kidnapping ransoms, and corrupt government officials. Although this sum paled in comparison to U.S. spending in Iraq, it was sufficient to continue a low-tech insurgency indefinitely. Critically, by the fall of 2006 insurgents no longer relied on foreign donors or funds of the former regime and were able to finance themselves through indigenous criminal activities and corruption.[63]

Even after U.S. commanders began attacking the funding network, analyses suggested that it was so well established that only a vast effort could dent it. In the first several years of the resistance, the capture of high-level financiers and cross-border shipments resulted in the confiscation of large amounts of cash that would otherwise fuel attacks. These financiers and their infiltration routes were a crucial chokepoint for targeting, though when the resistance became financially self-sufficient within Iraq, the funds were increasingly harder to cut off. These roots in the society were extremely difficult to extinguish through military action.

Insurgent groups were successful in networking for collaboration and support. They found willing recruits, both through parochial motives of the Sunni sub-state power structure and the powerful pull of religion. Average citizens, conditioned by years of survival in Saddam's police state, either openly supported the violent resisters or maintained an apolitical passivity that harmed the Iraqi government and its partners more than the resistance.

In this state, the resistance was akin to a tumor. It lived in the state, capable of drawing all that it needed from the populace and the network it embedded within. The network nurtured the resistance like a body's blood vessels feed the tumor. Medical professionals have found that a novel way of starving a tumor is to attack the fast-growing blood vessels that sustain it. Similarly, when an insurgent's connection to society is cut off, he rapidly becomes a dead-ender. Without support, concealment, and new recruits from society, the resister is trapped. Some resisters will lay down their arms and retreat back into society. Others will fight to the death. When the violence of al Qaeda isolated the extremist resistance from Iraqi society, many resisters laid down their arms or joined in the fight against the foreign terrorists, leading to a significant decline in insurgent violence.

Some groups chose to fight on, however, and not all of the remaining fighters were religious zealots. Payment continued to be a major motivation behind ongoing attacks; as many as three-quarters of detainees were motivated by money, rather than religious ideology. Foreign donations continued to flow into Iraq, supplementing domestic income sources ranging from kidnapping and theft to mafia-like skimming of profits from oil refineries and industrial enterprises. In one of the more audacious schemes, criminal dons built gas stations at a cost of up to $100,000 in order to be eligible for shipments of government-subsidized fuel, which they could then sell at substantial profits. Their $100,000 investment could be recouped in as little as six or seven tanker trucks' worth of gas and the profits were often funneled to pay for attacks. Instead of capitalizing on ideology, recruiters capitalized on unemployment, paying men to plant IEDs or initiate attacks.[64] While this economic motive kept the insurgency going, it also meant that loyalties could be bought, which is precisely what tribal leaders and American troops demonstrated in 2007 and 2008.

Sunni Politics and the Way Ahead

Violent attacks by Sunni resisters seemed to be on an unending upward climb well into 2007. The daily average of attacks topped 180 by the end of 2006, well over double the figure from early 2004. Multiple-casualty bombings showed a clear rising trend throughout 2006, reaching an all-time high of 69 in December 2006. Whereas the monthly count of these attacks had only exceeded 40 twice previously (in the second half of 2005), the count stayed above 50 from May 2006 into 2007. Even at the new lows in late 2007, there were still 20 to 30 multiple fatality bombings per month. Iraqi fatalities, topping 3,500 per month at the outset of 2007, were somewhat lessened by security measures in the early part of the year. Even so, the monthly level stayed above 2,000 deaths until the fall. Enemy-initiated attacks against Coalition troops likewise dropped throughout 2007. Finally, in 2008 indicators of violence fell the levels they had been at in mid-2006 and earlier.[65]

U.S. forces reached their highest levels in the summer of 2007, yet the collapse of the insurgency in Anbar Province, as will be described more fully later, had more to do with Sunni rejection than U.S. action. Though the American campaign must be credited with setting the conditions that enabled Sunni tribes and other local groups to stand up against the violent extremists, the success in Anbar would not have happened had tribes not turned against the insurgents. This success, unfortunately, is deceptive. Many of the Sunni tribes and other local groups that rebelled against the insurgency were once insurgents themselves. While these groups aligned against the violent extremists, they openly stated that their truce with the Coalition and the Iraqi government was temporary. Their campaign against the extremists was successful, however. On September 1, 2008, the unthinkable happened as security control of a pacified Anbar Province, the one-time heart of violence in Iraq, was transferred from the American troops that had fought and died there since 2003 to the Iraqi government. Violent attacks had fallen so sharply (by 90 percent) that American troops marched without weapons or body armor in the parade that accompanied the transfer of control.[66]

Deeper structural changes are required to turn Anbar's temporary calm into a lasting peace. Permanent stability will not be realized until the Sunnis have fully bought into a peaceful Iraqi political process, through which their interests can be achieved and their grievances redressed. Sunnis have not received the assurance that they will be partners in Iraq's government, not simply a disenfranchised minority. Some concessions were granted in late 2007 and early 2008, yet the lull in violence removes much of the pressure on the Shi'a to give significant ground. As will be discussed more thoroughly in the next chapter, all sides involved must sacrifice in order for the adventure to work. Success in the political arena, or more simply, the perception that the Sunni voice can make a difference politically, is a necessary factor in permanently removing the support for resistance.

Much of the blame for failure in the political arena lies on the shoulders of the Sunnis. The majority decision to boycott the political process until the constitution was written ensured that there would be little concern for Sunni points of view in Iraq's new political system. This inaction owed significantly to the fact that there was no shrewd Sunni leader with the stature of an Ayatollah Sistani in Iraq. Al-Sistani was instrumental in forcing relative Shi'a unity and non-violence, while the Sunni political voice was lost through disunity and insurgent violence. Since 2003, the Sunni political field has developed somewhat, though the damage done to Sunni leadership by Saddam's reign, the rejection of the Shi'a-dominated political process, and the high levels of violence in Sunni areas crippled Sunni political efforts.

While several personalities eventually rose to prominence in the Arab Sunni areas, none had the stature of Iraq's top Kurdish and Shi'a leaders. The state of Sunni politics was well described by Talat Wazan, head of a Mosul-based Sunni political party. "No one represents the Sunnis. Many of these people act like they are talking on behalf of the Sunni people and are a hero to them. But let me tell you that the Sunni people are divided into many branches and subgroups, so nobody can say that [he] can represent them."[67]

In turn, Sunni politicians' lack of control over the various factions, tribal confederations, and insurgent groups made them virtually powerless in negotiations with Shi'a and Kurdish leaders. Kurdish politician Ala Talabani laid out the problem. "If you ask Sunnis on the street what they think about these guys, no one will answer. What we have since the liberation is that people claim to represent this group or this constituency, and then when it comes to elections they don't get any votes."[68] Unable to control their own population, these Sunni politicians could not deliver cooperation, allowances, or any promise of reduced violence to Iraq's government and the other ethno-sectarian blocs. Therefore, Sunni politicians were unable to secure any concessions for their constituents and even the most powerful and popular Sunni politicians were forced to the fringes of government, opposing the Shi'a majority. The decline of Sunni insurgent violence, however, has provided a window for Sunni politicians to make gains in the official process.

There were several common themes in Sunni disenchantment with the new order that fed self-destructive political stances. As stated above, Sunnis believed that they were the rightful rulers of Iraq and that they could best guide the country they had controlled since Ottoman times. Even in the face of a new democratic system, they claimed that they had the right to remain at the helm of government. A major aspect in explaining this sentiment is the Sunni-Arab view of demographics in Iraq. There has not been a recent, comprehensive census to provide exact data, but estimates widely accepted outside of Sunni Iraq pin Sunni Arabs at approximately 20 percent of the Iraqi population. Shi'a are the majority, with an estimated 60 percent of the population, and Kurds make up the remaining 20 percent. Despite their low percentage, Sunni Arabs have long lived under the myth that they constitute the majority of Iraq's population, leading them to think that they are being cheated out of their majority power by a sinister Shi'a plot, perhaps in collusion with the occupiers.

Sunni political figures only fanned these beliefs, which, in turn, gave rise to claims that Sunnis had been swindled out of their share of government positions, their voting power in the constitutional referendum, and their rightful bloc of seats in the National Assembly. Saleh al-Mutlak in a January 2006 interview insisted that former Iraqi Planning Minister Mahdi al-Hafiz gave statistics that "confirm that the Sunni Arabs form more than forty-two percent of the Iraqi society." Other Sunni leaders put forth similar claims. Adnan Dulaimi boldly stated, "There are some voices who say that Sunni Arabs are a minority.... We want to prove to them that we are not a minority. We are the sons of the country.

We are responsible for the history of Iraq." This view was inflamed in popular opinion by pamphlets and books made available outside Sunni mosques; they presented "facts" to prove the Sunni majority and conspiracy theories to explain its erosion. An article in an Association of Muslim Scholars magazine pointed to Coalition plots to bring "Iranians, Kurds, and Turks" into the country to create "dangerous demographic changes" to the Sunnis' detriment. Sunni cleric Harith al-Dhari asserted, "Sunnis in Iraq are more than half of the population," calling statistics to the contrary "a lie which we have not disputed until now for the sake of national unity." Iraq expert Ahmed Hashim explained that this view was prevalent among most Sunnis he spoke with during his time in Iraq. Many Arab Sunnis believe that they constitute at least a plurality in Iraq (i.e., the largest single group but perhaps less than 50 percent), and even those that accede to the internationally accepted view that Shi'a are the majority believe that the Sunni still hold claim to their historical position at the helm of Iraq's government.[69]

These firmly held beliefs contrasted starkly with the growing reality of Shi'a majoritarian dominance in the new Iraqi political system. The growing gap between Sunnis' desire for a prominent role in Iraq and the reality of a Shi'a majority unwilling to loosen their grasp on power left little hope for a positive political outcome, even in the minds of the most moderate. Events in 2006 and 2007, most prominently the poorly handled execution of Saddam Hussein, compelled many Sunnis to look to the Shi'a government as corrupt, ruthless, and intransigent. Even as violence wound down in Sunni areas, skepticism about the government dominated by Shi'a politicians remained. There was still little political compromise in sight.

For many Sunnis, the new Iraqi government is a second-best solution, but it is a much better future than continued violence and extremism. As we will see, the political process in Iraq has left much to be desired for the once-dominant Sunni community. Iraq's official political process presents Iraq's last, best hope for peace. Yet, looking back on the experience of the United States, it is important to remember that the U.S. political process drove the nation into a cataclysmic civil war that almost destroyed it completely. Only out of the ashes of this civil war did America rebuild itself into the superpower it is today. Likewise, it may take more upheaval before Iraqis are able to come to permanent terms of agreement.

7
Building a New Order

So intricate is the interplay between the political and the military actions [in an insurgency] that they cannot be tidily separated; on the contrary, every military move has to be weighed with regard to its political effects, and vice versa.[1]
—DAVID GALULA, COUNTERINSURGENCY EXPERT, 1964

The Lockean American is so fundamentally anti-government that he identifies government with restrictions on government. Confronted with the need to design a political system that will maximize power and authority, he has no ready answer. His general formula is that governments should be based on free and fair elections. In many modernizing societies this formula is irrelevant. . . . The problem is not to hold elections but to create organizations. In many, if not most, modernizing countries elections serve only to enhance the power of disruptive and often reactionary social forces and to tear down the structure of public authority.[2]
—SAMUEL P. HUNTINGTON, POLITICAL SCIENTIST, 1968

From the close of World War I until the fall of Saddam's regime, state power in Iraq rested in Sunni hands. Presidents, prime ministers, generals, police chiefs, and executioners were drawn almost exclusively from the Sunni population. While some Shi'a climbed to positions of authority, these postings were the exception rather than the rule, despite the fact that the Shi'a composed 60 percent of the population. In Iraq, Sunni elites were the rulers. Shi'a, Kurds, and everyone not tied to the ruling Sunni clique were the ruled. This order stood for more than eighty years.

By late December 2006, this order had obviously been overturned, though a new, unified Iraqi political community had not replaced it. The new order was a sectarian arrangement, dominated by the Shi'a majority and resisted by the Sunni minority. At no time were these facts more viscerally clear than at the execution of Saddam Hussein. Saddam was reportedly the only Sunni present at the former intelligence headquarters where he was hanged. His hooded executioners were dark, burly men with strong southern Iraqi accents, undoubtedly Shi'a. The room rang with chants praising radical Shi'a leader Muqtada al-Sadr and his uncle, Ayatollah Muhammad Baqir al-Sadr, whom Saddam had put to death after a gruesome torture session in 1980.

The Sunni tyrant, once the undisputed leader of Iraq, was executed at the hands of the Shi'a whom his regime had dominated. Had Saddam been put to death by a true government of national unity, had the attendants of his execution represented Iraq's varied communities, the event may have truly marked the end of Saddam's sway over Iraq. Instead, the execution came at the hands of squad consisting solely of Shi'a politicians and a police unit that some labeled a death squad.

In the days following the execution, there was uproar over the way in which it was carried out and the speed and apparent disregard for legal procedure with which the death sentence was handed down following the denial of Saddam's appeal. Saddam was transferred from American custody only after the exhaustion of vigorous U.S. efforts to convince the Iraqi government to delay the hanging in order to rigorously follow legal procedures. When the Iraqi government could not persuade the chief judge of Iraq's Supreme Judicial Council to issue a ruling approving the execution, leaders turned instead to the highest ranking Shi'a clerics in Najaf to issue approval. Once the clerics assented, the government forged ahead.[3] This string of events illustrated the nature of the Shi'a dominated government and the power of religious leaders in the new Iraq.

With the fall of the Ba'ath regime, a new era in Iraqi politics arrived. Prior to the rise of the Ba'ath Party, Iraqi politics had been a complex interaction between pan-Arab and Iraqi nationalist themes. Once the Ba'athists took power in 1968, the pan-Arab discourse won out, yet this ideology gradually faded away into a cult of personality centered on Saddam Hussein and his immediate family. What remained of the pan-Arab ideology was a conception of an "Arab-Islamic Golden Age" and "a strong sense of conspiracy and victimization."[4] By 2004, the pan-Arab legacy had completely collapsed, though new champions had taken up the mantle of paranoid politics.

With the benefit of a clean slate, many hoped that a liberal and inclusive vision of Iraqi nationalism would take hold in the political sphere. While some politicians returned from exile promoting such a vision, they were often mistrusted and unable to connect with a broad constituency. Other groups were much more successful in capitalizing on existing institutions to mobilize supporters and dominate the political scene. Although these groups were based nominally on sectarianism, in reality, they were a narrow and ruthless group of elites that used identity and religion as means to promote themselves in what became a contest for the spoils of the Iraqi government. They, much more than the bulk of Iraqi society, played on sectarian identity and ethnicity to define a new order in Iraq in which they would hold the reins of power.

The sectarian divisions opened by decades of Sunni rule and made raw by Saddam's reign became institutionalized by the new political order in Iraq as groups campaigned on identity. Shi'a religious leaders demanded the unity of their followers at the ballot box, Kurds ensconced in their autonomous region consolidated their parties into a bloc and enshrined their status with constitutional concessions, and Sunnis rejected the whole process as illegitimate. Despite the fact that many Iraqis may have been receptive to more inclusive arrangements, such efforts did not serve the interests of the existing leaders and time was not sufficient for the rise of new ones. As a result, ethno-sectarian identity openly defined Iraqi politics for the first time.

This was the culmination of Iraq's new official political process, which played out over three years. Begun by the Coalition Provisional Authority (CPA), the process soon took on a life of its own as Coalition officials were surprised time and again by the strange ways of Iraqi politics. Sovereignty was handed back to an Iraqi government in June 2004, after which Iraqi leaders and politicians, coached by U.S. officials and international experts, crafted their own constitution, ran a national election, and formed a uniquely Iraqi government. Throughout this course of events, narrow concerns dominated national interests, resulting in a weakened central government rife with divisions and corruption. Large blocs rode identity into power, yet once in government, these blocs fought among themselves over political issues and power, even as their militias came into armed conflict in the streets. This partisan process was both a victim of and a contributor to the intractable violence that has gripped Iraq since 2003.

Experts and officials discussing Iraq often fell into the age-old chicken-or-egg debate, arguing whether security or political development had to come first. According to Amb. L. Paul Bremer III, Gen Peter Pace (then Vice Chairman of the Joint Chiefs of Staff) stated in a November 2003 National Security Council meeting, "The most important military strategy is to accelerate the governance track." In his book, Bremer counters by writing, "Central to all was better security." Shortly thereafter, in a meeting with the president and a number of key deputies in Washington, Bremer laid out his position. "Mister President, we have to deal more effectively with the security situation. The intelligence is just not good. And I'm personally not persuaded that the military has a strategy to win." Straining credulity, he continued, "You know, Mr. President, one of my favorite presidential moments was when McClellan was marching the Army of the Potomac up and down and refusing to give battle to the Confederates. Lincoln cabled him, 'If you're not going to use the army, could I borrow it?'" The president laughed, yet gave no comment.[5] Neither governance nor security was being provided, though officials responsible for one aspect often pointed the finger at those responsible for the other.

Regardless of what any pundit or official may assert, there are no simple solutions in Iraq, nor can the finger be pointed solely at one agency, department, or individual. A heightened military campaign could not salvage the nation alone, nor could elections or constitutional amendments. Iraqis needed both concrete improvements in security and government services and more abstract assurances that the official political process would guard their interests and their very existence. Nowhere has this been more plainly evident than at the lowest levels of interface between young U.S. military officers and local Iraqi leaders.

In the far western reaches of Anbar Province, only miles from the Syrian border, a Marine lieutenant met in November 2005 with a low-level sheikh to discuss grievances and attempt to build a working relationship. The lieutenant was surprised to find the sheikh's grievances not only reasonable but, more importantly, easily addressable. First, the sheikh was agitated because the local mosque's generator had been stolen. The lieutenant promised to do his best to have the generator returned. He later discovered that it had been appropriated by an Iraqi Army unit working in the area (whom the sheikh himself referred to as "Ali Babas"—the term U.S. troops coined for thieves). The lieutenant had it returned to the sheikh the next day, proving that he was a man of his word.

The second order of business was similar. "Your men have been taking chickens for their meals. We understand that they are hungry, but we ask that you pay for the chickens." Embarrassed that what his Marines thought of as foraging (the birds were free-ranging) was seen as stealing, the lieutenant replied, "Yes, sir. We will pay you for the chickens that you have lost up to now and we will buy any chickens that we may need in the future."

After a few more fruitful items, the lieutenant really sensed that he was making progress with the sheikh. There was dialogue, and the sheikh had reasonable demands on which the lieutenant could deliver. Then came the brick wall. "And finally, you know . . . the government in Baghdad is overrun with Iranians. This must be fixed." The lieutenant, taken aback by this demand, protested, "*Ana mulazim,* I'm only a lieutenant." Unfazed, the sheikh insisted that the lieutenant advise his commander to pass his demand up the chain of command.

There is only so much that can be accomplished at the concrete, local level. Projects can be completed. Agreements can be reached. Insurgents can be killed or run out of town. But at day's end, there must be success at both this level and at the larger and more abstract level of the national political system. For the sheikh, tangible achievements were important to maintain control of his regional domain, but he also feared a more conceptual political threat.

To him, perceived Iranian dominance of the central government in Baghdad posed real fears that life, as he understood it, would soon end under sectarian tyranny and persecution. Many Sunnis did not fear the Shiʻa, but rather the Iranians—a critical distinction. In a country where Sunnis were once preeminent, he and his people needed reassurance that the central government would not exclude or persecute them and that they would be included in the distribution of government spoils. The sheikh likely knew that the lieutenant did not have sway over goings-on in Baghdad. Still, he wished for his grievances to be heard and respected.

The official political process is the center stage of transition in Iraq. From the start, the end goal of the Coalition intervention in Iraq has been the establishment of a stable representative form of government. The sole route for consolidation of this transition is through the official political process. Peaceful and inclusive political engagement is the only way to avoid perpetual conflict in Iraq. If Iraq's ethno-sectarian groups believe that they can attain their needs through politics, then they will remain within the system; however, if they believe that they will not be treated fairly within the system, then they will seek alternative means to attain their goals. If used, these other means will most likely result in bloody and protracted insurgency or civil war.

Although Iraq's political process has made amazing progress given the circumstances, the country is hardly a budding democratic utopia. After the implosion of the central government in 2003, Iraq's state powers were scattered to the various local and sectarian groups that had grown up in Saddam's Iraq. Once this power was stripped from the central government, restoring unity to Iraqi politics would prove exceptionally difficult. The single factor that has most affected the process is the double division of political groups along and within ethno-sectarian lines. The local groups that received the windfall of powers arising from the crisis of governance became incredibly strong after 2003, often behind a narrow agenda. In addition, the Iraqi public was atomized from the start and, despite their brave turnouts for elections, not overwhelmingly interested in mass politics in the wake of the invasion. The country also lacked strong political parties and unifying leaders who could have campaigned for the support of broad national blocs reaching across geographic and ethno-sectarian boundaries. As a result, Iraqis were instead organized in support of several sectarian blocs that successfully carved up the government among them. That these grand sectarian blocks were riven with fractures and power struggles only deepened the political impasse that ensued. The prominence of sectarianism as a defining factor in Iraqi politics is a major legacy of this process and will continue to present difficulties for Iraq's fledgling government in the years ahead.

Ultimately, the goal of democratic transition in Iraq is to place in power a government elected by the people, based on a peaceful, democratic, and sustainable political process. In order for this system to survive, the actors in Iraq's three dominant communities must agree that their interests are best served by such an arrangement. Because the Kurds, the Arab Sunni, and the Arab Shi'a hold conflicting visions for the future of Iraq, a great deal of compromise will be required to sort out a solution amenable to all. Furthermore, even within the ethno-sectarian blocs, there is bitter dissent over the way ahead. Thus, negotiators must bargain not only with counterparts from other blocs, but also with the constituents of their own bloc to find potential common ground.[6] An eventual solution will require powerful local and sectarian groups to acquiesce to joint bargaining positions and will force local groups and leaders to return the state powers they claimed in the wake of the old regime's collapse. From court-like mediation to the provision of services and security, these powers are a major source of legitimacy and income for local power groups and will not be easily relinquished. These issues all rob the central government of power and legitimacy and exacerbate the tensions between sects and regions. Lasting solutions to these problems can be found only through the official political process. All other paths lead to continued warfare.

Hatred alone does not cause a civil war. There are several ways in which shortcomings in political engagement can feed conflict. First, if any group sees the process as illegitimate, it is unlikely to participate. By declaring the process illegitimate, some groups justified their attacks on the system and the government in Iraq. Second, if the process does not produce the desired outcome, groups may opt to defect from the system, as many Sunni and some Shi'a groups have repeatedly. Once spurned and outside the system, these groups are much more likely to come into conflict. Third, if groups feel that they are closed out of the process, they may decide that their views and desires cannot be expressed and their needs will not be provided for, prompting them to look for alternate means of reaching their goals. In Iraq, backroom deals and powerful, but arbitrary, political groups threaten to close many voices out of the process, pushing them toward aggressive means of pursuing their goals. These three shortcomings explain not only the violence between the sects, but also the growing clashes within Shi'a and Sunni political factions.

The ethno-sectarian and geographic makeup of Iraq presented particularly difficult ground for democratic transition. Two factors, in particular, have combined to make Iraq prone to conflict. First, Iraq's three ethno-sectarian groups fall roughly into three separate regions of Iraq, which has led many observers to suggest that a breakup of the country into three states may be the easiest way to end the fighting. Beyond the troubling fact that most Iraqis are staunchly against this proposition, the catch is that the sectarian populations are intermixed in many critical areas along the borders of these regions and in the capital. Second, the vast oil resources of the country are not equally distributed among these three groups, and some of the oil lies in hotly contested areas of diverse ethno-sectarian composition. This alone is a recipe for ethnic conflict. In addition, Iraq has a long history of tension among the three communities and sectarian fighting is ongoing, making reconciliation even more difficult.

The pre-eminent scholar of democratic transition observed "conflict and reconciliation are essential to democracy."[7] To this point, there has been much of the former in Iraq, but little of the latter. Iraq's political blocs have been slow to come to terms with the second-best solutions critical to the process of reconciliation. A major obstacle to reconciliation has been the entrenchment of ethno-sectarian parties in the political process. No major Iraqi political parties (and precious few minor ones) are defined primarily according to their stances on economic or social issues. Their defining characteristic is usually their sectarian composition and their allegiance to key leaders in that population. Thus, as of 2008, no organizations were capable of uniting Iraqis of different backgrounds under one political banner. The lack of unifying parties and the relatively clear delineation of Iraq's parliamentary lists along ethno-sectarian lines yielded hardened positions and little compromise. In this condition, instead of being a vessel for the provision of security and progress, the government is an arena where the sectarian groups and subgroups fight over the spoils of ministries and national resources, feeding violence in the process. In 2008, some parties began to align on issue, more than sect, which created loose cross-sectarian alliances. Although this was a step in the right direction, the moves have been informal and have not produced a major shift in political organization as of yet.

While ethnically mixed countries can avoid civil war and attain economic prosperity in most cases, there are critical caveats that predispose Iraq for ethno-sectarian troubles. First, in a study of ethnically diverse societies, noted economist Paul Collier found that ethnic dominance, where one group is larger than the others, doubles the risk of civil war. While Iraq's Shi'a, constituting more than 60 percent of the population, have been unable to dominate in the past, the fear of such domination was drilled into Sunnis by the Ba'ath regime. Furthermore, the success of Shi'a leadership in mobilizing voters along identity lines and their apparent lack of interest in granting concessions to the Arab Sunnis reinforced these fears.

Second, when a state relies on a natural resource such as oil for a great portion of its revenues, the risk of ethnic conflict increases dramatically. Often what seems like conflict based on primordial hatred is at root a battle over resources. Oil has historically accounted for more than 90 percent of Iraq's foreign exchange income and more than 60 percent of its total gross domestic product. Further, Iraq's oil fields are located largely in the Kurdish north and the Shi'a south, leaving the Sunni west virtually devoid of resources.[8] Control of the government means control of oil revenues that are the lifeblood of the state. This factor turned seemingly arcane legal discussions about federalism into matters of economic life or death.

The uneven distribution of Iraq's oil led to acrimonious debates on how the resource would be controlled and the revenues doled out. These were not resolved during the writing of Iraq's temporary or permanent constitutions, and the details were left to Iraq's parliament. In the absence of a law governing this issue, the Sunnis' lack of oil resources makes them particularly afraid that federalism and populist majoritarian politics will cut them off from the source of wealth that has sustained them for many years. If written properly, this law may allay Sunni fears, a key step in reconciliation.

Finally, the distribution of oil further complicated Iraqis' responses to federalism. Secession of the Shi'a or the Kurds threatens to take away large sources of revenue from the rest of the country. Due to the oil resources that lie below the contested ground, all parties will scrutinize the boundaries of any regional federation or breakaway state. Specifically, the disputed northern city of Kirkuk is a growing center of sectarian tension, a situation aggravated by the riches beneath its soil.

The official political process, the only peaceful way of dealing with these issues, has consisted of several stages. In 2003, Coalition and Iraqi leaders began to stake out the path of transition in Iraq, actively guided by Ambassador Bremer and the CPA. The main focus of this process was the creation of a constitution and a government to which sovereignty could be handed at an early date. The burgeoning insurgencies and condemnation of occupation demanded quick action in order to return Iraq's sovereignty and nullify the resisters' grievances. Thus, the process was characterized by haste, plagued by sectarian tensions, and hampered by violence.

As negotiations progressed, the CPA's original plans for the drafting of a permanent constitution by an appointed body were derailed. Shi'a Ayatollah Sistani demanded that a freely elected body write a legitimate constitution. These demands resulted in an agreement to appoint an interim governing body ruled under a transitional administrative law (TAL) followed by national elections for the assembly that would draft the permanent constitution. These national elections were held in January 2005, after which the elected assembly drafted Iraq's permanent constitution, which was ratified in an October 2005 referendum. The establishment of Iraq's permanent government pursuant to the constitution began in December 2005 with another round of general elections for National Assembly members.

In the end, the process resulted in the formation of a freely elected Iraqi government. Sadly, though, due to the vagaries of the Iraqi political process, the resulting government was weak and wracked by infighting and corruption. Maybe this should not be much of a surprise, however. In 1968, political scientist Samuel P. Huntington warned that Americans are most likely to build limitations on government, rather than government itself. He argued that underdeveloped political systems, rather than economic woes, were at the root of the developing world's problems. Because of America's unique experience, Americans worried more about controlling government than establishing a powerful government capable of quashing internal discord. Thus, "asked to design a government, [an American] comes up with a written constitution, bill of rights, separation of powers, checks and balances, federalism, regular elections, competitive parties—all excellent devices for limiting government." Yet, Huntington argues, such limitations are irrelevant if the government has no authority over the competing groups in society and is unable to establish order.[9]

American and other Western advisors lived up to Huntington's prediction almost exactly. They built limits on government before order had been established in Iraq. The resulting government has not had the power or authority to bring about order in the time since its formation. It has proved incapable of securing the country or providing for its citizens. Many Iraqis took security and justice into their own hands, bringing the country closer to civil war with each turn of violence and vengeance. In this regard, the political process failed to deliver the reconciliation required for the country to move toward peace and stability. Returning to Huntington's warning, though, with the initial lack of trust among Iraq's major communities, there seems to have been no way to build a government agreeable to all without placing severe limits on its power. This is the catch-22 of Iraqi politics. A powerful government is required to maintain order, but none of the players is willing to place such power in any other group's hands. Unless voters and politicians can exceed the bounds of the current sectarian-dominated political alliance system to create a broader coalition, the central government is likely to remain weak and the parliament gridlocked, as Iraq sputters along from crisis to crisis.

Staking Out the Official Political Process

The establishment of an official political process in Iraq began at the national level, under the auspices of the CPA, which defined the boundaries of the process and selected the Iraqis who would provide early official leadership. Early candidates for such positions were primarily exiles who had been living outside Iraq during the latter years of Saddam's rule. Elected by a conference of Iraqi exiles held in London in December 2002, the Iraqi Leadership Council (ILC) consisted of the most prominent of these exiles who expected to head the new Iraq. Although they were mostly educated men and staunch supporters of a new way in Iraq, the group did not fully represent Iraq's communities. Additionally, as previously mentioned, many Iraqis who had suffered under Saddam's hand until 2003 did not view these leaders as legitimate, desiring instead those who had shared in their harrowing experiences.

Political opposition to the official process emerged at the start. Many in Iraq did not view the CPA, the ILC, or their plans as legitimate, because they were products of a foreign invasion and occupation. Sunnis, in particular, were disenfranchised by the de-Baʻathification edict and the disbanding of the military and security forces that set the tone for the new era. At a more basic level, they were highly suspicious of Shiʻa and Kurdish motives in the new Iraq. A common Sunni refrain was that any government set up under an illegal occupation was illegitimate, advocating the unreasonable position that the Coalition should withdraw immediately to allow Iraqis to form a new government with no outside interference. Continuing insurgent violence and Shiʻa and Kurdish fears of a Baʻathist resurgence ensured that a quick withdrawal would not occur. The Sunni opposition to the occupation would produce a boycott of politics, marginalizing the Sunni effect on the new government, empowering the Shiʻa majority, and feeding the Sunni resistance.

Some Shiʻa, particularly Muqtada al-Sadr and his followers, opposed the new political process as illegitimate. Al-Sadr admitted that, although religiously Shiʻa, "politically I am closer to the Sunnis,"[10] demonstrating that sectarianism was not always predominant in Iraqi politics. Although he would go on to become heavily engaged in the Iraqi government, al-Sadr was initially willing to use force and thuggish tactics of intimidation and religious manipulation to advance his own power in southern Iraq. These twin threats to the official political process, the Sunni resistance and the Sadr movement, would combine in 2004 to nearly derail the entire political venture in Iraq.

The most influential Shiʻa figure, Grand Ayatollah Ali Sistani, exerted massive influence from the fringes of the political process. Although he refused to engage firsthand in the process, al-Sistani's statements and religious decisions, or *fatwa*, carried great weight and guided his followers' interpretation of and interaction with the political process. Although he turned down direct contact with the Coalition, al-Sistani's support or objection to the path of politics was critical in shaping the trajectory of transition and opposition, as will be detailed.

Kurdish leaders were the closest to the Coalition, owing to years of U.S. support for de-facto Kurdish autonomy, yet these leaders also carefully staked out positions on many issues in opposition to the CPA's wishes. In particular, the Kurds desired to maintain autonomy in a new Iraq, which presented problems for consensual politics. Although Kurdish politicians remained engaged the political process of a united Iraq, many of their constituents voiced a strong sentiment for independence. This fueled Sunni fears that federalism was a formula for the breakup of Iraq. It also hardened the Kurdish negotiators' positions in the struggle over the formation of Iraq's new regime. Given their common goal of continued Kurdish autonomy under a federal solution, Kurdish parties unified as an ethnic bloc for the elections and worked with the Shi'a majority to further their ends.

Many advisors in the CPA understood that the country needed time to grow the sorts of broad and inclusive party organizations that would lead Iraq out of the narrow politics of its past. Yet the slow, incremental progress desired by the CPA was a source of irritation to members of the ILC, and indeed some in the U.S. government who wished a rapid turnover and withdrawal from Iraq. By the early summer of 2003, the pressure was on the Coalition to return sovereignty to Iraq. The Supreme Council for Islamic Revolution in Iraq's (SCIRI) Abd al-Aziz al-Hakim expressed to Ambassador Bremer, "If the Iraqi people convened a national conference now, we could write a constitution within three months . . . without foreign assistance. We have a great tradition of scholarship, you know."[11] The Coalition had concerns about the inclusiveness of such a process, however. Shi'a opposition groups that had existed in exile for years dominated the ILC. There was little representation of Arab Sunnis or of Iraq's smaller ethnic and sectarian communities.

Even though ILC members generally resisted broadening their ranks into a Governing Council (GC), the CPA pressed the issue in a major diplomatic effort to convince Iraq's key leaders to participate in a broader interim governing body. By July 13, 2003, the CPA had assembled twenty-five prominent Iraqis to constitute the GC. The Council's membership was overtly defined by the sectarian communities each represented, a development in politics reviled by many Iraqis. Thirteen of the twenty-five seats were allocated to Shi'a, five to Arab Sunnis, and five to Kurds. One Turkoman and one Assyrian Christian represented Iraq's smaller communities.[12] This allocation mirrored Iraq's ethno-sectarian makeup, rather than socio-economic or other political distinctions. Though the Council shepherded the transition to sovereignty and attempted to draft an interim constitution, its success was limited by bitter infighting between headstrong leaders unwilling to compromise with the other groups in Iraq. These traits were both a product of Iraq's troubled past and a sign of things to come.

Mostly exiles, Shi'a politicians held a one-seat majority in the new GC and quickly organized to take advantage of their position. The Shi'a Islamists in the GC prompted the founding of a caucus, known as the Shi'a House (*al-Bayt al-Shi'i*). The caucus's key leaders held regular meetings and focused on gaining a Shi'a consensus on pressing issues. The Shi'a House was intimately tied into the Shi'a clerical powers in Najaf, most prominently Ayatollah Sistani. Together, the clerics and politicians ensured that no disunity would ruin their chance to rise to majoritarian power in the new Iraq.[13]

The CPA initially planned to select a convention of "representative Iraqis" to draft the new constitution. This plan unraveled as al-Sistani, in a June 2003 statement, demanded that a nationally elected Iraqi body draft Iraq's permanent constitution. Labeling the CPA plan as "unacceptable," al-Sistani stated that the Coalition had "no right to appoint members of the constitutional drafting committee." He expressed doubts that an appointed assembly would create a constitution that would serve Iraqis' "best interests" or "express their religious identity whose pillars are true Islamic religion and noble social values." Therefore, al-Sistani called for a general election to choose the constitutional convention's delegates and a referendum to confirm the draft constitution.[14] This simple one-paragraph statement profoundly impacted the path of Iraqi transition. Although it placed the Coalition in the awkward position of being questioned on democratic principles, the CPA eventually came around to the idea of deferring the drafting of a permanent constitution until after an elected body had convened.

The next step to a new Iraqi form of government was creating a transitional assembly. Initially, the CPA and many Iraqi politicians advocated elections for the assembly, an option that would have required intricate preparations on a short timeline. Early elections also tilted the playing field in favor of the existing ethno-sectarian groups and against broader parties and coalitions, which would take more time to organize and for their constituents to coalesce. The Coalition was caught in a delicate position, desiring free and fair elections, which required lengthy preparations, but wishing to move forward as rapidly as possible in creating a sovereign and legitimate Iraqi government. In the end, it was decided that holding elections by June 2004, right before the transfer of sovereignty to an Iraqi government, would not be feasible. Instead, Bremer advocated a caucus system to select the transitional assembly members. Though the option was not ideal, according to Bremer, it could act as "a way station to full democratic elections to a permanent government."[15] Even this caucus idea foundered, however, and the interim government was also a Coalition-appointed body.

Many Iraqi leaders accepted the new plan. For them, as long as an elected body drafted the constitution, the interim assembly was acceptable. On November 15, 2003, the GC approved the plan for selection of the transitional assembly by caucus, though the opposing votes of influential Shi'a members signaled problems ahead. The November 15 Agreement provided the roadmap for the transfer of sovereignty to an Iraqi government, the election of an assembly that would draft a permanent Iraqi constitution, and the election of a permanent National Assembly based on that constitution. The agreement set a February 28, 2004, deadline for the existing Council to draft and approve the "Law of Administration for the State of Iraq for the Transitional Period," popularly known as the Transitional Administrative Law, or TAL. The TAL was to "define the structures of a transitional government and the procedures for electing delegates to a constitutional convention" in addition to "guarantee[ing] certain basic rights for all Iraqis during [the] transition."[16]

The CPA was to turn over sovereignty to a representative body selected by Iraqis no later than June 30, 2004. "Direct one-man, one-vote elections" for the constitutional convention were to be held no later than March 15, 2005. Though the deadline for the constitution was not specified in the November 15 Agreement, the TAL later set it for August 15, 2005. The agreement did stipulate that national elections for a new Iraqi government based on the approved constitution would be held by December 31, 2005. The November 15 Agreement was a key timeline for the progression of Iraqi sovereignty and transition to democracy, yet there were many obstacles to be overcome along the way.

Following on the heels of the November 15 Agreement, the GC convened a drafting committee in December 2003 to come up with the TAL. From the beginning, the differing desires of Iraq's major communities clashed, complicating the creation of a new constitutional document. The TAL paved the way for sovereignty and was also the basis for much of Iraq's permanent constitution, written roughly a year later, although it did little to solve Iraq's deeper political conflicts. Ali Allawi summed up the feelings of those who felt that the TAL was essentially an American, not an Iraqi document. "The TAL embodied western, specifically American notions, and was carefully supervised by the CPA. Each significant point had been pre-cleared with the NSC [National Security Council] in Washington."[17] Drafting the TAL was a tortuous process as the various parties struggled to come to terms on critical issues. Federalism, the status of the Kurdish region, the relationship of Islam to the laws of Iraq, and the status of oil resources and revenues were critical areas of conflict. While vague, basic agreement was reached in most areas, the details were left to a permanent constitution.

A difficult issue for the TAL in the short term proved to be crafting the provision for a veto of the constitution during the referendum. Besides the national majority yes-or-no vote, the draft could be defeated if two-thirds of the voters in three or more governorates rejected the draft. This was seen by all sides as a specific Kurdish veto power and was a point of no compromise for the Kurdish delegates. Although the Shi'a council members agreed to the provision during the course of negotiations, al-Sistani strongly opposed the provision when he reviewed the document prior to giving counsel to his GC followers. Al-Sistani viewed the veto as an affront to the majoritarian powers that should be afforded to the demographically superior Shi'a. In the face of Sistani's opposition, many of the Shi'a members would not sign the document and requested concessions from the Kurds.

The matter came to a head on March 5, 2004. The completed TAL was to be signed at a high-profile afternoon ceremony in Baghdad; instead, the members entered into heated negotiations over al-Sistani's new demands. The Kurds refused to agree to any changes, and several Shi'a council members were determined to sign the agreement regardless of al-Sistani's reservations. The time of the signing came and went. It was not until late in the night that the Shi'a delegates persuaded their Kurdish counterparts to allow them two days to review the document with al-Sistani. After two days of arduous deliberations in Najaf, Shi'a representative Mowaffaq Rub'aie reported to Ambassador Bremer that the council members had convinced al-Sistani to allow the delegates to sign the existing document. The TAL was signed on March 8, 2004, marking the way toward a sovereign Iraqi government. Ambassador Bremer chalked up the successful signing of the document as a "significant round won in favor of a secular Iraq."[18]

Shi'a politician Ali Allawi provided a different perspective. "The TAL was deeply resented by a large majority of Iraqis. Its obviously western provenance and its Kurdo-centrism seemed to open the country to dismantling its Arab identity and to partition." This belief, coming from a Shi'a politician, not a Sunni, shows that the TAL was not the victory some considered it to be. Allawi asserted that it was seen as "a flawed document, written by a foreign occupier with Iraqi fellow-travelers in tow." His impression may not have been far off the mark. One official stated that Ambassador Bremer had "a tremendous investment in [the TAL] as one of his prized accomplishments" and had no interest in exploring any modifications to his vision.[19] This was hardly the inclusive framework that many hoped would usher in a new era of Iraqi politics.

The TAL formed the basis for sovereignty in the transitional period and heavily influenced much of the permanent constitution. The document also provided details on the timeline to a new, permanent Iraqi government that were only broadly outlined in the November 15 Agreement.[20] The document specified that a National Assembly of 275 members be chosen by a general election no later than January 31, 2005. The assembly was charged with drafting the permanent Iraqi constitution, which was to be completed no later than August 15, 2005, with a referendum on the constitution to be held by October 15, 2005. Ratification of the constitution required a simple majority vote nationwide. A two-thirds vote against the constitution in any three provinces would veto the constitution. If the constitution were approved in this referendum, the general elections for the permanent government would be held on December 15, 2005, with the government to be seated by December 31, 2005. The timeline was fairly straightforward, though it would severely test the limits of Iraqi politics.

Although the deadlines were required to keep Iraq moving toward a permanent, fully functioning government, they placed immense pressure on the political process. There was no room for error in the short schedule. It tended to favor the already extant, largely sectarian political parties and left the Sunnis at a serious organizational deficit. Both the Shi'a and the Kurds had the benefit of longstanding organization and leadership, albeit mostly in exile or underground. In contrast, there was no real Sunni political leadership or organization outside of the old regime. Critically, the deadlines offered little time for engaging the public, building consensus, and educating voters on the facts behind the many troublesome issues. Under these constraints Iraq's religious and ethnic parties would write the constitution, rather than a convention representing the best of Iraq. Votes would be cast based primarily on what local leaders communicated to their constituents about the constitution, rather than on a balanced public education campaign aimed at gaining broad support for the constitution and its articles. The timeline had serious repercussions for Iraq's political future and the resolution of difficult issues to be covered by the permanent constitution.

Iraq regained its sovereignty on June 28, 2004, as Bremer and the CPA furtively departed Iraq. The transfer occurred two days prior to the deadline in order to throw off any attacks timed to cripple the new government on the anticipated June 30 transfer date. Upon the transfer of sovereignty to the new government headed by Shi'a Prime Minister Ayad Allawi, the CPA and the Governing Council ceased to exist and Iraq forged ahead into new territory. Allawi was a noted exile politician with a secular program that many outsiders hoped would be an example for the new political system of Iraq. Allawi's dominance of Iraqi politics was short, however, as the power of Iraq's sub-state groups pulled and shaped the new government and the constitutional process.

Elections in the New Iraq: Obstacles and Outcomes

The next major step in Iraq's political transition was the January 2005 election. Though elections would be a major step in creating a more representative government, a number of issues worked against the credibility and success of the transitional government. First, the new government still lacked widespread acceptance. The government was chosen by the Coalition and composed the TAL under occupation, which prompted many leaders to label both as illegitimate. Moreover, the elections for the National Assembly would occur under occupation, a condition that many self-servingly decried as an obstacle to a legitimate outcome. Therefore, most Sunnis boycotted the elections, forfeiting their ability to significantly affect the drafting of the permanent constitution. By choosing not to participate in the official political process, the Sunnis restricted themselves to working outside the wire, often in the form of violent resistance.

Sunnis were not the only Iraqis continuing to snipe at the political process. Despite al-Sistani's apparent acquiescence to Shi'a GC members signing the TAL, he opposed its provisions because an appointed body had drafted it. On June 2, 2004, he released a statement highlighting the new government's shortfalls. "A new government was appointed without gaining the legitimacy of elections. Furthermore, the segments and political forces of Iraqi society are not suitably represented. Nonetheless, it is hoped that this government will prove its fitness and integrity and its certain resolve to carry out the momentous task that rests on its shoulders."[21] Al-Sistani followed this statement up with another on June 6 that railed against any reference to the TAL in an upcoming UN Security Council (UNSC) resolution recognizing Iraq's sovereign government:

> We have been informed that there are those who intend to mention the so called "Law of Administration for the State of Iraq for the Transitional Period" in the new UNSC Resolution on Iraq, with the intent of granting it international legitimacy. This "law" that has been passed by an un-elected council under the auspices and direct influence of occupation charges the National Assembly, which is due to be elected early next year, with the drafting of the permanent Iraqi constitution. This edict is illegal and is rejected by most Iraqi people. Therefore, any attempt to confer legitimacy

upon this "law" by including it in the international resolution is considered as contrary to the desire of the Iraqi people and may have dangerous consequences.[22]

Al-Sistani's statement caused a dilemma. Although he was staunchly against any reference to the TAL in the resolution, the Kurds were demanding that the TAL be mentioned to ensure that the Shiʻa would be bound to its clauses. In the end, Bremer proposed a compromise under which the UN resolution would not mention the TAL, but would include a reference to federalism to placate the Kurds. President Bush's weekly radio address endorsed the TAL in order to demonstrate the U.S. resolve to back the law and make certain that all players continued to respect it during the transitional period.[23] Once again, the different communities were held together only by a thread as they fought over the rules of the game.

The drafting of the electoral law that governed the January 2005 election was the last major hurdle the CPA faced before the transfer of sovereignty. Election experts from the International Foundation for Election Systems (IFES) and the UN Electoral Assistance Division (UNEAD) were consulted to determine the best electoral method and guarantee that the mechanism carried international support and credibility. Because of several shortcomings—including the lack of reliable census data, the short timeline for establishing complex electoral procedures, and the security problems in Iraq—the UN's election expert, Carina Perelli, recommended that the elections be conducted in a single nationwide district.

Perelli explained her reasoning in a June 2004 press conference.

There are a lot of communities that have been broken and dispersed around Iraq and these communities wanted to be able to accumulate their votes and to vote with like-minded people . . . . These communities of interest, by using a national district will be able to accumulate votes . . . to basically aggregate interests, which at the end of the day is what this assembly is all about.[24]

Unfortunately, the communities that aggregated interests were not broad, inclusive, or unified across ethno-sectarian lines. According to democracy expert and former CPA consultant Larry Diamond and political scientist Adeed Dawisha, the absence of districts made the elections "almost purely a national-identity referendum."²⁵ In contrast, a vote with smaller districts may have forced voters to choose between multiple candidates of the same ethnic and sectarian background, pushing them to vote based on issues rather than identity.

Ambassador Bremer signed this process into law on June 15, 2004, as CPA Order Number 96, "The Electoral Law," which stated that the 275 National Assembly members would be chosen by direct secret ballot in a single district. The members would be chosen from ranked lists, on which every third candidate was female. As lists received votes, the members of their list would be allocated seats proportional to their list's share of the vote.²⁶ In reality, this meant that only a few candidates at the tops of the lists were really known by the public. The rest received their seats based on the notoriety of the list and its top members. It was a process that confirmed the power of large, sectarian parties and their leaders, while making all but the most prominent list members beholden to the masters of the list that provided them with their assembly seat.

A major obstacle to politics of unity was the lack of known and acceptable national leaders. Iraq had only a handful of widely recognized leaders, most of whom were viewed with skepticism. When asked to name the leader that they trusted most, the top response, Ibrahim Jafari, was named by only 12 percent of respondents. The next closest leaders came in at 3 to 4 percent and an overwhelming 64 percent of Iraqis polled declined to name a trusted leader. Focus-group interviewers found that participants in the summer of 2003 "generally [had] more negative than positive things to say in reaction to a list of emerging political and religious leaders in Iraq." The researchers noted a particular distaste for exiled leaders and attributed this aversion to "vilification campaigns led by the previous regime," yet judging from many other Iraqi statements, exiled leaders were distrusted because they were often seen as traitors to the Iraqis that continued to suffer under Saddam's rule. In any case, Iraqis' recent experiences with Saddam's leadership will make them cynical for some time to come.²⁶ An Iraqi political analyst succinctly explained Saddam's effect on political organization in Iraq. "Over the period of the past thirty-five years, the Ba'ath Party destroyed the national Iraqi political movement and no political parties remained on the Iraqi scene." He continued, expressing that in the new Iraq, "the Islamic political parties and movements have indeed reorganized, whether they be Shi'a or Sunni, but they have been limited to a narrow sectarian framework" without wide popular support across the nation.²⁷

Many Iraqis mistrusted political parties, feeling that the parties worked "for their own benefit."²⁸ This opinion may have been a critical factor in the shape of post-invasion politics. Since many Iraqis were cynical and did not trust the programs of the political parties, they were much more likely to throw their lot in with the established credentials of local religious leaders and grass-roots organizations (also often religious) that demonstrated their ability to deliver goods and services to the people. National political parties stood little chance of gaining traction in such an environment.

While religious political parties had great power at their disposal, many Iraqis also expressed disdain for what they viewed as opportunistic use of religion for political power. A Shi'a man commented, "Religious political parties corrupt the reputation of the religion." A Sunni woman articulated a similar sentiment, "There is no party carrying out religion. They use the name of religion only. Where are the principles of forgiveness, honesty, and altruism by these parties?" Another added that the parties "used religion as a means to reach specific goals and those parties created differentiation between the Iraqi sects." Perhaps the most damning comment came from a Kurdish man: "The Islamic parties are merchants. They are making trade of the Islamic religion and religion is free for them."[29] Few Iraqis were impressed with the choices before them, but lacking attractive alternatives, they supported the sectarian groups that most resembled them and were promoted by their local, religious, and tribal leaders.

Because the voting public was atomized and dissatisfied, many parties decided campaign on sectarian identity, rather than cobble together support from the broader population on any given set of issues. The major parties of Iraq's largest ethno-sectarian groups combined into three large lists. Each bloc consisted of multiple major parties that could have campaigned alone. By joining forces, they took the safe bet to guard sectarian interests, yet also erased the need for major inter-sectarian coalition-making in the new government. The power of sectarian identity at the ballot box was surprising for many. Ali Allawi recounted a conversation with a young Iraqi who returned with the CPA after growing up in Europe. Allawi described him as "totally irreligious, an avid partygoer" who could barely speak Arabic. After the vote, the young man admitted he had cast his ballot for the Shi'a United Iraqi Alliance (UIA), saying, "I had planned to vote for one of the liberal parties, but when the time came, I could not betray my Shi'a origins." Although many cast a historic vote for identity, it was not always a vote for a religious vision and the reality of poor performance in government caused serious regrets.[30]

The UIA, a predominately Shi'a list that grew out of the Shi'a House caucus of the Governing Council, won 140 of 275 seats. A major force behind the unity of the Shi'a vote, and indeed the creation of the UIA itself, was the voice of al-Sistani and the traditional clerical hierarchy or *marji'iya*. The marji'iya ordered the formation of a six-member council that outlined the details of the alliance and the allocation of positions on the list between the existing parties. To dilute the power of the standing parties, al-Sistani insisted that half the candidates be independents, although they were ultimately vetted by the parties. This list included al-Da'wa and SCIRI, as well as most of the Sadrists. Al-Sadr himself hedged his bets by sprinkling his loyalists between multiple lists and not explicitly committing himself to the UIA. Second, with seventy-five seats, was the Kurdistan Alliance. Finally, the Iraqi List, a secular group, came in with forty seats. This list fared so well only because of the Sunni boycott. The way that Iraqis lined up behind identity-linked lists is striking. Dawisha and Diamond estimated that more than 95 percent of Kurds voted for the Kurdistan Alliance and around 75 percent of Shi'a voted for the UIA. Seventy-five percent of Arab Sunnis chose to boycott the elections, thus only seventeen Sunni members were elected, mostly as part of secular or nationalist lists. Sunnis who made up 20 percent of the population won only 6 percent of the 275 seats.[31]

A major beneficiary of this identity-based voting was SCIRI. As noted above, SCIRI did not return from exile in 2003 to a whirlwind of popular support. Yet, through a shrewd set of tactical alliances, SCIRI won the trust of the United States, the cooperation of several other Shi'a Islamist parties, and the hand of al-Sistani. Because of superior political acumen and organizational discipline, and in no small part to the party members' insinuations that they were al-Sistani's candidates, SCIRI entrenched itself as the leader of the UIA, even though it was not the most popular party on the list. These tactics also allowed SCIRI to fare well at the provincial level, a result that would give SCIRI control over most of the southern provinces and their security forces.[32]

It took three months for the blocs to cobble together a new government, mainly owing to stubborn competition for key positions and accommodation of the obstinate Sunnis. Although they gained only seventeen seats in the January elections and only two of fifty-five seats on the constitutional drafting committee, a constitution drafted without Sunni representation was clearly a recipe for disaster. Thus, fifteen voting and ten non-voting Sunni delegates were added to the constitutional drafting committee.[33] The delay in creating the government robbed the assembly of precious time, further contributing to the difficulties of the tight timeline for drafting the constitution.

The January election had another ominous effect on the drafting of the constitution. The list system rested on only a few powerful names. The remaining representatives rode the coattails of the headliners and their popular and organizational backing. Once in office, these powerful leaders dictated to the other members of the list how to act and vote in the assembly. Many Iraqis, especially Sunnis, felt that their voice was not expressed under the system and that the constitution was essentially completed as a backroom deal, with heavy Iranian influence.[34]

The Constitution

Iraqis longing for the sovereignty promised since 2003 looked to the permanent constitution as the document that would bring their struggles to fruition. Seeing the constitution as the basis for all else, many Iraqis expected the document to lead to security, the delivery of services, the alleviation of corruption, and even the end of unemployment.[35] More critically, Iraq's different communities viewed the constitution as a document that would secure majority rule, preserve minority rights, and provide for the realization of narrow sectarian goals of key political parties. In short, the constitution was the political battleground for Iraq's most contentious issues.

In the end, an overwhelming majority of Iraqis approved the vaguely-worded constitution. The draft had narrowly escaped defeat as two Sunni provinces voted heavily against it. The constitution enshrined the power of sub-state groups, creating a weak and restrained central government. It catered to sectarian interests at the detriment of national unity and postponed the most treacherous key issues for later resolution. While the constitution may be suitable over the long term, it certainly was not the answer to all of Iraq's hopes or needs.

The TAL decreed that "the system of government shall be republican, federal, democratic, and pluralistic, and powers shall be shared between the federal government and the regional governments, governorates, municipalities, and local administrations." Despite this provision, federalism continued to be an issue during negotiations for the permanent constitution. Arab Sunnis were suspicious of provisions that allowed for the creation of Kurdish and Shi'a regions. Conversely, the Kurds desired to maintain their autonomy and the Shi'a were wary of restoring too much power to a central government in Baghdad. They had lived for nearly a century under the oppression of such a government and were in no hurry to reinstate it, even if they were demographically at the helm.

Sunnis wished to maintain a strong central government, insisting that federalism would lead to a breakup and civil war. Their fear of federalism can also be understood in light of Iraq's oil resources and the well-ingrained specter of Iranian dominance over a Shi'a region in the south. Sunnis feared that the creation of Kurdish and Shi'a super-regions, along with the decentralized control of oil revenues at the regional level, would result in these two rich regions starving the Sunni west. Add to this issue the Sunni mistrust of Iranian designs on southern Iraq and animosity fueled by the bloody eight-year conflict between the two states, and federalism became a redline issue for Sunni negotiators. Despite Sunni wishes, once the powers of the central government were dispersed, there was little or no desire on the part of sheikhs, imams, and other local leaders to return power to the center. As a result, the Kurds and the leaders of the Shi'a bloc agreed to protect these sub-state powers while heavily restraining the powers of the central government in the constitution. The product, on paper at least, was what one observer deemed "possibly the weakest [central government] of any federal model in the world."[36]

The constitution was a design of the Shi'a majority, especially the well-organized SCIRI, with a number of overt concessions to the Kurds. It created a weak central government that prolonged Iraq's problems of governance and threatened fragmentation of the country. The constitution contained a number of provisions meant to empower the provinces at the expense of the federal government, apparently handing control over oil revenues, taxation, and legislation to the provinces.[37] In practice, however, the National Assembly had to legislate the details of these provisions. The glacial pace of that body, in addition to rising power of an anti-decentralization bloc, served to moderate the constitutional vision to a degree. If nothing else, the slow pace of legislation and political development put a brake on regional autonomy and kept the provinces as weak as or weaker than the central government.

The Kurds were most vocal and successful in realizing their demands for regional powers as they sought to protect their de-facto autonomous status. In fact, many Kurds openly stated their desire to press beyond autonomy and establish an independent state. The old regime had waged a brutal campaign against the Kurds in the 1980s, culminating in chemical weapons attacks on the city of Hallabjah in 1988. Additionally, Saddam used an "Arabization" campaign and moved Arabs into the Kurdish north, especially around Kirkuk, to dilute Kurdish influence in the area. After the instatement of a northern no-fly zone after the 1991 Gulf War, the Kurdish north was able to rule itself and establish state-like institutions. After 1997, the Kurds also were able to sell their oil independently, reaping 13 percent of the total Iraqi revenue.[38] These factors played strongly into the Kurds' longing for continued autonomy and suspicion of a central government in Baghdad.

Fears of Kurdish secession fueled Sunnis' opposition to federalization and decentralization. Even as Kurdish politicians negotiated on the premise of remaining in a united Iraq, an unofficial referendum in early 2004 demonstrated that the Kurds almost unanimously desired independence. The status of the disputed city of Kirkuk and its oil-rich environs further complicated the picture. Mustafa Barzani, a famous Kurdish leader and father of one of the Kurds' two main contemporary politicians, declared long ago that he was willing to allow U.S. development of the Kirkuk area's oil fields if the United States in turn supported his claims on Kirkuk. In the 2005 analysis of two political scientists, "the Iraqi Arabs had reason to believe that, given the Kurdish links to the United States and Israel, handing Kirkuk to the Kurds, in effect, would be giving it and its rich oil reserves to the United States and Israel."[39] The status of this divided city may well fuel sectarian conflict in the coming days.

The status of Kirkuk was addressed in the TAL, if only to put off resolution of the thorny issue until later. Article 58 of the TAL calls for various measures to remedy the injustices of Saddam's Arabization campaign, to include resettlement or compensation, as well as readjustment of administrative boundaries. There was then to be a census and a final resolution of the issue. All of these particulars were vaguely treated in the TAL. The permanent constitution continued deferment of the solution, simply stating that "the Executive Authority shall undertake the necessary steps to complete the implementation of the requirements of all subparagraphs of Article 58" of the TAL. The constitution stipulated that there shall be "normalization and census" in the region, culminating in a referendum that was to be completed by December 31, 2007, to decide whether the Kirkuk area will be associated with the Kurdish region, or will remain separate.[40]

Although the issue of Kirkuk loomed through 2007, a deferment of the referendum on its status has delayed any explosions until sometime in the future. To the end of 2008, there was little fighting between Iraq's well-developed Kurdish forces and the various Sunni and Shi'a militias. The eventual decision on the status of the divided city of Kirkuk threatens to change that situation. The issue of Kirkuk's sectarian "identity" is a point of great contention. Kurds feel strongly that Kirkuk should be part of their larger region. Kurdish leader Mustafa Barzani stated in a June 1973 interview with the *Washington Post* that the oil in the Kirkuk fields was the sole property of the Kurds and offered the U.S. oil concessions if it would help to protect the Kurds from the government in Baghdad. Kurdish politicians have referred to the city as "our Jerusalem." At the same time, the other Iraqi groups scrambled to ensure that their constituents were not expelled or mistreated, all the while maintaining a claim over the region and its resources, as the Kurds attempted to exert their influence over the contested city. Fears abound that Kirkuk may be the flashpoint at which the Kurds, the Shi'a, and the Sunni all come into open warfare.[41]

Religion also played into appeals for federalism. Some Shi'a politicians called for provisions for a Shi'a super-region in the eleventh hour of the negotiations. On August 11, 2005, SCIRI's Abd al-Aziz al-Hakim laid out a vision for a Shi'a region of nine provinces in the south, labeling this a "sacred" goal. When faced with the new demand, a Sunni politician explained, "We interpreted this as an Iranian push." Many of the motives behind these actions lie in Iraq's troubled past. Shi'a have long seen the revenues from the oil under their lands distributed to Sunni areas while their southern areas were poor and neglected. Of course, in a new Iraq they desire more control over the revenues derived from their resources and for their region to benefit. They also aspire for local control to ensure that they can allocate resources in a manner consistent with their religious and cultural principles. Sunnis, conversely, fear these super-regions will shut them off from governance, resources, and services, eventually leaving Sunni Iraq with nothing.[42]

A Kurdish northern region and a Shi'a southern region would control nearly all of Iraq's oil resources, leaving Sunnis with a barren shell of a region. The majority of Iraq's oil reserves lie in the Shi'a south. Basra alone holds 59 percent of Iraq's reserves. Together, the Shi'a-dominated provinces of Nasiriya, Maysan, and Basra hold 79.4 billion barrels of reserves, constituting 71 percent of Iraq's oil. The heavily disputed Kirkuk region holds approximately 12 percent of Iraq's reserves, although the supergiant Kirkuk field is nearing the end of its life, meaning that extraction will become increasingly difficult. The three predominately Kurdish provinces have 5.9 percent of Iraq's reserves. What is more, the southern oil fields accounted for 85 percent of total Iraqi production in 2005, due in part to the greater stability in the south and the higher incidence of insurgent sabotage in the north. Critically, the Sunni-dominated areas are virtually devoid of oil. Anbar Province has no active or proven oil fields. Salah al-din has 2.5 percent and Diyala only 0.6 percent of Iraq's reserves.[43]

Although new oil discoveries could change the geopolitical situation over the long term, there are no oil resources immediately at hand in western Iraq. Providing hope for future development in the Sunni regions, the consulting company IHS Incorporated announced in May 2007 the first detailed analysis of Iraqi oil reserves since the invasion. IHS conjectured that the Western Desert could hold up to one hundred billion barrels of oil.[44] If these estimates prove to be even remotely true, they will provide the Sunni lands with more than enough resources for self-sufficiency; however, the political fate of Iraq will be decided before such developments take hold.

If Iraq breaks up, it appears that the Sunnis would be left with nothing, at least in the short term. The ambiguity of key constitutional articles did little to assuage these fears. The constitution mandated that oil and gas revenues must be distributed

> in a fair manner in proportion to the population distribution in all parts of the country with a set allotment for a set time for the damaged regions that were unjustly deprived by the former regime and the regions that were damaged later on, and in a way that assures balanced development in different areas of the country, and this will be regulated by law.[45]

Another article stipulated, "Regions and governorates shall be allocated an equitable share of the national revenues sufficient to discharge its responsibilities and duties, but having regard to its resources, needs and the percentage of the population."[46] These clauses were the source of much controversy in Iraq since they seemed to justify steering money away from the Sunni areas, as will be addressed below.

Iraq's oil resources were subject to strong central control by previous regimes; therefore, discerning oil production and reserves on a governorate basis was never an important issue. In light of the new constitutional provisions for more decentralized control and distribution of oil resources, determining "ownership" of the various fields is likely to cause acrimony. While both the interim and permanent constitutions addressed the control and distribution of Iraq's oil wealth, these documents did not broach the technical, yet critical, subject of determining exactly where fields are situated with respect to provincial borders. These determinations will be the subject of political dispute as technocrats attempt to determine the exact lie of fields that cross over political boundaries.[47]

In the end, the Kurds were given the right to maintain their existing region by article 116 of the constitution. The constitution also required the National Assembly to enact "a law that defines the executive procedures to form regions, by a simple majority" within six months of its first session. Governorates may request regional status by the voice of one-third of the council members or one-tenth of the voters of each affected governorate, leaving the door open for further regionalization of Iraq.[48]

Besides fueling the federalism debate, religion continued to provide difficulties as it had during the drafting of the TAL. The vast majority of Iraqis are Muslims, yet their views on the position of religion in government vary between sects. Many Shi'a politicians supported a strong role for Islam in government. Sunnis, both Arab and Kurd, and Christians were more wary of Shi'a religious dominance of politics, which posed the threat of Shi'a religious hegemony and Iranian-style theocracy in Iraq. One Kurdish woman explained the problem with great clarity. "If it is an Islamic government, there will be divisions between religions. The religion doesn't create this division, but the people in power use it to create divisions."[49]

Many Shi'a interviewed by the National Democratic Institute shortly after the invasion were convinced that Islamic democracy was the way ahead for their country. Although different lines of reasoning were used to express why Islamic democracy was the best solution, a major problem in sorting these views out is divining what principles of Islam are being referenced. It is common among both Westerners and Muslims to refer to the teachings of Islam as if they are universally understood and interpreted. As with all religions, Islam is interpreted in a variety of ways. Islamic democracy can mean a fully functioning liberal democracy to one person and to another a fundamentalist regime in which everyone is "free" to live by a narrowly interpreted set of prescriptions at pain of physical punishment or death. Despite the positions of clerics and politicians, a focus-group interviewer in the summer of 2005 found that "a majority of focus group participants . . . say that religion, specifically *Sharia* [Islamic law], should be an important influence, but not the only one." Furthermore, the minority Arab Sunnis and Kurds articulated strong desires for the constitution to provide for religious freedom.[50]

A critical debate in the negotiations for both the TAL and the permanent constitution regarded a difference of only one word. While Islamists, especially Shi'a Islamist politicians, argued for the text to read that Islam was "*the* fundamental source of legislation" for Iraq, others insisted that it should be "*a* fundamental source." In the end, the semantics of the constitution set forth wide room for interpretation. Article 2 of Iraq's constitution designates Islam as the official religion of the state and "a fundamental source of legislation." The first sub-articles state that "no law that contradicts the established provisions of Islam" or "the principles of democracy may be established."[51]

Without enumeration of these provisions and principles, the wording of the article, like many others, opened the subject to later interpretation and debate. The wording did not provide the guarantees or peace of mind that could lead to a de-escalation of apprehension and tension between Iraq's various blocs. While more precise wording would have been impossible to pin down given the timeline and actors involved, these vague clauses reinforced the minority's fears and emboldened radical or majority segments to press hardline positions.

Some argue that Sunni fears regarding federalism, oil, and religion may have been overcome had more time been given to the negotiating process. Additionally, experienced Sunni constitutional lawyers were excluded from the drafting process, further alienating the Sunni sector of the population. Perhaps these technical experts could have convinced the Sunni population that federalism is a means for protecting the interests of Iraq's communities. This was certainly not the understanding many Sunnis had of federalism. In interviews conducted by the United Nations Office for Project Services, 51.7 percent of Sunnis contacted believed that federalism would lead to a division of Iraq and 46.8 percent believed it would lead to civil war. United States Institute of Peace scholar Jonathan Morrow points to similar misunderstandings in the Shi'a population a year earlier. These misunderstandings were generally corrected by "several months of Shi'a strategizing on constitutional matters."[52] Perhaps more time could have convinced Sunnis to support provisions of federalism.

The Sunnis were also put at a disadvantage in terms of capacity and capability to compete with the more established Shi'a and Kurdish parties and positions. Because of the short timeline, the Sunnis were unable to coalesce behind a coherent constitutional position. In Morrow's eyes, this "further isolated and radicalized Sunni Arab positions." To worsen matters, Sunnis were certain that the Shi'a and Kurds were making deals and decisions behind closed doors, leaving the Sunnis out of the process.[53] Former ambassador and Iraq expert Peter Galbraith blamed many of these problems on the firm deadline that the TAL set for the constitution's completion. "By insisting on the deadline, there wasn't time to work out the differences. . . . And there was no opportunity for the public to participate . . . . You have another constitution written in secret" like the TAL.[54]

Iraq's constitutional draft was completed at the eleventh hour. After twice surreptitiously extending the August 15 deadline stipulated by the TAL, negotiators announced a completed draft on August 22. The United States and supporters of the constitution in Iraq greeted the draft with fanfare; however, both Sunnis and Shi'a radicals attacked the product. Negotiators continued to hash over the document and consider changes and other deals up until the referendum. One last concession from Shi'a and Kurdish negotiators may have saved the constitution from a Sunni veto. On October 12, the Iraqi Islamic Party (IIP), the Sunnis' largest political party, was able to gain concessions from Shi'a and Kurdish negotiators that a committee would be formed after the December elections to address possible amendments. This mechanism was laid out in article 142 of the constitution, added at the last minute. The article stipulates that the committee would announce its recommendations for amendments within four months of the seating of the assembly. These amendments were then to be presented for national referendum within two months of the committee's completion. The amendments were to be considered as a bloc. A majority yes vote would approve all amendments, though no amendment could be approved separately from the others. Only after this concession was granted did the IIP urge its followers to participate in the referendum and vote for the constitution.[55] The Sunnis sought this concession in hopes that they could capitalize on larger numbers in the National Assembly after the December general elections specifically to readdress the issue of federalism. The concession may well have saved the constitution from veto, yet there has been little movement on constitutional amendments since the election, fueling Sunni discontent with the political process.

Iraq's constitutional referendum was held on October 15, 2005, and was a close-run contest, with nearly ten million Iraqis turning out to vote. The final results suggest a lopsided victory for the new constitution, with 78.59 percent of votes being cast for acceptance of the draft. In light of the veto clause, however, the draft squeaked by with only the smallest margin. Three provinces witnessed majority votes against the constitution, and one province was almost equally split. Of these, two provinces surpassed the two-thirds rejection threshold stipulated in article 61 of the TAL. Had one more province passed this threshold, the constitution would have been scuttled. Anbar Province residents voted 96.96 percent against the draft. Salahaddeen Province cast an 81.75 percent vote against. Although Ninewa Province residents voted 55.08 percent against the draft, this number fell below the two-thirds threshold and allowed the constitution to be ratified.[56] The close-run vote caused many Sunnis to cry foul and turn to a number of conspiracy theories to explain how they had been cheated out of their veto right. Though this was hardly the ringing endorsement that would bring the Sunnis decidedly into the official political process, Iraq had a new constitution.

The weak central government resulting from the constitution, its lukewarm endorsement, and the elections that ensued enshrined the diffusion of state powers that occurred when the old regime collapsed. Iraq's local powers reigned triumphant at the expense of national unity. Perhaps the most tragic aspect of this diffusion of power was that it deprived the central government of its ability to handle the growing sectarian violence and reduced the political sphere from a potential arena of national unity to a fighting ground for dividing the spoils of Iraq.

The December 2005 Election and Iraq's Permanent Government

Time was short between the October 15 referendum and the December 15 general election. Final arrangements and official announcements for the election stretched well into the month of December. While the December vote involved many more Sunni voters than did the one in January, Shi'a dominance was unaffected. Disgruntled Iraqis of all backgrounds hoped that people would vote for a new set of politicians the second time around, but the major parties were too well established. The same cast of parties and blocs dominated and, once elected, wasted precious months in haggling over key positions within the government. By the time the government was seated and began to work, the political process had been all but overwhelmed by rising sectarian violence.

The final regulation regarding the allocation of assembly seats was issued on December 6, little over a week before the election. The regulation allocated 230 seats to be decided at the governorate level, with the remaining 45 slated as compensatory and national seats. The 230 governorate seats were allocated proportionally to the governorates based on the numbers of registered voters (food-ration card holders) in each governorate. The governorate seats were to be issued in proportion to the votes received by governorate lists. If a political party did not win any governorate seats, but received enough national votes to rise above a calculated threshold, then compensatory seats would be awarded. In actuality, only one such seat was awarded. Finally, national seats would then be allocated to the political parties that won governorate seats, based on their national vote totals.[57] For example, candidates for the UIA won 109 seats in various governorates and their combined national total of votes allowed them to take an additional 19 seats from the national seat quota. According to the approved constitution, the resultant National Assembly sits for a four-year term and is responsible for establishing the Presidency Council, selecting the prime minister, and choosing the cabinet.

Realizing their error in boycotting the January elections, Sunnis participated heavily in the December vote. In addition to the lessons of their earlier mistake, the Sunnis were also encouraged by the new electoral system. The allocation of governorate seats guaranteed that Sunnis would be represented with a minimum block of seats proportional to their numbers in several, mainly Sunni provinces.[58] Sunni leaders, many of whom had not yet seen a copy of the disputed constitution, clamored for the text, even asking U.S. military patrols for copies to distribute.

Despite the different electoral methods, the voting still fell almost exclusively along ethno-sectarian lines. The local strength of ethno-sectarian lists, the coincidence of provincial and ethno-sectarian borders, the security situation, and the various difficulties of nation-wide campaigning on such a short timeline all worked against the prospects of uniting Iraqis behind any national list based on issues rather than identity. Moreover, campaigning hit on many issues prone to contribute to sectarian tensions, including federalism and Kurdish autonomy, Shi'a-Iranian ties, sectarian death squads, and the creation of a Shi'a super-region. Thus, instead of being a nationally unifying event, the elections further factionalized Iraqi politics along confessional lines.[59]

On December 15, 2005, twelve million voters, 77 percent of those registered, turned out to select their state's permanent government. The Sunni provinces of Salahaddeen and Anbar saw turnouts of 98 and 86 percent respectively. These impressive figures were up from 29 and 2 percent turnout for the January elections. Together, the three Kurdish provinces boasted the highest voter turnouts, with 92 percent in Dohuk, 95 percent in Erbil, and 84 percent in Suleymania. The Shi'a provinces averaged a lower, but respectable, 71 percent. Baghdad came in at 70 percent. By contrast, the U.S. presidential elections of 2004 witnessed a turnout of 60.7 percent, the highest in the States since 1968. The Iraqi election was the subject of both high participation and close observation by international authorities.[60]

The Shi'a UIA won 128 seats, making it the most powerful bloc once again. The "Kurdistan Alliance" gained a total of 53 seats, coming in as the second largest force, and the Sunni Arab "Iraqi Accord Front" won 44 seats. The secular "Iraqi National List" won only 25 seats. The remaining groups were all based on identity.[61]

The success of the Shi'a in remaining united under one list ensured Shi'a majority control of the government. Al-Sistani stressed the importance of Shi'a unity and voter turnout, even telling women that it was their duty to vote regardless of whether their husband wanted them to or not. To encourage women to go to the polls, he invoked the powerful image of Zaynab, the sister of Husain, riding into battle. In a statement released just days before the election, al-Sistani emphasized the necessity of "both men and women to participate widely" in the elections, warning followers to "avoid splitting [their] votes and subjecting them to loss." Pictures of al-Sistani had been used in UIA campaign materials for the January 2005 elections, though he clarified before the December elections that he did not support any political faction within the Shi'a bloc, only peaceful political involvement and Shi'a unity.[62] Al-Sistani was a primary driving force behind Shi'a unity, yet unity only went so far.

The UIA was far from being a monolithic bloc. SCIRI leader al-Hakim was the most vociferous politician in the UIA, and SCIRI ended up with the largest bloc of seats in the list; however, this was only 23 percent of the UIA's seats. The list also included the al-Da'wa Party, the al-Da'wa Party Iraqi Organization, Iraqi *Hizb Allah*, and two Turkoman movements. Al-Da'wa and its splinter group consisted of 20 percent of the bloc. Loyalists of Muqtada al-Sadr won 22 percent of the UIA's seats. The Fadhila Party, followers of the Sadr legacy, but not of Muqtada himself, made up another 13 percent of the list. The remaining seats were filled by independents.[63]

A closer look at how seats were allocated within the UIA gives insight into the list's dynamics. The list won 109 governorate seats, plus an additional 19 national seats, based on the overall vote total. When the governorate seats were allocated sequentially to the members of the UIA list, Muqtada al-Sadr's supporters were the largest bloc at 23 percent. The two al-Da'wa parties received 23 percent combined. SCIRI won only 19 percent. Although the method of allocation of the 19 national seats was not set by law, the most representative method would be to maintain the same proportion as in the governorate seats. Instead, the UIA gave nearly half of its national seats to SCIRI, bringing them to parity with the Sadrists. While it is impossible to determine whether this was a pre-agreed formula or the product of a SCIRI power grab, like many other political decisions in Iraq, it was made with little transparency and apparent disregard of the voters' wishes.[64]

The Kurdistan Alliance gained the second largest bloc of seats (fifty-three), owing to the Kurds ability to create a unity coalition and produce the highest turnout of any of the Iraqi ethno-sectarian groups. Similar to the UIA, however, the Kurdistan Alliance was not monolithic. The alliance was the product of the ability of the two towering figures of Kurdish politics, Masaoud Barzani and Jalal Talabani, to put aside their differences and run on one list. Barzani's Kurdish Democratic Party (KDP) and Talabani's Patriotic Union of Kurdistan (PUK) had come into open conflict in the past and physically controlled separate areas of the Kurdish autonomous region. Despite their past differences, however, the parties' similar short-term goals of ensuring Kurdish rights and autonomy under a federal arrangement made the Kurdistan Alliance a powerful bloc.[65]

Two lists, the Iraqi Accord Front (IAF) and the Iraqi National Dialogue Front (INDF), represented the Sunnis. The IAF showed more power by garnering forty-four seats. IAF was not founded until October 26, 2005, which demonstrated the last-minute nature of Sunni political organization. It included one of the oldest Sunni political parties, the Iraqi Islamic Party (IIP). The party was instituted in 1960 and operated in secrecy until the fall of the Ba'ath regime in 2003. The IIP first re-emerged in Mosul, where it undertook charity and public service projects, much like the Shi'a religious groups discussed earlier. This party may have tipped the scale in favor of the constitutional draft offered for the October 2005 elections when it called for Sunnis to vote yes. The IIP went on to become the largest Sunni party in the permanent National Assembly and one of Iraq's vice presidents, Tariq al-Hashimi, came from this bloc. According to the "Guide of Iraqi Parties," published in an Iraqi newspaper in December 2005, even the IAF "considers itself a peaceful extension of the resistance and this Front consists of tribal sheikhs and former officers [of the Iraqi forces]."[66]

The other Sunni list, the INDF, which gained eleven seats, was more vitriolic. A main figure of the INDF was Saleh Mutlak, who described his political program as resembling that of the armed resistance, but without arms. Mutlak founded the Iraqi National Dialogue Council in April 2005 as one of the first serious Sunni political groupings to engage in the new order. Mutlak became a member of the constitutional drafting committee, though in the end he campaigned against the draft before the October 2005 referendum. Because the Iraqi National Dialogue Council aligned with the INDF, which supported the new constitution, Mutlak left the Iraqi National Dialogue Council and ran as part of the INDF in the December 2005 national elections.[67]

The Iraqi National List was the only politically secular, non-sectarian list to make a significant showing, winning twenty-five seats to make it the fourth-largest bloc. The major names of the list were Adnan Pachachi and Ayad Allawi.

The list included the Iraqi Communist Party, a longstanding Iraqi political opposition force, as well as a number of titular democratic parties. The other major politically secular list in the election was the Iraqi National Council, led by Ahmed Chalabi.[68] Chalabi was a major driver behind regime change in 2003, yet by 2005 a series of scandals ranging from accusations of fraud to sharing sensitive information about U.S. intelligence efforts with Iran had severely tarnished his image. Once expecting to triumphantly ride the wave of the American-led invasion to the halls of government in Iraq, Chalabi watched as his list failed to win a single seat in the election.

Despite the clear victory for identity politics, the establishment of a government and several other significant votes required a two-thirds majority. Thus, the list members were, at times, forced to cooperate across identity lines in government. Dawisha and Diamond also noted that "while the various party lists seem to be fairly cohesive on matters of identity, they differ within themselves on other issues."[69] The requirement for coalition-making and the experience of four years of governing produced some weakening of blocs, but no new coalitions by mid-2008.

For the time being, Iraq has a defined official political process. It has been agreed on by most major actors and has resulted in relatively peaceful elections. Yet the resulting government presided over a near miss with all-out civil war. While sectarianism was surely a factor in the divvying-up of ministries in the wake of the identity referendum that the national elections became, the truth is more complicated. The ministries became "fiefdoms" of multiple sectarian parties more than purely sectarian institutions. While this made little difference in the incitement of sectarian violence, it is important to realize that the sectarian blocs are far from monolithic.[70]

The Official Political Process at Work

It took months for Iraq's elected politicians to form a cabinet to govern Iraq. Ibrahim al-Jafari, an al-Da'wa member and the UIA candidate for prime minister, was seen as too strongly linked to Tehran and ineffectual at any rate. His candidacy met strong opposition from the national assembly's other sectors, which produced a months-long standoff. Near the end of April 2006, the UIA replaced al-Jafari with Nouri al-Maliki, another longstanding member of the al-Da'wa Party. Al-Maliki proved to be sufficiently acceptable. The parties spent the next several weeks wrangling over the ministerial spoils before agreement was reached and the formation of the government was announced on May 20, 2006.[71] While this government has been called a government of national unity, the reality of politics under the al-Maliki government has been far from uniting.

Despite numerous security plans instituted throughout 2006, the government and its American supporters were unable to get a handle on the spiraling internecine violence. One of the most difficult topics for Iraqi politicians to cope with in this environment was the debate on federalism. Although Sunni representatives resisted further moves toward federalism, a strange alliance of SCIRI and the Kurds aggressively pushed the issue. The most bellicose politician on this front was SCIRI leader Abd al-Aziz al-Hakim of the UIA. In September 2006, al-Hakim attempted, but initially failed, to push a bill through the assembly that would provide a legal basis for the Shiʻa provinces to create an autonomous region in the south. While Sunnis were naturally opposed to the bill, even large portions of al-Hakim's own UIA failed to back his bid, demonstrating the nuances of Iraqi politics.

The SCIRI push was a plan for a Shiʻa super-region consisting of up to nine provinces. SCIRI had fared especially well in the January 2005 provincial elections, leaving the group in control of all the southern provinces except Maysan and Basra. Furthermore, it controlled local security forces and the Ministry of the Interior forces, which it used, according to many accusations, to further tilt the political playing field in its favor. With such power, SCIRI felt that it could run a massive southern province that included not only the two powerful, money-making shrine cities of Najaf and Karbala, but also Basra, its ports, and its massive oil wealth. Yet, other parties of the UIA were highly opposed to such an idea. The Fadhila Party and Muqtada al-Sadr, specifically, wanted no part of a Shiʻa super-region. Even though this was overtly explained with reasonable nationalist language, al-Sadr was still at a deficit as he attempted to expand his offices across Shiʻa Iraq and Fadhila was comfortably ensconced in the jewel of Basra, though in no position to contest SCIRI for control of a greater region. Al-Daʻwa was likewise against the SCIRI plan and its rough handling of the agenda.

Internal conflict over the federalism issue was driven by the competing ambitions and differing geographic locations of the parties' bases of support. As tensions grew, the hostility simmered behind closed doors, according to UIA sources. Muqtada al-Sadr's followers and the smaller Fadhila Party joined Sunnis in rivaling al-Hakim's move. This stance pulled the rug out from under al-Hakim's proposal, if only for a short while. On the federalism issue, SCIRI and the Kurdish parties were opposed by a coalition of Sadrists, Sunnis, and secular parties.[72] Not all the fault lines in Iraq fell along sectarian divisions, although at the same time, grand nationalist language is often a cover for narrower political calculations.

For example, Fadhila played a beautiful hand, denouncing SCIRI's maneuvering and later withdrawing from the UIA in objection to sectarian politicking, but all the while eyeing the prize of Basra. In the economic keystone of a "Shiastan," Fadhila occupied the governor's office, the chairmanship of the provincial council, a large portion of the police, and provided the security forces and other key positions for Basra's Southern Oil Company. Unsurprisingly, Fadhila called for a federalism model in which Basra could stand on its own. In the words of Aqeel Talib, a senior Fadhila official, "We want to make our province our own region. We have two million people, an airport, a port and oil—everything we need to be a state."[73]

Regardless, the federalism law was not long delayed. In a parliamentary session boycotted by the Sunni IAF as well as the Fadhila and Sadr parties, the remaining representatives voted unanimously to pass a law outlining the mechanics of federalism. This came only after an agreement that implementation of any further regions would be delayed for eighteen months (until April 2008). This stripped down vote demonstrated the SCIRI-Kurdish alliance that really drove the government. The voting coalition claimed that 140 representatives of the 275-member assembly were present for the vote, over the 138-member requirement for a quorum. Sunnis, however, accused their counterparts of fudging the count and pushing the vote through against parliamentary procedures. In return, SCIRI's al-Hakim labeled them as "Saddamists, Baathists, and Takfiris [Sunni Islamist extremists]."[74]

This vote was not purely sectarian. Several Shi'a parties stood by the Sunnis in fighting the measure. Yet, Sunnis as a whole were of the opinion that they were being wrongly excluded from a say in government. Al-Hakim's dismissal of them as terrorists only rubbed salt in the wounds. Many Sunnis felt that, in the face of a SCIRI-Kurdish alliance and an increasingly hostile cast of Shi'a militias, they were to be a perpetually dominated minority. Donald Horowitz, an expert on ethnic conflict, explained how ethnic democratic politics can quickly become perpetual majority domination. If after an election

> the majority and minority are fixed rather than fluid, because each thinks of itself as a group defined by birth and possessing affinities and interests

not shared across group lines . . . two consequences follow. Parties that span group lines will be difficult to organize, and . . . alternation in office is highly improbable. The textbook case of democratic majority rule turns quickly into a case of egregious minority exclusion. In ethnically divided societies, majority rule is not a solution; it is a problem, because it permits domination, apparently in perpetuity.

Perpetual domination seems especially likely to Sunnis because numerous (but not all) Shi'a leaders have announced on several occasions that they have no intentions of allowing any changes to the constitution.[75]

While the Sadrists were joined with Sunnis in opposing the SCIRI plan, they were also engaged in a sectarian war of the streets, negating any opportunity for broader sectarian cooperation. In 2007 and 2008, though, there was a glimmer of hope for greater cooperation across group lines; however, powerful cross-sectarian parties seem to still be a long way off. These uncompromising positions gave Sunnis little incentive to come more fully into the political arena.

In February 2006, Sunni leaders devised an unofficial list of eight points on which they desired changes to the constitution. Five key points caused great acrimony. First, Sunnis desired that moves toward federalism should be delayed for a period of time to allow the country to stabilize. Second, they argued for national ownership of Iraq's natural resources, managed and distributed by the central government, a point that was hotly contested by both the Kurds and some Shi'a. Third, Sunnis wanted a clause stating that Iraqi armed forces and security services would consist of all Iraqis, regardless of sect or ethnicity. In a fourth, related point, they desired a repeal of the de-Ba'athification articles (7 and 135), which they viewed as a legal tool for their exclusion from key government posts. Legislation was passed to reverse some de-Ba'athification measures, yet Sunnis questioned its effectiveness. In any case, the measure did not give the finality of a constitutional amendment. Finally, they argued that Kirkuk should not be annexed to any region, a red line with the Kurds. At the bottom line, the constitution came out largely as desired by the ruling Shi'a and the Kurds, and amending it along all of the points desired by the Sunni will prove to be a non-starter. A constitutional amendment committee was formed in September 2006, but it missed a December 2007 deadline due to gridlock between the parties and was granted a six-month extension. The attitude of the committee's chair, a member of SCIRI, made it clear that reconciliation was not a major concern in any case. "What is there to reconcile? Sunnis are unwilling to acknowledge their minority status and act accordingly." By the end of 2008, though the committee had progressed on largely technical issues, it was still unable to come to consensus on the key issues.[76]

While Iraq's official political process offers the only hope for avoiding violent conflict, it also contributed to the animosity that nearly plunged the land into civil war. It is still unclear whether Iraq's political bosses have looked into the abyss and blinked, or if the gains made in 2007 and 2008 were only a temporary respite. Success in Iraq will require many years of delicate political work and will be impossible without greater and more permanent cross-ethno-sectarian cooperation for the good of the nation, rather than more narrow agendas. Groups within Iraq must come to terms with each other and find acceptable, second-best solutions that they can all live with regarding the gamut of contentious issues that have been discussed. This consensus-building effort will require many compromises and probably painful reshaping of political alliances. The key will be convincing the involved parties to work within the democratic and constitutional rules of the game, rather than choosing to defect through means of violence or secession. Even once this choice is made, the nation will still have an extremely long row to hoe in order to create a productive and self-sustaining socio-economic entity. This entity can only happen if the violence that engulfed Iraq between 2003 and 2007 can be curbed long enough for lasting political progress to be made, which is no sure thing. The specter of civil war, though, may have been the impetus Iraq's politicians needed to slowly begin exceeding their sectarian bounds.

8
Iraq Looks into the Abyss of Civil War

This is the wounded human material out of which a new order in Iraq has to be fashioned. The poison of Sunni-Shi'i sectarianism, and of Arab-Kurdish bitterness, either one of which is enough to kill Iraq, are today working together to tear the country apart. The division of the country is being acted out in people's hearts, before it is played out on the ground at the cost of untold numbers of new Iraqi dead.[1]
—KANAN MAKIYA, IRAQI EXILE AUTHOR, 1993

I'm living here in the middle of shit, a civil war will happen I'm sure of it. . . . You can't be comfortable talking with a man until you know if he is Shia or Sunni. . . . People don't trust each other. . . . Now Shia are Iranians for the Sunni, and Sunni are Salafi terrorists for the Shia.[2]
—SUNNI BAGHDADI, 2006

In the years after the fall of Baghdad, the eyes of the world focused on the Sunni insurgency in Iraq. All along, however, the greatest danger for Iraq was the lurking specter of sectarian violence and civil war that Kanan Makiya perceived as far back as 1993. Despite Sunni insurgents' efforts, most notably Abu Musab al-Zarqawi's al Qaeda in Iraq, Shi'a leaders were highly successful in preventing sectarian reprisals until February 2006, when a bomb destroyed the al-Askariyya Shrine in Samarra, the resting place of the revered tenth and eleventh Shi'a Imams and one of the holiest Islamic sites in the world. Sectarian violence soared, turning Iraq, and especially Baghdad, into a killing ground. In

2009, it seems that the vast majority of Iraqis have recoiled at the thought of sectarian civil war, though it only takes a minority to re-ignite chaos.

Sectarian tension and mistrust was present prior to the invasion and grew quickly thereafter; outright sectarian war, however, was never a foregone conclusion. Even Iraq's most bellicose actors were loath to stir the sectarian pot prior to 2006. Although Shi'a radicals such as Muqtada al-Sadr and die-hard supporters of Sunni resistance such as Harith al-Dhari spewed vitriol at the occupiers and their Iraqi collaborators, they also extended a hand across sectarian lines in mutual disdain of the greater enemy. Ayatollah Sistani vehemently denounced sectarian violence and many Iraqis called for national unity. While hatred was not a common theme, mistrust was, and that was all that was needed for terrorists to kick off a wave of sectarian violence that nearly tore the country apart.

Once started, the violence escalated as reprisal and counter-reprisal brought ever-greater levels of barbarity. For a time, Iraq teetered on the brink of civil war, yet it appears that the majority of Iraqis looked into the abyss and blinked. The violence that gripped Iraq in 2006 and 2007 was not purely sectarian, however. Every tortured body that was found, every militia attack, and every bombing was attributed to sectarian hatred. There is no denying that countless killings were motivated by sect as the violence of Sunni extremists and Shi'a death squads seeking vengeance against Ba'athists spread. This narrative, however, covered up a much more complex truth. The work of murderous robbers and organized crime figures could not be differentiated from sectarian reprisals. Political violence was also a contributor to the toll, as militias and their parties jostled for control of territory and power, particularly in the Shi'a world. Iraq's divisions are not as straightforward as they may seem.

The division between the sects has dominated Iraqi politics and the discourse on Iraq since the fall of Saddam. Though there was ample fuel for sectarian violence in Iraq, the core of national identity and unity was present to a certain degree as well. A wide-ranging series of focus-group discussions with Iraqis conducted in the summer of 2003 determined Iraqi national identity to be stronger than many expected. Interviewers asked the respondents to choose the title that best identified them from a list that included Iraqi, Arab or Kurd, Muslim, member of a family or tribe, or Sunni, Shi'a, or Christian. The leading response was "Iraqi." Even many of those who supported apparently sectarian insurgent attacks distinguished between attacking rival political parties and militias and attacking civilians based on sect. A resident of Baquba stated that "targeting the Shiites at large, rather than the Shiite parties that came atop American tanks, was . . . unpopular."[3]

Even the political groups that openly supported the insurgency had little stomach for sectarian violence. The Association of Muslim Scholars (AMS) built its position around outright hostility to the foreign occupation and believed that Sunnis should rule Iraq; AMS, however, was not openly hostile to the Shi'a and disparaged sectarianism as an organizing principle of politics. In a February 2005 statement addressing a number of topics, the group, in association with other members of the resistance, called for the end of ethno-sectarianism in favor of nationalism and legal equality. Though the AMS and its allies supported violent resistance to the occupation, they also refuted the "terrorism that targets innocent Iraqis and the establishments and institutions for the public good, and the targeting of places of worship to include mosques, *husseiniyas* [Shi'a religious centers], churches, and all holy places."[4]

Throughout the post-invasion period, Iraqi identity remained strong. Sectarian violence created fear and suspicion among Iraqis, yet it also produced a backlash and an emphasis on Iraqi identity in many of the innocent citizens caught between the extremes. Demonstrating the complexity of the issue, Sunni and Shi'a residents of the al-Ghazalia neighborhood of Baghdad were forced into segregation by sectarian militias under threat of death. Despite these circumstances, the victims' reaction showed, according to one Iraqi blogger, "the union and love between the real Iraqis whether Shiite or Sunni because the people of al-Ghazalia have agreed on a specific square where displaced people (Shiite and Sunni) meet to exchange houses . . . how sad and how nice at the same time."[5] Many condemn the sectarian violence and call for Iraqi unity. Iraqi nationalism is incredibly important to Iraq's future. Outside of Kurdistan, most Iraqis believe in a united Iraq, yet they are at odds over who should control that Iraq and were forced to retreat into a sectarian-Iraqi identity to protect themselves during the height of the violence. Even within the sectarian communities, power brokers have frequently resorted to armed conflict, or the threat of it, to advance their political standing. While the violence abated in 2008, should future unrest resurrect calls to divide Iraq, that solution may be as bloody as a battle for dominance in a unified Iraq.

The Rise of Communal Identity

As laid out in chapter 2, Iraq has a long history of sectarian tension, which has broken out into violence at times. The majority of Iraqis, however, were able to live together with few issues until 2006. Ethno-sectarian hatred was not a constant in Iraq and the brutality that occurred was never a given. Insecurity in uncertain times, political manipulation, and terrorist targeting all served to stretch sectarian relations to the breaking point.

The problem of balancing the wants and needs of various communities is not new to the Middle East, nor is it restricted to Iraq. Noted scholar of the Middle East Vali Nasr observed, "The Bush administration thought of politics as the relationship between individuals and the state, and so it failed to recognize that people in the Middle East see politics also as the balance of power among communities."[6] As noted in the last chapter, the official political process succumbed to this tendency to balance, rather than integrate, communities. Despite this balancing act and the increasing prominence of sectarian identities, an Iraqi national identity exists as well. This Iraqi identity may provide hope for the unity of Iraq, or it may simply intensify a fight over the future of what each community sees as its Iraq.

The emergence of sectarian identity during times of upheaval and crisis is to be expected. CPA staffer Noah Feldman explained that the re-emergence of old categories of identity, which may appear to be "ancient hatreds," is actually an act of self-preservation. Faced with an outside threat, people find that the "shortest and best route to self-protection" is to rely on associations based on identities such as race, ethnicity, or sect. In the absence of "an external power capable of maintaining the balance," these identity-based protective associations may spiral toward civil war, because "the uncertainty of who will dominate whom is so high." It is difficult to trust "the other" in uncertain times, especially as people feel that the other is out to kill members of their identity group. In Iraq, any new institutions of civil society that sprang up once the dictatorship was removed were far too weak and untested to be relied on for protection when institutions of primary identity were available. What is more, political leaders were more than willing to use these institutions to their advantage.[7]

Scholar of ethnic conflict Donald Horowitz put forth a similar view of the security provided by primary identity groups. "Ethnic affiliations provide a sense of security in a divided society, as well as a source of trust, certainty, reciprocal help, and protection against neglect of one's interests by strangers."[8] From this initial springboard, communal identities were further boosted by the evolution of electoral and political processes in Iraq. United Nations officials, among others, were worried early on about "'Lebanonization' of politics" where political positions were determined by ethnic and sectarian proportions. For this reason, UN experts favored providing time for the development of cross-cutting political parties based on political and economic issues rather than sect or ethnicity.[9]

A UN fact-finding mission to Iraq in February 2004 revealed that

> sectarianism is becoming entrenched and inter-communal politics more polarized, all within a context of a political process that remains limited to a few actors. . . . The competition among the elite is taking place against a backdrop of massive unemployment, particularly among a large young male population. Many interlocutors also speak of rising disillusionment and anger.

The sectarian competition was a political one, played out by close-minded elites, though they used angry and unemployed Iraqis as their foot soldiers in the high-stakes game. As governmental ministries were doled out to various Shiʿa groups, many purged their newly won ministries of non-Shiʿa employees based on security justifications and de-Baʿathification claims.[10] In this way, not only the political arena but also the institutions of government became narrow and nominally ethno-sectarian in nature. In reality, they were divided by political faction, rather than by sect. Ministries were transformed into lairs for semi-official militias and some harbored death squads.[11] Sectarian identity became a tool for making distinctions, though beneath it lay a multitude of conflicts among parties, militias, and even bloodthirsty individuals, both within and across sectarian lines.

Taking the Gloves Off

Despite Iraq's history of mixed towns and even mixed families, violence quickly opened deep rifts. While most Iraqis may not have held any deep sectarian malice prior to 2003, the armed minority that manned roving death squads and identity checkpoints drove wedges in Iraqi society. Iraqis crossing battle lines were quizzed on their identity, starting with names, which sometimes give sectarian clues; the inquisitors then looked to dress, jewelry, and even cell phone ring tones and other media to differentiate. They tested people on details of prayer and belief to root out the other. In their zealotry, they terrified innocents of both sects. Neighborhoods, and even families, that had been mixed for ages were forced into segregation by these zealots. Manal Omar, a human rights activist in Iraq, explained:

Mixed families played a crucial role in preventing civil war. Iraqis, especially in Baghdad, were very proud of the mix in their communities and the fact that Sunnis, Shiʻas, and Kurds married so frequently. Now the barrier has significantly eroded and the wheels for the civil war have already begun to turn. . . . The sad reality is that most of us still don't believe we have seen the worst yet.[12]

Numerous factors exacerbated the tensions. Iraqi media sources and political groups often published inflammatory coverage with the effect of increasing sectarian tensions between Sunnis and Shiʻa. The proliferation of satellite TV channels added fuel to the fire as partisan programming highlighted sectarian violence. The Shiʻa SCIRI party and a major Sunni party each created their own network, often spewing inflammatory commentary on violent events. In response to such exposure and in the face of random killings that were most easily labeled as sectarian violence, Iraqis were driven to move into homogenous sectarian communities in search of safety. In addition to the threat of bloodshed, the imposition of harsh Shiʻa or Sunni visions of Islamic propriety by extremists was another reason for citizens of the other sect to flee. Some departed early on, while others only evacuated their homes after an escalating series of threats. These often started when militias posted lists of families that were to vacate, followed by more pointed personal "night letters," direct and explicit warnings left on doorsteps in the middle of the night, and all too often culminated in an attack on the home or the murder of a family member.[13]

The hostility forced ordinary Iraqis to align with local sectarian militias for protection. These militias were often organized around mosques, a common target of sectarian attacks. One Sunni who was married to a Shiʻa shortly after the invasion found himself patrolling his neighborhood with other Sunnis. He explained, "We had no other choice but to protect ourselves" after numerous Sunni mosques in the area were assailed. Iraqis bought weapons in increasing numbers and at staggering prices on the black market. Reporter C. J. Chivers found weapons sellers to be ubiquitous, doing brisk business in groceries, tea shops, and the like. Western pistols commanded up to $1,800, sniper rifles were available for $1,100 to $2,000, and even the AK-47 could bring as much as $800 in parts of Iraq. A security chief in the Sulaimaniya area clarified, "Now the Sunni want the weapons because they fear the Shiʻa, and the Shiʻa want the weapons because they fear the Sunni . . . so prices go up."[14]

Even formerly upscale neighborhoods were not immune to the problem. Baghdad's famed Mansour district was home to the middle and upper class, composed of an ethno-sectarian mix of residents. In June 2006, residents warned that the posh neighborhood was "falling to the terrorists." Bombings damaged its storefronts and kidnappings targeted its affluent residents. Living only three miles from the Green Zone, residents and businessmen were forced to hire guards to protect them. While some of the violence was nominally sectarian, a business owner named Omar had a different account. When Shi'a business owners were warned to remove pictures of Shi'a saints or face retribution, he remarked, "It's all about money. The pictures are just an excuse." By January 2007, the storefronts were all but vacant as many moderate and middle-class Iraqis had been killed or chased away to safer areas or neighboring countries.[15]

Some Iraqis were relocated to refugee camps. In April 2006, Iraqi government figures put the number of displaced families at 14,000, or approximately 100,000 people, 80 percent of whom were Shi'a. By the end of July, the number had climbed to around 180,000 people. Over one week in mid-July 2006 alone, 1,117 families were forced to flee for sectarian enclaves. The majority of these families were displaced from the Baghdad area and the number seems to have risen rapidly throughout 2006. Between the bombing of the al-Askariyya Shrine in February 2006 and the end of October in the same year, the Office of the United Nations High Commissioner for Refugees (UNHCR) estimated that 418,392 people had been dislodged by sectarian violence, with another 15,000 by military operations. By the fall of 2007, up to 2.2 million Iraqis were internal refugees while as many as an additional 2.3 million had escaped the country altogether. Iraqis resorted to trading houses for de-facto segregation. One Sunni minority in a Shi'a village swapped houses with an old Shi'a friend in a Sunni town, even sharing a truck for the move. These two lived in one of the roughly twenty mixed areas around Baghdad that segregated under the pressure of the country's significant violence.[16]

In 2005, a non-governmental organization dedicated to the plight of refugees found that a total of almost 900,000 refugees had fled Iraq since 2003. Statistics suggest that this exodus shot sharply upward in 2005. By October 2006, the UNHCR put the estimate of Iraqi refugees in neighboring countries at 1.6 million. That figure had climbed to 2.2 million recognized refugees by September 2007, with the greatest population in Syria, then Jordan and Egypt. The commission stated that the exodus reached monthly totals of around 100,000 Iraqis leaving the country for the late summer and fall months of 2006.[17] Because of this exodus, Arab sports channels showed cuts of wild crowds in Amman, Jordan—not Baghdad—when the Iraqi national team won the Asia Cup in July 2007.

A poll conducted in the summer of 2006 indicated where this dislocation was mainly occurring. Fifty-one percent of Baghdad respondents personally knew someone who had been forced to move by sectarian violence, as did 38 percent of residents of the Sunni west. The violence and the segregation occurred predominately in the capital region and the outlying Sunni areas. Less than 12 percent of respondents in any other region of the country knew people who had been moved.[18]

The refugee flow slowed significantly at the end of 2007, though the numbers were still high. As many as 76,000 Iraqis were displaced monthly in the beginning of 2007; the rate slowed to just under 30,000 per month in the second half of the year. Although these figures reveal tremendous improvement, it is nonetheless a huge number of refugees. Many Iraqis outside of Iraq, faced with depleted resources, uncertain residency status abroad, and improved security in Iraq, returned to the country as well, beginning in the latter part of 2007. Those returning to the country discovered conditions to be much improved, although still harrowing.[19]

The level of barbarism in Iraq during the worst of the sectarian fighting was appalling. In May 2006, a twelve-year-old boy was abducted while walking from his home to work at his father's parking lot. His body appeared the next day, dumped in a largely Sunni district after he had been whipped with cables, tortured with electric drills, shot in the head, and dragged through the street. "This was definitely a sectarian killing," asserted the boy's uncle, a prominent Baghdad journalist.[20] With so many random killings in Iraq, the label of sectarian barbarism was simple to apply and almost impossible to refute.

Sectarian killings surged in the wake of the bombing of the Shi'a al-Askariyya Shrine in Samarra in February 2006. Undertaken by a seven-man al Qaeda cell consisting of two Iraqis, four Saudis, and a Tunisian, the attack was calculated to inflame sectarian tensions in order to cause a civil war in Iraq. Iraqi government estimates put the toll at approximately five hundred civilian deaths in the ten days following the bombing. The number of Iraqis killed in assassinations, mostly sectarian in nature, rose to four times those killed in other attacks in March. Sectarian incidents rose from around a hundred in January to four hundred and fifty in February, and then dipped to three hundred in April. The level of sectarian casualties climbed faster than the number of incidents, indicating deadlier attacks.[21]

Many of these murders were blamed on Shi'a militias that added "thousands of foot soldiers and gained new political stature" in the tense environment. The

Mahdi Army was believed to have in the vicinity of ten thousand members and the SCIRI's less vilified but equally barbarous Badr Brigades around five thousand. In addition to these large forces, there were countless local militias and neighborhood defense committees. In a country where almost every male has an AK-47 for self-defense, armed militias could form on the spot in response to a threat. For this reason, the power of the Mahdi Army was not in the full-time thugs who roamed the cities of Iraq, but in the thousands of other Iraqis who would pick up a rifle and come out into the streets when the clerics called (often through mosque loudspeakers).[22]

The CPA estimated in 2004 that there were sixty thousand to one-hundred thousand militia members belonging to nine different Shi'a and Kurdish groups across Iraq. Although the CPA recognized that the militias must be dealt with, there was little success in convincing the various leaders to disband their forces and little will to enforce any initiative that would forcibly disarm them. A prime reason for this is that most of Iraq's political bosses were backed by an armed contingent. Neutralizing these bands would have disgruntled staunch supporters and stripped political bosses of the muscle they needed in the territorial squabbles that characterized the underbelly of Iraqi politics. Many of these militias infiltrated government ministries under the aegis of political parties they supported, becoming semi-official in the process. Some Iraqis see the military and other security forces simply as a legal venue for taking revenge against other groups.[23]

The division of ministerial spoils following the elections placed single parties, and their militias, in charge of key functions. For example, Sadrists control the Health Ministry, as well as the agriculture, transport, and education portfolios. The Mahdi Army provided "security" for the Health Ministry buildings, and members of the militia were enlisted in the ranks of the ministry's official Facilities Protective Service (FPS). Sunnis alleged that FPS members frequently carried out rapes and sectarian killings at hospitals and morgues across the country, especially when Sunni family members came to claim the bodies of relatives slain in sectarian violence. FPS ranks were filled with Iraqis who had no more than a hasty three-week police-training class. Ambassador Bremer, acknowledging that these trainees were too poorly prepared for real police work, proposed that they be placed in the "Facilities Protection Service where training's less important."[24]

Even though Shi'a militias saturated the ministries, their leaders pointed the finger back at the Sunnis. A senior U.S. officer declared, "There are extremist elements of Badr and of the Mahdi Army who are using their positions in the police to carry out operations against the Sunni population." Another U.S. official observed, "The FPS has basically become a private army for the ministers. They have no accountability." Yet al-Hakim returned the blame to the Sunnis, "The problem is the Saddamists and the *takfiris*. These groups are committing genocide against the Shiite people."[25] These statements demonstrate the problems of inclusion and exclusion that Horowitz noted in ethnic majoritarian politics. The Shi'a, on the inside, blame security issues on the outsider Sunni rejectionists. The Sunnis, in turn, point the finger at the Shi'a forces within the government for barring them from the government and the state. It will be difficult to gain reconciliation from such an impasse.

Events such as a November 2006 coordinated multiple car-bomb assault on Sadr City that resulted in the deaths of more than two hundred residents and tit-for-tat killings served to empower militias such as the Mahdi Army at the expense of the national government. On the day of the Sadr City attack, the Mahdi Army came out in force to seal off the city, tend to casualties, and provide supplies to the local hospital. Within minutes, militia members had erected barricades, preventing all traffic from entering the neighborhood, and searched cars and unknown people at checkpoints. The militia succeeded in finding a seventh car filled with explosives and arresting the driver. In the days that followed, besides revenge operations, the Mahdi Army secured the funeral and memorial services and granted funds for burials. Residents' comments were telling. "The Mahdi Army are the people who helped us after the explosion. . . . They saved us." Another observed, "Yesterday was a good example of how we can handle security. Our city can protect itself better than the government." Because many Iraqi Shi'a viewed the militias as their only protector, it was impossible to disarm them before the populace felt more secure. Even Prime Minister Nouri al-Maliki said that he would not crack down on Shi'a militias as long as Sunni insurgent groups continued to pose a threat to security. Despite his stance, mourners at a memorial for the victims of the Sadr City attack shouted "coward" and "collaborator" when al-Maliki called for calm and national reconciliation. As he ignominiously drove away, his motorcade was pelted with rocks.[26]

Many killers were motivated more by greed than sectarian hatred. They could steal their victims' belongings, amassing tidy sums in short order. They used the cover of a supposed fatwa legitimating the seizure of goods of "those who oppose Ali's caliphate" to justify their activities. Some even bribed victims' families for the return of their bodies. The Mahdi Army also profited from renting seized Sunni real estate. As membership of the militia expanded and greed grew, bands took to robbing Shi'a as well. In majority Shi'a neighborhoods, the militia demanded protection money from residents to fund their activities. Many thugs in the Mahdi Army longed for Sadr's 2007 truce to be revoked so they could return to their lucrative trade. Furthermore, poor, opportunistic squatters from outside the cities took advantage of the violence to move into abandoned homes in middle-class districts. Demonstrating the complexities that are glossed over by sectarian labels, one Sunni man from the Amel neighborhood told his former Shi'a neighbor that the peasant Sunni squatters who had come to live in the neighborhood's empty Shi'a houses were "barbarian, dirty people."[27]

Sectarian violence was not limited to random acts of brutal retribution or crime. Some militias used the opportunity to expand their area of control and their political power base during the period. Mahdi Army bands made a calculated advance across the Tigris River, taking control of several Sunni neighborhoods in 2007. They were especially successful in middle-class areas, where residents had not organized militias. Through a steady encroachment into largely Sunni neighborhoods, the Mahdi Army forced the withdrawal of the Sunni Iraqi Islamic Party from its local headquarters in the Hurriya district. After a campaign of targeted sectarian killings aimed at removing Sunni businessmen and local leaders, the Sadrists set up offices to consolidate their gains. Through these methods, the Mahdi Army secured a large number of neighborhoods in the capital, even mixed middle-class areas, leaving only a few Sunni strongholds. Many of these advances were lost due to the U.S. troop surge and Sadr's truce of 2007.[28]

All eyes were turned on inter-sectarian violence, yet there was significant intra-sectarian political conflict during the same period. Shi'a parties jostled for territory and the political power and control that came with it. In Sunni areas, too, intra-sectarian violence was a significant contributor to the toll of deaths. Al Qaeda waged a campaign of assassinations against local leaders and their families. Insurgent groups turned on one another, with many siding against the global Islamist ideology of al Qaeda and its allies. These intra-sectarian splits, along with the diplomatic and military efforts of the Coalition, led to a significant change in the tenor of conflict in Iraq in 2007 and 2008. Intra-sectarian positioning resulted in the rise of Sunni tribes and urban groups against al Qaeda, in a shaky alliance with the U.S. military. At the same time, Shi'a political concerns caused Muqtada al-Sadr to declare a truce with his rivals and the Coalition. These factors created a major improvement in the security situation, but the wounds caused by Iraq's brush with civil war are far from healed.

9
Prospects for Stability, Prospects for Democracy

> Nobody says anything about turning corners, seeing lights at the ends of tunnels. You just keep your head down and keep moving.[1]
> —GENERAL DAVID PETRAEUS, COMMANDER OF COALITION FORCES IN IRAQ, DECEMBER 2007

In 2006 and 2007, while pundits and politicians debated academic definitions of civil war, U.S. officials and Iraqi leaders desperately sought to steer the country away from it, however it was termed. The lack of governance, the proliferation of armed groups, and the sectarian domination of the official political process brought Iraq to the brink of civil war. Key initiatives on these fronts combined to bring universally recognized improvement in 2007 and 2008, securing much-needed breathing room for the Iraqi government and its beleaguered American supporters in Washington. The improvements were not yet backed by enduring systemic changes, however, and though violence was at a relative low for Iraq, it was still quite bloody on an absolute level. Without more permanent improvements in governance, security, and political reconciliation, violence is likely to flare once again. Beyond stability, it will take time and work to bring something resembling democracy, or at least a stable, representative government, to Iraq, yet there are some bases for hope.

With the reduced levels of violence came a renewed focus on political progress. While movement was slow and the legislation far from earth shattering, political maneuvering produced signs that new, non-sectarian coalitions could be in the offing. The Maliki government also showed resolve in going after Shiʻa militias with the increasingly capable Iraqi security forces, a move applauded by Sunnis. Muqtada al-Sadr, while crying foul, was forced to cede ground to official forces. Oil flowed more steadily, given increased redundancy and security of pipelines. The windfall of revenues due to extremely high prices enabled more rapid reconstruction and economic development efforts. At the grassroots level, too, Iraqis worked to rebuild their media, educational, and cultural organizations. All of these phenomena were marked improvements over the situation in the first four years after the invasion, but years of work are still ahead.

In an acknowledgment that change was desperately needed in Iraq, President Bush announced new strategic guidance in a January 10, 2007, address to the nation.[2] Shortly thereafter, the president appointed GEN David Petraeus, a noted combat leader and strategic thinker, to head the Multi-National Forces in Iraq. The military shift, which took place on February 10, 2007, was followed shortly by the appointment of Amb. Ryan Crocker as Chief of Mission in Baghdad in March. The two were an excellent pairing of the best the United States had to offer. Each had a broad vision that exceeded the narrow parochial bounds that often hamper inter-agency coordination in the U.S. government. In addition to extensive combat leadership experience in Iraq and the Balkans and high-profile postings in the military bureaucracy, Petraeus held a doctorate in international relations from Princeton University. Between 2005 and 2007, Petraeus and Marine LtGen James Mattis oversaw the writing of the military's new joint publication on counterinsurgency operations, which would be the model for his new strategy. For Crocker's part, he was vastly experienced in the Middle East, having been posted to six Arab countries and Iran. He was previously ambassador in Syria, Kuwait, Lebanon, and Pakistan and, critically, was the International Affairs Advisor at the U.S. military's National War College in 2003 and 2004, gaining insight and credibility in the military world. The new Iraq team was not coming in empty handed: their appointments came on the heels of President Bush's announcement of the decision to deploy an extra twenty-thousand troops to Iraq. The plan became known as the Surge.

Petraeus entered Iraq with a handpicked team of military and academic experts ready to analyze the situation on the ground and adapt the best strategic practices to these conditions. Because of the recommendations of Petraeus and his team, the Surge was expanded and extended. At its peak, there were over thirty thousand additional troops in Iraq compared to the pre-Surge strength, yet the downturn of violence in Iraq did not owe solely to higher troop levels. Though the additional troops were sorely needed, so were the tactical, operational, and strategic shifts that came with them. Soldiers pushed farther out into cities and worked more closely with Iraqi forces from the government and the tribes. The renewed offensive was instrumental in putting extremists on their heels. More significantly, it may have convinced Iraqis that their only chance to avoid descent into hell was at hand.

As the Surge forces rolled into the country, another phenomenon was already taking root in Anbar Province. Internecine warfare was bringing about significant changes in Sunni points of view. Fed up with al Qaeda's extreme violence and the undercurrent of intra-sectarian violence between urban and rural Sunnis, sheikhs and poor tribesmen, and Islamic nationalist and global Islamist groups, Sunnis were forced to choose sides. Sheikhs turned their tribesmen, many of whom had been insurgents, into local defense forces to cast out the extremists. By late 2007, they had all but chased al Qaeda out of their lands. On the other side of the sectarian divide, as rising tensions between Shi'a factions broke out into fighting, Muqtada al-Sadr announced a six-month truce of his Mahdi Army in August 2007, leading to a sharp drop in inter-sectarian violence.

The synergy of these three phenomena produced tangible results for the first time since 2003. The Surge, and preceding American military pressure on al Qaeda, allowed Sunni tribes to organize and begin to retaliate against the terrorists. Likewise, the pressure on the Mahdi Army and other sectarian death squads helped effect Sadr's truce and curbed the sectarian violence gripping the capital. Together, these factors caused a marked decrease in violence and a return to a remote semblance of normalcy in many areas, although gunfire and explosions never ceased to be a common occurrence. By the spring of 2008, 73 percent of Iraqis felt safe in their neighborhood, although only 37 percent felt safe traveling outside their neighborhood. While the polling questions differed slightly, a similar poll conducted in the fall of 2007 showed much lower confidence in the security situation. Estimates of civilian casualties dipped from monthly highs well over three thousand in the summer and fall of 2007 to less than a thousand each month through the first half of 2008. Though the situation remained unstable, the improvement was undeniable.[3]

The additional troops began flowing into Iraq in January 2007. The full strength of the surge was not reached until mid-June, however. More than fifteen thousand additional troops flooded the streets of Baghdad by mid-2007. Significantly, this commitment was for the first time matched by Iraqi units near their promised strength. Six U.S. combat brigades occupied Baghdad by the summer of 2007, with another six brigades in the surrounding areas, for a total strength of nearly fifty thousand troops. In addition, the Iraqis committed twenty-two brigades of military and police forces for a total strength of nearly seventy-nine thousand. Together, these troops departed from their major bases to blanket the city with patrols and combat outposts in a presence that significantly impacted the insurgent and sectarian violence that had gripped the city since early 2006.[4] The increased U.S. presence provided the space needed for Iraqis to begin taking responsibility for their future, and the results may have saved Iraq.

The Awakening

The declining fortunes of the Sunni insurgency in Iraq owed to more than simply the Surge, or even the decision of tribesmen and former insurgents to band together in local defense groups. The "Awakening" was, at root, the product of internal divisions among the Arab Sunni. In the end, most Arab Sunnis turned on al Qaeda and other insurgent groups for numerous reasons, not the least of which were these conflicts within Iraqi society.

The rise of the Awakening groups should not be boiled down to an Iraqi rejection of a foreign jihadist group's Islamic extremism. Though the Awakening was a rejection, in part, of the global Islamic extremism brought in by foreigners, Iraqis constituted the bulk of al Qaeda. It is also true that the extreme version of the "Islamic State of Iraq" was an anathema to the many nationalist tribesmen and former regime members who chose to align against the extremist insurgents. Yet the struggles in Anbar Province and other Sunni areas that triggered the Awakening were much more complex.

Divisions between urban and rural Sunnis, poor tribesmen and domineering sheikhs, Islamic zealots and more parochial tribal Sunnis, collaborators with the old regime and those wronged by it, and old and new generations were all at work in the Sunni areas after Saddam's fall. These divisions, in addition to al Qaeda's quest for domination in Anbar, generated a deadly mix of violence driven by greed, ambition, and vengeance that burned on behind the veil of the insurgency. Beyond vague dreams of an Islamic caliphate, many al-Qaeda foot soldiers were drawn from a peasantry that targeted the land-owning sheikhs and the educated classes that had oppressed them for ages. Sheikhs eager to protect themselves and their tribes' lucrative enterprises had little choice but to unite their tribesmen and ally themselves with their recent enemy, the Coalition, against the greater threat to their existence.[5]

Few Iraqis had any interest in living under the absurd conditions of the so-called Islamic Republics imposed by the brainwashed zealots of al Qaeda. In the tribal milieu of western Iraq, there was little common ground between local views of religion and the Salafi way. David Kilcullen, a former Australian Army officer with a doctorate in politics who recently served as a counterinsurgency advisor to the Coalition, commented on the tensions that caused the break. He observed from extensive conversations with Iraqis that al Qaeda's view of Islam, which he described excellently as a "hyper-reductionist version of 'Islam' stripped of cultural content," was "utterly foreign to [the tribes'] traditional and syncretic version of the faith." In turn, the al-Qaeda zealots discounted tribal Iraqis' views of Islam as "ignorant, stupid, and sinful." Further, the common tactic of al-Qaeda leaders to marry into the host population in order to literally embed themselves into society was an anathema to Iraqi tribal sensibilities. This was in addition to general cultural differences between the mostly urban foreigners in the upper ranks of al Qaeda and the Iraqi tribes.[6]

Even before the Awakening movement came into its own, Iraqi insurgent groups had begun to revolt against al Qaeda's attempt to monopolize the insurgency. In April 2007, nine insurgent groups issued a statement announcing the formation of the Office for Coordination of the National and Islamic Iraqi Resistance. These groups denounced foreign connections and stated their intention to isolate al Qaeda's Islamic State of Iraq and the extremist groups that shed Muslim blood. In the same month, another group posted a nine-page letter to Osama Bin Laden, demanding that he rein in the violence of al Qaeda in Iraq. Islamic Army commander Abu Mohammad al-Salmani stated, "Al Qaeda has killed more Iraqi Sunnis in Anbar province during the past month than the soldiers of the American occupation have killed within three months. People are tired of the torture." Khalid Awad, commander of another resistance group, delved further. "We must confess that if it was not for al Qaeda, neither Iraq nor Afghanistan would have been occupied. For al Qaeda has awakened the American ogre against the Islamic nation." The April moves were followed by a cascade of realignments of most Iraqi insurgent groups, all in defiance of al Qaeda.[7] This break in the insurgency paved the way for many members of the same groups to turn completely, siding with the occupier against al Qaeda.

The Awakening movement (variously known by its Arabic name *Sahwa* or the Sons of Iraq) had its roots in the far western reaches of Iraq when a small tribe that lived off of smuggling was squeezed out by another tribe that had allied with al Qaeda. The Albu Mahal of the huge Dulaimi tribal confederation initially approached U.S. Marines for help against al Qaeda in May 2005, though real cooperation did not begin until August. With U.S. assistance, the tribe pushed back the extremists, and the successful model slowly began to spread in Anbar Province. The movement is about more than setting up local vigilante groups, however. Along with these groups, the government is providing police and other civil service jobs, and increased stability has brought rebuilding and new commercial life. It has also allowed American units to concentrate more time and funds on reconstruction projects, rather than fighting insurgents. All combine to give men jobs and income, keeping them away from the monetary lure of the insurgency.[8]

The movement really came into its own when a number of sheikhs, tired of extremist violence, formed the al-Anbar Salvation Council in late 2006. This tribal grouping made significant strides in banishing al Qaeda from Anbar and provided an incentive and a protective shield for recruitment of tribesmen into the official police force. Sheikh Abdul Satar Abu Reisha headed the Council until his death on September 13, 2007. Reisha, head of the Abu Reisha tribe of the Dulaimi tribal confederation, created this league after his father and brother were assassinated and two other brothers were kidnapped, never to be seen again. Reisha was the target of numerous car bombings before he was killed. The Council reportedly represented twenty-five tribes, helped in recruiting six thousand tribesmen into the provincial police, and formed a twenty-five-hundred-man "emergency brigade." After Reisha's death, his brother Ahmad Abu Reisha, led the Council. In April, two hundred tribal sheikhs announced the development of the Iraqi Awakening (*Sahwa*) Party, based around the successes of the Anbar Salvation Council.[9]

The U.S. military jumped on this phenomenon, offering a monthly stipend of around $300 for more than sixty-five thousand of the volunteers by the end of 2007. This was in addition to over twenty thousand Sunnis that joined the police forces in Anbar at the behest of their tribes. The Awakening groups spread to eight provinces, with the total strength reaching almost one-hundred thousand by the fall of 2008, with as many as six thousand Shi'a members and thousands more unpaid volunteers organized by tribal and religious leaders. The groups were no collection of angels, however. In urban areas, especially, leaders of the groups tended to be officers of the former Iraqi army and many of the sheikhs running tribal Awakening councils had previously been associates of al Qaeda. In Diyala Province, the 1920 Revolution Brigades, an insurgent group, made up much of the new Awakening movement. To keep tabs on the force, who were armed only with the AK-47 that each household is authorized, U.S. troops catalogued members' fingerprints, photos, and retinal scans. This work yielded over sixty high-value detainees in Diyala Province alone between the fall of 2007 and the spring of 2008.[10]

'Ali Hatem Al 'Ali Suleiman, the young sheikh of the huge Duleimi tribal confederation, was one of the leaders who tentatively accepted American assistance. While 'Ali consented to American aid against the "al-Qaeda dogs" that tried to kill him on more than one occasion, he maintained his distance. "I am not a puppet of the invaders," he avowed in February 2008. His differentiation between "the terrorists who have killed so many Iraqis, Shi'a and Sunni alike" and "the honorable resistance to the occupation" demonstrated that the alliance between the tribes and U.S. forces is a day-by-day affair. The alliances between Awakening tribes are fleeting as well. Suleiman heads the al-Anbar Tribal Council and is allied with another prominent Anbari sheikh, Hamid Farhan al-Hayis. Al-Hayis was formerly a member of the Anbar Salvation Council until Abdul Satar Abu Reisha ejected him in 2007. Al-Hayis has since been strongly allied with Suleiman.[11]

These two tribal leaders have been at the forefront of conflict with other Sunni political forces, particularly the Accord Front and the Iraqi Islamic Party (IIP), which composes a sizable part of the Front. When the Accord Front withdrew from government in 2007, al-Hayis criticized its "closed-minded policies and radical stance." Sniffing an opportunity, he offered his own candidates to replace the cabinet vacancies left by the Accord pullout. In February 2008, the political conflict escalated with the two sheikhs chastising the IIP for its domination of political posts, especially those on the electoral commission that shaped the 2009 provincial elections. The matter came to a head when the two sheikhs gave the IIP thirty days to leave Anbar under threat of force, calling it the "the political wing of al Qaeda." The IIP, headed by Vice President Tariq al-Hashimi, responded with a lawsuit that resulted in arrest warrants being issued for both Suleiman and al-Hayis.[12]

Although the acrimony between the IIP and the sheikhs was another manifestation of the conflict between urban (IIP) and rural (Awakening) groups, it also reflected divisions between those who benefited from the 2005 elections and those who did not. The IIP, in particular, stands to lose significantly if the Awakening groups become a political force. As one of the few Sunni parties to take part in the political process from the start, the IIP held almost all the Anbar provincial posts awarded in the 2005 election. In Baghdad, too, Awakening groups are mobilizing politically, uniting with former army officers to form the Iraqi Dignity (*Karama*) Front, based on a political platform opposed to extremism, but assertive of an Arab identity for Iraq.[13] The new groupings may expand political involvement in Iraq and provide a basis for broader coalition-making, though the existing political order will not make room for them willingly.

Many officials acknowledged that organizing and paying Awakening groups was a risk. In the long run, the lack of political reconciliation and development may eclipse the gains secured by the Awakening. The groups and the tribal sheikhs and former officers who control them have no loyalty to the national Iraqi government. One sheikh summed up his view of the government simply: "They are working only for the Shiites." This view was exacerbated as Sunnis witnessed Shi'a militias that fought the Mahdi Army praised and quickly inducted into the Iraqi Army. The induction of Sunnis is much slower, officially owing to background checks, if it happens at all. The Iraqi government, which began to assume control of the groups in October 2008 starting with fifty-four thousand members in and around Baghdad, has stated that it can only induct around 25 percent of the hundred thousand Sunnis in the Awakening movements. Thus, more than seventy-five thousand will be cashiered back into unemployment in the near future.[14]

The Awakening strategy had other drawbacks. It carved up many areas into fiefdoms managed by the sheikh or former officer who ran the local Awakening militia. Rivals jostled for control of territory and the power that came with it. In a number of these areas, conditions were less violent, but not much more liberal than they were under al Qaeda. Women, in particular, were threatened by Awakening gunmen if they violated the tenets of the Islamic code of conduct as imagined by the local powers. Another complaint was that these "concerned local citizens" often were not locals. Urban residents and officers of the old regime grew increasingly irritated with the rural tribesmen that now walked their city streets. Some warned that yet another conflict was brewing. Activists complained that the strategy ceded powers to illiberal forces that drew Iraq away from the central, liberal vision laid out by its constitution. Insiders, however, argue that the United States initially refused help from the sheikhs only to spend the next four years battling an insurgency to no avail. They were forced to ally with the powers that could stop the killing, even if they were not ideal democrats.[15]

The contradictions inherent in this policy were demonstrated by an incident in September 2007 when American troops were forced to rush to the aid of a Sunni sheikh from an Awakening group in the south of Baghdad. In a tense standoff, the Americans rescued him, not from the grasps of al Qaeda, but from an official Iraqi police checkpoint. The Shi'a police had taken custody of the sheikh, who was in danger of being turned over to the Mahdi Army and almost certain death. The American troops sided with a tribal leader of a non-governmental militia against a unit of official government police. The government police, however, were likely to surrender the sheikh to another non-government militia, the Mahdi Army.[16] Counterinsurgency and nation-building require a complex and often contradictory set of policies and actions, the results of which are often clear only in hindsight.

Shi'a Maneuvering and Broader Political Developments

Shi'a militias, political parties, and their backers in the security forces turned on each other during the same period. In October 2006, members of al-Sadr's Mahdi Army clashed in Amara with Iraqi police who were said to be members of the Badr Organization, ISCI's armed wing, after a tit-for-tat escalation of bombings and killings between the two groups. Splits between ISCI and the Sadrists continued to grow and the Fadhila Party, an ally of the Sadrists, withdrew from the United Iraqi Alliance (UIA) in early 2007. By that time, the Shi'a political environment had become so acrimonious that a UIA spokesman acknowledged that a February 2007 assassination attempt on a Shi'a politician may have been an attempt to settle accounts within the UIA, rather than attributing it to sectarian violence. The flashpoint for much of this intra-Shi'a tension was in Basra, where political animosity broke out into gunfights in March 2007 between followers of Muqtada al-Sadr and members of the Fadhila Party.[17] The violence belied the lack of Shi'a political unity and the continued problems presented by inclusion of some forces in official roles and the exclusion of others, even when those groups arise from the same sectarian background.

Increased pressure on the Mahdi Army in Baghdad drove some commanders to move to the south, especially to the poorer neighborhoods of Basra where inhabitants tended to be sympathetic to al-Sadr. Mahdists' encroachment on the more middle-class areas of Basra and the Badr strongholds of Najaf and Karbala (important for their religious prestige and revenues) was fiercely resisted. Fighting ensued between the organizations in 2007, leading disillusioned residents to decry the hostility that some said was "all for the oil in Basra." They accused the many formerly exiled leaders of these groups of returning to Iraq "for revenge, not to help the people." One resident noted with disgust that it was safer for Shiʻa in the formerly Sunni-extremist–controlled Dora neighborhood than in their own enclaves because of the infighting between Shiʻa factions. "It's not sectarian, it's within sects," one man observed.[18]

Facing violence that was spreading out of control and jeopardizing his political status, Muqtada al-Sadr called for a six-month truce with American and Iraqi troops and other Shiʻa groups on August 29, 2007. As in previous strategic climb-downs, al-Sadr showed a savvy that contradicted the common perception of him as a simpleton. Realizing that continued violence would justify stronger U.S. and Iraqi government strikes against him, al-Sadr lay low and issued instructions for a crackdown on rogue elements. The political maneuvering continued, however. Other than occasional firefights, after the truce was announced the contest took on subtler dimensions. Arrests of Mahdi Army members, presumably legal detentions of militia members, were often carried out by Iraqi police who were also Badrists. ISCI also attempted to undercut the Sadrists' popular support in the poorer classes by competing on the provision of social services, charities, and mosques.[19]

Al-Sadr's truce led to a nearly instant drop in sectarian violence. Mahdi Army checkpoints reduced in number and roving religious squads were far less intrusive. One Sadrist who preferred the more acerbic interpretation of Islam the Mahdi Army was able to enforce prior to the truce moaned, "Today, weddings once again take place to the sound of music, and alcohol vendors have reopened their shops."[20] Al-Sadr kept his army and his political clout, however, all the while staying legitimate enough to maintain ties with the strengthening government.

By 2008, the Iraqi government attempted to lead major operations against militias and insurgents with its fledgling army. The military demonstrated significant improvement in its capabilities by 2008, although the progress was spotty. Iraqi units still relied heavily on American troops for additional firepower, as well as a range of support functions. Some units were aggressive and disciplined, while others refused to go on missions or fled at first contact. In Mosul, the Iraqis pressed an offensive against a well-armed and organized insurgent enemy. While Iraqi units performed many functions on their own, they required considerable American fire support to face al Qaeda head on. Elsewhere, American officers reported that some experienced Iraqi units held the line well, but other units deserted critical posts. As many as one thousand troops deserted during the assault in Basra. Another complaint was the lack of

Iraqi fire discipline. Soldiers shot everywhere when under fire, threatening civilians, their own comrades, and their American allies. Americans referred to the Iraqi response to incoming fire as the "death blossom": they sprayed AK-47 rounds in a 360-degree arc around them.[21]

The government used the increasingly capable troops to hunt down rogue elements of Muqtada al-Sadr's Mahdi Army in 2008. Sadrists accused the Maliki government of using the assaults to weaken Muqtada's political power ahead of the provincial elections scheduled for the fall. Mahdi Army fighters believed that ISCI and al-Da'wa were behind the attacks, exclaiming that the Shi'a parties had become bigger enemies than the Sunnis. An assault in Basra showed that government forces were still incapable of dealing speedily with the Shi'a militias, although Muqtada al-Sadr ordered his forces to stand down after the assault's sixth day. Prime Minister Maliki was forced to stem losses from desertions by inducting Shi'a tribal forces into the security forces, a move that angered Sunnis demanding official status for their tribal forces. The move may have been the key to the government's qualified success in Basra, though, and the simple fact that the Shi'a-dominated government was finally taking on Shi'a militias won points with many Sunnis. Deputy Prime Minister Barham Salih, a Kurd, observed of al-Maliki's confrontation with the Sadrists, "What he did in taking on his own constituents can give him the credentials to be a national leader rather than the leader of a Shia sect."[22]

Although the forces were not tactically victorious, they produced a strategic withdrawal of the militias that had gripped the city. Life returned to a semblance of normalcy and people felt relief from the pressure of militia checkpoints and patrols. Residents praised the strength of the government and Prime Minister Maliki, while Muqtada al-Sadr's face was scratched out on many posters around the city. The Iraqi Army, which performed questionably during the initial assault, improved its image as thirty thousand troops presided over a peaceful city. Over time, continued calm may win residents' trust and loyalty to the central government. The Mahdi Army, however, continued to dole out threats of retribution should it return to prominence there. Fearing that their respite would be fleeting, tribal militias formed to guard against the day when the Iraqi Army would pull out and the Mahdi Army might return.[23]

An assault on Sadr City ended similarly. Tactically, the battle was little more than a stalemate, but strategically it forced al-Sadr to retreat. Facing growing discontent over the civilian toll of his fight, al-Sadr acceded to a ceasefire with the government. Despite ceding control of Sadr City to government forces, in doing so he escaped the destruction of his army and won concessions from the government, which promised not to arrest his followers unless directly implicated in the fighting. After the dust settled, the U.S. military applied its tried and tested Awakening model and found residents eager to step up for the $300 monthly stipend. After successes in Basra and Sadr City, Iraqi and U.S. troops rolled into the Sadrist stronghold of Amara in Maysan Province, where many of Sadr City's residents have their roots, with virtually no resistance.[24] If the Iraqi government and the Coalition are able to supplant al-Sadr as the main provider and protector in such troubled areas as Sadr City, they will make great strides in gaining the trust and support of the populace.

Improving fortunes on the security side, however, will not last long without increased political cooperation and reconciliation. Hopes were raised in December 2006 that a new coalition of moderate Iraqi politicians could join hands across sectarian lines and lead the country away from the brink. These hopes were dashed at the end of December when Shi'a politicians failed to gain Ayatollah Sistani's support for their involvement in such a coalition. Al-Sistani, valuing Shi'a unity above all, refused to back a government of unity if it did not include the entire Shi'a bloc. An official who attended the meeting between Shi'a politicians and al-Sistani said he "does not approve any alliance that would break the United Iraqi Alliance up."[25] Instead of supporting a coalition between the mainstream parties, al-Sistani may have encouraged a stronger cross-sectarian coalition of the opposition parties.

Growing tired of the dominance of ISCI, al-Da'wa, and the Kurds, Sadrists, secular parties, and some Sunnis increasingly cooperated on legislation, staking out opposition stances on federalism, amnesty, and other issues.[26] One of the first parties to claim opposition to sectarianism was the Fadhila Party, whose fifteen representatives withdrew from the UIA in March 2007, declaring in a party statement that "the first step on the path of saving Iraq from its choking crisis begins with the breakup of these blocs and barring the formation of blocs on ethnic or sectarian bases."[27] The party's withdrawal likely had as much to do with blocking ISCI aspirations for including Basra in a super-region as any ambition for a greater good, but it was the first significant fracture in the UIA. As the Maliki government staggered under the weight of continued violence and political deadlock, groups maneuvered to prepare themselves to take advantage of any turn of events. The upshot of this maneuvering was that the sectarian bloc system that had dominated the 2005 elections was weakened somewhat, leaving the government essentially adrift throughout the critical events of 2007.

The debate over federalism drove groups to align by issue rather than identity. Along with the Kurds, who already had regional status in their three provinces, the powerful Shi'a group ISCI was the prime driver behind decentralized federalism. ISCI politicians touted grand plans of founding a nine-province super-region in the south as soon as the law allowed in April 2008. Some analysts believed that ISCI would use their alliance with the Kurds to create twin super-regions, each gobbling controversial territory such as Kirkuk and other extensions in the Kurdish north and encroachments into Sunni territory by a southern Shi'a region.[28]

In January 2008, though, a quiet yet significant event occurred. Shi'a politicians from the Sadrist bloc, al-Da'wa, and independents joined with Sunnis, Turkomen, secularists, and other minorities to call for limits on ambitious regional plans and powers. In its "memorandum of understanding" published on January 13, the bloc also united behind a demand that provincial elections be held before any further developments take place. The coalition stood strongly against decentralization in Iraq. Although its members have little contact with the United States and many are far from liberal in outlook, they may present the beginnings of a turn away from sectarian blocs and toward the issue-based coalitions needed to move legislation through parliament. Conversely, the Kurds and ISCI, who maintain strong contacts with the United States, are pushing for a decentralized ethno-sectarian federation, often by distinctly un-democratic means.[29]

The loose coalition came to the fore again in February during a parliamentary vote on three crucial and controversial laws that had failed to be considered previously. The parliament demonstrated initiative and creativity in packaging these laws into one up-or-down vote in February 2008. Prior to the package deal, political blocs had dueling walkouts, each refusing to vote on bills important to the other before their own bill was brought up. Fearing that their colleagues would renege on agreements and scuttle their bill, lawmakers found an ideal middle ground. By packaging the three laws, each of which had strong backing from a different bloc, they assured a yes vote for all three and a compromise with little risk of defection. Sunni parties and the Sadrists strongly supported an amnesty law that freed Iraqi detainees under certain conditions. The Kurds demanded passage of the national budget law with a controversially high 17 percent allocation of the budget to Kurdistan. Most interestingly, a broad coalition of interests aligned against ISCI in favor of the Provincial Powers Act that maintained a relative centralization of powers and specified October 1, 2008, as the date for provincial elections, although squabbling over the election law forced a postponement until 2009.[30]

The negotiation and the fact that parties were beginning to form voting blocs on issues rather than identity were a massive step in the right direction, yet this was not solely a good-news story. First, the three-bill package was necessitated, because the various blocs had virtually no trust in one another. Each feared that if they voted for the other's bill first, there would be no reciprocity. Second, Vice President Adel Abd al-Mahdi, a member of ISCI, invoked his veto power as part of the Presidency Council in an attempt to scuttle the Provincial Powers Act. The veto was withdrawn after the Sadrists threatened protests and strikes and the United States reportedly pressured al-Mahdi to do so. The memory of this veto attempt may inhibit future compromise deals. Yet if Iraqi politicians can continue to cooperate to pass important legislation, they will not only be reconstructing the institutions of their government, but they will also be rebuilding the trust required for reconciliation and continued transition toward a more capable and democratic form of government.[31]

Unfortunately, reconciliation to this point has often been only window dressing. The Iraqi parliament passed a January 2008 law aimed at easing restrictions on former Ba'athists' employment in the government; one of the U.S.-defined benchmarks for progress in Iraq. While it promised to make former Ba'athists more eligible for government positions, the details of the law and its implementation opened up many currently employed Ba'athists to sacking, reducing its value as a tool of reconciliation. The law did allow pension payments for forcibly retired Ba'athists, however.[32] In a more general sense, implementation of legislation is difficult due to a lack of trained personnel and institutions used to carrying out large-scale projects and spending large amounts of money in a rapid, but accountable, way. Thus, even with the passage of key legislation, it will be some time before Iraqis see that their politicians have worked toward improving their lives and reconciling their needs.

At present, the system is too gridlocked for real reconciliation to be seen soon. Only time will tell if greater trust and legislative frequency can be had after new elections. The outcomes of the second round of provincial and national elections will be a critical marker in determining the trajectory of Iraq's transition. Democracy, even a relatively illiberal democracy, will not be possible unless Iraqis can exceed the bounds of confessional politics and the resulting legislative standstill. For power to be transferred democratically, the electoral rules of the game must first be agreed to. Although parliament has made some strides in this direction, the groups currently atop the system seem uninterested in elections that may unseat them or clarify that the sources of their power do not lie in their popularity.

The first provincial elections were held in January 2005. Because of the early date of these elections, many of the current political parties had not yet coalesced, and most Sunnis were still boycotting the political process. Despite many groups' eagerness to hold new provincial elections as a first step toward reshuffling the political power structure, the parties that made the strongest showing in the first election, especially ISCI, have little interest in other parties gaining seats at their expense.

The Provincial Powers Act laid basic ground rules for the provincial elections, although these caused as much controversy as they settled. A clause stipulating requirements for candidacy was sure to cause squabbles over interpretation. Candidates must have been residents in the province for no less than ten years or be registered as originating from the province.[33] While not completely ruling powerful former exiles out, this certainly presented a pretext for excluding some from the elections.

The deadlines stipulated by the act presented more fundamental problems. The law required that a provincial elections act be passed within ninety days of its effective date, yet this May 17 deadline came and went with no legislative action. Without detailed legislation, preparation for the elections could not begin, making it impossible to meet the October 1, 2008 deadline set in the Provincial Powers Act. It was a welcome delay to many politicians who believed their positions were threatened by new elections. Those who stood to lose in new elections rallied around a major sticking point in the fight over the electoral law: whether the vote would be by an open list, in which specific candidates could be chosen, or a closed list where only parties could be.[34]

ISCI, a party that had benefited from Sunni and Sadrist boycotts of the 2005 provincial elections and later manipulation of the UIA list behind closed doors, favored using a closed list for the provincial elections. ISCI spokesman Hamid al-Ma'ala used the constitution to justify this position, arguing that open lists do not ensure the representation of women and minorities in government as required by the constitution. This statement is quite disingenuous considering ISCI's narrow sectarian base and its followers' general disregard for women's rights. ISCI also contended that the employment of open lists would delay the election for technical reasons. Other parties claimed that closed lists lead to the election of unknown representatives. ISCI member Jalal al-Din al-Saghir was defter in his comments. He asserted that while ISCI and the UIA supported open lists, the technical requirements would require delaying the election. The party's recognition that its popularity has slid significantly caused ISCI's reticence in legislating a date for provincial elections in the Provincial Powers Act.[35] Since ISCI desired delayed elections and closed lists, al-Saghir's position seemed to be an attempt to hedge ISCI's bets.

ISCI was not the only party to shy away from elections. The Sadrists, in a bombshell move in June 2008, vowed not to participate in the provincial vote, although they would back independent candidates. This decision came shortly after Muqtada al-Sadr announced that he was forming a new, elite force to confront the American occupation. It seemed that this strategy was shrewdly calculated by the Sadrists to maintain resistance credentials and to stake out a position in opposition to Nouri al-Maliki, whose assaults on Basra, Sadr City, and Amara struck at the heart of al-Sadr's power. With cracks spreading in the ruling coalition, al-Sadr's announcement and his pledge of support for Allawi or al-Jafari instead of al-Maliki suggest that he was playing an astute political hand. Additionally, by withdrawing participation in elections, al-Sadr was heading off threats to disallow Sadrist candidates unless his militia was disbanded. Aides quickly clarified that Sadrists could run as technocrats, but not Sadr Party members. Further, the move to isolate resistance to a new, elite force may actually have been an effort to conserve the bulk of his forces for an eventual U.S. drawdown.[36]

Though the Sadrists' denouncement of alliance with al-Maliki came in part owing to the government's campaign of assaults on Sadr strongholds, it also targeted splits in al-Maliki's own al-Da'wa Party. In an apparent contest for control of al-Da'wa's supporters, former Prime Minister Ibrahim al-Jafari created a new political front called the National Reform Movement (*Tayar al-'Islah al-Watani*). This was more than a simple parting of ways. The rump Da'wa headed by Maliki issued a statement cutting all ties with Jafari, and pro-Maliki sources called the move a "bloodless coup." Supporters of al-Jafari accused al-Maliki of using his position as prime minister to woo supporters with money and government positions, thereby buying control of the party. Al-Jafari's new movement retained control of key Da'wa offices and replaced the old Da'wa signs in the key headquarters of Najaf, across other southern cities, and in the Kadhimiya neighborhood of north Baghdad.[37]

Al-Jafari's followers reportedly joined a new parliamentary bloc consisting of the Sadrists, the Fadhila Party, the National Dialogue Front, and the Iraqi List. This bloc consisted of eighty representatives, to which al-Jafari's group was expected to add at least ten. The bewildering maze of splits and new alliances belied the fact that, while many Iraqi politicians pledged new nationalist fervor in 2008, the incoherent political field was unlikely to unify behind a strong, new vision.[38]

The elections of 2009 are an opportunity to see if changing attitudes about religion affect electoral outcomes. Many Iraqis, including Shiʻa, were disappointed by the success of religious parties even after the first vote in 2005. Reflecting broader attitudes, one religiously liberal Shiʻa blogger expressed sheer dismay at the victory of the "Iranian mullahs" in the December 2005 elections. He claimed that many Shiʻa said they would not vote for the UIA again after the first vote in January 2005 and was incredulous at their continued success in December, even claiming Iranian vote rigging.[39]

Anti-clerical sentiment rose as the UIA failed to produce results. Iraqis, especially young adults, confessed to reporters their disillusionment with religion and religious leaders who had brought them only suffering in the years after Saddam's fall. The inability of religious parties to improve life in Iraq and the misery of life under "virtue patrols'" constant threats, which ranged from breaking fingers for smoking to killing for greater "transgressions," initiated a backlash against religion. Journalists and imams, alike, noted dropping attendance at Friday prayers, and the esteemed position of religious leaders slipped significantly.[40]

Despite this, some parties continued to employ religion as a source of legitimacy. Opponents of the UIA said that its use of mosques and pictures of Ayatollah Sistani for campaigning was "an indicator of its lack of a political program" to attract voters. Secular parties and a number of Kurds spoke out against this use of mosques and images of religious figures for campaigning, though an ISCI spokesman made it clear that the religious parties had no intention of forgoing their use. In a Friday sermon after parliamentary debate on a law regarding the use of religious materials in campaigns, a key aide of Ayatollah Sistani restated the Ayatollah's position that he did not support any political faction and refused the use of his picture for campaigning.[41]

Even though religious considerations will continue to figure heavily in Iraqi political calculations, many wish that the upcoming rounds of elections will produce bodies capable of enacting a broad political program and producing real improvement in stability, security, and governance, rather than a body of narrow groups that used religion to enter into office and raid the spoils. Many more groups have entered the political arena and hopes are high that the elections will generate real change. These aspirations are a double-edged sword, however. Similar hopes were raised ahead of the December 2005 elections, only to be dashed.[42] The inclusion of more actors in the process raises expectations, but may also deepen discontent if the current powers are successful in blocking a new direction in Iraq's politics. Balloting alone cannot solve Iraq's problems, though electing the right cast of characters may go a long way in breaking the current legislative malaise. The groups currently in power, however, have attempted to delay and resist the sorts of electoral mechanisms that will loosen their grip on the system.

Although parliament first passed a provincial election law on July 22, 2008, the event was far from a clear endorsement of a democratic future. The vote was boycotted entirely by the Kurds, along with many of their ISCI supporters, leaving (perhaps) the minimum for a quorum, which consisted primarily of the cross-sectarian opposition bloc that figured in earlier 2008 votes. In the wake of the provincial election law vote, this bloc took on a greater prestige and became known as the "July 22 Force."[43]

The law provided for open lists, yet the system still favored parties. While votes for candidates determined the order of the seats awarded, the proportion of the seats awarded to a given list still depended on the overall votes to all candidates in the list. Thus, unpopular candidates could ride into the council on the extra votes of popular candidates in their list. The provisions regarding Kirkuk held the law up for months, however. Elections in Kirkuk were to be postponed until the city's status could be determined and the law specified that the area should be secured by military and security units from the "south and center of Iraq" and a committee formed to arbitrate the city's future. The act also stipulated that security and civil service positions in the city should be divided by a 32-32-32-4 formula among Arabs, Kurds, Turkomen, and Christians, respectively. This was not the only provision for what one observer termed the "Lebanonization" of Iraqi politics: the establishment of quotas based on identity. Minority seats were also to be allocated in Baghadad, Ninewa, Kirkuk, Dohuk, Irbil, and Basra Provinces.[44]

Besides taking healthy cuts at the Kurds, the act also undercut religious parties. It forbade images of any non-candidate in campaign materials, meaning ISCI could not display pictures of Ayatollah Sistani and the Sadrists could not display images of their leader or his ancestors either. It also prohibited campaigning in any government or religious building and proscribed the use of public or *waqf* (Islamic charitable) funds for campaigning purposes.[45]

Because of the controversial provisions, Kurdish President Jalal Talibani's veto sent the law back to the parliament, where debate centered on the disposition of Kirkuk. After several hopeful moments, the bill was shelved while parliamentarians took their summer recess, thwarting any possibility of on-time elections. For the groups in power, this was a comfortable arrangement, but patience was wearing thin.[46] For the Sunni Awakening groups, especially, time seemed to be running out as the government planned to cashier them before they could turn their story into electoral success.

In September 2008, the parliament passed an amendment to Article 24 of the provincial elections law, regarding Kirkuk. Passed by a consensus vote of the 190 representatives present, the amendment deferred local elections in Kirkuk until a parliamentary committee reviewed the situation there and made recommendations for normalization of the situation and division of government among the three major ethnic blocs in the region: Kurds, Turkomen, and Arabs. The committee's report to the parliament is due no later than March 31, 2009. Once the report is accepted, parliament is to create a special law, providing for a single round of elections in Kirkuk. Presumably, once all adjustments are completed, Kirkuk will fall under the country-wide provincial elections law for subsequent rounds.[47]

In the same session, the National Assembly set the stage for provincial elections in the rest of Iraq to take place no later than January 31, 2009. Representatives passed slight modifications to several articles, allowing the use of non-candidates' images, except for religious leaders, and of government facilities and religious places in support of election-related activities, but not active campaigning. The importance of this event cannot be overemphasized. It demonstrated the ability of Iraq's political groups to reach compromise within the bounds of their political system. The compromise dealt significant blows to some, particularly minorities, and the parties that desired retention of the closed list system. Yet the ability to peacefully compromise was a major step in the right direction.

On January 31, 2009, Iraqis once again went to the polls, this time under much better security conditions. While the situation allowed for a more vibrant campaign and dialogue, the opportunity was not grasped as enthusiastically as was hoped. Sunnis' participation was much heralded, but the anemic turnout in the Sunni stronghold of Anbar Province was matched only by Baghdad's 40 percent to be the lowest in the country. Of a total of 14.9 million voters registered, only 7.5 million (51 percent) turned out to cast their ballot. By comparison, over 15.5 million Iraqis were registered for the historic December 2005 vote, of whom over 12.2 million (77.7 percent) voted. When corrected for the nearly 2.8 million votes cast in Tamim Province (home of the contested city Kirkuk) and the three Kurdish provinces that did not vote in the 2009 election, the turnout for the December 2005 poll was still much higher. The previous provincial elections, held in January 2005, saw nearly 8.3 million votes cast, of which 2.2 million were cast in the four provinces that did not vote in the January 2009 elections. Despite great improvements across Iraq, the 2009 turnout was not dramatically higher than the 2005 figure.[48]

The low turnout could not be blamed on apathy alone, however. Iraq continued to rely on ration cards for voter registration rolls, leading to critical complications at polling stations. Many displaced families could not vote in the elections because they did not re-register in their new districts and could not return to their old ones. Other Iraqis who had moved shorter distances found problems as well. A journalist who had moved several miles from his parents' home updated his address with authorities, but still had to go to several polling stations to find that the change had not made its way to the voter rolls. Many in this situation gave up after they were turned away at the first station. Rejection rates due to such complications cannot be definitively stated, but anecdotal figures run as high as 35 percent for some polling stations.[49]

Four hundred and one political organizations and a total of 14,800 candidates participated in the elections, chasing 440 seats. Campaigning took on many forms, from animated banners on Iraqi websites to outright bribes. The great strides made in calming the violence in most areas of Iraq allowed candidates to get out among their potential constituents and it also facilitated the creation of a number of nationwide lists. In all, the elections slightly restructured the existing order, reducing the influence of key parties, particularly ISCI in Shi'a-dominated provinces and the IIP in Sunni areas. The legacies entrenched in the early development of post–2003 politics could not be erased by a single election, however. Due to the local nature of the elections and the organizational advantages enjoyed by the existing sectarian religious parties, the elections did not mark a significant turn toward secular national parties. Furthermore, the profusion of entities running in opposition to these established parties scattered votes of dissent. The loose grouping of the July 22 Force did not carry over from parliamentary wrangling to electoral alliances and no other broad coalition emerged. Over three hundred new groups professing liberal outlooks registered for the elections, yet no major alternative could contest the name recognition and organizational backing that the existing parties had built up since 2003.[50]

Critically, the method for distribution of seats favored the biggest winners and left the many opposition candidates without seats. Due to the small number of seats in many provinces, the electoral threshold required to win a single seat was between 1 and 3.8 percent of the total vote. The large number of candidates and lists meant that significant proportions of the vote were as wasted on candidates that did not make the threshold to gain a seat. For example, 18.8 percent of the votes went unrepresented in Baghdad, 25.9 percent in Anbar, and 30.7 percent of the vote in Basra. Wasit Province had an amazing 60.2 percent of the vote go unrepresented, marking a high number of dissent votes and a profusion of candidates.[51]

The United Iraqi Alliance, the Shi'a bloc that had dominated previous elections, broke into several blocs. Prime Minister Nouri al-Maliki's "State of Law Alliance" (*I'tilaf Dowla al-Qanoon*) rose above the other factions in many areas on the wave of relative satisfaction with the improvements made over the previous year. Al-Maliki's alliance included both the Da'wa Party and the Da'wa Party Iraqi Organization, as well as a group headed by powerful Shi'a politician Hussain al-Shahristani, and Fayli Kurd (a predominantly Shi'a subgroup located in Baghdad and Diyala Provinces) and Turkoman parties.[52] State of Law dominated much of the south, coming out on the top position in nine provinces and winning seat in every province except Anbar and Nineveh. The list gained large pluralities in Basra (37 percent), Dhi Qar, (23.1 percent), and Qadissiya (23.1 percent) and won a critical 38 percent in Baghdad. The allocation of seats, however, made this coup even more dramatic. In Baghdad, State of Law's yield increased to 49 percent with 28 of 57 assembly seats.

The State of Law List's strongest competition came from ISCI, whose members had dominated earlier provincial elections. ISCI and its allies ran under the "Martyr of the Mihrab and Independent Force List," a reference to Ayatollah Mohammed Baqir al-Hakim who was martyred in an explosion at the Imam Ali Mosque in Najaf in 2003. The mihrab is the alcove in the wall of a mosque that indicates the direction of Mecca and thereby the direction of prayer. The list included ISCI, the Badr Organization, an organization aligned with Vice President Adel Abd al-Mahdi, and two smaller ISCI-allied parties.[53]

ISCI was significantly weakened by the vote, but retained some power throughout the south, with their Martyr of the Mihrab and Independent Force List finishing second to State of Law in six provinces and registering a third place ranking in two more. In Baghdad, though, the list's 5.4 percent of the vote placed it behind five others. This was a crushing blow for a party that had controlled 54.9 percent of the Baghdad council for the three years prior.[54] To make matters worse, the system for distributing seats meant that, while ISCIs 5 percent vote equated to approximately the same percentage of seats, State of Law's 38 percent of the vote won 49 percent of the seats, putting ISCI even farther out of dominance.

The Sadrists, whose stature had been significantly impacted by the government's campaign to extend its reach into strongholds such as Sadr City, did not participate in the elections as a bloc. Sadrist candidates, mostly billed as technocrats and independents, did participate in other lists, however. Muqtada al-Sadr's representatives openly supported two lists, Integrity and Construction (*Nazaha' wa al-Bina'a*) and the Liberals' Independent Trend (*Tayaar al-Ahrar al-Mustaqil*). Banned from running openly under their own party list, Sadrists chose a spoiler strategy, aiming to break up the councils into blocs of five to ten seats per party, in addition to supporting many independents for seats. A Sadrist spokesman in Najaf stated, "We realized that the best way to make provincial councils more effective is to demolish majority rule and to leave councils without the control of any one party."[55] This strategy was definitely self-serving and, while it may have been one contributor to the reduction of ISCI's dominance on politics in the south, it also allowed State of Law to gain a larger percentage of seats as the small parties and independent candidates failed to meet the threshold required to win a seat.

The Sadrists made a modest showing, but their Liberals' Independent Trend won seats in ten provinces, placing in the top three in Baghdad, Babel, Dhi Qar, Maysan, Najaf, Qadissiya, and Wasit. In a striking turn of events, the Sadrists, outspoken opponents of Nouri al-Maliki, were a central focus of the State of Law list's coalition-making efforts. State of Law formed a central subcommittee charged with approaching the other lists to form coalition governments in the nine provinces where State of Law won. According to a State of Law representative, the two lists have "made great strides" toward agreement on the conditions that would underlie a ruling coalition.[56]

Rounding out the major factions of the fragmented Shi'a political field were several parties that ran on middle class roots and opposition to the major Islamist parties, but missed the threshold to win a seat in most provinces. These lists included the Iraqi Constitutional Party of Interior Minister Jawad al-Bolani, (won seats in only one province), former prime minister Ibrahim al-Jafari National Reform Current (won seats in eight provinces), and the Fadhila Party (won seats in only three provinces).[57]

The Sunni political field was cacophonous as well. Although the resurgent tribal politicians agreed that the Iraqi Islamic Party's (IIP) days in power must end, they failed to create a cohesive political opposition. Members of the Awakening Councils split their lot among several lists and parties, with one influential Awakening figure, Ahmed Abu Risha (brother of slain Awakening leader 'Abd al-Sattar Abu Risha), even allying with the IIP under the Alliance of Intellectuals and Tribes for Development list. The IIP's established name and organization were significant advantages. This, plus the IIP's urban constituency in Ramadi and Falluja, allowed it to do relatively well in polling.[58]

In Anbar Province, Saleh al-Mutlak's relatively moderate Iraqi National Project Gathering took the top spot, with 17.6 percent of the vote and 27.6 percent of the seats. The Alliance of the Awakening of Iraq and Iraqi Independents, a political movement resulting from one faction of the tribal Awakening groups, followed closely with 17.1 percent of the vote and 20.7 percent of the seats. Ahmed Abu Risha's tribal candidates and the IIP were relegated to the third position with 15.9 percent of the vote and 20.7 percent of the seats. Interestingly, a list reportedly consisting of former Baathists and insurgents, the National Movement for Reform and Development (known as *al-Hal*, the solution) garnered fourth place and 7.8 percent of the vote.

The results in Anbar were quickly denounced by many of the participants. Even as talks began on building a coalition provincial government, tribal leaders-turned-politicians threatened to return to violence due to their discontent with the outcome of the vote. Tribal politicians claimed that the Iraqi Islamic Party's list "does not deserve even 1 percent of the vote" while IIP members claimed that the results were fraudulent and that they had actually won some 40 percent.[59]

The largest victory came in Nineveh Province, where the National Hudaba' List garnered 48.4 percent of the total vote, which made them the only list to win an outright majority of seats. When the allocations were made, list members were granted 51 percent of the provincial seats. The list consisted primarily of prominent Arabs and a few Kurds running on a platform of resisting the absorption of Nineveh, or parts of it, into a Kurdish region.[60] A Kurdish coalition, the Nineveh Brotherly List won another 25.5 percent (32 percent of the seats), relegating the formerly dominant Sunni Iraqi Islamic Party to a mere 6.7 percent.

The elections were relatively successful, but allegations of fraud and the large proportion of unrepresented votes do not bode well for satisfaction with the electoral process. One report in an Iraqi newspaper alleged that as many as 250 of the winning candidates in the elections (out of a total of 440) provided forged diplomas when they applied for their candidacy. The electoral law required that candidates have at least a high school diploma, so these winners would be ineligible for their seats on the councils on the face of it. A council member quoted in the article also stated that the votes of up to thirty election centers in Baghdad, Mosul, and Diyala were discounted due to fraud. It seems that some of these stations' votes were discounted because the voting totals there exceeded 100 percent of the registered voters in the district, indicating that ballot boxes were being stuffed.[61]

While these violations may not have significantly affected the outcome of the election, they will heighten the discontent of those who feel that they have been cheated out of their representation. Even where these feelings are completely unfounded, the hint of irregularities opens the way for people to challenge the validity of the whole process. Accompanied by high handedness of the victors in distributing the spoils or prolonged quarreling over ruling coalitions, these allegations of electoral fraud could be a major incitement toward defection from the political process. In short, while the fraud may be statistically insignificant, it could be turned by wily politicians into a major factor in driving discontented Iraqis to obstruct the political process, to return to violence, or to justify other non-democratic tactics to get their way in the future.

The most positive outcome of the provincial elections may be the experience gained by the newer political parties. These entities gained organizational and campaigning ability that may be used in the upcoming national elections. What is more, the bitter memory of thousands of wasted votes may prompt greater cooperation among the opposition groups and candidates. Without a more unified opposition, there is little hope that the character of government and the corrupt contest for spoils will change. Iraqis, however, seem to be breathing a sigh of relief that the elections went off nearly free of violence and that their country is returning to some semblance of normalcy in many areas.

Looking past the January 2009 provincial elections, the key event in any transition is the first transfer of national power. In late 2009, a second round of elections for the National Assembly will be held. A new government will be formed based on the outcome of those elections and a new prime minister will be chosen. There are several stumbling blocks that may hinder the political environment in the meantime. The handling of the Kirkuk issue and the absorption of the Awakening groups into Iraqi government control will go a long way toward determining the future of Iraq. Handled well, they could provide Iraqis with a feeling of certainty about their future going into the national vote. Handled poorly, they could derail the whole project of transition in Iraq. Once those obstacles are cleared, the completion of a peaceful transfer of power following free and fair national elections will be one of the surest markers that Iraq is marching steadily on the path toward true democracy. Much is yet to be seen, however.

Development from the Bottom Up

The reality of life in Iraq is that political leaders, insurgents, and militia members have been in the driver's seat since 2003. The focus of this book has been, of necessity, on the small minority of Iraqis that drive politics and violence. The majority of Iraqis are silent victims to the hell that their country has become, yet, despite the violence, Iraqis have been struggling to rebuild the country's social and cultural institutions, see beyond the attempts to create sectarian chaos, and live in defiance of the horrific conditions imposed on them. There are numerous signs of change and hope, but unless these bottom-up reforms can be transmitted into the political realm, they will have little bearing on Iraq's future path. Should Iraq's future elections produce positive change, bottom-up development of civil society will be critical to linking the political realm to the society.

The most critical role Iraqi society has to play at current is in healing the wounds opened by years of violence, sectarian and otherwise. As noted earlier, sectarianism is a phenomenon with an extensive history in Iraq but the worst of it has tended to be at the political level, as opposed to the social or interpersonal level. The success of radical elements in creating sectarian war in Iraq has undoubtedly created a great deal more sectarian tension and mistrust than there was before, but many Iraqis realize that, beyond the armed groups, there are other Iraqis of the opposite sect in similar, miserable situations with no way to stop the violence perpetrated by a minority. Even among the armed groups, there have been numerous examples of cross-sectarian cooperation. In 2004, sermons from radical Sunni cleric Harith al-Dhari drew both Sunni and Shi'a Iraqis opposed to the occupation. Shi'a Sadrists and Sunnis offered mutual support during the Fallujah and Najaf crises of 2004, offering fighters, blood, and medical supplies.[62] Many Iraqi nationalists oppose the occupation above all.

The decline in sectarian violence in 2007 and 2008 gave Iraqi society space to reach across lines and rebuild old ties. Local community leaders began holding neighborhood-level meetings in which they discussed security measures and negotiated the return of families displaced by sectarian violence and threats.[63] If local-level initiatives such as these can expand into broader organizations and offer their own neighborhoods collective services, they could displace the militias and party and clerical offices that use services to buy loyalty and territory for their own ends. Such development would give ordinary Iraqis a degree of independence from the ruthless groups that have ruled Iraq since 2003 and could blossom into more inclusive political organizations. This process would take time, however, and the resistance from standing groups would be merciless.

Another key institution required for democratic society is the press. The Iraqi press underwent a booming revival after 2003. Iraqi historian Jassim Mohammed al-'Azawi discovered that an amazing 764 daily and weekly newspapers and magazines had been established since April 2003. These ran the gamut from independent dailies to party papers and even publications issued by individuals from all of Iraq's communities. He found that the independent papers enjoyed wide freedom in their commentary and criticism, which was quite a development considering the complete lack of press freedom only a few years earlier. The fledgling press is far from refining its coverage, though. Al-'Azawi found that most papers relied on online reports from other agencies without referencing their sources, failed to abide by professional journalistic standards, and tended to publish political and religious statements and speeches selectively. Many papers were the mouthpieces of religious or political groups, which tended to use their front pages to publicize their leadership.[64]

Voters in the first round of elections often knew little about the lists, candidates, and issues they were voting for, beyond what was preached to them in sermons and other forums. The experience of nearly four years of Iraqi government, fully exposed to the spotlight of Iraqi and international media, has raised awareness of the cast of characters and their strengths and failings. The growth of the press and their coverage of key issues has established a better-informed electorate than was the case four years ago. It is for this reason that some parties wish to limit voters' latitude by keeping closed lists for elections.

Going hand-in-hand with the issue of the media, Iraqis are seeking not only more information but more education as well. Despite Iraq's ills, demand for education was rising even before the latest downturn in violence. Enrollment increased markedly in primary and middle schools across the country following the invasion. In large part, this growth seems to have been driven by the improved salaries seen by civil servants under the new regime, allowing their children to turn from subsistence living to education. Even older students, unable to complete their education under Saddam, have returned to school. This progress was uneven, however. Violence-ridden areas, such as Baghdad, witnessed drops in enrollment while stable regions such as the south had much higher increases than the national average. This local growth was partly driven by rising numbers of internally displaced families. Unfortunately, this growth and its uneven nature taxed infrastructure and teaching capacity in many areas.[65]

Iraq has a relatively well-developed higher education sector, with twenty-one public universities and nine private universities. The country was a major center of academic production through the early years of Saddam's reign, but quality fell sharply with the strain of wars and economic crisis. Since 2003 there has been re-growth, with two of the nine private universities being established after the fall of the old regime. These universities offered a large number of different programs and enrolled a relatively high number of Iraqis, yet years of neglect and the looting and attacks in 2003 and later took their toll on facilities and personnel.[66]

Hundreds of university professors have been killed since the invasion in acts of political, sectarian, class, and simply criminal violence. One report put the number of dead at 550 by January 2007. In the year between September 2006 and September 2007 alone seventy-eight professors were assassinated. John Agresto, a former advisor to the Ministry of Higher Education, said that the academics were targeted, because they tended to be more secular and open-minded than the general population. This posed a threat to those who would use fear and distrust to control the population and attain their narrow ends. Students were frequently unable to attend class due to security concerns and road closures. Adding to the sense of insecurity, militia members often monitored professors' lectures for offensive content. Intimidation of professors was commonplace, whether for political reasons or simply for grades and other preferential treatment. Student organizations became polarized and hostile, with violence breaking out frequently on campus among students and between students and faculty. Many universities became segregated by sect and even political faction as groups attempted to impose their religious and political program on students, including dress codes for female students and inspection of cell phones for songs or other evidence that students support the wrong faction. Academic posts previously held by Baʻathists were now doled out according to sectarian and party affiliation. Despite the mostly negative trends, some student associations do promote understanding and dialogue.[67]

Education is the cornerstone of any society's campaign for self-improvement. Universities, especially, are critical to providing qualified employees for both the public and the private sector. What is more, the congregation of students of varied backgrounds enriches the educational experience and encourages more open and tolerant viewpoints in the future. Indeed, in Arabic, the word for university, *jami'a,* is a derivation of "to congregate" and is very similar to the word for mosque, *jami'*. The balkanization of Iraq's university system by political thugs deprives the nation of a well-educated and integrated professional class, blocking a major arena in which social reconciliation could be taking place. With increased security and pressure on the militias, perhaps the government will be able to retake the educational system in the coming years.

Despite the problems with the university system, Iraqis are demanding access to more social and cultural output. Bookstores have proliferated since 2003. Demand is returning for works of Iraqi authors, especially the sociologist Ali al-Wardi and Hassan al-Allawi, an author and politician, as Iraqis struggle to come to a better understanding of their own society. Many bookstores, meeting places of poets and intellectuals before their closure due to economic strain and government surveillance, have recently re-opened. Iraq's associational life flourished in these stores in the 1950s and '60s, and many hope for a similar rebirth in the coming years. Beyond cultural works, demand remains high for the Islamist works that were banned under the old regime. Art and film have likewise bloomed, with artists' groups that hid under Saddam holding open shows and festivals focusing on indigenous works.[68]

In order for Iraq to inch back from the brink of civil war, much more will have to be accomplished at both the social and political levels to re-integrate society. Although violence is down sharply, Iraq's society and polity are still highly balkanized. From the National Assembly to university halls and coffee shops, only increased contact, rebuilt cross-sectarian institutions, and time will heal the wounds of mistrust and reorient Iraqi political and social activity toward a broader and more inclusive future. This will be resisted, however, by the ruthless opportunists who inflamed sectarian differences into sectarian fear and hatred. The political bosses that caused Iraq's descent into hell, directly or indirectly, are still at the top of a sectarian political system, fighting against any trends that may unseat them. Electoral politics must cause a change in the top of the system if bottom-up reconciliation is to have a chance to work. The road to stability will be long and fraught with pitfalls. Though the road to democracy is longer still, it is not completely blocked off yet for Iraq.

10
Whither Transition?

> Above all else, the criteria governing intervention should recognize that, as we learned in Vietnam, military force has only a limited capacity to facilitate the process of nation building. Military force, by itself, cannot rebuild a "failed state."[1]
> —Robert S. McNamara, former secretary of defense, 1995

> The situation is now too critical and the investment too great for us to longer tolerate a directionless and floundering effort that is losing the population, hence the war.[2]
> —John Paul Vann, advisor in Vietnam, 1965

The case of transition in Iraq is as unique as it has been tragic. In one of the world's few cases of externally imposed transition, and the only case in the Arab world, America hoped to quickly create an unprecedented paragon of democratic virtue in the Arab world. Instead, it created a nightmare of competing illiberal groups and a focus for jihadist and anti-American sentiment in the region. Despite the American missteps and Iraqi obstacles, Iraq has a much better chance at mid-term stability and long-term democracy today than it did in the first four years of its transition. Yet, the outcome hangs in the balance. It could swiftly and decisively turn to chaos and illiberalism, yet it will take considerable time and work to build stability. Democracy is a possible, but distant, prospect.

Two sets of conclusions arise for consideration when one looks at the experience in Iraq to date. The first set offers insight into the specifics of the Iraqi case and can help to partly illuminate the road ahead in Iraq. The second is a broader set of cautions regarding transition in general, which must be heeded when the world confronts its next crisis of transition. While few people have a taste for another adventure of regime change, dictators fall, regimes crumble, and popular sentiments change. Policymakers and scholars must not bury their heads, saying, "Never again." Transitions will pop up again, and the many lessons of Iraq should be analyzed for warning signs and examples of what did work.

Perhaps the biggest lesson of all is that, while the international community must assist states in transition, the project must be guided from within. In the end, the solutions in Iraq must be Iraqi solutions, which means that the initially lofty American goals in Iraq were forced to become much more circumscribed. America removed the dictator. It caused some, but not all, of the chaos that followed. America must now stand back and allow Iraqis to build their own order. General Petraeus acknowledged the limits of American policy in Iraq during testimony before Congress in early 2008. "We're not after the Holy Grail in Iraq," he said. "We're not after Jeffersonian democracy. We're after conditions that would allow our soldiers to disengage."[3]

The challenge in Iraq today is much the same as that outlined by Hanna Batatu. Writing at a time when the barbarian nature of the Baʻath regime had not yet become fully apparent, Batatu wondered if Iraq would be able to

> contribute, in a creative manner, to the process of nation-state building that the 1920 Revolt had set afoot. This will involve . . . the necessity of binding the peasants to the townsmen and the Shiʻis to the Sunnis; and creating mutually advantageous relations between the Kurds and the Arabs; and, at the same time, raising qualitatively the standard of living and level of culture of the mass of Iraqis—all of which presupposes . . . the ability to channel into agricultural and industrial development the wealth that oil generates instead of largely dissipating it, as in past years, in unproductive consumption.

He closed his eleven-hundred-page tome by writing that these tasks "can be accomplished only if the country's principal political forces pull together and work hand-in-hand for the good of their people."[4] Some thirty years later, it is still unclear if the country's principal political forces will pull together. Regardless of surges, American policy shifts, Awakenings, or international commitments, the only ones who can salvage transition in Iraq and slowly work toward democracy are Iraqis.

The fundamental flaw of early U.S. policy in Iraq was the use of the paradigm of regime change. From the idea that the Ba'ath regime could be surgically replaced with a friendly democratic regime sprung many of the mistakes and misconceptions that led to the Iraq's crisis of governance and chaos. If future interventions are to succeed, whether they stem from invasion, internal conflict, state collapse, or self-initiated change, the concept of transition, rather than sharp regime change, must be embraced along with its implications of major commitments in the arenas of security and state-building.

At the bottom line, policy guidance for transition situations must start with a pragmatic assessment of the former regime's legacy, which affects the institutions and servants of the state, the social structures within the state, and the individuals of that society. Those who enjoyed power and status under the old order are likely to reject a transition that robs them of that power. Even in the most repressive regimes, there must be a base of support in the state and society. Security forces must be staffed, societal structures and leaders must be co-opted, and the rest of society must be cowed into obeisance. These are not legacies that can be erased overnight.

The United States liberated Iraq expecting that regime change would be a simple matter of removing Saddam Hussein, assisting Iraqis to create a new government over a period of months, and then leaving a new democratic state by the fall of 2003. The contentious legacy of Saddam's rule confounded these expectations and proved their naivety. A key lesson from the Iraqi conflict is that transition from oppressive rule to democracy is not a simple task of regime change, but rather demands a careful and long-term change of societal and political structures heavily damaged by years of mistreatment.

Much of the planning for operations in Iraq rested on faulty assumptions about the character of the social and political landscape in Iraq. While policymakers hoped to find a welcoming and relatively intact Iraq, they found that Iraq was much more complex and broken than had been expected. Most of the criticism leveled at the actors and actions in Iraq since 2003 has likewise failed to fully explore the intricate legacy that confronted Iraqi transition. Instead, commentators have chosen to dissect the Bush administration's ideological background, slam military planning, detail operational execution, and provide venues for officials to lay blame at each others' feet and the feet of the media.

Although many of these critiques are warranted, they fall into the comfortable realm of superficial introspective study, rather than a frank admission of our American failure to understand many of the societies that inhabit our world and an attempt to rectify that shortcoming. All of these endeavors fall short of our duty to the many Soldiers, Sailors, Airmen, and Marines who have died in individually noble attempts to contribute to Iraq's liberation. The critiques also fall short of our debt to the innocent Iraqis who have died, caught in the crossfire of a war brought on them by a sadistic madman and continued by many more that emerged in his wake.

The Lessons of Iraqi Transition

Concepts of insurgency and sectarian violence dominate narratives about the conflict in Iraq. Of course, while these are major aspects of the conflict and have been a central part of this book, it is important to look beyond these broad themes to the complexities that churn beneath them. Most Iraqis hold a strong sense of nationalism. Beyond this, however, they are divided by complex layers of loyalty and identity. Although some of these divisions fueled insurgency and sectarian violence, they are only the broadest categories of fault lines in Iraqi society. The factionalized nature of Iraqi society is a key factor in politics and violence.

For instance, with the Sunni, the only façade of Sunni unity was in their near-universal rejection of the occupation and the new political process in its first two years. As we have seen, there was no one "Sunni insurgency," but rather many groups fighting different insurgencies for different ends. These groups were divided along multiple lines: ideological, religious, class, tribal, urban versus rural or tribal, tribal sheikhs versus tribal peasants, and old regime supporters versus their opponents, to name a few. Even at the height of the insurgency from 2004 through 2006, intra-Sunni conflict simmered along these divisions, and, by 2007, they had crystallized, sidelining the insurgencies as tribal and urban groups organized to drive out extremists. With the decline of the extremist threat, however, divisions among Awakening groups and between the Awakening and the established Sunni political elites came to the surface once again.

On the Shi'a side, despite the early internecine violence in which Sadrist under-classes confronted the established clerical hierarchy and their middle class supporters, politicians quickly chose a tactical unity with the active guidance of Ayatollah Ali al-Sistani. Yet, as the mud that patched together the United

Iraqi Alliance dried, cracks soon appeared. Parties withdrew ministers, walked out of the alliance, and even splintered into competing factions. By 2008, parliamentarians of the Alliance were aligned against each other on key votes, seeking new allies from outside their list. In the streets, ISCI and Sadr supporters competed for new territory and supporters behind the veil of sectarian war, even coming into direct conflict in key Shi'a areas. Only the Kurds were relatively unified at the national political level.

In this divisive environment lay both pitfalls and promise. The pitfalls are numerous. Each invites more violence should bosses find themselves unable to navigate through the peaceful political system. Even if the fault lines do not flare into violence, Iraqi disunity cripples attempts at political progress and national reconciliation. There is promise, however. The fragmentation of Iraq's ethno-sectarian communities along class and issue lines provides a potential basis for new political coalitions formed around issues other than identity. This is Iraq's only hope for exceeding the bounds of the confessional politics that will undoubtedly lead the nation to disaster.

Political maneuvering in 2008 demonstrated the willingness of some parties to exceed sectarian boundaries and unite on certain issues. The cross-sectarian bloc that has formed thus far, however, is united on little more than opposition to the occupation, the ruling elites, and the ISCI-Kurd alliance pushing for increased federalism. For a more permanent coalition to successfully break the mold of the sectarian bloc system, parties will have to gather around a positive set of principles (as opposed to the negative principles of opposition) and demonstrate an ability to break the current ruling elites' grasp on government. The opposition bloc as it currently stands holds a good number of vocal outsiders and political extremists. It is doubtful that the Sadrists and their Sunni former insurgent allies will bring the country to a stable democracy. Yet, if moderates from all parts of Iraq find that they must join hands in parliament to overcome this opposition, the beginnings of democratic politics may begin to materialize.

Western analysts have put forth a number of benchmarks for progress in Iraq. Even though many of these are absolute requirements for a stable democratic order, it may be years before Iraq's political sphere develops the confidence, credibility, and mutual trust required to lay such issues to rest. The clearest indicators of Iraq's path will be the effects of the 2009 elections on the party and coalition systems and their eventual performances in government. If these elections are delayed or disrupted, there is a chance of Iraq slipping back into a form of authoritarian government. If the elections go well and the power structure in Iraq is changed peacefully, there will be hope for a slow, painful march toward democracy. If the elections produce political stagnation or continued sectarianism in government, there is a great risk of state failure and/or civil war.

If the Iraqi people are given a fair chance to express their political desires in a timely manner, some recent bottom-up developments may bode well for electoral changes. Many, especially in the younger generation, have grown tired of the sectarian violence and disgusted with the politicians who have failed to improve conditions in Iraq. These sentiments show promise for a political shake-up and a demand for greater accountability and pragmatism. Further, growing distrust of religion and religious parties may force politicians to campaign behind real political programs, rather than relying on religious solidarity and allegiance to clerics such as al-Sistani to ensure them votes. Some groups, most notably ISCI, have refused to consider removing religious symbols and pictures from their campaign, however. The development of the press and other social organizations in the years since the last votes may help voters to become more informed on candidates and issues as well. Finally, the greater inclusion of nearly all groups in the political sphere, to include former Sunni insurgents, tribal figures, and a more developed set of Sadrist figures, tends to suggest that the upcoming elections are an opportunity for a much fuller accounting of the population's political desires than the earlier votes. Despite these advancements, successful elections are not the end point of Iraqi transition. In reality, it is only the beginning of a progression toward more representative form of government.

While political activity may placate the majority, it only takes a small minority to derail politics through violence. Policymakers must remain focused on long-term deterrence or destruction of these actors. Violence in Iraq has been fueled by a diverse mix of nationalist and Islamist insurgents, militia thugs, and criminals. Several of these actors cannot be deterred by any means, yet they represent the smallest minority of the lot. Many insurgents have already been lured away from the fight by political concessions and the enticement of a monthly paycheck. Others continue to attack simply for the attractive pay offered by extremists and opportunists. Economic development and the provision of jobs is a central component to robbing violent groups of their manpower and inviting opportunists to turn to more legitimate enterprises. Political engagement, too, is crucial to forcing bosses to rein in their followers. The remaining extremist minority must simply be hunted down by Iraqi security forces amid a population hostile to their continued campaign of terror. Missteps can easily return the initiative to the violent groups, however.

Should elections fail to produce political movement, or should renewed violence intervene, calls for "soft partition" of Iraq may increase. The Biden Resolution, an amendment to the 2008 National Defense Authorization Act, is held up by both sides of the debate over the partitioning of Iraq as a key document. Yet, Amendment Number 2997, the "Sense of Congress on Federalism in Iraq," really offers little about soft partition. In the context of earlier drafts and comments during floor debate, the amendment's promotion of a federal solution to Iraq's woes was originally meant to be a soft division of Iraq into ethno-sectarian regions under a weak federal government. The amendment in its final approved version contains no such explicit language, however.[5]

Even with the watered-down language of the final text, Iraqi politicians were quick to condemn the resolution as unwelcome meddling based on a faulty interpretation of Iraq's history and its future desires.[6] As noted in the previous chapter, only ISCI and the Kurds are strong proponents of more extensive regionalization of Iraq at the current time. Many other Iraqi politicians of both Shi'a and Sunni backgrounds have strongly opposed moves to create new regions. Iraqi politicians know that, while the idea of federalism gives the illusion that Iraq could easily be carved up into three large, peaceful enclaves for Kurds, Sunni, and Shi'a, the reality on the ground is nowhere near as neat.

Some have pushed the dangerous idea that, because Iraq is an amalgam of three separate Ottoman provinces, the best solution is to allow the country to return to its natural form of the three provinces of Mosul, Baghdad, and Basra that existed prior to the machinations of the European powers. Others argue that the lines of division have already been drawn and that the majority of the displacement, ethnic cleansing, and realignment was completed in the bloody months of 2006. The reality of the situation, as laid out earlier, is not so simple. Iraqi regions have become increasingly segregated, yet partition would still require a massive amount of relocation. Moreover, several key areas including Kirkuk, Mosul, Baquba, and the entire capital region would be hotly disputed, leading to a civil war among all three of the country's major groups. Finally, while the Kurds will be quite happy with the partition of Iraq, neither most Iraqi Arabs, nor Iraq's neighbors will accept such a solution.[7]

Even were Iraqis and their neighbors to agree to partition, evidence is dubious that it would stop the violence. A recent study of seventeen ethnic civil wars since 1945 showed that partition correlated with a drop in violence only where populations could be significantly segregated, such as Cyprus in 1974, Ethiopia-Eritrea in 1991, and Pakistan-Bangladesh in 1971.[8] In Iraq, populations are still highly mixed in a number of areas, not least of which are Baghdad and Kirkuk. Barring an all-out civil war that would bloodily redraw Iraq's demographic boundaries, the state will continue to be unified and its population significantly intermixed.

Iraq will not be "soft partitioned." Therefore, another way must be found to stabilize the country. One way is the slow process of transition toward democracy. The other is a relapse into dictatorship, in which a strongman would brutally quell the violence. Otherwise, Iraq, the land of many of the world's most storied civilizations with a veritable treasure beneath its soil, may be headed for state collapse. The enormity of the work to be accomplished to overcome violence, corruption, and institutional incapacity is such that a weak government staggering on incoherently is doomed for failure. If Iraq does not begin to tread decisively down the path of democracy or regress into dictatorship in the coming one to two years, it risks becoming the world's most strategically important failed state. The outcome will rely on the Iraqi leadership, as there is no way for outsiders to force greater democratic development and the international community surely cannot encourage a strongman to step up in Iraq. Even once a course is chosen, though, Iraq must complete the nation-building of which Hanna Batatu spoke. In these challenges, Iraq joins a host of countries trying to find stability and prosperity without a strong sense of nation.

The Broader Lessons of Iraqi Transition

Experiences gained in Iraq reach well beyond the country's borders, and even beyond cases of transition. Scholars and policymakers alike have a duty to study and heed the often-tragic lessons gained in the years since Saddam's fall and to apply them, not only to future transitions to democracy, but also to the host of states around the world that are desperately attempting to modernize their governments, economies, and societies. Many of the problems in Iraq, while often simplistically portrayed as arising from ancient and immobile hatreds, are actually a product of the upheaval that is modernization.

Modernity in a socio-political sense is a loaded term that can be seen as dismissive of older, particularly non-Western forms of social and political organization. Yet, it is the simplest term we can use to refer to the milieu of concepts that underpin the modern state system. The clash between modern social and political loyalties and older forms of organization and association are at the heart of Iraq's tortured response to transition and are characteristic of the broader struggle of modernizing societies. Samuel Huntington wrote that "political modernization involves the rationalization of authority, the replacement of a large number of traditional, religious, familial, and ethnic political authorities by a single, secular, national political authority." Huntington continues to argue that government must be a result of humanity, not God or nature, and that "a well-ordered society must have a determinate human source of final authority, obedience to whose positive law takes precedence over other obligations." In his view, modernization is the process of centralization of power in a single national body, with sovereignty against both internal and external forces. On an individual level, these changes require broadened loyalties, expanding from entities such as family, clan, or sect to class and nation.[9] Batatu refered to this process of nation-building, in which all groups are assimilated into the political arena, their desires reconciled, and their loyalties realigned to a newly constructed national identity.

In Iraq, as in many other modernizing societies around the world, allegiance is torn between the traditional and the modern. Transition in Iraq is much more than the creation of new laws and institutions. It is the process of reorganizing a society factionalized into sects, tribes, families, and other local power groups into a political body with national loyalty, divided along modern lines of identity such as class and political outlook. Although a complete break with traditional social identity will never be realized anywhere in the world, identities must be realigned enough to build a national, consensual political sphere. This movement is strongly resisted by conservative forces in Iraq, for both ideological and self-serving reasons. The grip of these conservative forces can only be weakened over time through broadened political participation. If Iraq continues its electoral and legislative work in the coming years, rather than lapsing back into authoritarianism, repeated popular and legislative votes will tend to realign political organization on these modern lines of class and issue to a degree. The tentative first steps of this realignment have already been seen in the parliament. This shift is critical to build a more fluid and adaptable socio-political order, capable of dealing peacefully with the demands of representative government, rather than a fixed and antagonistic system of ethno-sectarian blocs or a cacophony of tribal candidates unable to work toward common ends.

In 2003, Iraq was thrust into the most radical process of modernization in a region that is already witnessing one of the fastest rates of sociological change in history. Less than a century ago, the vast majority of Arabs were living in a stateless, tribal society that had changed relatively little in over a millennium. Today, the Arab world is thoroughly penetrated with the newest technological, political, and social phenomenon. The mind-boggling rapidity of change plays no small part in the upheaval found in the region today. While Iraq has a longer history of modernizing development than other Arab states, there remains a great deal of conflict between traditional and modern socio-political loyalties.

Beyond the clash between modern and traditional loyalties lies the confrontation between positive and divine laws. Huntington's assertions regarding the centrality of positive law, written by humans, to modern political organization are problematic for many societies, not least of which the Islamic and tribal societies of the Middle East. Huntington asserts that a stable society must have a definite, human source as its final authority. Positive law can be endlessly debated and modified, yet as long as political actors work within an agreed system, conflicts over this positive law can be peacefully resolved through elections, legislation, judicial proceedings, and the like.

In a modern society, many citizens hold divine law to be the ultimate source of inspiration and arbitration, though they generally agree to operate within a system defined by positive law. Such a system is fluid, adaptable, and open to criticism and amendment. Yet, others reject such a system out of hand, charging that humans cannot defy law handed down from God. Many Islamists would argue that Islamic society can only be governed by the immutable religious *shari'a* law. As the law of God, shari'a is not open to amendment or debate, although Islamic scholars do have some latitude for interpretation and adaptation to new social circumstances. Yet, even interpretation of religious law is highly contentious and rarely leads to consensus, because opponents can always argue that they know the higher truth intended by God and refuse to be bound to others' "faulty interpretation" of that law. With positive law, there is no higher truth to contest. It is a man-made law that can be contested in a man-made system.

Conflicts between positive and divine laws, secularism and religious politics, and modern and traditional identities are at the root of reform in many developing countries today. While Huntington's prescriptions worked for the West, other societies must come to a solution with which they can live. While such a solution may not fully reflect the modernity Huntington had in mind, for those wishing to maintain a highly traditional society, the genie is out of the bottle in Iraq. If diverse groups and ideologies are not reconciled in a representative political system, the only alternatives will be draconian rule or outright chaos.

Countries on the path of modernization are often struggling against strong conservative forces defending a comfortable status quo. What is more, these states do not have the level of institutional development needed to supplant the older forces. In the past, nation-states were built slowly, upon layers of previous socio-political development. Strong institutions were established and then used to draw or force allegiance to a constructed national identity. Furthermore, the development of nation-states was driven by necessity. In the ruthless environment of Europe, states were forced to develop institutions and loyalties capable of sustaining the state in the face of nearly constant military threats. Governmental institutions, schools, infrastructure, and industry were all products of a fierce military and economic competition in which the defeated were incorporated into states more successful at development.[10] Today, no such competitive environment exists for budding nation-states.

Iraq and the many other states created in the course of the last century never went through the long crucible of state-making that European states did, nor are they longstanding political entities like China or Japan. Many of them have been able to rely on resource revenues rather than entering an industrial competition that has similar state-making pressures to the conflictual environment of Europe over the past several centuries. To compete industrially or militarily, a country must construct institutions, facilities, and infrastructure. It must have a government capable of managing these assets, produce an educated citizenry with national loyalty and a sense of cooperation to fill factories or military formations, and an economy that provides this interested community with jobs and income. Iraq's development on all these fronts is stunted. Thus, the state has never had to force its citizens to redirect their loyalties to the center. It has never built the infrastructure that makes central control and balanced economic development possible. Saddam was able to rule through terror and manipulation of traditional loyalties. Freedom does not translate to democracy in these conditions. It becomes chaos.

Corruption and lawlessness are two of the main drivers of persisting insecurity and are major drains on governmental capacity. Virtually nothing can be achieved in Iraq without a bribe, and every government program leaks huge amounts of money through various forms of corruption. Of 180 countries surveyed by Transparency International, only Somalia and Myanmar fare worse on measures of corruption.[11] People need to learn how to deal with freedom: to share the road, stand in line, abide by ethics and the rule of law without someone standing over them with a club. The government must be rebuilt, yet so too must the will to be governed by rules and norms. The ruthless opportunists who emerged as political leaders in the new Iraq were often the worst violators of the lot. Much more than the average citizen, these leaders instigated Iraq's descent into sectarian peril and transformed the political arena into a trough of spoils.

This is a phenomenon that the U.S. military has faced and recognized before, most recently in Vietnam. A major problem that the United States faced in winning the support of the South Vietnamese was the rotten government in Saigon, consisting of elite crooks competing in a race to line their own pockets before the inevitable, self-induced fall of their regime. Even though high-level military professionals, including the Marine Corps' LtGen Victor Krulak, recognized that their efforts were being greatly damaged by Saigon's lack of legitimacy, their observations were drowned out by the high command's desire for a solely military solution to what was misperceived as a solely military problem. One of the most outspoken critics of this solely military solution was the legendary, controversial, and tragic figure of John Paul Vann.

During the opening days of America's involvement in Vietnam, Vann was there as an advisor. Disapproving of the Army's approach to the war, he retired but returned to the country as a civilian advisor. During this period, Vann and some of his colleagues perceived that the corrupt and worthless regime in Saigon was driving young men toward the Viet Cong (VC). Vann viewed the challenge as nothing less than formulating a new strategy in 1965. Instead of focusing on destroying the VC, America needed to build South Vietnam into a nation to which its citizens would rally. U.S. forces would secure Saigon and protect the regime while America gradually rebuilt it, rooting out corruption and incompetence. In a strategic proposal written in 1965, Vann warned that "a successful military venture will be negated by a continued failure of [the Government of Vietnam] to win its own people." Vann went on to write, "The situation is now too critical and the investment too great for us to longer tolerate a directionless and floundering effort that is losing the population, hence the war."[12]

Vann and others advocated that the United States take over and rebuild the South Vietnamese government essentially as a colonial power. Of course, this never happened in Vietnam and it certainly should not happen in Iraq. There is a popularly elected, sovereign government there and the United States has no right to take back that sovereignty. Yet, the basic premise of Vann's argument holds true in Iraq as it did in Vietnam. As long as the government fails to take the strides required to win public support and confidence, democracy can never flourish. Many of the current Iraqi politicians have no sense of national interest, but rather use slogans about the nation to wrap up their narrow interests. While many Iraqis are fed up, it is yet to be seen whether or not future elections will sufficiently express the public's desires for accountability, stability, and progress.

Looking for the Future in Our Past

Looking forward, scholars, analysts, and statesmen must examine beyond the surface of troubled regimes. Whether looking for a change of regime, or attempting to assist others in their quest for a better future through democratic opening, they will find that simple solutions are unlikely to last. Transition is a complex event, in which the lasting legacies of the old regime confront the new realities that demand change. To help others navigate the contentious path that such a transition must travel, we must examine not only problematic leadership, but also the troubles that lie beneath.

In the end, we, as Americans, may need to reevaluate how we desire to promote our beloved democracy around the world. Germany and Japan are shining examples of the true greatness of America. We fought and defeated them in a total war. Then, in a spirit that was not only self-interested, but also noble and charitable, we undertook massive programs of reconstruction and state-building in both countries These countries' prominent positions in today's world is in no small part due to the effort of Americans. Our own position, too, is a product of the decisive end of the war and the aggressive policies that followed to exploit our victory for the good of our own country and theirs. Since then, our record has been more checkered. A trail of broken bodies and troubled states marks the path of American armed intervention since the close of World War II. The most prominent of these was our involvement in Vietnam. Both Americans and Iraqis draw frequent comparison between that war and the one ongoing today. Many of the staunchest supporters of the war despise such comparisons, but veterans of both conflicts are often the first to admit the parallels.

Many of these comparisons are simplistic; there is a story, however, of one Marine officer's last day in Vietnam that illustrates a critical parallel. Having come to the end of his year-long tour in Vietnam, he sat in the China Beach Officers' Club in Danang, Vietnam, with a friend, basking in the glow of the afternoon sun and a few congratulatory beers as he awaited his flight home. An American civilian working in the area offered to give the two a ride to the airport.

This gracious offer allowed the two officers to relax a while longer, rather than having to head out to wait for a bus. As they sat in the dying afternoon light, the fatigue of a year of danger and exertion began to drain from them as they sipped their beers. As they were about to leave for the airport, their new acquaintance made a remark that the Marine would carry with him and pass on years later. It was at once a subtle, yet emphatic, punctuation of a year of his life. "The Vietnamese are mostly poor farmers. Their main concern is their rice paddies and not the government in control in Saigon. Democracy means almost nothing to them in their daily struggle to make ends meet."

This was not American arrogance. In reality it was a mark of humility. We believe so fundamentally in the power of democracy that we often think that it will cure all ills. Most Americans have never seen firsthand the crushing poverty and insecurity of many parts of the developing world. Those who have know that political activity is the furthest thing from the minds of families trying to feed a starving baby or to guard themselves against ethnic or sectarian violence. Only years of institutional and political development can help people in such situations. Elections are not a silver bullet.

Echoing this sober departure of my father from Vietnam, I read a hauntingly familiar comment from a young Baghdadi girl's diary, recorded by Anthony Shadid. "What are we going to do with democracy when we don't have anything?"[13] There is so much more that must go with democracy in order for it to be meaningful, for it to work. Security, economic development, institutions and laws must accompany it. While all of these things are improving in Iraq, are they improving quickly enough for a stable and beneficial democracy to take root?

If we had approached the termination of World War II in the same manner as we approached the termination of this war, the remainder of the last century would have been one vast paroxysm of violence. However, we did not. We committed the mass of our resources and our strengths to creating a lasting peace. In Iraq, we should have done the same. Had policymakers recognized the lasting legacies of Iraq's troubled past and called for a massive and enduring commitment to rebuilding the state and slowly fostering democracy, the outcome may have been much different. Surely, Americans would have been much more willing to commit to such a plan while the impact of 9/11 was still fresh than they were years into a seemingly failed campaign. While Iraq has been at least temporarily rescued from catastrophe, there will clearly be no Iraqi Marshall Plan. The future of Iraq rests mostly on the shoulders of Iraqis now.

Looking into my father's past, I see a reflection of our future in Iraq. Iraq's fate is still uncertain. I hope for the best there, yet I fear the worst. Our experience in Iraq should underscore the difficult legacies that transition must overcome. It should also serve as a warning against rosy hopes for best-case outcomes. Success is built on preparation, planning, and complete commitment—not hope.

As for the people of Iraq, they struggle on through days of fear and insecurity. For four years, Iraqis lived in constant dread of the insurgents, the death squads, the Iraqi forces, and the Coalition. While their lot has improved greatly since 2007, they still live in the most dangerous place in the world. For the civilians caught in the line of fire, bombs and bullets are equally deadly, though life in Iraq continues day after day.

Little more than a month after the fall of Saddam's statue in Firdaus Square, a new statue stood in its place. The statue depicts a father, mother, and child. They hold aloft the Islamic crescent moon and the sun, a symbol of Iraq's proud and ancient Sumerian legacy. The sculpture was erected by a group of Iraqi artists who initially came together and worked, often secretly, in the wake of the 1991 Gulf War. A legacy of Saddam's manipulation and repression of culture and art, they were the first artists to work openly and freely in Iraq in decades as they undertook numerous projects in the spring and summer of 2003. Their sculpture represents Iraqis' hopes for a new future and pride in their storied past. It also represents the crucibles that have formed the Iraq of today.

The statue is commonly known by the same name as the artists' group, *al-Najeen*: The Survivors. Iraq is a nation of survivors, who have endured every trial and tribulation thrown at them for centuries, although each one has left its mark. Each time Iraqis have been pulled into the depths, they have bounced back to the surface, battered, but alive and gasping for air. For all those caught in the current struggle, I hope that history does not pull Iraq back into the depths once again.

Bibliography

Official Documents and Key Statements

Coalition Provisional Authority. *Order Number 2: Dissolution of Entities.* May 23, 2003. http://www.cpairaq.org/regulations/20030823_CPAORD_2_Dissolution_of_Entities_with_Annex_A.pdf (accessed May 5, 2008).

———. *Law of Administration for the State of Iraq for the Transitional Period* (Transitional Administrative Law). March 8, 2004. http://www.cpairaq.org/government/TAL.html (accessed May 4, 2008).

———. *Order Number 96: The Electoral Law.* June 7, 2004. http://www.iraqcoalition.org/regulations/20040615_CPAORD_96_The_Electoral_Law.pdf (accessed May 5, 2008).

Coalition Provisional Authority and Iraqi Governing Council. *November 15 Agreement: Timeline to a Sovereign, Democratic, and Secure Iraq.* November 15, 2003. http://www.cpa-iraq.org/government/AgreementNov15.pdf (accessed May 4, 2008).

Government of Iraq. *Constitution of Iraq.* October 2005. *Constitution of Iraq*, available in Arabic, http://www.cabinet.iq/dostor.htm, and English, http://portal.unesco.org/ci/en/files/20704/11332732681iraqi_constitution_en.pdf/iraqi_constitution_en.pdf (accessed May 5, 2008).

Iraq Study Group. *Iraq Study Group Report.* December 2006. http://www.usip.org/isg/iraq_study_group_report/report/1206/iraq_study_group_report.pdf (accessed May 5, 2008).

Woods, Kevin M., Michael R. Pease, Mark E. Stout, Williamson Murray, and James G. Lacey. *Iraqi Perspectives Project: A View of Operation Iraqi Freedom from Saddam's Senior Leadership.* Washington, DC: Joint Center of Operational Analysis, U.S. Department of Defense, 2006. http://www.jfcom.mil/newslink/storyarchive/2006/ipp.pdf (accessed May 5, 2008).

Books and Journal Articles

Allawi, Ali. *The Occupation of Iraq: Winning the War, Losing the Peace*. New Haven, CT: Yale University Press, 2007.

Baram, Amatzia. "Neo-Tribalism in Iraq: Saddam Hussein's Tribal Policies 1991–96." *International Journal of Middle East Studies* 29, no. 1 (February 1997): 1–31.

———. "Saddam's Power Structure: The Tikritis Before, During, and After the War." In *Iraq at the Crossroads: State and Society in the Shadow of Regime Change*. International Institute for Strategic Studies Adelphi Paper No. 354. Edited by Toby Dodge and Steven Simon. New York: Oxford University Press, 2003.

Batatu, Hanna. *The Old Social Classes and the Revolutionary Movements of Iraq: A Study of Iraq's Old Landed and Commercial Classes and of Its Communists, Ba'thists, and Free Officers*. Princeton, NJ: Princeton University Press, 1978.

Bremer III, L. Paul, and Malcom McConnell. *My Year in Iraq: The Struggle to Build a Future of Hope*. New York: Simon and Schuster, 2006.

Burke, Jason. *Al-Qaeda: The True Story of Radical Islam*. New York: I. B. Tauris, 2004.

Casper, Gretchen. *Fragile Democracies: The Legacies of Authoritarian Rule*. Pittsburgh, PA: University of Pittsburgh Press, 1995.

——— and Michelle Taylor. *Negotiating Democracy: Transitions from Authoritarian Rule*. Pittsburgh, PA: University of Pittsburgh Press, 1996.

Chandrasekaran, Rajiv. *Imperial Life in the Emerald City: Inside Iraq's Green Zone*. New York: Alfred A. Knopf, 2006.

Cockburn, Patrick. *Muqtada: Muqtada al-Sadr, the Shia Revival, and the Struggle for Iraq*. New York: Scribner, 2008.

Davis, Eric. *Memories of State: Politics, History, and Collective Identity in Modern Iraq*. Los Angeles: University of California Press, 2005.

Dawisha, Adeed, and Larry Diamond. "Iraq's Year of Voting Dangerously." *Journal of Democracy* 17, no. 2 (April 2006): 89–103.

Diamond, Larry. *Squandered Victory: The American Occupation and the Bungled Effort to Bring Democracy to Iraq*. New York: Times Books, 2005.

Etherington, Mark. *Revolt on the Tigris: The Al-Sadr Uprising and the Governing of Iraq*. Ithaca, NY: Cornell University Press, 2005.

Fallows, James. "Why Iraq Has No Army." *Atlantic Monthly* (December 2005): 60–77.

Farouk-Sluglett, Marion, and Peter Sluglett. *Iraq Since 1958: From Revolution to Dictatorship*. 3rd Ed. New York: I. B. Tauris, 2003.

Galula, David. *Counterinsurgency Warfare: Theory and Practice*. Westport, CT: Praeger Security International, 2006. First published 1964.

Gordon, Michel R., and Bernard E. Trainor. *Cobra II: The Inside Story of the Invasion and Occupation of Iraq*. New York: Pantheon Books, 2006.

Hashim, Ahmed S. *Insurgency and Counter-Insurgency in Iraq*. Ithaca, NY: Cornell University Press, 2006.

Horowitz, Donald L. "Democracy in Divided Societies." In *Nationalism, Ethnic Conflict, and Democracy*. Edited by Larry Diamond and Marc F. Plattner. Baltimore, MD: Johns Hopkins University Press, 1994.

Huntington, Samuel P. *Political Order in Changing Societies*. New Haven, CT: Yale University Press, 1968.

Ibn Khaldun. *The Muqaddimah: An Introduction to History*. Translated by Franz Rosenthal. Princeton, NJ: Princeton University Press, 1967.

Inglehart, Ronald, Mansoor Moaddel, and Mark Tessler. "Xenophobia and In-Group Solidarity in Iraq: A Natural Experiment on the Impact of Insecurity." *Perspectives on Politics* 4, no. 3 (September 2006): 495–505.

Jabar, Faleh A. "Sheikhs and Ideologues: Deconstruction and Reconstruction of Tribes under Patrimonial Totalitarianism in Iraq, 1968-1998." In *Tribes and Power: Nationalism and Ethnicity in the Middle East*. Edited by Faleh Abdul-Jabar and Hosham Dawod, 69-109. London: Saqi Books, 2003.

———. "The Worldly Roots of Religiosity in Post-Saddam Iraq." *Middle East Report* 227 (Summer 2003): 12.

Linz, Juan J. and Alfred Stepan. *Problems of Democratic Transition and Consolidation: Southern Europe, South America, and Post-Communist Europe*. Baltimore, MD: Johns Hopkins University Press, 1996.

Makiya, Kanan. *Republic of Fear: The Politics of Modern Iraq*. Berkeley: University of California Press, 1989.

———. *Cruelty and Silence: War, Tyranny, Uprising, and the Arab World*. New York: W. W. Norton and Company, 1993.

Marr, Phebe. *The Modern History of Iraq*. 2nd ed. Boulder, CO: Westview Press, 2004.

Munson, Peter J. "What Lies Beneath: Saddam's Legacy and the Roots of Chaos in Iraq." (Montery, CA: Masters Thesis, Naval Postgraduate School, 2005), available at http://bosun.nps.edu/uhtbin/hyperion-image.exe/05Dec_Munson.pdf.

Nakash, Yitzhak. *Reaching for Power: The Shi'a in the Modern Arab World.* Princeton, NJ: Princeton University Press, 2006.

———. *The Shi'is of Iraq.* Princeton, NJ: Princeton University Press, 1994.

Nasr, Vali. *The Shia Revival: How Conflicts within Islam Will Shape the Future.* New York: W. W. Norton and Company, 2006.

O'Donnell, Guillermo, Philippe C. Schmitter, and Laurence Whitehead, eds. *Transitions from Authoritarian Rule: Prospects for Democracy.* Baltimore, MD: Johns Hopkins University Press, 1986.

Packer, George. *The Assassins' Gate: America in Iraq.* New York: Farrar, Straus and Giroux, 2005.

Ricks, Thomas. *Fiasco: The American Military Adventure in Iraq.* New York: Penguin Press, 2006.

Rustow, Dankwart A. "Transitions to Democracy: Toward a Dynamic Model." *Comparative Politics* 2, no. 3 (April 1970): 337–63.

Shadid, Anthony. *Night Draws Near: Iraq's People in the Shadow of America's War.* New York: Henry Holt and Company, 2005.

Tripp, Charles. *A History of Iraq.* 2nd ed. New York: Cambridge University Press, 2002.

———. "After Saddam." *Survival* 44, no. 4 (November 1, 2002): 22–37.

Wardi, Ali. *Understanding Iraq: Society, Culture, and Personality.* Translated by Fuad Baali. Lewiston, NY: Edwin Mellen Press, 2008. First published 1965 as *Dirasah fi Tabi'a al-Mujtama' al-'Iraqiya.*

West, Bing. *No True Glory: A Frontline Account of the Battle for Fallujah.* New York: Bantam Books, 2005.

Wiley, Joyce N. *The Islamic Movement of Iraqi Shi'as.* Boulder, CO: Lynne Rienner Publishers Inc., 1992.

Notes

Chapter One: Introduction
1. Kanan Makiya, *Cruelty and Silence: War, Tyranny, Uprising, and the Arab World* (New York: W. W. Norton and Company, 1993), 218.
2. General David H. Petraeus, Letter to Troops of Multi-National Force Iraq, September 15, 2008, http://graphics8.nytimes.com/images/2008/09/15/world/20080915petraeus-letter.pdf (accessed September 16, 2008).
3. Saddam or Saddam Hussein will be used throughout to refer to Iraq's former ruler. See Blair Shewchuk, "Saddam or Mr. Hussein," *CBC News Online*, February 2003, http://www.cbc.ca/news/indepth/words/saddam_hussein.html (accessed June 23, 2008).
4. David Levering Lewis, *God's Crucible: Islam and the Making of Europe 570–1215*, (New York: WW Norton, 2008), 272.

Chapter Two: A Crushing Legacy
1. John Agresto's "All Hands" email to the CPA quoted in Rajiv Chandrasekaran, *Imperial Life in the Emerald City: Inside Iraq's Green Zone* (New York: Alfred A. Knopf, 2006), 283.
2. General George Casey quoted in Damien Cave, "New Boss Takes Reins of U.S. Forces in Iraq," *New York Times*, February 11, 2007.
3. In addition to viewing the video, available from several websites, this account also draws from John F. Burns, "Hussein Video Grips Iraq; Attacks Go On," *New York Times*, December 31, 2006. Marc Santora, "On the Gallows, Curses for U.S. and 'Traitors,'" *New York Times*, December 31, 2006. "*Juthman al-Ra'es al-Sabiq Saddam Hussein Yuara al-Taree fi Balda al-'Aouja wa Radud al-Fa'l Tatawala 'Ala I'adamihi*," [Body of Saddam Hussein Buried in Town

of Aouja and Television Channels Transmit Details of His Execution] *Radio Sawa*, December 31, 2006, http://www.radiosawa.com (accessed December 31, 2006). "*I'adam Saddam . . . Hal Saqatat al-Hakuma al-'Araqiya fi al-Fakh?*" [Saddam's Execution . . . Has the Iraqi Government Fallen into the Trap?] *al-Majalla*, no. 1404 (January 7–13, 2007): 36–42.

4. Chandrasekaran, *Imperial Life in the Emerald City*, 42–43.
5. Marion Farouk-Sluglett and Peter Sluglett, *Iraq Since 1958: From Revolution to Dictatorship*, 3rd ed. (New York: I. B. Tauris, 2003), 2. Hanna Batatu, *The Old Social Classes and the Revolutionary Movements of Iraq: A Study of Iraq's Old Landed and Commercial Classes and of Its Communists, Ba'athists, and Free Officers* (Princeton, NJ: Princeton University Press, 1978), 16–17. Batatu said Iraq could be divided into roughly three religious zones along these same lines, 37.
6. See Clifford Geertz, "Primordial Loyalties and Standing Entities: Anthropological Reflections on the Politics of Identity" (lecture, Collegium Budapest, Budapest, Hungary, December 13, 1993), http://www.colbud.hu/main_old/PubArchive/PL/PL07-Geertz.pdf (accessed May 15, 2008). In using the term primordial, Geertz does not mean ancient and unchanging, although other scholars view the term negatively as it suggests that identities are fixed. The bottom line is that primordial/primary identities change continuously as they are reinterpreted by the people who are loyal to them, but they are based on ethnicity or language rather than social class or citizenship. Ascriptive identity may be a better term, but I use primary identity here for simplicity of terminology. Also Eric Davis, *Memories of State: Politics, History, and Collective Identity in Modern Iraq* (Los Angeles: University of California Press, 2005), 23–24.
7. Construction of identity and how primary identity becomes salient under certain conditions pertaining to civil war, see Carter Johnson, "Partitioning to Peace: Sovereignty, Demography, and Ethnic Civil Wars," *International Security* 32, no. 4 (Spring 2008): 145–47 and associated notes.
8. Batatu, *Old Social Classes*, 17–18, 44–47. Davis, *Memories of State*, 36.
9. Batatu, *Old Social Classes*, 649, 1116. Phebe Marr, *The Modern History of Iraq*, 2nd ed. (Boulder, CO: Westview Press, 2004), 8. Charles Tripp, *A History of Iraq*, 2nd ed. (New York: Cambridge University Press, 2002), 37–47, 208. Sluglett, *Iraq Since 1958*, 192. Davis, *Memories of State*, 56–58.
10. Davis, *Memories of State*, 55–81, 101.
11. Davis, *Memories of State*, 49–53, 71–73. Ali Allawi, *The Occupation of Iraq: Winning the War, Losing the Peace* (New Haven, CT: Yale University Press, 2007), 235.

12. Saeid N. Neshat, "A Look into the Women's Movement in Iraq," *Farzaneh* 6, no. 11 (Spring 2003): 54–65. Human Rights Watch, "Background on Women's Status in Iraq Prior to the Fall of the Saddam Hussein Government," November 2003, http://www.hrw.org/backgrounder/wrd/iraq-women.htm (accessed June 28, 2008).
13. Batatu, *Old Social Classes*, 36. Nakash, *Reaching for Power*, 86–87.
14. Batatu, *Old Social Classes*, 1078–1079. Davis, *Memories of State*, 122, 131, 184–85, 273. Said K. Aburish, *Saddam Hussein: The Politics of Revenge* (New York: Bloomsbury, 2000), 123. Nakash, *Reaching for Power*, 87–93.
15. Sociologist Ihsan al-Hassan quoted in Babak Deghanpisheh, "Love in a Time of Madness," *Newsweek*, International Edition, March 13, 2006, http://www.newsweek.com/id/46871 (accessed May 15, 2008). International Crisis Group, (ICG), "The Next Iraqi War? Sectarianism and Civil Conflict," *Middle East Report*, no. 52 (February 27, 2006): 6–7, http://www.crisisgroup.org/library/documents/middle_east___north_africa/iraq_iran_gulf/52_the_next_iraqi_war_sectarianism_and_civil_conflict.pdf (accessed May 15, 2008). Ghaith Abdul-Ahad "Iraq's Deepening Sectarianism," *The Hindu*, April 5, 2005, http://www.thehindu.com/2005/05/04/stories/2005050404371100.htm (accessed May 15, 2008). Allawi, *Occupation of Iraq*, 127. For the view of an Iraqi who grew up in a mixed environment see Iraqi Rebel, "Sunni and Shi'i," weblog post, December 2, 2005, http://iraqirebel.blogspot.com/2005/12/sunni-and-shii.html (accessed May 19, 2008).
16. Allawi, *Occupation of Iraq*, 74–75. "Declaration of the Shi'a of Iraq," July 2002, http://www.al-bab.com/arab/docs/iraq/shia02a.htm (accessed May 6, 2008). Davis, *Memories of State*, 228, 261.
17. See Allawi, *Occupation of Iraq*, 135–36. For Sunni solidarity, see next paragraph and note 17.
18. Ronald Inglehart, Mansoor Moaddel, and Mark Tessler, "Xenophobia and In-Group Solidarity in Iraq: A Natural Experiment on the Impact of Insecurity," *Perspectives on Politics* 4, no. 3 (September 2006): 498–500. Davis, *Memories of State*, 7–8.
19. Ali Wardi, *Understanding Iraq: Society, Culture, and Personality*, trans. Fuad Baali (Lewiston, NY: Edwin Mellen Press, 2008), originally published in 1965 as *Dirasah fi Tabi'a al-Mujtama' al-'Iraqiya*. See also Ibn Khaldun, *The Muqaddimah: An Introduction to History*, trans. Franz Rosenthal (Princeton, NJ: Princeton University Press, 1967).
20. Tripp, *A History of Iraq*, 51–52, 139. Sluglett, *Iraq Since 1958*, 172. Marr, *Modern History of Iraq*, 159–61.

21. Marr, *Modern History of Iraq*, 166–67. Sluglett, *Iraq Since 1958*, 174, 193, 227, 246–47.
22. Sluglett, *Iraq Since 1958*, 217.
23. Sluglett, *Iraq Since 1958*, 173, 230.
24. Marr, *Modern History of Iraq,* 144–45.
25. Tripp, *A History of Iraq*, 190–96, 208, 215, 222–23. Sluglett, *Iraq Since 1958*, 121.
26. Kevin M. Woods, et al., *Iraqi Perspectives Project: A View of Operation Iraqi Freedom from Saddam's Senior Leadership* (Joint Center of Operational Analysis, U.S. Department of Defense: 2006): 4, 56, http://www.jfcom.mil/newslink/storyarchive/2006/ipp.pdf (accessed May 19, 2008). Aburish, *Saddam Hussein*, 171–73.
27. U.S. Department of State, *Country Reports on Human Rights Practices, 2005: Iraq*, March 8, 2006, http://www.state.gov/g/drl/rls/hrrpt/2005/61689.htm (accessed May 19, 2008). Larry Diamond, *Squandered Victory: The American Occupation and the Bungled Effort to Bring Democracy to Iraq* (New York: Times Books, 2005), 125.
28. Amatzia Baram, "Between Impediment and Advantage: Saddam's Iraq," *USIP Special Report* 34 (June 1998), http://www.usip.org/pubs/specialreports/early/baram/Baram.html (accessed May 19, 2008).
29. Ibrahim al-Marashi, "Iraq's Security and Intelligence Network: A Guide and Analysis," *Middle East Review of International Affairs* 6, no. 3 (electronic version September 2002): 1–2, http://www.ciaonet.org (accessed October 7, 2005). Central Intelligence Agency, *Iraq: Foreign Intelligence and Security Services*, August 1985, http://www.gwu.edu/~nsarchiv/NSAEBB/NSAEBB167/05.pdf (accessed May 19, 2008).
30. Anthony Cordesman and Ahmed Hashim, *Iraq: Sanctions and Beyond* (Boulder, CO: Westview Press, 1997), 36–37.
31. "Iraq Battling More Than 200,000 Insurgents: Intelligence Chief," *Agence France-Presse North American Service*, January 3, 2005, http://www.informationclearinghouse.info/article7603.htm (accessed May 19, 2008).
32. Central Intelligence Agency, *Political and Personality Handbook of Iraq*, January 1991, 9, http://www.gwu.edu/~nsarchiv/NSAEBB/NSAEBB167/06.pdf (accessed May 19, 2008). Sluglett, *Iraq Since 1958,* 184–85. Marr, *Modern History of Iraq*, 149. For the Iraqi Communist Party's structure, see Batatu, *Old Social Classes*, 637, for older Ba'ath Party structure 744–45. For Algerian resistance structures see Alf Andrew Heggoy, *Insurgency and*

Counterinsurgency in Algeria (Bloomington: Indiana University Press, 1972), 122–27.
33. al-Marashi, "Iraq's Security and Intelligence Network," 2–7. Kanan Makiya, *Republic of Fear: The Politics of Modern Iraq* (Berkeley: University of California Press, 1989), 12–14. Amatzia Baram, "The Iraqi Political Scene Eleven Years After the Gulf War," in *The Future of Iraq Conference Proceedings*, eds. Lyle Goldstein and Ahmed Hashim (Newport, RI: Center for Naval Warfare Studies, United States Naval War College, December 2002), 22. Alexis Debat, "Vivisecting the Jihad," *The National Interest* 76 (Summer 2004): 22. Cordesman and Hashim, *Iraq: Sanctions and Beyond*, 46–47.
34. Makiya, *Republic of Fear*, 76–77. Joseph Braude, *The New Iraq: Rebuilding the Country for Its People, the Middle East, and the World* (New York: Basic Books, 2003), 46–49, 61. Marr, *Modern History of Iraq*, 150.
35. Sluglett, *Iraq Since 1958*, 175. Marr, *Modern History of Iraq*, 151, 210. Chandrasekaran, *Imperial Life in the Emerald City*, 48, 72–73.
36. Braude, *The New Iraq*, 46–49, 61. Baram, "Between Impediment and Advantage: Saddam's Iraq." Saddam Hussein quoted in Bob Woodward, *State of Denial: Bush at War, Part III* (New York: Simon & Schuster, 2006), 88.
37. Quote from Makiya, *Republic of Fear*, 16. Baram, "Between Impediment and Advantage: Saddam's Iraq."
38. Quoted in Amatzia Baram, "Who Are the Insurgents?: Sunni Arab Rebels in Iraq," *USIP Special Report* 134 (April 2005): 5, http://www.usip.org/pubs/specialreports/sr134.html (accessed May 19, 2008). Kalshan al-Beyait, "*Al-Dur M'aql 'Izzat al-Duri Yakhdh'a li-Hamla Amaniya Mushadada*, Al-Dur, Fortress of Izzat al-Duri, Subject to Harsh Security Campaign," *al-Hayat*, April 3, 2007.
39. Woods, *Iraqi Perspectives Project*, 64.
40. Makiya, *Republic of Fear*, 21, 25–27. Sluglett, *Iraq Since 1958*, 120. Cordesman and Hashim, *Iraq: Sanctions and Beyond*, 50–56. Marr, *Modern History of Iraq*, 151. Batatu, *Old Social Classes*, 1094–95. See Staff General Nizar al-Khazraji quoted in Ahmed Hashim, *Insurgency and Counter-Insurgency in Iraq* (Ithaca, NY: Cornell University Press, 2006), 5.
41. Al-Marashi, "Iraq's Security and Intelligence Network," 10.
42. Iraqi National Congress, "Structure of Special Republican Guard," FBIS transcript of website, May 14, 1998. Global Security summary available at http://www.globalsecurity.org/wmd/library/news/iraq/1998/srg.htm (accessed May 19, 2008).

43. Quote from Amatzia Baram, "Saddam's Power Structure: The Tikritis Before, During, and After the War," in *Iraq at the Crossroads: State and Society in the Shadow of Regime Change*, International Institute for Strategic Studies Adelphi Paper, no. 354, eds. Toby Dodge and Steven Simon (New York: Oxford University Press, 2003), 109. Isam al-Khafaji, "A Few Days After: State and Society in Post-Saddam Iraq," in *Iraq at the Crossroads*, 84. Guillermo O'Donnell, Philippe Schmitter, and Laurence Whitehead, eds., *Transitions From Authoritarian Rule: Prospects for Democracy* (Baltimore, MD: Johns Hopkins University Press, 1986), 32.
44. Cordesman and Hashim, *Iraq: Sanctions and Beyond*, 57. Makiya, *Republic of Fear*, 16, 43–44, 47, 58, 117, 119.
45. Makiya, *Republic of Fear*, 61.
46. Thomas Melia and Brian Katulis, "Iraqis Discuss their Country's Future: Post-War Perspectives from the Iraqi Street, Findings from Focus Groups with Iraqi Men and Women Conducted June 29–July 9, 2003," (Washington, DC: National Democratic Institute for International Affairs, July 28, 2003), 30–31, http://www.peacewomen.org/resources/Iraq/FullNDI.pdf (accessed May 5, 2008).
47. Makiya, *Republic of Fear*, 77–78. Twelve-year-old and father quoted in Anthony Shadid, *Night Draws Near: Iraq's People in the Shadow of America's War* (New York: Henry Holt and Company, 2005), 120.
48. "*5,000,000 Tilmeeth 'Iraqi Yuwajjhun 'Ila Madarsihim al-Yawm*" [Five Million Iraqi Students Head to Their Schools Today] *Al-Dustour*, August 16, 1995. Marr, *Modern History of Iraq*, 295–96.
49. Davis, *Memories of State*, 3.
50. Davis, *Memories of State*, 3, 7–9, 12, 184–85, 273. Inglehart, Moaddel, and Tessler, "Xenophobia and In-Group Solidarity in Iraq," 497–98.
51. Marr, *Modern History of Iraq*, 206.
52. Cordesman and Hashim, *Iraq: Sanctions and Beyond*, 136. Sluglett, *Iraq Since 1958*, 283–84. Marr, *Modern History of Iraq*, 205, 219–21.
53. Davis, *Memories of State*, 226–31. Tripp, *A History of Iraq*, 255–56.
54. Tripp, *A History of Iraq*, 256–57.
55. Davis, *Memories of State*, 227–28. Tripp, *A History of Iraq*, 255–57.
56. Cordesman and Hashim, *Iraq: Sanctions and Beyond*, 124–27, 140.
57. World Bank, "World Bank Data Sheet for Iraq," January 29, 2004, http://lnweb18.worldbank.org/mna/mena.nsf/Attachments/Datasheet/$File/iraqprototype.pdf (accessed October 31, 2005).
58. L. Paul Bremer III and Malcom McConnell, *My Year in Iraq: The Struggle to Build a Future of Hope* (New York: Simon & Schuster, 2006), 67.

59. 1991 statistics in Isam al-Khafaji, "Repression, Conformity, and Legitimacy: Prospects for an Iraqi Social Contract," in *The Future of Iraq*, ed. John Calabrese (Washington, DC: Middle East Institute, 1997), 21. CPA estimates in Bremer, *My Year in Iraq*, 67. Reinoud Leenders and Justin Alexander, "Case Study: Corrupting the New Iraq," in *Global Corruption Report 2005*, ed. Transparency International (2005), 84, http://www.globalcorruptionreport.org/download.html (accessed November 1, 2005). 1995 salary Sluglett, *Iraq Since 1958*, 294. 1995 and 1991 figures, Graham-Brown, *Sanctioning Saddam*, 185. Robert Looney, "Corruption's Reflection: Iraq's Shadow Economy," *Strategic Insights* 4, no. 3 (electronic journal, March 2005), http://www.ccc.nps.navy.mil/si/2005/Mar/looneymar05.pdf (accessed October 20, 2006).

60. Bremer, *My Year in Iraq*, 62–65.

61. Looney, "Corruption's Reflection." Braude, *The New Iraq*, 118.

62. Sluglett, *Iraq Since 1958*, 294. Cordesman and Hashim, *Iraq: Sanctions and Beyond*, 15. Qais al-Nouri, "The Impact of the Embargo on Iraqi Families: Re-Structuring of Tribes, Socio-Economic Classes and Households," *Journal of Comparative Family Studies* 28, no. 2 (1997): 99. Graham-Brown, *Sanctioning Saddam*, 180–82. Quote from Robert Tomes, "Schlock and Blah: Counter-insurgency Realities in a Rapid Dominance Era," *Small Wars and Insurgencies* 16, no. 1 (March 2005): 45. For details on oil-smuggling network see Central Intelligence Agency, "Comprehensive Report of the Advisor to the DCI on Iraq's WMD," Annex F (September 30, 2004), https://www.cia.gov/library/reports/general-reports-1/iraq_wmd_2004/index.html (accessed May 10, 2008).

63. Graham-Brown, *Sanctioning Saddam*, 170–71. Braude, *The New Iraq*, 99.

64. Graham-Brown, *Sanctioning Saddam*, 171. Iraqi merchant quoted in Braude, *The New Iraq*, 121.

65. Graham-Brown, *Sanctioning Saddam*, 172, 186, 191. Debat, "Vivisecting the Jihad," 20. Col. David Teeples quoted in Patrick McDonnell, "Coalition Gains Insight into Iraq's Foreign Insurgents," *Los Angeles Times*, February 9, 2004.

66. For a discussion of the effect of rent seekers on transition, see Anders Aslund, *How Capitalism Was Built: The Transformation of Central and Eastern Europe, Russia, and Central Asia* (New York: Cambridge University Press, 2007), 47–53. Toby Dodge, "Prepared Testimony for Senate Committee on Foreign Relations," April 20, 2004, http://foreign.senate.gov/testimony/2004/DodgeTestimony040420.pdf (accessed May 10, 2008). al-Nouri, "The Impact of the Embargo," 104–11. Sarah Graham-Brown, "War and Sanctions: Cost to Society and Toll on Development," in *The Future of Iraq*, ed. John Calabrese

(Washington, DC: The Middle East Institute, 1997), 37. Larry Johnson, "A Nation Sagging under the Weight of Sanctions: Iraq's Youth Faces a Bleak Future," *Seattle Post-Intelligencer*, May 11, 1999. Marr, *Modern History of Iraq*, 295.

67. Allawi, *Occupation of Iraq*, 127–28. Batatu, *Old Social Classes*, 1131.
68. Quoted in Braude, *The New Iraq*, 114.
69. Adeed Dawisha, "Iraqi Politics: The Past and Present as Context for the Future," in *The Future of Iraq*, ed. John Calabrese (Washington, DC: Middle East Institute, 1997), 12.
70. The *al-Quds* Army was a regional militia force for putting down local uprisings. It consisted of as many as five-hundred thousand members of varying loyalties. Woods, et al., *Iraqi Perspectives Project*, 48.
71. Amatzia Baram, *Building Toward Crisis: Saddam Husayn's Strategy for Survival* (Washington, DC: Washington Institute for Near East Policy, 1998), 50. Cordesman and Hashim, *Iraq: Sanctions and Beyond*, 47–48. Kenneth A. Pollock, *The Threatening Storm: The Case for Invading Iraq* (New York: Random House, 2002), 123. "Saddam Ordered Training of Al-Qa'ida Members," *Al-Yawm Al-Aakher,* trans. Middle East Media Research Institute, (Iraq: October 16, 2003), http://www.memri.org/bin/latestnews.cgi?ID=SD59203 (accessed May 27, 2008). Mohammad Bazzi, "A Promise to Fight On: A Leader in Iraqi Militia Group Tells of Plans for Extended Guerrilla War," *New York Newsday*, July 10, 2003.
72. Woods, et al., *Iraqi Perspectives Project,* 52–54.
73. Woods, et al., *Iraqi Perspectives Project*, 52–54. Tactical intelligence from interviews, Michel R. Gordon and Bernard E. Trainor, *Cobra II: The Inside Story of the Invasion and Occupation of Iraq* (New York: Pantheon Books, 2006), 366, 372, 395, 445, 408, and note 27 from that page. For use of *Hizb Allah*, see author's note.
74. Many instances of Sunni FREs crossing over to insurgency will be documented below. For a Shi'a example see Anthony Shadid, "This is Baghdad. What Could Be Worse?" *Washington Post*, October 29, 2006.
75. Patrick Lang quoted in Sydney J. Freedburg Jr., "Chess With the Sheiks," *National Journal*, April 12, 2008, http://www.njdc.com/njmagazine/print_friendly.php?ID=nj_20080412_5305, (accessed July 22, 2008).
76. Batatu, *Old Social Classes*, 68–70.
77. Sluglett, *Iraq Since 1958*, 12. Batatu, *Old Social Classes*, 88–89 (note 125), 95. British forces were significantly drawn down after 1920, forcing commanders to rely on tribes, locally recruited forces, and air power.

78. Wardi, *Understanding Iraq*, 61–62. Batatu, *Old Social Classes*, 78–120.
79. Faleh A. Jabar, "Sheikhs and Ideologues: Deconstruction and Reconstruction of Tribes under Patrimonial Totalitarianism in Iraq, 1968–1998," in *Tribes and Power: Nationalism and Ethnicity in the Middle East*, eds. Faleh A. Jabar and Hosham Dawod (London: Saqi Books, 2003), 71, 81–82.
80. Toby Dodge, *Inventing Iraq: The Failure of Nation Building and a History Denied* (New York: Columbia University Press, 2003), 161. Cordesman and Hashim, *Iraq: Sanctions and Beyond*, 27, 29. Jabar, "Sheikhs and Ideologues," 81–83. Batatu, *Old Social Classes*, 1084. Graham-Brown, *Sanctioning Saddam*, 197.
81. Jabar, "Sheikhs and Ideologues," 89. Cockburn, *Muqtada*, 98. ICG, "Iraq After the Surge I: The New Sunni Landscape," *Crisis Group Middle East Report* 74 (April 30, 2008): 10, http://www.crisisgroup.org/home/index.cfm?id=5415 (accessed June 7, 2008).
82. Amir Taheri, "Saddam Husayn Tries To Revive the Tribal System Following the Collapse of the Party Control System," *Al-Sharq al-Awsat*, trans. FBIS (London: May 15, 1996). Davis, *Memories of State*, 239. Jabar, "Sheikhs and Ideologues," 95.
83. Taheri, "Saddam Husayn Tries To Revive the Tribal System." Andrew Terrill, *Nationalism, Sectarianism, and the Future of the U.S. Presence in Post-Saddam Iraq*, (Carlisle, PA: Strategic Studies Institute, U.S. Army War College, 2003), 24. Amatzia Baram, "Neo-tribalism in Iraq: Saddam Hussein's Tribal Policies 1991–1996," *International Journal of Middle East Studies* 29, no. 1 (1997): 12–13. Jabar, "Sheikhs and Ideologues," 96.
84. Baram, "Neo-tribalism in Iraq," 18, 21. Jabar, "Sheikhs and Ideologues," 97, 99.
85. Nir Rosen, "Fallujah: Inside the Iraqi Resistance Part 1: Losing It," *Asia Times*, July 15, 2004, http://www.atimes.com/atimes/Front_Page/FG16Aa02.html (accessed May 28, 2008).
86. ICG, "The New Sunni Landscape," 10–12. The new generation became known as the "sheikhs of the 2000s," in contrast to the "Taiwan sheikhs" or "sheikhs of the Nineties."
87. Makiya, *Republic of Fear*, 106–107.
88. Eric Foner, *Reconstruction: America's Unfinished Revolution, 1863–1877* (New York: Perennial Classics, 1989), 88–95. Gretchen Casper, *Fragile Democracies: The Legacies of Authoritarian Rule* (Pittsburgh, PA: University of Pittsburgh Press, 1995), 13. Juliet Johnson, "Path Contingency in Postcommunist Transformations," *Comparative Politics* 33, no. 3 (April 2001): 254.

89. It should be noted that militant politicization of religion is by no means limited to Islam and is a growing phenomenon around the world. See Karen Armstrong, *The Battle for God* (New York: Alfred A. Knopf, 2000).
90. Ahmed Hashim and Jerrold Post, "Saddam is Iraq: Iraq is Saddam," *The Counterproliferation Papers: Future Warfare Series*, no. 17 (Maxwell Air Force Base, AL: Air University, United States Air Force, December 2002), 50. Ahmed S. Hashim, "Iraq's Chaos." David Thaler, "The Middle East: The Cradle of the Muslim World," in *The Muslim World After 9/11*, ed. Angel M. Rabasa (Santa Monica, CA: RAND Corporation, 2004), 125. Marr, *Modern History of Iraq*, 297.
91. Allawi, *Occupation of Iraq*, 56–57. Kim Ghattas, "Religion—Iraq: Saddam Embraces Islam in Time of Crisis," *Global Information Network*, July 3, 2002. Hashim and Post, "Saddam is Iraq," 51. Graham-Brown, *Sanctioning Saddam*, 191.
92. Ghattas, "Religion—Iraq." Jason Burke, "Saddam Wields Sword of Islam," *Guardian*, December 19, 1999. Shadid, *Night Draws Near*, 36.
93. Iraqi quoted in al-Nouri, "The Impact of the Embargo," 110. Ghattas, "Religion-Iraq." Baram, "Who Are the Insurgents?" 10. Burke, "Saddam Wields Sword of Islam."
94. Interview by Muhammad al-Baqali, "Iraq's Muslim Ulema Council Aide: Every U.S. Solider is Legitimate Target," *Al-Quds al-Arabi*, trans. by FBIS (London: April 23, 2004).
95. ICG, "The Next Iraqi War? Sectarianism and Civil Conflict," February 27, 2006, 21–22, http://www.crisisgroup.org/library/documents/middle_east__north_africa/iraq_iran_gulf/52_the_next_iraqi_war_sectarianism_and_civil_conflict.pdf (accessed June 28, 2008).
96. Baram, "Who are the Insurgents?" 10–11.
97. Vali Nasr, "Regional Implications of Shi'a Revival in Iraq," *The Washington Quarterly* 27, no. 3 (Summer 2004): 7–8, 18–20.
98. Quintan Wiktorowicz, "Anatomy of the Salafi Movement," *Studies in Conflict and Terrorism* 29, no. 3 (April–May 2006): 207–39.
99. Marc Lynch, "Beyond the Arab Street: Iraq and the Arab Public Sphere," *Politics and Society* 31, no. 1 (March 2003): 67–82.
100. Braude, *The New Iraq*, 54.
101. Iraqi at democracy seminar in Baghdad, January 15, 2004, quoted in Larry Diamond, *Squandered Victory: The American Occupation and the Bungled Effort to Bring Democracy to Iraq* (New York: Times Books, 2005), 107.
102. Ammar al-Shahbander quoted in Packer, *The Assassins' Gate*, 178.
103. Etherington, *Revolt on the Tigris*, 147, see also 114–15.

Chapter Three: Iraq's Collapse and the Crisis of Governance

1. Nicias quoted in Thucydides, *The Peloponnesian War*, bk. 6.23.
2. John Paul Vann quoted in Neil Sheehan, *A Bright and Shining Lie: John Paul Vann and America in Vietnam* (New York: Random House, 1988), 67.
3. Quoted in Michael R. Gordon and Bernard E. Trainor, *Cobra II: The Inside Story of the Invasion and Occupation of Iraq* (New York: Pantheon Books, 2006), 493.
4. The democratic transition literature is extensive. For a brief overview of how the Iraqi case fits into the literature see Peter J. Munson, "What Lies Beneath: Saddam's Legacy and the Roots of Chaos in Iraq" (master's thesis, Naval Postgraduate School, Monterey, CA, 2005), 10–15, available at http://bosun.nps.edu/uhtbin/hyperion-image.exe/05Dec_Munson.pdf. This book draws most heavily on: Guillermo O'Donnell, Philippe Schmitter, and Laurence Whitehead, eds., *Transitions from Authoritarian Rule: Prospects for Democracy* (Baltimore, MD: Johns Hopkins University Press, 1986). Gretchen Casper, *Fragile Democracies: The Legacies of Authoritarian Rule* (Pittsburgh, PA: University of Pittsburgh Press, 1995). Dankwart A. Rustow, "Transitions to Democracy: Toward a Dynamic Model," *Comparative Politics* 2, no. 3 (April 1970): 337–63. Gretchen Casper and Michelle Taylor, *Negotiating Democracy: Transitions from Authoritarian Rule* (Pittsburgh, PA: University of Pittsburgh Press, 1996).
5. Di Rita quoted in George Packer, *The Assassins' Gate* (New York: Farrar, Straus and Giroux, 2005), 133. For a similar assessment of the optimism, see Bremer, *My Year in Iraq*, 12.
6. Donald Rumsfeld, "Speech to Veterans of Foreign Wars," (transcript of speech, San Antonio, TX, August 25, 2003), http://www.defenselink.mil/speeches/2003/sp20030825-secdef0403.html (accessed October 5, 2005).
7. Edward Wong, "Fearful Iraqis Avoid Mosques as Attacks Rise," *New York Times*, August 19, 2006. The government lags benchmarks and fails to provide sufficient services with regard to sewage treatment, fuel supplies, electricity, security, healthcare, etc. For some indicators see Brookings Institution, "Iraq Index," http://www.brookings.edu/iraqindex. U.S. Department of State, "Iraq Weekly Status Report," December 28, 2005, http://www.state.gov/documents/organization/58673.pdf (accessed July 27, 2006). *Iraq Study Group Report*, 20.
8. Quoted in Packer, *The Assassins' Gate*, 141.
9. Phebe Marr, *The Modern History of Iraq*, 2nd ed. (Boulder, CO: Westview Press, 2004), 244.
10. Quoted in Bremer, *My Year in Iraq*, 63.

11. This theme is discussed throughout Rajiv Chandrasekaran, *Imperial Life in the Emerald City: Inside Iraq's Green Zone* (New York: Alfred A. Knopf, 2006).
12. For a similar thesis and fuller exploration of Coalition policies and actions in this period see Gordon and Trainor, *Cobra II*. Ricardo S. Sanchez, *Wiser in Battle: A Soldier's Story* (New York: Harper, 2008), 179–80.
13. Packer, *The Assassins' Gate*, 139.
14. Quoted in Anthony Shadid, *Night Draws Near: Iraq's People in the Shadow of America's War* (New York: Henry Holt and Company, 2005), 131.
15. Gordon and Trainor, *Cobra II*, 459, 462. Sanchez, *Wiser in Battle*, 168.
16. General Paul Van Riper cited in Thomas Ricks, *Fiasco: The American Military Adventure in Iraq* (New York: Penguin Press, 2006), 84. Bing West, *No True Glory: A Frontline Account of the Battle for Fallujah* (New York: Bantam Books, 2005), 26. Gordon and Trainor, *Cobra II*, 459, 462.
17. Quoted in Gordon and Trainor, *Cobra II*, 463.
18. Chandrasekaran, *Imperial Life in the Emerald City*, 29–32. Media in Cooperation and Friedrich-Ebert Foundation, "*Daleel Lil-Ahzab al-Iraqiya 2005*, Guide of Iraqi Parties 2005," distributed as supplement to *al-Sabah al-Jadeed* newspaper, December 11-12, 2005, 25, http://www.niqash.org/intern/getBin.php?id=292 (accessed May 7, 2008). For a slightly more charitable version of Chalabi's background see Allawi, *Occupation of Iraq*, 40–42.
19. Packer, *The Assassins' Gate*, 168. For a Sunni example see Nir Rosen, "Fallujah: Inside the Iraqi Resistance Part 3: The Fallujah Model," *Asia Times*, July 20, 2004, http://www.atimes.com/atimes/Middle_East/FG20Ak01.html (accessed May 7, 2008).
20. Lt. Col. Mustafa Duleimi quoted in Chandrasekaran, *Imperial Life in the Emerald City*, 74. Sanchez, *Wiser in Battle*, 172.
21. Gordon and Trainor, *Cobra II*, 480–83. Garner quoted in James Fallows, "Why Iraq Has No Army," *The Atlantic Monthly* 296, no. 5 (December 2005): 65. Sanchez, *Wiser in Battle*, 176.
22. Walter Slocombe, *Frontline* interview, August 17, 2004, http://www.pbs.org/wgbh/pages/frontline/shows/pentagon/interviews/slocombe.html (accessed May 28, 2008). Bremer, *My Year in Iraq*, 53–57.
23. Gordon and Trainor, *Cobra II*, 480–83. Bremer states that he "reviewed every word of the order" with Paul Wolfowitz and Doug Feith at the Pentagon and that Lieutenant General McKiernan was consulted as well, *My Year in Iraq*, 224. Quote from Michael R. Gordon, "Fateful Choice on Iraq Army Bypassed Debate," *New York Times*, March 17, 2008.
24. Memo quoted in Gordon, "Fateful Choice on Iraq Army Bypassed Debate."

25. Coalition Provisional Authority, *Coalition Provisional Authority Order Number 2: Dissolution of Entities*, May 23, 2003, http://www.cpairaq.org/regulations/20030823_CPAORD_2_Dissolution_of_Entities_with_Annex_A.pdf (accessed May 28, 2008). Ahmed Hashim, "Military Power and State Formation in Modern Iraq," 38. Senior advisor quoted in Packer, *The Assassins' Gate*, 191–92.
26. Slocombe, *Frontline* interview. Gordon, "Fateful Choice on Iraq Army Bypassed Debate." Mattis quoted in Ricks, *Fiasco*, 161.
27. Gordon, "Fateful Choice on Iraq Army Bypassed Debate." Ricks, *Fiasco*, 161–62. Jay Garner, *Frontline* interview, July 17, 2003, http://www.pbs.org/wgbh/pages/frontline/shows/truth/interviews/garner.html (accessed June 2, 2008).
28. Gordon and Trainor, *Cobra II*, 485. Lt. Col. R. Alan King quoted in Ricks, *Fiasco*, 164.
29. Melia and Katulis, "Iraqis Discuss their Country's Future," 13–14.
30. Garner, *Frontline* interview. Robert Perito, "Policing Iraq: Protecting Iraqis from Criminal Violence," *USIP Briefing*, June 2006, http://www.usip.org/pubs/usipeace_briefings/2006/0629_policing_iraq.html (accessed May 28, 2008). Bremer, *My Year in Iraq*, 128.
31. For one influential account of these issues see Fallows, "Why Iraq Has No Army."
32. Perito, "Policing Iraq."
33. Ibid.
34. Edward Wong and Paul von Zielbauer, "Iraq Stumbling in Bid to Purge its Rogue Police," *New York Times*, September 17, 2006.
35. Ricks, *Fiasco*, 235, 238, *ff.* Michael Moss, "Iraq's Legal System Staggers Beneath the Weight of War," *New York Times*, December 17, 2006.
36. Department of Defense, *Measuring Security and Stability in Iraq*, Report to Congress (November 2006): 8, http://www.defenselink.mil/pubs/pdfs/9010Quarterly-Report-20061216.pdf (accessed May 13, 2008). Department of Defense, *Measuring Security and Stability in Iraq*, Report to Congress (March 2008): 4–6, http://www.defenselink.mil/pubs/pdfs/Master%20%20Mar08%20%20final%20signed.pdf (accessed June 11, 2008). Department of Defense, *Measuring Security and Stability in Iraq*, Report to Congress (June 2008): 5, http://www.defenselink.mil/pubs/pdfs/Master_16_June_08_%20FINAL_SIGNED%20.pdf (accessed June 27, 2008).
37. For example, see Brigardier General 'Abd al-Karim Khalaf quoted in Alissa J. Rubin, "Iraq Says Truck Bomb in North Killed 152," *New York Times*, April 1, 2007. Moss, "Iraq's Legal System."

38. For results of improvements in system see Walter Pincus, "U.S. Official Cites 'Hardening' of Iraqi Detainees," *Washington Post*, June 10, 2008. DoD, *Measuring Security and Stability* (March 2008): 4–6.
39. Ahmed Ali quoted in Shadid, *Night Draws Near*, 265.
40. Erdmann quoted in Packer, *The Assassins' Gate*, 144. Shiʻa woman quoted in Melia and Katulis, "Iraqis Discuss their Country's Future," 12.
41. Quoted in Sharon Behn, "Shiʻite Mosques Fill Void Left by Government," *Washington Times*, June 28, 2006.
42. Mathieu Guidere and Peter Harling, "Iraq's Resistance Evolves," *Le Monde diplomatique,* May 12, 2006, http://mondediplo.com/2006/05/02irak (accessed May 28, 2008).
43. Melia and Katulis, "Iraqis Discuss their Country's Future," 13–14, 31–32.
44. Department of Defense, Office of the Inspector General, "Contracts Awarded for the Coalition Provisional Authority by the Defense Contracting Command-Washington (D-2004-057),"March 18, 2004, 17–18, http://www.dodig.osd.mil/audit/reports/fy04/04-057.pdf (accessed May 19, 2008). Chandrasekaran, *Imperial Life in the Emerald City*, 130–35.
45. Chandrasekaran, *Imperial Life in the Emerald City*, 136. Don North quoted in Chandrasekaran, 136. Muntasar al-Amara quoted in Heidar Najam, *"Naʾib 'Araqi Sabiq Yedʾaou al-Hakouma Li-Iʾada Heykla Wizara al-Iʾalam"* [Former Iraqi Representative Calls for the Government to Re-establish the Ministry of Information] *Asharq Alawsat*, March 20, 2007.
46. Marr, *Modern History of Iraq*, 295. Eric Bauer, interview by Barbara Nielsen for USIP, October 21, 2004, 28, http://www.usip.org/library/oh/sops/iraq/gov/bauer.pdf (accessed May 28, 2008). Chandrasekaran, *Imperial Life in the Emerald City*, 150–51, UNDP report quoted 151.
47. Gordon and Trainor, *Cobra II*, 209. Bremer, *My Year in Iraq*, 18. Chandrasekaran, *Imperial Life in the Emerald City*, 150–51.
48. Eric Bauer, interview by Barbara Nielsen for USIP, October 21, 2004, http://www.usip.org/library/oh/sops/iraq/gov/bauer.pdf (accessed May 28, 2008). See also Chandrasekaran, *Imperial Life in the Emerald City*, 150.
49. Chandrasekaran, *Imperial Life in the Emerald City*, 110. Department of Defense, *Measuring Security and Stability in Iraq*, Report to Congress (November 2006): 15. New Electricity Plan—'Something Better than Nothing,'" *Voices of Iraq*, February 2, 2008, http://www.iraqupdates.com/p_articles.php/article/26894 (accessed May 28, 2008). Usama Redha, "Iraq: Vying for Power," *Los Angeles Times Babylon & Beyond Weblog*, May 12, 2008, http://latimesblogs.latimes.com/babylonbeyond/2008/05/iraq-vying-for.html (accessed May 28, 2008).

50. Brookings Institution, "Iraq Index," July 24, 2006, http://www.brookings.edu/iraqindex (accessed July 27, 2006). U.S. Department of State, "Iraq Weekly Status Report," December 28, 2005, http://www.state.gov/documents/organization/58673.pdf (accessed May 28, 2008).
51. Steven R. Hurst, "Iraqi Power Grid Nearing Collapse," *Associated Press*, August 5, 2007, http://www.abcnews.go.com/International/wireStory?id=3447819 (accessed May 28, 2008). Steve Negus, "Black-Outs Sap Public Faith in Baghdad," *Financial Times*, June 16, 2008, http://us.ft.com/ftgateway/superpage.ft?news_id=fto061620081757155229&page=1 (accessed June 23, 2008). Ben Lando, "Iraq with More Power, 'Angel of Light' Heads Home," *UPI* June 18, 2008, http://www.upi.com/Energy_Resources/2008/06/18/Iraq_with_more_power_Angel_of_Light_heads_home/UPI-15581213819691/ (accessed June 23, 2008).
52. James Glanz, "Inspectors Find Rebuilt Projects Crumbling in Iraq," *New York Times*, April 29, 2007.
53. Jeff Gerth, "Report Offered Bleak Outlook about Iraqi Oil," *New York Times*, October 5, 2003. Brookings Institution, "Iraq Index."
54. James Glanz and Robert F. Worth, "Attacks on Oil Industry in Iraq Aid a Vast Smuggling Network," *New York Times*, June 4, 2006. Department of Defense, *Measuring Security and Stability in Iraq*, Report to Congress (December 2007):10, http://www.defenselink.mil/pubs/pdfs/FINAL-SecDef%20Signed-20071214.pdf (accessed June 11, 2008).
55. Glanz and Worth, "Attacks on Oil Industry."
56. Oliver quoted in Bremer, *My Year in Iraq*, 66, see also 110.
57. Mark Etherington, *Revolt on the Tigris: The Al-Sadr Uprising and the Governing of Iraq*, (Ithaca, NY: Cornell University Press, 2005), 156–57.
58. Etherington, *Revolt on the Tigris*, 85. For a similar assessment, see Edwin O. Rueda, "Tribalism in the Al Anbar Province," *Marine Corps Gazette* 90, no. 10 (October 2006): 11. Also Ali Wardi, *Understanding Iraq: Society, Culture, and Personality*, trans. Fuad Baali (Lewiston, NY: Edwin Mellen Press, 2008), 3–4, 10–11, 110.
59. Major General Diamond quoted in Moni Basu, "General Warns of Graft in Iraq," *Atlanta Journal-Constitution*, June 22, 2006. Senior Iraqi official referenced in *Iraq Study Group Report*, 20.
60. Marc Santora and Damien Cave, "Banned Station Beams Voice of Iraqi Insurgency," *New York Times*, January 21, 2007.
61. Constitution of the Commonwealth of Massachusetts, art. 30, sec. 1.
62. For the CPA's shortcomings, see Chandrasekaran, *Imperial Life in the Emerald City*. Unnamed aid quoted therein, 277.

63. Chandrasekaran, *Imperial Life in the Emerald City*, 226, 277, 283–84, 286–87. American general quoted therein, 289.
64. Condoleezza Rice, "Remarks with British Foreign Secretary Jack Straw," April 3, 2006, http://www.state.gov/secretary/rm/2006/64036.htm (accessed May 28, 2008). Department of Defense, *Measuring Security and Stability in Iraq*, Report to Congress (May 2006): 29, http://www.defenselink.mil/news/may2006/d20060530SecurityandStabiltyRptFinalv2.pdf (accessed May 28, 2008).
65. Megan Stack, "Fear and Posing in Baghdad," *Los Angeles Times*, June 28, 2006. This continued to be the case in some areas of Iraq into 2008, although the situation had generally improved.

Chapter Four: The Rise of Shi'a Power in Iraq

1. Anthony Shadid, *Night Draws Near: Iraq's People in the Shadow of America's War* (New York: Henry Holt and Company, 2005), 173.
2. Marion Farouk-Sluglett and Peter Sluglett, *Iraq Since 1958: From Revolution to Dictatorship*, 3rd ed. (New York: I. B. Tauris, 2003), 193, 227. Patrick Cockburn, *Muqtada: Muqtada al-Sadr, the Shia Revival, and the Struggle for Iraq* (New York: Scribner, 2008), 91. Sadr City is tribally linked to Maysan Province. Ali Allawi, *The Occupation of Iraq: Winning the War, Losing the Peace* (New Haven, CT: Yale University Press, 2007), 267–68.
3. George Packer, *The Assassins' Gate* (New York: Farrar, Straus and Giroux, 2005), 108.
4. This is a point made in numerous instances by Mark Etherington, *Revolt on the Tigris: The Al-Sadr Uprising and the Governing of Iraq* (Ithaca, NY: Cornell University Press, 2005).
5. For one concise account of the early events of Shi'ism and their political effect see Augustus Richard Norton, "Musa al-Sadr," in *Pioneers of Islamic Revival*, ed. Ali Rahnema (Atlantic Highland, NJ: Zed Books, 1994), 186–90. Quote from Reza Aslan, *No god but God: The Origins, Evolution, and Future of Islam* (New York: Random House, 2005), 178, account of the origins of the Shi'a: 171–93.
6. Ahmed H. al-Rahim, "The New Iraq: The Sistani Factor," *Journal of Democracy* 16, no. 3 (July 2005): 52.
7. "Shared sense of grievance" in ICG, "Iraq's Shiites Under Occupation," September 9, 2003, 5, http://www.crisisgroup.org/library/documents/report_archive/A401120_09092003.pdf (accessed October 14, 2006). Joyce N. Wiley, *The Islamic Movement of Iraqi Shi'as* (Boulder, CO: Lynne Rienner Publishers, Inc., 1992), 107.

8. Wiley, *The Islamic Movement of Iraqi Shi'as*, 73–74.
9. Ibid., 113.
10. Max van der Stoel, UN Special Rapporteur of the Commission on Human Rights, "Situation of Human Rights in Iraq," United Nations General Assembly Document A/53/433, September 24, 1988, http://daccessdds.un.org/doc/UNDOC/GEN/N98/282/89/PDF/N9828289.pdf?OpenElement (accessed May 9, 2008). Cole, "The U.S. and Shi'ite Religious Factions in Iraq," 549. For coup preference see Sarah Graham-Brown, *Sanctioning Saddam: The Politics of Intervention in Iraq* (New York: I. B. Tauris, 1999), 19.
11. Vali Nasr, *The Shia Revival: How Conflicts within Islam Will Shape the Future* (New York: W. W. Norton & Company, 2006), 170.
12. For the Iranian case, see Kenneth M. Pollack, *The Persian Puzzle: The Conflict Between Iran and America* (New York: Random House Paperbacks, 2004), 142–43.
13. Larry Diamond, *Squandered Victory: The American Occupation and the Bungled Effort to Bring Democracy to Iraq* (New York: Times Books, 2005), 221. Nicholas Blanford, "Iraqis Battle Gangs in Basra," *Christian Science Monitor*, March 24, 2004.
14. The group will be refered to as SCIRI unless discussing events after the May 2007 change to ISCI.
15. Ahmed Hashim, *Insurgency and Counter-Insurgency in Iraq* (Ithaca, NY: Cornell University Press, 2006), 252.
16. Cockburn, *Muqtada*, 14. Hashim, *Insurgency and Counter-Insurgency in Iraq*, 252–53.
17. Mahan Abedin, "The Sadrist Movement," *Middle East Intelligence Bulletin* 5, no. 7 (July 2003), http://www.meib.org/articles/0307_iraqd.htm (accessed May 20, 2008). Cole, "The U.S. and Shi'ite Religious Factions," 552. Allawi, *Occupation of Iraq*, 58, 268. Cockburn, *Muqtada*, 98–99.
18. Cockburn, *Muqtada*, 105–107. Shadid, *Night Draws Near*, 170–71. Faleh A. Jabar, "The Worldly Roots of Religiosity in Post-Saddam Iraq," *Middle East Report* 227 (Summer 2003): 16. ICG, "Iraq's Muqtada al-Sadr: Spoiler or Stabilizer?" July 11, 2006, 3–5, http://www.crisisgroup.org/library/documents/middle_east___north_africa/iraq_iran_gulf/55_iraq_s_muqtada_al_sadr_spoiler_or_stabiliser.pdf (accessed July 21, 2008). Allawi, *Occupation of Iraq*, 59–61.
19. ICG, "Iraq's Muqtada al-Sadr," 5. Cockburn, *Muqtada*, 109. Allawi, *Occupation of Iraq*, 58–59.
20. Allawi, *Occupation of Iraq*, 268. Shadid, *Night Draws Near*, 174–75.

21. Abbas quoted in Cockburn, *Muqtada*, 117. Mohammed Sadiq is often referred to as Sadr II. In Arabic this is *al-Sadr al-Thani*, which translates as "the second Sadr" or "Sadr the second," not "Sadr Two."
22. Cole, "The U.S. and Shi'ite Religious Factions," 554–55, 565. Cockburn, *Muqtada*, 112–13, 117.
23. Shadid, *Night Draws Near*, 175. Cockburn, *Muqtada*, 127 *ff*.
24. Hashim, *Insurgency and Counter-Insurgency in Iraq,* 254. 42-year-old resident quoted in Anthony Shadid, "For Rebuilders of Sadr City, Gratitude Tainted by Mistrust," *Washington Post*, December 17, 2004. Local resident quoted in ICG, "Iraq's Muqtada al-Sadr," 20. Craig S. Smith, "In Hotbed of Shi'ite Emotion, Clerics Jockey for Leadership," *New York Times*, April 23, 2003.
25. Reidar Visser, "The Sadrists of Basra and the Far South," 2008, 9, http://www.historiae.org/documents/Sadrists.pdf (accessed June 3, 2008). ICG, "Iraq's Muqtada al-Sadr," 7–8. Cockburn, *Muqtada*, 113, 117.
26. Etherington, *Revolt on the Tigris*, 188.
27. Sadr quoted in Shadid, *Night Draws Near*, 179.
28. Shadid, *Night Draws Near*, 185.
29. Dan Murphy and Awadh al-Taiee, "Seeking Safety, Iraqis Turn to Militias," *Christian Science Monitor* July 24, 2006. ICG, "Iraq's Muqtada al-Sadr," 19–20.
30. Shadid, *Night Draws Near*, 186. L. Paul Bremer III and Malcom McConnell, *My Year in Iraq: The Struggle to Build a Future of Hope* (New York: Simon & Schuster, 2006), 191. ICG, "Muqtada al-Sadr," 14, 19–20. Ellen Knickmeyer, "'Shiite Giant Extends Its Reach," *Washington Post*, August 24, 2006. 'Abd al-Latif al-Mosawi, 'Ali Khalil, and Mohammed Hamid, "*Insihab al-Sadriyeen Yaqt'a Awsal Hakouma al-Maliki*" [Withdrawal of the Sadrists Dismembers Maliki Government] *Azzaman*, April 16, 2007.
31. ICG, "Iraq's Muqtada al-Sadr," 14, footnote 100.
32. Visser, "The Sadrists of Basra and the Far South," 7. Media in Cooperation, "Guide of Iraqi Parties 2005," 19. Cockburn, *Muqtada*, 173.
33. The most complete account is Cockburn, *Muqtada*, 123–26. For two different accounts, see Shadid, *Night Draws Near*, 191–92. Meg Laughlin and Soraya Sarhaddi Nelson, "Mosque Custodian Gives Account of Shiite Cleric's Assassination," *Knight Ridder Newspapers*, April 27, 2003.
34. Cole, "The U.S. and Shi'ite Religious Factions," 557. Cockburn, *Muqtada*, 130–31.
35. Quoted in Craig S. Smith, "In Hotbed of Shiite Emotion, Clerics Jockey for Leadership," *New York Times*, April 23, 2003.

36. Jay Garner, *Frontline* interview, July 17, 2003, http://www.pbs.org/wgbh/pages/frontline/shows/truth/interviews/garner.html (accessed June 2, 2008).
37. Aslan, *No god but God*, 250–51.
38. Shadid, *Night Draws Near*, 255–56. The saying is a common comfort at times of death, *Koran* 2:156.
39. Mary Anne Weaver, "The Short, Violent Life of Abu Musab al-Zarqawi," *Atlantic Monthly*, June 8, 2006, http://www.theatlantic.com/doc/print/200607/zarqawi (accessed May 20, 2008). Shadid, *Night Draws Near*, 256–57.
40. Allawi, *Occupation of Iraq*, 27. Roger Shanahan, "Shi'a Political Development in Iraq: The Case of the Islamic Da'wa Party," *Third World Quarterly* 25, no. 5 (2004): 944–49. Cockburn, *Muqtada*, 41–42. According to Cockburn, the Islamic Action Organization was founded in Karbala in the 1970s. When in exile in Lebanon, the group mixed and trained with the Palestinian Fatah movement and the Lebanese Shi'a Amal militia.
41. Quoted in Shanahan, "Shi'a Political Development in Iraq," 952.
42. Shanahan, "Shi'a Political Development in Iraq," 950. Media in Cooperation, "Guide of Iraqi Parties 2005," 18.
43. Reidar Visser, "Beyond SCIRI and Abd al-Aziz al-Hakim: The Silent Forces of the United Iraqi Alliance," January 20, 2006, http://historiae.org/uia.asp (accessed May 8, 2008). Shanahan, "Shi'a Political Development in Iraq," 950–51.
44. Shanahan, "Shi'a Political Development in Iraq," 947. Mahan Abedin, "SCIRI: An American Ally in Iraq?" *The Jamestown Foundation Terrorism Monitor* 1, no. 5 (November 7, 2003): 4–5, http://jamestown.org/terrorism/news/uploads/ter_001_005.pdf (accessed May 9, 2008). Media in Cooperation, "Guide of Iraqi Parties 2005," 16. Marr, *Modern History of Iraq*, 197. ICG, "Shiite Politics in Iraq: The Role of the Supreme Council," November 15, 2007, http://www.crisisgroup.org/library/documents/middle_east___north_africa/iraq_iran_gulf/70_shiite_politics_in_iraq___the_role_of_the_supreme_council.pdf (accessed June 28, 2008).
45. Abedin, "SCIRI: An American Ally in Iraq?" 6. Hashim, *Insurgency and Counter-Insurgency in Iraq*, 247–49. "Badr Commander Killed in Baghdad," *Middle East Online*, July 6, 2005, http://www.middle-east-online.com/english/?id=13948 (accessed May 9, 2008). Media in Cooperation, "Guide of Iraqi Parties 2005," 15. ICG, "Shiite Politics in Iraq," 5–6.
46. Khomeini and Sadr telegram quoted in Aburish, *Saddam Hussein*, 183. Sluglett, *Iraq Since 1958*, 256.
47. ICG, "Shiite Politics in Iraq," 9–11.
48. Allawi, *Occupation of Iraq*, 206–209.

49. Mehdi Khalaji, *The Last Marja: Sistani and the End of Traditional Religious Authority in Shiism*, (Washington, DC: Washington Institute for Near East Policy, September 2006), 7–10, http://www.washingtoninstitute.org/pubPDFs/PolicyFocus59final.pdf (accessed May 7, 2008). Babak Rahimi, "Ayatollah Ali al-Sistani and the Democratization of Post-Saddam Iraq," *Middle East Review of International Affairs* 8, no. 4 (December 2004): 13.
50. Hashim, *Insurgency and Counter-Insurgency in Iraq*, 241. Rahimi, "Sistani and the Democratization of Post-Saddam Iraq," 13.
51. Abdulaziz Sachedina, "What Happened in Najaf?" undated, http://www.uga.edu/islam/sachedina_silencing.html (accessed May 10, 2008).
52. Quoted in Rod Nordland and Babak Dehghanpisheh, "What Sistani Wants," *Newsweek*, February 14, 2006, http://www.newsweek.com/id/48716 (accessed May 19, 2008).
53. Sharistani and Sistani quoted in Norland and Dehghanpisheh, "What Sistani Wants." Ryan Lenz, "Top Shiite Cleric: End Sectarian Bloodshed," *Miami Herald*, July 21, 2006. Grand Ayatollah Ali al-Hussaini al-Sistani, *"Risala lil-Sh'ab al-'Araqi Howl al-Fitna al-Tai'ifiya"* [Message to the Iraqi People Regarding Sectarian Strife] http://www.sistani.org/local.php?modules=extra&eid=2&sid=67 (accessed May 21, 2008).
54. ICG, "Shiite Politics in Iraq," 19.
55. Gen. George Casey, Transcript of Press Conference, June 22, 2006, http://www.defenselink.mil/transcripts/2006/tr20060622-13318.htm (accessed June 23, 2006).
56. ICG, "Iraq's Civil War, the Sadrists, and the Surge," February 7, 2008, 8, 11 (note 64), 18, http://www.crisisgroup.org/home/index.cfm?id=5286 (accessed May 24, 2008). Department of Defense, *Measuring Security and Stability in Iraq*, Report to Congress (June 2008): 6, 7, 22, http://www.defenselink.mil/pubs/pdfs/Master_16_June_08_%20FINAL_SIGNED%20.pdf (accessed June 27, 2008).
57. Department of Defense, *Measuring Security and Stability in Iraq*, Report to Congress (June 2008): 6, 7, 22, http://www.defenselink.mil/pubs/pdfs/Master_16_June_08_%20FINAL_SIGNED%20.pdf (accessed June 27, 2008). ICG, "Iraq's Civil War, the Sadrists, and the Surge," 8, 15–16.

Chapter Five: Setting the Stage for Insurgency

1. This passage is closely paraphrased, omitting "Spanish" twice, changing "French" to "the occupiers" and replacing a phrase about the guerillas' "mountain fastnesses" with elipses. David G. Chandler, *The Campaigns of Napoleon*, (New York: Scribner, 1966), 659-660.

2. Many officers have used the Sopranos or mafia reference. See also Specialist Khaled Dudin quoted in Bing West, *No True Glory: A Frontline Account of the Battle for Fallujah* (New York: Bantam Books, 2005), 29–30. Amit R. Paley, "Iraqis Joining Insurgency Less for Cause than Cash," *Washington Post*, November 20, 2007.
3. Isma'il Haqqi Bey Baban Zadeh quoted in Hanna Batatu, *The Old Social Classes and the Revolutionary Movements of Iraq: A Study of Iraq's Old Landed and Commercial Classes and of Its Communists, Ba'athists, and Free Officers* (Princeton, NJ: Princeton University Press, 1978), 21.
4. Captain Bassim Hassan quoted in Alissa J. Rubin, "3 Suspects Talk After Iraqi Soldiers Do Dirty Work," *New York Times*, April 22, 2007.
5. Ahmed Hashim, "The Insurgency in Iraq," *Small Wars and Insurgencies* 14, no. 3 (2003). Peter Maass, "The Way of the Commandos," *New York Times Magazine*, May 1, 2005. Steven Metz, "Insurgency and Counterinsurgency in Iraq," *The Washington Quarterly* 27: 1 (Winter 2003–2004): 28. Anthony Cordesman, "Iraq's Evolving Insurgency," working paper, Center for Strategic and International Studies, Washington, DC, August 5, 2005, 37, 41, http://www.csis.org/media/csis/pubs/050805_iraqi_insurgency.pdf (accessed July 21, 2008). John F. Burns, "Iraq's Ho Chi Minh Trail," *New York Times*, June 5, 2005. Dan Murphy, "Iraq's Foreign Fighters: Few But Deadly," *Christian Science Monitor*, September 27, 2005. Richard A. Oppel, "Foreign Fighters in Iraq Are Tied to Allies of U.S.," *New York Times*, November 22, 2007.
6. W. Patrick Lang quoted on weapons caches in Eland, "Occupied Iraq," 13. Nir Rosen, "Fallujah: Inside the Iraqi Resistance Part 3: The Fallujah Model," *Asia Times* July 20, 2004, http://www.atimes.com/atimes/Middle_East/FG20Ak01.html (accessed June 5, 2006). Mohammed quoted in Patrick Graham, "Beyond Fallujah," *Harper's Magazine* 308, no. 1849 (June 2004): 43. Weapons market: Robert E. Looney, "The Business of Insurgency: The Expansion of Iraq's Shadow Economy," *The National Interest* 81 (Fall 2005): 67.
7. Edward T. Pound, "Seeds of Chaos: The Baghdad Files," *US News and World Report*, December 20, 2004, 20. "Incriminating Evidence Shows that Saddam Ordered the Training of Al-Qa'ida Elements Two Months Prior to the Bombings of the Twin Towers in New York on 11 September," *Al-Yawm al-Akhar*, trans. by FBIS (Iraq: October 16, 2003).
8. Bob Woodward, *State of Denial: Bush at War, Part III*, (New York: Simon & Schuster, 2006), 184. L. Paul Bremer III and Malcom McConnell, *My Year in Iraq: The Struggle to Build a Future of Hope* (New York: Simon & Schuster, 2006), 126–27.

9. Intelligence operative quoted in Mohammad Bazzi, "A Promise to Fight On: A Leader in Iraqi Militia Group Tells of Plans for Extended Guerrilla War," *New York Newsday*, July 10, 2003. Baʿath memo: Pound, "Seeds of Chaos," 20. Abu Omar quoted in Henry Schuster, "Iraq Insurgency 101," October 12, 2005, http://www.cnn.com/2005/WORLD/meast/10/12/schuster.column/index.html (accessed July 21, 2008).
10. Kevin M. Woods, et al., *Iraqi Perspectives Project: A View of Operation Iraqi Freedom from Saddam's Senior Leadership* (Joint Center of Operational Analysis, Department of Defense: 2006), 25-27, *ff*, http://www.jfcom.mil/newslink/storyarchive/2006/ipp.pdf (accessed May 19, 2008). Ann Scott Tyson, "FBI Agent: Hussein Didn't Expect Invasion," *Washington Post*, January 26, 2008.
11. W. Patrick Lang quoted on weapons caches in Eland, "Occupied Iraq," 13. Nir Rosen, "Fallujah: Inside the Iraqi Resistance Part 3: The Fallujah Model," *Asia Times* July 20, 2004, http://www.atimes.com/atimes/Middle_East/FG20Ak01.html (accessed June 5, 2006). Mohammed quoted in Patrick Graham, "Beyond Fallujah," *Harper's Magazine* 308, no. 1849 (June 2004): 43. Weapons market: Robert E. Looney, "The Business of Insurgency: The Expansion of Iraq's Shadow Economy," *The National Interest* 81 (Fall 2005): 67.
12. Buying weapons: Anthony Shadid, *Night Draws Near: Iraq's People in the Shadow of America's War*, (New York: Henry Holt and Company, 2005), 22Samir Haddad and Mazin Ghazi, "Who Kills Hostages in Iraq?" *Al-Zawra*, trans. FBIS (Iraq: September 19, 2004). C. J. Chivers, "Black-Market Weapon Prices Surge in Iraq Chaos," *New York Times* December 10, 2006.
13. Jeffrey White quoted in Eland, "Occupied Iraq," 9. Also Ali Allawi, *The Occupation of Iraq: Winning the War, Losing the Peace* (New Haven, CT: Yale University Press, 2007), 244–45.
14. Jeffrey White and Michael Schmidmayr, "Resistance in Iraq," *Middle East Quarterly* (Fall 2003): 5, http://www.washingtoninstitute.org/opedsPDFs/4224efa51926d.pdf (accessed September 28, 2006).
15. Jabbar Kadhim quoted in Rajiv Chandrasekaran, *Imperial Life in the Emerald City: Inside Iraq's Green Zone* (New York: Alfred A. Knopf, 2006), 49. Bremer, *My Year in Iraq*, 40. CIA station chief quoted in Thomas Ricks, *Fiasco: The American Military Adventure in Iraq* (New York: Penguin Press, 2006), 159 and similarly quoted in Chandrasekaran, *Imperial Life in the Emerald City*, 71. ICG, "The Next Iraqi War? Sectarianism and Civil Conflict," February 27, 2006, 9–10, http://www.crisisgroup.org/library/documents/middle_east_

__north_africa/iraq_iran_gulf/52_the_next_iraqi_war_sectarianism_and_civil_conflict.pdf (accessed June 28, 2008).

16. Kareem Fahim, "Playing With Soldiers: Is the Cost Rising on CPA Bungling?" *The Village Voice*, July 2–8, 2003, http://www.villagevoice.com/news/0327,fahim,45232,1.html (accessed October 31, 2005). Iraqi general and Major General Marks quoted in Schuster, "Iraq Insurgency 101."
17. Richard A. Oppel Jr., "In Northern Iraq, the Insurgency Has Two Faces, Secular and Jihad, but a Common Goal," *New York Times*, December 19, 2004.
18. DIA report quoted in Pound, "Seeds of Chaos." James Glanz, "Insurgents Wage Precise Attacks on Baghdad Fuel," *New York Times*, February 21, 2005.
19. Bremer, *My Year in Iraq*, 180.
20. Schuster, "Iraq Insurgency 101." Quote from Ahmed Hashim, *Insurgency and Counter-Insurgency in Iraq*, (Ithaca, NY: Cornell University Press, 2006), 85. Thomas Ricks, "General: Iraqi Insurgents Directed from Syria," *Washington Post*, December 17, 2004. Keshlan al-Bayati, *"Al-Dur M'aql 'Izzat al-Duri Yakhda' li-Hamala Aminiya Mushedida"* [al-Dur, Fortress of Izzat al-Duri, Is Subject of Harsh Security Campaign] *Al-Hayat*, April 3, 2007.
21. Schuster, "Iraq Insurgency 101." Multi-National Force-Iraq, "Iraq's 55 Most Wanted," http://www.defendamerica.mil/iraq/iraqi55/ (accessed May 28, 2008). Casey quoted in Ricks, "General: Iraqi Insurgents Directed from Syria." Annia Ciezadlo, "Fragmented Leadership of the Iraqi Insurgency," *Christian Science Monitor*, December 21, 2004. Al-Duri is named as the Deputy Secretary-General of the Arab Socialist Ba'ath Party and signatory to a Febuary 7, 2005, message encouraging resistance, "Statement from the Arab Ba'ath Socialist Party of Iraq," http://comitesirak.free.fr/baath/baath-050207-en.htm (accessed May 28, 2008).
22. Sa'id al-Qaysi, "'Reform' Is New Name for Ba'ath Party's Political Wing, Armed Resistance Is Military Wing," *Al-Bayyinah*, trans. FBIS (Iraq: October 17, 2004).
23. Parker, "Iraq Battling More Than 200,000 Insurgents: Intelligence Chief."
24. Pound, "Seeds of Chaos," 20. Cordesman, "Iraq's Evolving Insurgency," 44.
25. M'ad Feadh, *"Hal Ya'oud al-Ba'ath?"* [Will the Ba'ath Return?] *Asharq Alawsat*, February 9, 2007. Munthar al-Shoufi, Ibrahim Bou 'Azi, and 'Ali al-Mousawi, *"Al-Hashimi Yuwassat Dimashq lil-Tafawwadh ma' al-Ba'athiyeen al-'Araqiyeen"* [Al-Hashimi Seeks Damascus's Mediation for Negotiations with the Iraqi Ba'athists] *Azzaman*, March 5, 2007, http://www.azzaman.com/index.asp?fname=2007\03\03-05\999.htm&storytitle (accessed May 28, 2008).

26. Quoted in Dexter Filkins, "Votes Counted. Deals Made. Chaos Wins," *New York Times*, April 30, 2006.
27. Quoted in Shadid, *Night Draws Near*, 324.
28. Samir Haddad and Mazin Ghazi, "Who Kills Hostages in Iraq?" *Al-Zawra*, trans. FBIS (Iraq: September 19, 2004). Kenneth Katzman, *Iraq: U.S. Regime Change Efforts and Post-Saddam Governance* (Washington, DC: Congressional Research Service, March 4, 2005), 28. Mashriq Abbas, "Maliki Government Is Amidst a Grave Problem of Militias and Mafia Corruption," *Al-Hayat*, May 27, 2006. Zaki Chehab, *Inside the Resistance: The Iraqi Insurgency and the Future of the Middle East* (New York: Nation Books, 2005), 59.
29. Pound, "Seeds of Chaos," 20. Bazzi, "A Promise to Fight On." "Commander of Saddam Hussein's 'The Army of Muhammad' Confesses," *al-Fayha TV* (Iraqi station operating from UAE), transcript trans. by MEMRI, , January 14, 2005, http://www.memritv.org/clip_transcript/en/492.htm (accessed July 21, 2008). Also Bobby Ghosh, "Professor of Death," *Time*, October 16, 2005.
30. Marc Santora, "Beyond Baghdad, Beyond the Surge, War Still Simmers," *New York Times*, February 25, 2007.
31. Donald Rumsfeld, "Speech to Veterans of Foreign Wars," Transcript of Speech, San Antonio, TX, August 25, 2003, http://www.defenselink.mil/speeches/2003/sp20030825-secdef0403.html (accessed May 28, 2008).
32. Perry Biddiscombe, *Werewolf! The History of the National Socialist Guerilla Movement, 1944–1946*, (Buffalo, NY: University of Toronto Press, 1998), 279–81.
33. See quotes in Hashim, *Insurgency and Counter-Insurgency in Iraq*, 29.
34. Hashim, "The Insurgency in Iraq," 12.
35. Marion Farouk-Sluglett and Peter Sluglett, *Iraq Since 1958: From Revolution to Dictatorship*, 3rd ed. (New York: I. B. Tauris, 2003), 267.
36. Metz, "Insurgency and Counterinsurgency in Iraq," 28.
37. "War against the Sunnis" White quoted in Eland, et al., 9. Hashim, "The Insurgency in Iraq," 4. "The Cycle" in Graham, "Beyond Fallujah," 42.
38. Amatzia Baram, "Who Are the Insurgents?: Sunni Arab Rebels in Iraq," *USIP Special Report* 134 (April 2005): 7, http://www.usip.org/pubs/specialreports/sr134.html (accessed May 19, 2008).
39. George Packer, *The Assassins' Gate* (New York: Farrar, Straus and Giroux, 2005), 223.
40. Brian Bender, "Condolence Payments to Iraqis Soar," *Boston Globe* (June 8, 2006), http://www.boston.com/news/world/middleeast/articles/2006/06/08/condolence_payments_to_iraqis_soar/ (accessed May 28, 2008).

41. Author interview.
42. Shadid, *Night Draws Near*, 241–43.
43. Abd al-Zahra Abid quoted in Packer, *The Assassins' Gate*, 204.
44. Shadid, *Night Draws Near*, 223–24.
45. U.S. and Iraqi soldier quoted in Shadid, *Night Draws Near*, 208–210. Hashim, "Iraq's Chaos."
46. See Hashim, *Insurgency and Counter-Insurgency in Iraq*, 20, for an Iraqi's explanation of Coalition treatment.
47. Nir Rosen, *In the Belly of the Green Bird: The Triumph of the Martyrs in Iraq* (New York: Free Press, 2006), 89–91.
48. Alf Andrew Heggoy, *Insurgency and Counterinsurgency in Algeria*, (Bloomington: Indiana University Press, 1972), 265. For a brilliant treatise on the problems of asymmetric warfare, see Andrew Mack, "Why Big Nations Lose Small Wars," *World Politics* 27, no. 2 (January 1975): 175–200.
49. "Abu Abdul Rahman" quoted in Rory McCarthy, "For Faith and Country: Insurgents Fight On," *Guardian,* December 16, 2004.
50. Quoted in Parker, "Iraq Battling More Than 200,000 Insurgents: Intelligence Chief."

Chapter Six: The Widening Insurgencies

1. Quoted in Henry Schuster, "Iraq Insurgency 101," October 12, 2005, http://www.cnn.com/2005/WORLD/meast/10/12/schuster.column/index.html (accessed July 21, 2008).
2. Nir Rosen, *In the Belly of the Green Bird: The Triumph of the Martyrs in Iraq* (New York: Free Press, 2006), 147–48.
3. Ahmed Hashim, *Insurgency and Counter-Insurgency in Iraq* (Ithaca, NY: Cornell University Press, 2006), 25–26.
4. Rashid Khalidi, "Fallujah 101: A History Lesson About the Town We Are Currently Destroying," *In These Times*, November 14, 2004, http://www.inthesetimes.com/site/main/article/1683/ (accessed November 12, 2006). Rosen, *In the Belly of the Green Bird*, 62.
5. Joseph Felter and Brian Fishman, "The Demographics of Recruitment, Finances, and Suicide," in *Bombers, Bank Accounts & Bleedout: Al-Qai'da's Road In and Out of Iraq*, ed. Brian Fishman (West Point, NY: Combating Terrorism Center, 2008), 45–46, http://www.ctc.usma.edu/harmony/pdf/Sinjar_2_July_23.pdf (accessed August 9, 2008).
6. See Hanna Batatu, *The Old Social Classes and the Revolutionary Movements of Iraq: A Study of Iraq's Old Landed and Commercial Classes and of*

its Communists, Ba'athists, and Free Officers (Princeton, NJ: Princeton University Press, 1978), 85.

7. Battles of Fallujah: Bing West, *No True Glory: A Frontline Account of the Battle for Fallujah* (New York: Bantam Books, 2005), 316.
8. For the demise of Arab nationalism and the rise of political Islam, see Giles Kepel, *Jihad: The Trail of Political Islam*, trans. Anthony F. Roberts (Cambridge, MA: Belknap Press, 2002), 61–80. For the "nationalization" of political Islam, see Olivier Roy, *Globalized Islam: The Search for a New Ummah* (New York: Columbia University Press, 2004), 62–65.
9. Baghdadi quoted in Dan Murphy, "Radical Islam Grows Among Iraq's Sunnis," *Christian Science Monitor*, July 28, 2004. Islam has long been the "dominant idiom through which the populace mediated reality and the primary locus of historical memory." Eric Davis, *Memories of State: Politics, History, and Collective Identity in Modern Iraq* (Los Angeles: University of California Press, 2005), 47.
10. Anthony Shadid, *Night Draws Near: Iraq's People in the Shadow of America's War* (New York: Henry Holt and Company, 2005), 232. Toby Dodge, "Prepared Testimony for Senate Committee on Foreign Relations," April 20, 2004, http://foreign.senate.gov/testimony/2004/DodgeTestimony040420.pdf (accessed May 10, 2008).
11. Kubaysi quoted in Muhammad al-Baqali, "Iraq's Muslim Ulema Council Aide: Every U.S. Soldier Is Legitimate Target," *Al-Quds al-Arabi*, trans. FBIS, London, April 23, 2004, http://www.fbis.gov. Power of religion: Christian Smith, "Correcting a Curious Neglect, or Bringing Religion Back In," in *Disruptive Religion: The Force of Faith in Social Movement Activism*, (New York: Routledge, 1996), 5–6, 9–10. Ron Aminzade and Elizabeth J. Perry, "The Sacred, Religious, and Secular in Contentious Politics: Blurring Boundaries," in *Silence and Voice in the Study of Contentious Politics*, ed. Ron Aminzade (New York: Cambridge University Press, 2001), 162.
12. Smith, "Correcting a Curious Neglect," 9–10. Carrie Wickham, *Mobilizing Islam: Religion, Activism, and Political Change in Egypt* (New York: Columbia University Press, 2002), 15, 120. Scholars quoted in Steven Stalinsky, "Leading Egyptian Islamic Clerics on Jihad Against U.S. Troops in Iraq: March–April 2003," *MEMRI Inquiry and Analysis Series*, no. 145 (August 14, 2003), http://memri.org/bin/opener.cgi?Page=archives&ID=IA1 4503 (accessed May 7, 2008).
13. Ali Allawi, *The Occupation of Iraq: Winning the War, Losing the Peace* (New Haven, CT: Yale University Press, 2007), 183. "Saudi Terrorist: I Waged Jihad in Iraq Because of the Communique of the 26 Clerics and Because

of Dr. Yousuf al-Qaradhawi's Fatwa That Any American in Iraq Should Be Killed," Transcript of Interrogation, *Al-Iraqiya TV*, trans. by MEMRI, March 31, 2005, http://www.memritv.org/clip_transcript/en/629.htm (accessed May 15, 2008). "Iraqi Terrorist Talal Ra'ad Sleiman Yasin: Saudi-Sanctioned Fatwa Permits Killing Iraqi Security Personnel," *Al-Iraqiya TV*, trans. by MEMRI, February 9, 2005, http://www.memritv.org/clip_transcript/en/602.htm (accessed May 15, 2008). "Terrorist Confessions Aired on Al-Iraqiyah TV," FBIS Feature, June 10, 2005, http://www.fbis.gov. Shahid, *Night Draws Near*, 291–92, 303. Abu Musab al-Zarqawi, "Message to the Fighters of Jihad in Iraq on September 11, 2004," trans. by MEMRI, http://memri.org/bin/opener.cgi?Page=archives&ID=SP78504 (accessed May 15, 2008).

14. Smith, "Correcting a Curious Neglect," 12. Roy, *Globalized Islam*, 247–48.
15. Quoted in Shadid, *Night Draws Near*, 288–89.
16. Quoted in Patrick Graham, "Beyond Fallujah," *Harper's Magazine* 308, no. 1849 (June 2004): 47.
17. Quoted in Patrick Cockburn, *Muqtada: Muqtada al-Sadr, the Shia Revival, and the Struggle for Iraq* (New York: Scribner, 2008), 159.
18. Smith, "Correcting a Curious Neglect," 13, 21. Mosques not fully controlled in Baram, "Who Are the Insurgents?" 10. Importance of religious leaders in Shadid, *Night Draws Near*, 36.
19. Rosen, *In the Belly of the Green Bird*, 48, 140–41.
20. Smith, "Correcting a Curious Neglect," 15–16. Doug McAdam, "Recruitment to High-Risk Activism: The Case of Freedom Summer," *American Journal of Sociology* 92, no. 1 (July 1986): 64, 70. "Saudi Terrorist: I Waged Jihad in Iraq." "Amjad Uraibi, A Terrorist Captured in Iraq, Tells of Massacres and His Training." "Top Iraqi Terrorist Shihab al-Sab'awi Tells of His Training in Syria and Activity in Iraq," trans. by MEMRI, http://www.memritv.org/clip_transcript/en/573.htm (accessed May 15, 2008). Numerous transcripts and summaries of interviews from the *Al-Iraqiya TV* show "Terrorism in the Hands of Justice" are available at http://www.fbis.gov and http://www.memritv.org. See also Andrea Elliot, "Where Boys Grow Up to Be Jihadis," *New York Times Magazine*, November 25, 2007, http://www.nytimes.com/2007/11/25/magazine/25tetouan-t.html (accessed May 15, 2008). Felter and Fishman, "The Demographics of Recruitment, Finances, and Suicide," 45–46.
21. Eli Berman and David D. Laitin, "Religion, Terrorism, and Public Goods: Testing the Club Model," *National Bureau of Economic Research Working Paper* 13725 (January 2008), http://www.nber.org/papers/w13725.pdf (accessed April 28, 2008).

22. François Labrouillère and Olivier O'Mahony, "A Mother's Angry Cry: 'The Islamists Stole My Son's Soul!'" *Paris-Match*, trans. by FBIS, February 17, 2005, http://www.fbis.gov. Peter Taylor, "Radicalizing Europe's Young Muslims," *BBC Online*, September 1, 2006, http://news.bbc.co.uk/2/hi/programmes/5301512.stm (accessed May 15, 2008). Molly Moore, "7 Convicted in France on Terrorism Charges," *Washington Post*, May 15, 2008. Gregory Viscusi, "French Iraq Insurgents Get Up to Seven Years in Prison," *Bloomberg.com*, http://www.bloomberg.com/apps/news?pid=20601090&sid=a42QRtqpqhd0&refer=france (accessed May 15, 2008).
23. Labrouillère and O'Mahony, "A Mother's Angry Cry." Taylor, "Radicalizing Europe's Young Muslims."
24. Caleb Temple, Defense Intelligence Agency, Testimony Before the House Financial Services Subcommittee on Oversight and Investigations and the House Armed Services Subcommittee on Terrorism, July 28, 2005, http://financialservices.house.gov/media/pdf/072805ct.pdf (accessed May 15, 2008).
25. Vice Adm. Lowell E. Jacoby, Director, Defense Intelligence Agency, "Current and Projected National Security Threats to the United States," statement for the record, Senate Select Committee on Intelligence, February 16, 2005, http://www.dia.mil/publicaffairs/Testimonies/DIA_DR_WWT_20050216U.pdf (accessed May 15, 2008), 8.
26. Milton Bearden, "Afghanistan, Graveyard of Empires," *Foreign Affairs* 80, no. 6 (November/December 2001). Jason Burke, *Al-Qaeda: The True Story of Radical Islam* (New York: I. B. Tauris, 2004), 60–61.
27. Dan Murphy, "Iraq's Foreign Fighters: Few but Deadly," *Christian Science Monitor*, September 27, 2005. Dexter Filkins, "Foreign Fighters Captured in Iraq Come From 27, Mostly Arab Lands," *New York Times*, October 21, 2005. Handler quoted in Bobby Ghosh, "Professor of Death," *Time*, October 16, 2005. Joseph Felter and Brian Fishman, "Al-Qa'ida's Foreign Fighters in Iraq: A First Look at the Sinjar Records" (West Point, NY: Combating Terrorism Center, December 19, 2007), 18, http://www.ctc.usma.edu/harmony/pdf/CTCForeignFighter.19.Dec07.pdf (accessed May 25, 2008).
28. "A Saudi Seriously Injured in Suicide Bombing in Iraq Tells His Story," *MEMRI TV*, September 18, 2005, http://www.memritv.org/clip_transcript/en/861.htm (accessed May 15, 2008).
29. Filkins, "Foreign Fighters." Maj. Gen. William B. Caldwell IV, "Multi-National Force Iraq Situational Update," Briefing Slides, July 5, 2006, http://www.mnf-iraq.com/Transcripts/Slides/060705.pdf (accessed July 5, 2006, link inactive). "*200 M'ataqal 'Arabi fi Sajun al-Ihtilal fi al-'Araq*" [200 Arab

Prisoners in the Prisons of the Occupation in Iraq] *al-Khaleej*, Dubai, United Arab Emirates, May 2, 2008, 25. Alissa J. Rubin, "U.S. Remakes Jails in Iraq, but Gains Are at Risk," *New York Times*, June 2, 2008. Detailed spring of 2008 statistics: Felter and Fishman, "The Demographics of Recruitment, Finances, and Suicide," 35–36.

30. Richard A. Oppel, "Foreign Fighters in Iraq Are Tied to Allies of U.S." *New York Times*, November 22, 2007. Felter and Fishman, "Al-Qa'ida's Foreign Fighters in Iraq," 7–17.

31. Ahmed S. Hashim, "Iraq's Chaos: Why the Insurgency Won't Go Away," *Boston Review*, October/November 2004, http://bostonreview.net/BR29.5/hashim.html (accessed July 21, 2008). Al-Shami quoted in Nimrod Raphaeli, "'The Sheikh of the Slaughterers: Abu Mus'ab Al-Zarqawi and the Al-Qa'ida Connection," *MEMRI Inquiry and Analysis Series*, no. 231, (July 1, 2005), http://memri.org/bin/opener.cgi?Page=archives&ID=IA23105 (accessed May 8, 2008).

32. ICG, "Radical Islam in Iraqi Kurdistan: The Mouse That Roared?" (February 7, 2003), 3–5, http://www.crisisgroup.org/library/documents/report_archive/A400885_07022003.pdf (accessed May 8, 2008).

33. "Radical Islam in Iraqi Kurdistan," 3–6. Anthony Cordesman, "Iraq's Evolving Insurgency," working paper, (Washington, D.C.: Center for Strategic and International Studies, August 5, 2005), 49, http://www.csis.org/media/csis/pubs/050805_iraqi_insurgency.pdf (accessed July 21, 2008). U.S. Department of State, *Country Reports on Terrorism, 2004* (Washington, D.C.: U.S. Department of State, April 2005), 95, http://www.state.gov/documents/organization/45313.pdf (accessed May 8, 2008).

34. Mary Anne Weaver, "The Short, Violent Life of Abu Musab al-Zarqawi," *Atlantic Monthly*, June 8, 2006, http://www.theatlantic.com/doc/print/200607/zarqawi (accessed May 20, 2008). Jordanian intelligence official quoted therein. Nir Rosen, "Iraq's Jordanian Jihadis," *New York Times Magazine*, February 19, 2006, http://www.nytimes.com/2006/02/19/magazine/iraq.html?_r=1&oref=slogin&pagewanted=all (accessed May 8, 2008). Nimrod Raphaeli, "Islamist Pressures in Iraq," *Middle East Media Research Institute Inquiry and Analysis Series*, no. 190 (September 29, 2004), http://memri.org/bin/opener.cgi?Page=archives&ID=IA19004 (accessed May 8, 2008). U.S. Department of State, *Country Reports on Terrorism, 2004*, 111. Thomas Ricks, "Military Plays Up Role of Zarqawi," *Washintgon Post*, April 10, 2006.

35. Weaver, "The Short, Violent Life of Abu Musab al-Zarqawi." The meeting between Bin Laden and Zarqawi was termed "loathing at first sight." Rosen,

"Iraq's Jordanian Jihadis." Raphaeli, "The Sheikh of the Slaughterers." Matthew Levitt, "Untangling the Terror Web: Identifying and Counteracting the Phenomenon of Crossover Between Terrorist Groups," *SAIS Review* 24, no. 1 (Winter–Spring 2004): 40.

36. Weaver, "The Short, Violent Life of Abu Musab al-Zarqawi." Raphaeli, "The Sheikh of the Slaughterers." Greg Miller and Tyler Marshall, "More Iraqis Lured to Al Qaeda Group," *Los Angeles Times*, September 16, 2005.
37. Mathieu Guidère and Peter Harling, "Iraq's Resistance Evolves," *Le Monde diplomatique*, May 12, 2006, http://mondediplo.com/2006/05/02irak (accessed May 8, 2008).
38. John F. Burns, "U.S. Strike Hits Insurgent at Safehouse," *New York Times*, June 8, 2006. Brian Fishman, "After Zarqawi: The Dilemmas and Future of Al-Qaeda in Iraq," *Washington Quarterly* 29, no. 4 (Autumn 2006): 28.
39. Sharon Behn, "Zarqawi Backers Lay Down Shariah Rules," *Washington Times*, May 25, 2006. Heidar Najam, "*Qadmun min Samarra': al-Medina fi Tareqiha lil-tahaul ila Kandahar au Kabul Ayam Taliban*" [Those Coming from Samarra: The City Is on Its Path of Transformation to Kandahar or Kabul in the Days of the Taliban] *Asharq Alawsat*, February 24, 2007. Marc Santora, "Beyond Baghdad, Beyond the Surge, War Still Simmers," *New York Times*, February 25, 2007.
40. Alexis Debat, "Vivisecting the Jihad," *The National Interest* 76 (Summer 2004): 22. Burke, *Al-Qaeda*, 269.
41. Shadid, *Night Draws Near*, 288.
42. Shadid, *Night Draws Near*, 288–289, leaflet quoted, 312.
43. Graham, "Beyond Fallujah," 38, 42. "Mohammed" quoted in Graham, 41.
44. Michael Ware, "Meet the New Jihad," *Time*, July 5, 2004.
45. Former officer quoted in Ware, "Meet the New Jihad." Al-Tamimi quoted in Ghosh, "Professor of Death." Major General Gardner quoted in Michael Moss, "Iraq's Legal System Staggers Beneath the Weight of War," *New York Times*, December 17, 2006. Bob Woodward, *The War Within* (New York: Simon & Schuster, 2008), 34–35.
46. Rashid Khalidi, "The PLO and the Uprising," *Middle East Report* 154 (September–October 1988): 21. Ware, "Meet the New Jihad." Alissa J. Rubin, "U.S. Remakes Jails in Iraq, but Gains Are at Risk," *New York Times*, June 2, 2008. See also Jeffrey Goldberg, *Prisoners: A Muslim & a Jew Across the Middle East Divide* (London: Picador, 2007), 145–162, especially 154. If Israeli jailors did not stop Palestinian organization and education in their camps, American jailors never will.
47. Ellen Knickmeyer and K. I. Ibrahim, "Bombing Shatters Mosque in Iraq,"

Washington Post, February 22, 2003. Joshua Partlow, "Iraqi Official Says Insurgent Cell Bombed Shiite Shrine," *Washington Post*, June 29, 2006. Edward Wong, "Prisoner Links Iraqi to Attack on Shiite Shrine, Official Says," *New York Times*, June 29, 2006.

48. Rubaie quoted in Miller and Marshall, "More Iraqis Lured to Al Qaeda Group."
49. Cordesman, "Iraq's Evolving Insurgency," 12, 41, 45.
50. Jeffrey Record and W. Andrew Terrill, *Iraq and Vietnam: Differences, Similarities, and Insights* (Carlisle, PA: U.S. Army War College Strategic Studies Institute, May 2004), 2.
51. Ghosh, "Professor of Death." Daniel Glaser, Acting Assistant Secretary, Office of Terrorist Financing and Financial Crimes, U.S. Department of the Treasury, Testimony Before the House Financial Services Subcommittee on Oversight and Investigations and the House Armed Services Subcommittee on Terrorism, July 28, 2005, http://financialservices.house.gov/media/pdf/072805dg.pdf (accessed May 7, 2008). Hashim, "Iraq's Chaos." Col. Stephen Twitty quoted in Amit R. Paley, "Iraqis Joining Insurgency Less for Cause than Cash," *Washington Post*, November 20, 2007.
52. "Saudis Reportedly Funding Iraqi Sunnis," *USA Today*, December 8, 2006, http://www.usatoday.com/news/world/iraq/2006-12-08-saudis-sunnis_x.htm (accessed May 8, 2008).
53. Toby Dodge, "Prepared Testimony for the Senate Committee on Foreign Relations." Steven Metz, "Insurgency and Counterinsurgency in Iraq," *The Washington Quarterly* 27, no. 1 (Winter 2003–2004): 34. Chris Dishman, "The Leaderless Nexus: When Crime and Terror Converge," *Studies in Conflict and Terrorism* 28 (2005): 237–252.
54. Quoted in James Glanz and Robert F. Worth, "Attacks on Oil Industry in Iraq Aid a Vast Smuggling Network," *New York Times*, June 4, 2006.
55. Teeples quoted in Patrick McDonnell, "Coalition Gains Insight into Iraq's Foreign Insurgents," *Los Angeles Times*, February 9, 2004. L. Paul Bremer III and Malcom McConnell, *My Year in Iraq: The Struggle to Build a Future of Hope*, (New York: Simon & Schuster, 2006), 80.
56. Debat, "Vivisecting the Jihad," 19, 22. Sudarsan Raghavan, "Sunni Factions Split with al-Qaeda Group," *Washington Post*, April 14, 2007.
57. Abu Qaqa al-Tamimi quoted in Ghosh, "Professor of Death."
58 Glaser, testimony. Looney, "The Business of Insurgency," 71–72. Hashim, "Iraq's Chaos." Graham, "Beyond Fallujah," 43.
59. Bruce Hoffman, *Insurgency and Counterinsurgency in Iraq* (Santa Monica, CA: Rand National Security Research Division, 2004), 12. Anthony

Shadid, "'They Deal in Danger': Iraqi Militiaman's Fatal Error Offers Look into Anti-Occupation Campaign," *Washington Post*, September 4, 2003. "Terrorists Caught in Iraq Confess," *Al-Arabiya TV*, trans. by MEMRI, January 10, 2005, http://www.memritv.org/clip_transcript/en/481.htm (accessed May 7, 2008). "Iraqi Terrorist Talal Ra'ad Sleiman Yasin: Saudi-Sanctioned Fatwa Permits Killing Iraqi Security Personnel," *Al-Iraqiya TV* and "Amjad Uraibi, A Terrorist Captured in Iraq, Tells of Massacres and His Training," *Al-Iraqiya TV*. Eric Schmitt and Thom Shanker, "Estimates by U.S. See Rebels with More Funds," *New York Times*, October 22, 2004. Fahim, "Playing With Soldiers." Coalition Provisional Authority, *Coalition Provisional Authority Order Number 30: Reform of Salaries and Employment Conditions of State Employees,* September 8, 2003, http://www.cpairaq.org/regulations/20030908_CPAORD_30_Reform_of_Salaries_and_Employment_Conditions_of_State_Employees_with_Annex_A.pdf (accessed May 7, 2008). "Life in Iraq: The Cost of Living," *BBC Online*, http://news.bbc.co.uk/2/shared/spl/hi/in_depth/post_saddam_iraq/html/6.stm (accessed May 7, 2008).

60. Schmitt and Shanker, "Estimates by U.S." Charles Tripp, *A History of Iraq*, 2nd ed. (New York: Cambridge University Press, 2002), 217. Glaser, testimony. Schmitt and Shanker, "Estimates by U.S." Salah Nasrawi, "Hussein Nephew Arrested in Iraq," *Boston Globe*, October 20, 2005, http://www.boston.com/news/world/middleeast/articles/2005/10/20/hussein_nephew_arrested_in_iraq/ (accessed May 7, 2008). Cordesman "Iraq's Evolving Insurgency," 44, 53.
61. Cordesman, "Iraq's Evolving Insurgency," 51. "Saddam's Cousin Blasts 'Illegal' Trial," *Al-Jazeera* website, December 16, 2003, http://english.aljazeera.net/NR/exeres/DF1DD10A-B7B9-4F07-BF36-39AEC9AFE7E7.htm (accessed November 9, 2005, link inactive). "Saddam's Cousin: No Link to Fighters," *Al-Jazeera* website, December 16, 2004, http://english.aljazeera.net/English/archive/archive?ArchiveId=8303, (accessed May 7, 2008). Raphaeli, "The Sheikh of the Slaughterers." Glaser, testimony.
62. Hazem al-Amin, "The Resistance in the 'Sunni Triangle,'" *Al-Hayat*, November 10, 2003, http://english.daralhayat.com/Spec/11-2003/Article-20031110-c6a45ce3-c0a8-01ed-007c-ff663bd55a34/story.html (accessed May 8, 2008). Woods, *Iraqi Perspectives Project*, 54–55.
63. John Burns and Kirk Semple, "Iraq Insurgency Has Funds to Sustain Itself, U.S. Finds," *New York Times*, November 26, 2006.
64. Richard A. Oppel Jr., "Iraq's Insurgency Runs on Stolen Oil Profits," *New*

York Times, March 16, 2008. Sabrina Tavernese, "Violence Leaves Young Iraqis Doubting Clerics," *New York Times*, March 4, 2008.

65. Elaine M. Grossman, "New Bush Strategy in Iraq Will Aim to Shield Public from Insurgents," *Inside the Pentagon*, November 3, 2005. Brookings Institution, "Iraq Index," http://www.brookings.edu/iraqindex. Ghaith Abdul-Ahad, "The New Sunni Jihad: 'A Time for Politics'; Tour With Iraqi Reveals Tactical Change," *Washington Post*, October 27, 2005.
66. Dexter Filkins, "U.S. Hands Off Pacified Anbar, Once Heart of Iraq Insurgency," *New York Times*, September 1, 2008.
67. Wazan quoted in Borzou Daragahi, "The Puzzle of Sunnis' Leadership Vacuum," *Los Angeles Times*, July 5, 2005.
68. Talabani quoted in Daragahi, "The Puzzle of Sunnis' Leadership Vacuum."
69. Saleh al-Mutlak quoted in "*Saleh al-Mutlak: La 'Alaqa Li Bal-Harika al-Musellaha wa Lestu Wakeelan Li Zouja Saddam* Saleh al-Mutlak" [No Relations for Me to the Armed Movement and I Am Not an Agent of Saddam's Wife] *Asharq Alawsat* (January 12, 2006), http://www.aawsat.com/details.asp?section=4&article=342915&issue=9907 (accessed May 8, 2008). Dulaimi quoted in Daragahi, "The Puzzle of Sunnis' Leadership Vacuum." Dhari and AMS article quoted in Nir Rosen, "The Battle for Sunni Hearts and Minds," *Asia Times*, April 16, 2004, http://www.atimes.com/atimes/Middle_East/FD16Ak02.html (accessed May 8, 2008). Rosen, *In the Belly of the Green Bird*, 63. Hashim, *Insurgency and Counter-Insurgency in Iraq*, 74–75.

Chapter Seven: Building a New Order

1. David Galula, *Counterinsurgency Warfare: Theory and Practice* (Westport, CT: Praeger Security International, 2006; original edition 1964), 5.
2. Samuel Huntington, *Political Order in Changing Societies* (New Haven, CT: Yale University Press, 1968), 7
3. John F. Burns, "In Days Before Hanging, a Push for Revenge and a Push Back from the U.S.," *New York Times*, January 7, 2007.
4. Eric Davis, *Memories of State: Politics, History, and Collective Identity in Modern Iraq* (Los Angeles: University of California Press, 2005), 66.
5. L. Paul Bremer III and Malcom McConnell, *My Year in Iraq: The Struggle to Build a Future of Hope* (New York: Simon & Schuster, 2006), 223, 228.
6. For a general discussion of the problem of two-level negotiations at the international level see Robert D. Putnam, "Diplomacy and Domestic Politics: The Logic of Two-Level Games," *International Organization* 42, no. 3 (Summer 1988): 427–60. The problem in Iraq is essentially the same, with

negotiations between ethno-sectarian blocs depending significantly on the "domestic politics" of the members of the bloc.

7. Quote from Dankwart A. Rustow, "Transitions to Democracy: Toward a Dynamic Model," *Comparative Politics* 2, no. 3 (April 1970): 338.
8. Paul Collier, "Ethnic Diversity: An Economic Analysis," *Economic Policy* 32 (April 2001): 127–66. Iraq oil statistics from "Life in Iraq: Oil," *BBC News Online*, http://news.bbc.co.uk/1/shared/spl/hi/in_depth/post_saddam_iraq/html/4.stm (accessed May 7, 2008). Energy Information Administration, "Iraq Country Analysis Brief," August 2007, http://www.eia.doe.gov/emeu/cabs/Iraq/Background.html (accessed May 2, 2008). Central Intelligence Agency, "Iraq," *World Factbook* (2008) https://www.cia.gov/library/publications/the-world-factbook/geos/iz.html (accessed May 2, 2008).
9. Huntington, *Political Order in Changing Societies*, 7–8.
10. Quoted in "Maliki's Knights Fail to Shine," *Economist*, April 5, 2008, 52–53.
11. Quoted in Bremer, *My Year in Iraq*, 83.
12. "Iraqi Governing Council Members," *BBC News*, July 14, 2003, http://news.bbc.co.uk/2/hi/middle_east/3062897.stm (accessed May 7, 2008). ICG, "The Next Iraqi War? Sectarianism and Civil Conflict," February 27, 2006, 10–11, http://www.crisisgroup.org/library/documents/middle_east___north_africa/iraq_iran_gulf/52_the_next_iraqi_war_sectarianism_and_civil_conflict.pdf (accessed June 28, 2008).
13. Allawi, *Occupation of Iraq*, 205–206.
14. Bremer, *My Year in Iraq*, 224. Grand Ayatollah Ali al-Hussaini al-Sistani, "*Howl Mushrua' Kitaba al-Dustour al-'Araqi*" [Regarding the Drafting of the Iraqi Constitution] June 26, 2003, http://www.sistani.org/local.php?modules=extra&eid=2&sid=13 (accessed May 4, 2008). See also L. Paul Bremer III, "Iraq's Path to Sovereignty," *Washington Post*, September 8, 2003.
15. Bremer, *My Year in Iraq*, 226–28.
16. Coalition Provisional Authority and Iraqi Governing Council, *November 15 Agreement: Timeline to a Sovereign, Democratic and Secure Iraq*, November 15, 2003, http://www.cpa-iraq.org/government/AgreementNov15.pdf (accessed May 4, 2008).
17. Allawi, *Occupation of Iraq*, 222.
18. Bremer, *My Year in Iraq*, 302–308. Allawi, *Occupation of Iraq*, 222–224.
19. Allawi, *Occupation of Iraq*, 224. Unnamed "official involved in the process" quoted in George Packer, "Letter from Baghdad: Caught in the Crossfire," *New Yorker*, May 17, 2004, http://www.newyorker.com/archive/2004/05/17/040517fa_fact?currentPage=all (accessed May 8, 2008).

20. Coalition Provisional Authority and Iraqi Governing Council, *Law of Administration for the State of Iraq for the Transitional Period* (Transitional Administrative Law), March 8, 2004, http://www.cpa-iraq.org/government/TAL.html (accessed May 4, 2008).
21. Sistani, "*Istifta' Howl al-Hakuma al-Muwaqata aleti Shekeletha al-Umum al-Mutahida*" [Request for a Ruling Regarding the Temporary Government Formed by the United Nations] June 2, 2004, http://www.sistani.org/local.php?modules=extra&eid=2&sid=38 (accessed May 4, 2008).
22. Sistani, "*Risala 'Ila Ra'es Majlis al-'Amn al-Douli Tahthir Min al-'Ishara 'Ila Qanoon 'Idara al-Dowla fi al-Qirar al-Dowli 1546*" [Letter to the President of the United Nations Security Council Warning Against Reference to the Administrative Law in UN Resolution 1546] June 6, 2004, http://www.sistani.org/local.php?modules=extra&eid=2&sid=39 (accessed May 4, 2008).
23. United Nations Security Council, *Resolution 1546*, June 8, 2004, http://daccessdds.un.org/doc/UNDOC/GEN/N04/381/16/PDF/N0438116.pdf?OpenElement (accessed May 5, 2008). Bremer, *My Year in Iraq*, 380–82.
24. Carina Perelli, "UN's Perelli Discusses Iraqi Elections Preparations," Press Conference Transcript, June 4, 2004, http://www.iraqcoalition.org/transcripts/20040604_Perelli_Prep.html (accessed May 5, 2008). Adeed Dawisha and Larry Diamond, "Iraq's Year of Voting Dangerously," *Journal of Democracy* 17, no. 2 (April 2006): 93.
25. Coalition Provisional Authority, "Order Number 96: The Electoral Law," June 7, 2004, http://www.iraqcoalition.org/regulations/20040615_CPAORD_96_The_Electoral_Law.pdf (accessed May 5, 2008).
26. Thomas Melia and Brian Katulis, "Iraqis Discuss Their Country's Future: Post-War Perspectives from the Iraqi Street, Findings from Focus Groups with Iraqi Men and Women Conducted June 29–July 9, 2003," (Washington, D.C.: National Democratic Institute for International Affairs, July 28, 2003), 25, http://www.peacewomen.org/resources/Iraq/FullNDI.pdf (accessed May 5, 2008). Department of State Office of Research, "Opinion Analysis: Iraqi Public Has Wide Ranging Preferences for a Future Political System," 14, http://www.cpa-iraq.org/government/political_poll.pdf (accessed May 5, 2008).
27. Fadhil al-Rubi'aie quoted in M'ad Feadh, "*Hal Ya'oud al-Ba'ath?*" [Will the Ba'ath Return?] *Asharq Alawsat*, February 9, 2007, http://www.asharqalawsat.com/print/default.asp?did=405511 (accessed March 17, 2007, link inactive).
28. Melia and Katulis, "Iraqis Discuss Their Country's Future," 26.

29. Quoted David M. Dougherty, "Iraqi Voices: Religion, Rights and Responsibility in Transition, Findings from Focus Groups with Iraqi Men and Women Conducted June 21, and July 9, 2005," (Washington, D.C.: National Democratic Institute for International Affairs, August 2005), 21–22, http://www.accessdemocracy.org/library/1921_iq_focusgroups_060105.pdf (accessed May 5, 2008).
30. Young Iraqi quoted in Allawi, *Occupation of Iraq*, 391. Sabrina Tavernese, "Violence Leaves Young Iraqis Doubting Clerics," *New York Times*, March 4, 2008.
31. Dawisha and Diamond, "Iraq's Year of Voting Dangerously," 93–94. Allawi, *Occupation of Iraq*, 343–44.
32. ICG, "Shiite Politics in Iraq: The Role of the Supreme Council," November 15, 2007, 11–12, http://www.crisisgroup.org/library/documents/middle_east__north_africa/iraq_iran_gulf/70_shiite_politics_in_iraq__the_role_of_the_supreme_council.pdf (accessed June 28, 2008).
33. Neil Macdonald, "Kurds 'Up the Ante' in Iraqi Constitution Talks," *Financial Times*, July 27, 2005. Dawisha and Diamond, "Iraq's Year of Voting Dangerously," 94. Allawi, *Occupation of Iraq*, 403–405.
34. Jill Carroll, "Iraq's Democracy Dilemma: Iraq's Parliament is Stifled by Back-Room Deals and Lack of Attendance, Members Say," *Christian Science Monitor*, September 22, 2005.
35. These themes are taken from summer of 2005 Iraqi interview statements, Dougherty, "Iraqi Voices," 16.
36. Jonathan Morrow, "Weak Viability: The Iraqi Federal State and the Constitutional Amendment Process," *USIP Special Report* 168 (July 2006): 4, http://www.usip.org/pubs/specialreports/sr168.pdf (accessed May 5, 2008).
37. Constitution of Iraq, available in Arabic, http://www.cabinet.iq/dostor.htm, and English, http://portal.unesco.org/ci/en/files/20704/11332732681iraqi_constitution_en.pdf/iraqi_constitution_en.pdf (accessed May 5, 2008). An English translation was available at the Iraqi government's website in 2006 and 2007, yet was inaccessible at time of writing. See also Morrow, "Weak Viability," 3–4.
38. Michael M. Gunter and M. Hakan Yavuz, "The Continuing Crisis in Iraqi Kurdistan," *Middle East Policy* 12, no. 1 (Spring 2005): 123.
39. Gunter and Yavuz, "The Continuing Crisis in Iraqi Kurdistan," 127–28. Ashraf Khalil, "All Sides Weigh Losses, Gains in Iraqi Constitution," *Los Angeles Times*, August 21, 2005.
40. Constitution of Iraq, art. 140.
41. Marion Farouk-Sluglett and Peter Sluglett, *Iraq Since 1958: From Revolution*

to Dictatorship, 3rd ed. (New York: I. B. Tauris, 2003), 165. See ICG, "Iraq and the Kurds: The Brewing Battle Over Kirkuk," July 18, 2006, http://www.crisisgroup.org/library/documents/middle_east___north_africa/iraq_iran_gulf/56_iraq_and_the_kurds___the_brewing_battle_over_kirkuk.pdf (accessed May 18, 2008).

42. Iyad Samarrai quoted in Borzou Daragahi, "Sunnis See Iran's Hand in Call for Federalism," *Los Angeles Times*, August 21, 2005.
43. Kamil al-Mehaidi, "Geographical Distribution of Iraqi Oil Fields and Its Relation with the New Constitution," *Iraq Revenue Watch*, May 27, 2006, http://www.iraqrevenuewatch.org/reports/052706.pdf, (accessed May 5, 2008). Edward Wong, "Iraqis Near Deal on Distribution of Oil Revenues," *New York Times*, Decemberr 9, 2006.
44. IHS Press Release, April 18, 2007, http://www.ihs.com/News/Press-Releases/2007/IraqAtlas.htm (accessed May 5, 2008).
45. Constitution of Iraq, art. 111.
46. Constitution of Iraq, art. 120.
47. Al-Mehaidi, "Geographical Distribution of Iraqi Oil Fields."
48. Constitution of Iraq, arts. 116, 117, 118.
49. Quote and other interview data from this paragraph in Melia and Katulis, "Iraqis Discuss their Country's Future," 21.
50. Dougherty, "Iraqi Voices," 17–18.
51. Constitution of Iraq, art. 2.
52. Jonathan Morrow, "Iraq's Constitutional Process II: An Opportunity Lost," *USIP Special Report* 155 (November 2005): 11–12, http://www.usip.org/pubs/specialreports/sr155.html (accessed May 6, 2008).
53. Morrow, "Iraq's Constitutional Process II," 13. Ashraf Khalil, "All Sides Weight Losses, Gains in Iraqi Constitution.".
54. Quoted in Borzou Daragahi and Alissa J. Rubin, "Iraqi Constitution Panel Fails to Deliver a Draft," *Los Angeles Times*, August 15, 2005.
55. Dawisha and Diamond, "Iraq's Year of Voting Dangerously," 94–95. Constitution of Iraq, art. 142.
56. Independent Electoral Commission of Iraq, "Certification of the Constitutional Referendum Final Results," October 25, 2005, http://www.ieciraq.org/final%20cand/20051102%20Certified%20Referendum%20Results%20English.pdf (accessed October 14, 2006). Website not functioning at time of writing. Results also available in "Iraq Voters Back New Constitution," *BBC News*, October 25, 2005, http://news.bbc.co.uk/2/hi/middle_east/4374822.stm (accessed May 6, 2008).
57. Independent Electoral Commission of Iraq, "IECI Regulation 13-2005:

Allocation of Seats," November 13, 2005, http://www.ieciraq.org/final% 20cand/Regn13-2005AllocationofSeats_English-Dec6_[1].pdf (accessed October 14, 2006). Website not functioning at time of writing.
58. Dawisha and Diamond, "Iraq's Year of Voting Dangerously," 95.
59. Dawisha and Diamond, "Iraq's Year of Voting Dangerously," 96–98.
60. International Foundation for Election Systems Center for Transitional and Post-Conflict Governance, "Council of Representatives Election Composite Report," February 20, 2006, http://www.ifes.org/publication/ d2046fde59cd1eeda675eb611bfd4d9e/Council%20of%20Representatives %20Election%20Composite-Update20FebV3.doc (accessed May 6, 2008). Dawisha and Diamond, "Iraq's Year of Voting Dangerously," 99. Brian Faler, "Election Turnout in 2004 Was Highest Since 1968," *Washington Post*, January 15, 2005.
61. Independent Electoral Commission of Iraq, "Certification of the Council of Representatives Elections Final Results," February 10, 2006, http://www. ieciraq.org/final%20cand/IECI_Decision_Certified_Results_of_CoR_ Elections_En.pdf (accessed July 12, 2006). Website not functioning at time of writing. Results also available at "Iraqi Shias Win Election Victory," *BBC News*, January 21, 2006, http://news.bbc.co.uk/2/hi/middle_east/4630518. stm (accessed May 6, 2008).
62. Vali Nasr, *The Shia Revival: How Conflicts within Islam Will Shape the Future*, (New York: W. W. Norton & Company, 2006), 189. Media in Cooperation, "Guide of Iraqi Parties 2005," 15. Sistani, "*'Istifta' Howl al-Intikhabat al-'Araqiya*" [Response to Request for Legal Opinion Regarding the Iraqi Elections] December 10, 2005, http://www.sistani.org/local.php?m odules=extra&eid=2&sid=62 (accessed May 21, 2008).
63. Reidar Visser, "Beyond SCIRI and Abd al-Aziz al-Hakim: The Silent Forces of the United Iraqi Alliance," January 20, 2006, http://historiae.org/uia.asp (accessed May 6, 2008). Reidar Visser, "SCIRI, Daawa and the Sadrists in the Certified Election Results," February 11, 2006, http://www.historiae. org/sciri.asp (accessed June 1, 2008). Media in Cooperation, "Guide of Iraqi Parties 2005," 15.
64. Visser, "SCIRI, Daawa and the Sadrists in the Certified Election Results."
65. Media in Cooperation, "Guide of Iraqi Parties 2005," 20–22.
66. Media in Cooperation, "Guide of Iraqi Parties 2005," 11–14. Ahmed Hashim, *Insurgency and Counter-Insurgency in Iraq*, (Ithaca, NY: Cornell University Press, 2006), 21–22.
67. Media in Cooperation, "Guide of Iraqi Parties 2005," 11.
68. Media in Cooperation, "Guide of Iraqi Parties 2005," 5–7, 24–25.

69. Dawisha and Diamond, "Iraq's Year of Voting Dangerously," 101.
70. See ICG, "The Next Iraqi War?" 19.
71. Charles Recknagel, "Iraq: Formation of New Government Crippled by Sectarian Violence," *Radio Free Europe / Radio Liberty*, March 23, 2006, http://www.rferl.org/featuresarticle/2006/03/64f83917-e780-4819-b190-9b01f5d7c283.html (accessed May 7, 2008). John Burns, "For Some, a Last, Best Hope for U.S. Efforts in Iraq," *New York Times*, May 21, 2006.
72. ICG, "Shiite Politics in Iraq," 12–13, 17–18. "*Al-Fadhila Yansahib min al-I'tlaf al-'Iraqi Khalasan min al-Ta'ifea*" [Fadhila Withdraws from the Iraqi Alliance Forgoing Sectarianism] *Azzaman*, March 7, 2007, http://www.azzaman.com/index.asp?fname=2007\03\03-07\999.htm&storytitle (accessed May 7, 2008). Jonathan Finer, "At Heart of Iraqi Impasse, A Family Feud," *Washington Post*, April 19, 2006. Reidar Visser, "Basra Crude: The Great Game of Iraq's 'Southern' Oil," March 2007, 4, http://historiae.org/documents/oil.pdf (accessed May 7, 2008). Richard Oppel and Abdul Razzaq al-Saiedi, "Hard Lesson in Baghdad: Oops, There Goes Basra," *New York Times*, September 17, 2006. Reidar Visser, "The Law on the Powers of the Governorates Is Passed after Significant Cross-Sectarian Cooperation in the Iraqi Parliament," February 14, 2008, http://www.historiae.org/provinces.asp (accessed June 3, 2008).
73. Fadhila Party Statement, March 7, 2007, http://www.alfadhela.org/news/news_details.asp?field=general_news&id=356 (accessed June 28, 2008). Sabrina Tavernise and Qais Mizher, "Oil and Politics Corrupt Basra, a Once-Calm City," *New York Times*, June 13, 2006. Visser,"Basra Crude," 10, 12.
74. "Iraqi Parliament Approves Federal Law," *Reuters*, October 11, 2006. Hakim quoted in *Associated Press*, "Sunni Accuse Shiites of Dirty Tricks in Passing Controversial Federalism Law," (October 12, 2006) http://www.iht.com/articles/ap/2006/10/12/africa/ME_GEN_Iraq_Federalism.php (accessed May 7, 2008).
75. See Donald L. Horowitz, "Democracy in Divided Societies," in *Nationalism, Ethnic Conflict, and Democracy*, eds. Larry Diamond and Marc F. Plattner (Baltimore, MD: Johns Hopkins University Press, 1994), 36–37, 46. Morrow, "Weak Viability," 6–7. Ahmed Saleh, "*al-Barzani: Narfud al-Masalaha 'ala Hisab al-Kurd*, Al-Barzani" [We Refuse Reconciliation at the Expense of the Kurds] *Azzaman*, August 8, 2006, http://www.azzaman.com/azzaman/articles/2006/08/08-29/999.htm (accessed May 7, 2008).
76. Morrow, "Weak Viability," 9. Ali Khalil and Nidal al-Leithi, "*Teshkeel Lejna Barlimaniya L'I'ada al-Nathar fi al-Dustour*" [Parliamentary Committee Formed to Re-examine the Constitution] *Azzaman*, September 26, 2006,

http://www.azzaman.com/azz/articles/2006/09/09-25/878.htm (accessed May 7, 2008). Rend al-Rahim Francke, "Political Progress in Iraq During the Surge," *USIP Special Report* 196 (December 2007): 5, http://www.usip.org/pubs/specialreports/sr196.pdf (accessed May 25, 2008). Humam Hammudi quoted therein, 6. Department of Defense, *Measuring Security and Stability in Iraq*, Report to Congress, (June 2008): 3, http://www.defenselink.mil/pubs/pdfs/Master_16_June_08_%20FINAL_SIGNED%20.pdf (accessed June 27, 2008.

Chapter 8: Iraq Looks into the Abyss of Civil War

1. Kanan Makiya, *Cruelty and Silence: War, Tyranny, Uprising, and the Arab World* (New York: W. W. Norton and Company, 1993), 225.
2. Sunni Baghdadi quoted in Nir Rosen, *In the Belly of the Green Bird: The Triumph of the Martyrs in Iraq* (New York: Free Press, 2006), 247.
3. Thomas Melia and Brian Katulis, "Iraqis Discuss Their Country's Future: Post-War Perspectives from the Iraqi Street, Findings from Focus Groups with Iraqi Men and Women Conducted June 29–July 9, 2003," (Washington, DC: National Democratic Institute for International Affairs, July 28, 2003): 22. Also Eric Davis, *Memories of State: Politics, History, and Collective Identity in Modern Iraq*, (Los Angeles: University of California Press, 2005), 18. Baqubah resident quoted in "Iraq After the Surge I: The New Sunni Landscape," April 30, 2008, 3–4, note 18, http://www.crisisgroup.org/home/index.cfm?id=5415 (June 7, 2008).
4. February 15, 2005, statement quoted in Association of Muslim Scholars Press Release, "*Tasreeh Sahafi Howl al-Musharaka fi al-'Amaliya al-Siyasiya wa Kitaba al-Dustour*" [Press Release Regarding Participation in the Political Process and the Drafting of the Constitution], http://iraq-amsi.org/ (accessed May 10, 2008). Attempt to reach out to Sadrists: Ali Allawi, *The Occupation of Iraq: Winning the War, Losing the Peace* (New Haven, CT: Yale University Press, 2007), 183.
5. See Last-of-Iraqis, "Dentistry College Ordeal," weblog post, February 18, 2008, http://last-of-iraqis.blogspot.com/2008/02/dentistry-college-ordeal.html (accessed May 7, 2008).
6. Vali Nasr, "When the Shiites Rise," *Foreign Affairs* 85, no. 4 (July/August 2006): 58.
7. Noah Feldman, *What We Owe Iraq: War and the Ethics of Nation Building* (Princeton, NJ: Princeton University Press, 2004), 75–78.
8. Donald L. Horowitz, "Democracy in Divided Societies," in *Nationalism,*

Ethnic Conflict, and Democracy, eds. Larry Diamond and Marc F. Plattner (Baltimore, MD: Johns Hopkins University Press, 1994), 49.

9. Larry Diamond, *Squandered Victory: The American Occupation and the Bungled Effort to Bring Democracy to Iraq*, (New York: Times Books, 2005), 60.

10. United Nations, "The Political Transition in Iraq: Report of the Fact-Finding Mission," Security Council Document S/2004/140 (February 23, 2004): 3, http://www.un.org/News/dh/iraq/rpt-fact-finding-mission.pdf (accessed June 2, 2008). U.S. Department of State, *Country Reports on Human Rights Practices, 2005: Iraq* March 8, 2006, http://www.state.gov/g/drl/rls/hrrpt/2005/61689.htm (accessed June 2, 2008).

11. Dexter Filkins, "Armed Groups Propel Iraq Toward Chaos," *New York Times*, May 24, 2006.

12. Quoted in Babak Deghanpisheh, "Love in a Time of Madness," *Newsweek*, International Edition, March 13, 2006, http://www.newsweek.com/id/46871 (accessed May 15, 2008).

13. ICG, "The Next Iraqi War? Sectarianism and Civil Conflict," February 27, 2006, 4–5, http://www.crisisgroup.org/library/documents/middle_east_north_africa/iraq_iran_gulf/52_the_next_iraqi_war_sectarianism_and_civil_conflict.pdf (accessed June 28, 2008). Bassem Mroue, "As Iraqi Television Grows, So Does a Religious Divide," *Philadelphia Inquirer*, July 8, 2006. Nir Rosen, *In the Belly of the Green Bird*, 153. Ghaith Abdul-Ahad "Iraq's Deepening Sectarianism," *The Hindu*, April 5, 2005, http://www.thehindu.com/2005/05/04/stories/2005050404371100.htm (accessed May 26, 2006). Sharon Behn, "Zarqawi Backers Lay Down Shariah Rules," *Washington Times*, May 25, 2006. Sabrina Tavernise, "Sectarian Hatred Pulls Apart Iraq's Mixed Towns," *New York Times*, November 20, 2005.

14. Sunni quoted in Deghanpisheh, "Love in a Time of Madness." Department of Defense, *Measuring Security and Stability in Iraq*, Report to Congress, (May 2006): 29, http://www.defenselink.mil/news/may2006/d20060530SecurityandStabiltyRptFinalv2.pdf (accessed June 7, 2006). Sarkawt Hassan Jalal quoted in C. J. Chivers, "Black-Market Weapon Prices Surge in Iraq Chaos," *New York Times*, December 10, 2006. Rosen, *In the Belly of the Green Bird*, 136.

15. Sabrina Tavernise, "Fear Invades a Once-Comfortable Iraqi Enclave," *New York Times*, June 24, 2006. Sabrina Tavernise, "It Has Unraveled So Quickly," *New York Times*, January 28, 2007.

16. Dexter Filkins, "Votes Counted. Deals Made. Chaos Wins." *New York Times*, April 30, 2006. Damien Cave, "More Iraqis Fleeing Strife and Segregating by Sect," *New York Times*, July 20, 2006. Republic of Iraq Council of Ministers

Press Release, July 31, 2006, http://www.iraqigovernment.org/Content/Press%20release/English/31-7-2006/4.htm (accessed September 7, 2006, link active). United Nations Assistance Mission for Iraq, "Human Rights Report," September 1–October 31, 2006, 3, http://www.uniraq.org/documents/HR%20Report%20Sep%20Oct%202006%20EN.pdf (accessed June 2, 2008). Brookings Institution, "Iraq Index." United Nations High Commissioner for Refugees, "Statistics on Displaced Iraqis Around the World," September 2007, http://www.unhcr.org/cgibin/texis/vtx/home/opendoc.pdf?tbl=SUBSITES&id=470387fc2 (accessed June 2, 2008). Tavernise, "Sectarian Hatred Pulls Apart Iraq's Mixed Towns."

17. Sabrina Tavernise, "For Iraqis, Exodus to Syria and Jordan Continues," *New York Times*, June 14, 2006. UNAMI, "Human Rights Report," 3–4. International Republican Institute, "Survey of Iraqi Public Opinion: June 14–June 24, 2006," July 2006, http://www.iri.org/mena/iraq/pdfs/2006-07-18-Iraq%20poll%20June%20June.ppt (accessed June 2, 2008). UNHCR, "Statistics on Displaced Iraqis Around the World," September 2007.

18. IRI, "Survey of Iraqi Public Opinion."

19. Department of Defense, *Measuring Security and Stability in Iraq*, Report to Congress, (March 2008):10, http://www.defenselink.mil/pubs/pdfs/FINAL-SecDef%20Signed-20071214.pdf (accessed June 11, 2008). Returnee perspective: Mohamed Hussein, "Back From Syria," *New York Times Blog*, May 5, 2008, http://baghdadbureau.blogs.nytimes.com/2008/05/05/back-from-syria/ (accessed June 10, 2008).

20. Michael Georgy, "Sectarian Slaying of Boy Shows Level of Barbarism," *San Diego Union-Tribune,* May 24, 2006.

21. Details on AQI cell from Joshua Partlow, "Iraqi Official Says Insurgent Cell Bombed Shiite Shrine," *Washington Post*, June 29, 2006. Edward Wong, "Prisoner Links Iraqi to Attack on Shiite Shrine, Official Says," *New York Times*, June 29, 2006. Iraqi government statistics from Jonathan Finer, "Threat of Shiite Militias Now Seen as Iraq's Most Critical Challenge," *Washington Post*, April 8, 2006, and Dehghanpisheh, "Love in a Time of Madness." U.S. statistics from U.S. Department of Defense, *Measuring Security and Stability in Iraq*, Report to Congress, (May 2006): 40, http://www.defenselink.mil/news/may2006/d20060530SecurityandStabiltyRptFinalv2.pdf (accessed June 2, 2008).

22. Jonathan Finer, "Threat of Shiite Militias Now Seen as Iraq's Most Critical Challenge," *Washington Post*, April 8, 2006. "Near the Point of No Return," *Economist*, April 22, 2006, 48.

23. Bremer, *My Year in Iraq*, 274. For one example see Sabrina Tavernise, "Sectarian Hatred Pulls Apart Iraq's Mixed Towns."
24. Dan Murphy, "Sadr's Militia Tightens Grip on Healthcare," *Christian Science Monitor*, May 25, 2006. Edward Wong, "U.S. Troops Start Major Attacks on Shiite Insurgents in 2 Cities," *New York Times*, May 6, 2004. "*Quwat Khuta Baghdad Taghtasib Sayyida 'Araqiya*" [Forces of the Baghdad Plan Rape Iraqi Woman] *Azzaman*, February 20, 2007, http://www.azzaman.com/index.asp?fname=2007%5C02%5C02-20%5C999.htm&storytitle (accessed June 2, 2008). Bremer, *My Year in Iraq*, 186.
25. Quoted in Dexter Filkins, "Armed Groups Propel Iraq Toward Chaos," *New York Times*, May 24, 2006, and Scott Johnson, "Phantom Force: In the 'Year of the Police,' A Murky Security Groups is Mutating and Growing," *Newsweek*, International Edition, April 24, 2006, http://www.msnbc.msn.com/id/12335716/site/newsweek (accessed June 6, 2006).
26. Sudarsan Raghavan, "A Day When the Mahdi Army Showed Its Other Side," *Washington Post*, November 27, 2006. "Devastating Blasts Hit Sadr City," *BBC News*, November 23, 2006, http://news.bbc.co.uk/2/hi/middle_east/6177356.stm (accessed June 2, 2008). Kirk Semple and Omar al-Neami, "47 Sunni Militants Die in Iraq Gunfights," *New York Times*, November 26, 2006. Louise Roug, "Iraqi Shiites Vent Anger on Premier," *Los Angeles Times*, November 27, 2006.
27. ICG, "Iraq's Civil War, the Sadrists, and the Surge," February 7, 2008, 6–7, 9, 18, http://www.crisisgroup.org/home/index.cfm?id=5286 (accessed May 24, 2008). Cockburn, *Muqtada*, 178. Rend al-Rahim Francke, "Political Progress in Iraq During the Surge," *USIP Special Report* 196 (December 2007): 3–4, http://www.usip.org/pubs/specialreports/sr196.pdf (accessed May 25, 2008). Sabrina Tavernese, "Fear Keeps Iraqis Out of Their Baghdad Homes," *New York Times*, August 23, 2008.
28. ICG, "Iraq's Civil War, the Sadrists, and the Surge," February 7, 2008, 2–4, http://www.crisisgroup.org/home/index.cfm?id=5286 (accessed May 24, 2008).

Chapter Nine: Prospects for Stability, Prospects for Democracy
1. Quoted in Ann Scott Tyson, "Petraeus Says Cleric Helped Curb Violence," *Washington Post*, December 7, 2007.
2. The strategy, known as "The New Way Forward," was outlined in the January 10, 2007, address, http://www.whitehouse.gov/news/releases/2007/01/20070110-7.html (accessed June 27, 2008) and National Security Council, "Highlights

of the Iraq Strategy Review," January 2007, http://www.whitehouse.gov/nsc/iraq/2007/iraq-strategy011007.pdf (accessed June 27, 2008).
3. Department of Defense, *Measuring Security and Stability in Iraq*, Report to Congress, (June 2008): 30, http://www.defenselink.mil/pubs/pdfs/Master_16_June_08_%20FINAL_SIGNED%20.pdf (accessed June 27, 2008). Department of Defense, *Measuring Security and Stability in Iraq*, Report to Congress, (December 2007): 24, http://www.defenselink.mil/pubs/pdfs/FINAL-SecDef%20Signed-20071214.pdf (accessed June 27, 2008). Brookings Institution, "Iraq Index," http://www.brookings.edu/iraqindex.
4. Gen. David A. Petraeus, "Report to Congress on the Situation in Iraq," Testimony Before the House Foreign Relations and Armed Services Committees, September 10, 2007, http://www.internationalrelations.house.gov/110/pet091007.pdf (accessed May 23, 2008). Brookings Institution, "Iraq Index."
5. ICG, "Iraq After the Surge I: The New Sunni Landscape," *Crisis Group Middle East Report* 74 (April 30, 2008): 10–15, http://www.crisisgroup.org/home/index.cfm?id=5415 (accessed June 7, 2008).
6. David Kilcullen, "Anatomy of a Tribal Revolt," August 2007, http://smallwarsjournal.com/blog/2007/08/print/anatomy-of-a-tribal-revolt/ (accessed May 22, 2008). ICG, "The New Sunni Landscape," 4.
7. ICG, "The New Sunni Landscape," 6. Meisar al-Shamri, "*Yastahdif 'Azl al-Doula al-Islamiyya fi al-'Araq . . . 9 Fasa'il Muqawama 'Araqiya T'alan Ta'sees Maktab al-Tanseeq lil-Muqawama al-Islamiya wa al-Wataniya*" [Aiming to Isolate the Islamic State in Iraq, 9 Iraqi Resistance Groups Announce the Formation of the Office for Coordination of the Islamic and National Resistance] *al-Hayat*, April 13, 2007. Sudarsan Raghavan, "Sunni Factions Split with Al-Qaeda Group," *Washinton Post*, April 14, 2007.
8. Austin Long, "The Anbar Awakening," *Survival* 50, no. 2 (April 2008): 78–79. Alissa J. Ruben and Damien Cave, "In a Force for Iraqi Calm, Seeds of Conflict," *New York Times*, December 23, 2007.
9. Jaloud al-'Amari, "*Abu Reisha lil-Hayat: al-Tantheem Yahtadhar*" [Abu Reisha for al-Hayat: The Organization is Dying] *Al-Hayat*, March 19, 2007. The Sheikh is named as Abdul Sattar Bzaigh al-Rishawi in Edward Wong, "An Iraqi Tribal Chief Opposes the Jihadists, and Prays," *New York Times*, March 3, 2007. Chris Kraul, "Iraqi Tribal Chiefs Forming an Anti-Insurgent Party," *Los Angeles Times*, April 20, 2007. Joshua Partlow, Ann Scott Tyson, and Robin Wright, "Bomb Kills a Key Sunni Ally of U.S.," *Washington Post*, September 14, 2007. Fadhil Ali, "Sunni Rivalries in al-Anbar Province Threaten Iraq's Security," *Jamestown Foundation Terrorism Focus* 5, no. 10

(March 11, 2008) http://www.jamestown.org/terrorism/news/article.php?articleid=2374024 (accessed June 1, 2008).

10. Alissa J. Ruben and Stephen Farrell, "Awakening Councils by Region," *New York Times*, December 22, 2007. Michael R. Gordon, "The Former-Insurgent Counterinsurgency," *New York Times*, September 2, 2007. Walter Pincus, "U.S. Unsure About the Future of Iraq's Sons," *Washington Post*, March 31, 2008. Sudarsan Raghavan and Amit R. Paley, "Sunni Forces Losing Patience with U.S.," *Washington Post*, February 28, 2008. Sudarsan Raghavan, "New Leaders of Sunnis Make Gains in Influence," *Washington Post*, January 8, 2008. Erica Goode, "U.S. Military Will Transfer Control of Sunni Citizen Patrols to Iraqi Government," *New York Times*, September 1, 2008.

11. 'Ali Hatem Al 'Ali Suleiman quoted in Patrice Claude, "Ali Hatem Al-Ali Suleiman, un 'prince' contre Al-Qaida," *Le Monde*, February 15, 2008, http://www.lemonde.fr/proche-orient/article/2008/02/14/ali-hatem-al-ali-suleiman-un-prince-contre-al-qaida_1011339_3218.html#ens_id=981585 (accessed February 25, 2008). Ali, "Sunni Rivalries in al-Anbar Province."

12. Ali, "Sunni Rivalries in al-Anbar Province."

13. "Can a Lull Be Turned into a Real Peace?" *Economist*, December 15, 2007, 30. Farook Ahmed, "The Iraqi Accord Front's Return to Government," *Institute for the Study of War Backgrounder* 32 (May 2008) http://www.understandingwar.org/files/reports/The%20Iraqi%20Accord%20Front's%20Return%20to%20Government.pdf (accessed June 1, 2008). Ali, "Sunni Rivalries in al-Anbar Province."

14. Alissa J. Ruben and Damien Cave, "In a Force for Iraqi Calm, Seeds of Conflict." Mahmoud Abed Shabeeb quoted therein. Raghavan and Paley, "Sunni Forces Losing Patience with U.S." Sumedha Senanayake, "Iraq: Future of Awakening Councils in Limbo," *Radio Free Europe/Radio Liberty*, April 4, 2008, http://www.rferl.org/featuresarticle/2008/04/2e6ab5d3-b416-4366-93d0-283267676b60.html (accessed May 8, 2008). Goode, "U.S. Military Will Transfer Control of Sunni Citizen Patrols."

15. Silvia Spring and Larry Kaplow, "Sacrificed to the Surge," *Newsweek*, (April 5, 2008) http://www.newsweek.com/id/130602 (accessed June 6, 2008). ICG, "The New Sunni Landscape," 14-16.

16. Gordon, "The Former-Insurgent Counterinsurgency."

17. John F. Burns, "Precarious Cease-Fire in Amara Holds," *New York Times* (October 22, 2006). "*Al-Fadhila Yansahib min al-I'tlaf al-'Iraqi Khalasan min al-Ta'ifea,* Fadhila Withdraws from the Iraqi Alliance Forgoing Sectarianism," *Azzaman*, (March 7, 2007), http://www.azzaman.com/index.asp?fname=2007\03\03-07\999.htm&storytitle (accessed May 8, 2008).

Ned Parker and Christian Berthelsen, "Shiite Clash in Basra Injures 9," *Los Angeles Times*, March 23, 2007.

18. ICG, "Iraq's Civil War, the Sadrists, and the Surge," (February 7, 2008) http://www.crisisgroup.org/home/index.cfm?id=5286 (accessed May 24, 2008), 11-13. Quotes from Sudarsan Raghavan, "On a Baghdad Street, Palpable Despair," *Washington Post*, March 31, 2008.
19. Ewen MacAskill, "Mahdi Army Calls Six-Month Truce After Fighting Leaves 50 Dead," *The Guardian*, August 30, 2007. ICG, "Iraq's Civil War, the Sadrists, and the Surge," 16. Sudarsan Raghavan, "Shiite Contest Sharpens in Iraq," *Washington Post*, December 27, 2007.
20. ICG, "Iraq's Civil War," 17, Sadrist quoted on 18.
21. Solomon Moore, "In Mosul, New Test of Rebuilt Iraqi Army," *New York Times*, March 20, 2008. Michael R. Gordon, "Iraqi Unit Flees Post, Despite American's Pleas," *New York Times*, April 16, 2008. Sholnn Freeman, "Iraqi, U.S. Forces Put Pressure on Mahdi Army," *Washington Post*, April 19, 2008. Stephen Farrell and James Glanz, "More than 1,000 in Iraq's Forces Quit Basra Fight," *New York Times*, April 4, 2008. Michael R. Gordon and Alissa J. Rubin, "Operation in Sadr City Is an Iraqi Success, So Far," *New York Times*, May 21, 2008. Michael R. Gordon, Eric Schmitt, and Stephen Farrell, "U.S. Cites Planning Gaps in Iraqi Assault on Basra," *New York Times*, April 3, 2008.
22. Farrell and Glanz, "More than 1,000 in Iraq's Forces Quit Basra Fight." James Glanz and Steven Lee Myers, "Assault by Iraq on Shiite Forces Stalls in Basra," *New York Times*, March 28, 2008. Sudarsan Raghavan and Ernesto Londono, "Basra Assault Exposed U.S., Iraqi Limits," *Washington Post*, April 4, 2008. Sudarsan Raghavan, "Between Iraqi Shiites, a Deepening Animosity," *Washington Post*, April 7, 2008. Erica Goode and James Glanz, "Cleric Suspends Battle in Basra by Shiite Militia," *New York Times*, March 31, 2008. Salih quoted in James Glanz and Stephen Farrell, "Crackdown on Militias Raises Stability Concerns," *New York Times*, April 8, 2008. Ned Parker, "U.S. Is Entangled in Shiite Rivalry," *Los Angeles Times*, March 30, 2008.
23. Stephen Farrell and Ammar Karim, "Drive in Basra by Iraqi Army Makes Gains," *New York Times*, May 12, 2008. Sudarsan Raghavan, "Basra's Wary Rebirth," *Washington Post*, June 1, 2008. Sudarsan Raghavan, "Calm in Basra May Offer a Guide for Iraqi Security," *Washington Post*, June 21, 2008.
24. Alissa J. Rubin, "Sadrists and Iraqi Government Reach Truce Deal," *New York Times*, May 11, 2008. Amit R. Paley, "U.S. Enlists and Arms Patrols in

Sadr City," *Washington Post*, June 12, 2008. Ernesto Londono and Aahad Ali, "Iraq, U.S. Launch Crackdown," *Washington Post*, June 20, 2008.

25. Marc Santora, "Iraqi Government Officials Reach Out to Shiite Leaders," *New York Times*, December 24, 2006.
26. Reidar Visser, "The Law on the Powers of the Governorates Is Passed after Significant Cross-Sectarian Cooperation in the Iraqi Parliament," February 14, 2008, http://www.historiae.org/provinces.asp (accessed June 3, 2008).
27. Fadhila Party Statement, March 7, 2007, http://www.alfadhela.org/news/news_details.asp?field=general_news&id=356 (accessed June 28, 2008).
28. Reidar Visser, "Debating Devolution in Iraq," *Middle East Report Online*, March 10, 2008, http://www.merip.org/mero/mero031008.html (accessed June 5, 2008).
29. "*'Itifaq Beyn 145 Na'ib 'ala Rufdh Mutalib al-Akrad al-Muta'aliqa bi Kirkuk wa Mukhususat al-Beshmerka*" [Agreement of 145 MPs on Refusal of Kurdish Demands Regarding Kirkuk and the Peshmerga] *Radio Sawa*, January 12, 2008, http://www.radiosawa.com/arabic_news.aspx?id=1484394 (accessed June 5, 2008). Visser, "Debating Devolution in Iraq." Ned Parker, "Kirkuk Referendum Needed, Kurdish Leader Says," *Los Angeles Times*, January 15, 2008.
30. Jason Gluck, "From Gridlock to Compromise: How Three Laws Could Begin to Transform Iraqi Politics," USIP Briefing, March 2008, http://www.usip.org/pubs/usipeace_briefings/2008/0319_iraqi_politics.html (accessed June 4, 2008). Alissa J. Rubin, "Ending Impasse, Iraq Parliament Backs Measures," *New York Times*, February 14, 2008.
31. Gluck, "From Gridlock to Compromise." Political scientists have observed that repeated positive interactions and an improved understanding of the counterpart tend to increase the probability of cooperation and lessen the chances of defection. For one discussion, see Robert Axelrod and Robert O. Keohane, "Achieving Cooperation Under Anarchy: Strategies and Institutions," *World Politics* 38, no. 1 (October 1985): 226–54.
32. Richard A. Oppel Jr. and Steven Lee Myers, "Iraq Eases Curb for Former Officials of Hussein's Party," *New York Times*, January 13, 2008.
33. Article 5 (4), *Qanoon al-Muhafithat al-Gheyr Munathima bi-'Iqleem* [Law of the Provinces Not Organized in a Region] February 17, 2008, http://www.parliament.iq/Iraqi_Council_of_Representatives.php?name=articles_ajsdyawqwqdjasdba46s7a98das6dasda7das4da6sd8as dsawewqeqw465e4qweq4wq6e4qw8eqwe4qw6eqwe4sadkj&file=showdetails&sid=1433 (accessed June 8, 2008).

34. Law of the Provinces, arts. 54(1) and (2). Ahmed Rashid, "Iraq Electoral Commission Urges Speedy Poll Law," *Reuters*, May 23, 2008, http://www.reuters.com/article/middleeastCrisis/idUSL23853644 (accessed on May 25, 2008).
35. Hamid al-Ma ala quoted in Nidal al-Leithi, "*Al-Ahzab al-Diniya fi al- Iraq Tabashir Hamlatiha bi-'Istikhdam Sur al-Muraji a fi al-Da iya al-'Intikhabiya*" [The Religious Parties in Iraq Use Pictures of Religious Authorities in Their Campaign] *Azzaman*, June 4, 2008, http://www.azzaman.com/index.asp?fname=2008\06\06-04\999.htm&storytitle= (accessed June 5, 2008). Jalal al-Din al-Saghir quoted in "*Al-Saghir: Al-'Itilaf Yu'ayid Tutbeeq Nitham al-Qa'ima al-Muftouha fi al-'Intikhabat al-Mahaliya*" [Al-Saghir: The Alliance Supports Implementation of an Open List System in the Local Elections] *Iraq 'Ialan*, June 6, 2008, http://iraqalaan.com/bm/Politics/2524.shtml (accessed June 6, 2008). Gluck, "From Gridlock to Compromise."
36. Nidal al-Leithi, "*Al-Tayar al-Sadri: La Aouda Lil-Tahaluf ma al-Maliki wa Kheyarina al-Ja afari au Alawi*, The Sadr Movement: No Return to the Mailiki Coalition and Our Choice Is Jafari or Alawi," *Azzaman*, (June 15, 2008) http://www.azzaman.com/index.asp?fname=2008\06\06-15\999.htm&storytitle= (accessed June 16, 2008). Ned Parker and Raheem Salman, "Iraq: Sadr's Party Says It Won't Stand in Elections," *Los Angeles Times*, June 15, 2008. Amit R. Paley, "Aides to Sadr Refine Stance on Elections," *Washington Post*, June 16, 2008.
37. Nidal al-Leithi, "*Inqisam fi Hizb al-Da wa B ad Qarar al-Maliki Fasal al-Jafari*" [Split in the Da wa Party after Mailiki's Decision to Separate Jafari] *Azzaman*, June 6, 2008, http://www.azzaman.com/index.asp?fname=2008\06\06-06\999.htm&storytitle (accessed June 8, 2008). Jawdat Kadhim, "*Al-'Inqisam fi Hizb al-Da wa Yakhraj 'Ila al- Alan wa 'Ansar al-Jafari Yaseytarun Ala Makatib fi al-Najaf* [Split in Da wa Party Beomes Public and Supporters of Jafari Control Offices in Najaf] *al-Hayat*, June 7, 2008, http://www.daralhayat.com/arab_news/levant_ncws/06-2008/Item-20080606-5f4c17f3-c0a8-10ed-0165-7e5a4f5041b0/story.html (accessed June 8, 2008).
38. Kadhim, "Split in Da wa Party Becomes Public." See Reidar Visser, "Iraq's Regional Elections: Another D-Day Coming," June 16, 2008, http://www.historiae.org/provincial.asp (accessed June 18, 2008).
39. Iraqi Rebel weblog post, December 20, 2005, http://iraqirebel.blogspot.com/2005/12/can-somebody-tell-me-what-hell-just_20.html (accessed May 26, 2008). See also ICG,"The Next Iraqi War? Sectarianism and Civil Conflict," February 27, 2006, 29, notes 202, 203, http://www.crisis

group.org/library/documents/middle_east___north_africa/iraq_iran_gulf/52_the_next_iraqi_war_sectarianism_and_civil_conflict.pdf (accessed June 28, 2008).
40. Sabrina Tavernese, "Violence Leaves Young Iraqis Doubting Clerics," *New York Times*, March 4, 2008.
41. Hamid al-Ma ala quoted in al-Leithi, "Religious Parties in Iraq." Nidal al-Leithi, "Split in the Da wa Party after Mailiki's Decision."
42. ICG, "The Next Iraqi War?" 31.
43. Alissa J. Rubin, "Kurds Object to Iraqi Provincial Election Law," *New York Times*, July 23, 2008. Sudarsan Raghavan and Ernesto Londono, "Iraqis Take Flawed Step on Electoral Legislation," *Washington Post*, July 23, 2008.
44. "*Qanoon Intikhab Majalis al-Mahafithat wa al-Aqdhiya wa al-Nuwahi*" [Provincial, Judicial, and Local Elections Law] July 22, 2008, http://www.parliament.iq/Iraqi_Council_of_Representatives.php?name=articles_ajsdyawqwqdjasdba46s7a98das6dasda7das4da6sd8asdsawewqeqw465e4qweq4wq6e4qw8eqwe4qw6eqwe4sadkj&file=showdetails&sid=1910 (accessed July 23, 2008). "Lebanonization": Reidar Visser, "Iraqi Parliament Passes Provincial Elections Law," July 22, 2008, http://www.historiae.org/muhafazat (accessed July 23, 2008).
45. Provincial Elections Law.
46. Campell Robertson and Richard A. Oppel Jr., "Iraqis Fail to Agree on Provincial Election Law," *New York Times*, August 6, 2008.
47. Text of the amended article: Iraqi Parliament Press Release, "*Majlis al-Nuab Yusawwat ala al-Mowad al-Manqoudha li-Qanoon Intikhabat al-Muhafathat*" [Council of Representatives Votes on Abrogated Articles of the Provincial Elections Law] September 24, 2008, http://www.parliament.iq/Iraqi_Council_of_Representatives.php?name=articles_ajsdyawqwqdjasdba46s7a98das6dasda7das4da6sd8asdsawewqeqw465e4qweq4wq6e4qw8eqwe4qw6eqwe4sadkj&file=showdetails&sid=2006 (accessed September 24, 2008). Amr Suleiman, "*Iqrar Qanoon Intikhabat Majalis al-Muhafathat fi al- Araq Istithna' Kirkuk min al-Intikhabat fi Intithar Qanoon Khas 2009*" [Decision on Provincial Election Law in Iraq Excludes Kirkuk from Elections Pending a Special Law in 2009] *Azzaman*, September 24, 2008, http://www.azzaman.com/index.asp?fname=2008\09\09-24\998.htm&storytitle (accessed September 24, 2008). Erica Goode, "Iraq Passes Provincial Elections Law," *New York Times*, September 25, 2008.
48. Independent High Commission on Elections, Press Release, (February 2, 2009),

http://www.ihec.iq/Arabic/press_releases.aspx (accessed February 2, 2009). International Foundation for Election Systems Center for Transitional and Post-Conflict Governance, "Council of Representatives Election Composite Report," (February 20, 2006), http://www.ifes.org/publicationd2046fde59cd1eeda 675eb611bfd4d9e/Council%20of%20Representatives%20Election% 20Composite-Update20FebV3.doc (accessed May 6, 2008).

49. See for example, Stephen Farrell, "Election Reaction: Iraqi Journalists' Experiences," *New York Times Baghdad Bureau Blog*, (February 1, 2009), http://baghdadbureau.blogs.nytimes.com/2009/02/01/election-reaction-iraqi-journalists-experiences/ (accessed February 1, 2009).

50. ICG, *Iraq's Provincial Elections*, 22.

51. Electoral statistics throughout are drawn from official Independent High Electoral Commission documents published on February 22, 2009 and accessed on February 28, 2009. "*Isma' al-Fa'izeen bi al-Maqa d al- Am*, Names of the Winners of Open Seats," http://www.ihec.iq/content/file/Election_results/Assembly_seats.pdf; "*Isma' al-Keyanat al-Fa'iza wa Gher Fa'iza*, Names of Winning and Non-Winning Entities," http://www.ihec.iq/content/file/Election_results/Others_nominees_%2520winners_final_2009_ar.pdf. Preliminary electoral statistics were published on February 5, 2009, accessed February 28, 2009, and are available at the root http://www.ihec.iq/content/file/Election_results/ followed by the following suffixes for the corresponding provincial results: alanbar.pdf, deyala.pdf, salah_aldeen.pdf, karbla.pdf, naynua.pdf, alnajef.pdf, albasra.pdf, maysan.pdf, bable.pdf, baghdad.pdf, theykar.pdf, kadsya.pdf, almuthna.pdf, wast.pdf.

52. "State of Law Coalition," (January 28, 2009), http://www.niqash.org/content.php?contentTypeID=75&id=2362&lang=0 (accessed February 8, 2009). ICG, *Iraq's Provincial Elections*, 18.

53. "The Shaheed al-Mihrab List," (January 28, 2009) http://www.niqash.org/content.php?contentTypeID=75&id=2363&lang=0, (accessed February 8, 2009). ICG, *Iraq's Provincial Elections*, 15-16.

54. Riyadh Muhammad, "Election Results: Who's Up, Who's Down," *New York Times Baghdad Bureau Blog*, (February 6, 2009), http://baghdadbureau.blogs.nytimes.com/2009/02/06/election-results-whos-up-whos-down/ (accessed February 9, 2009).

55. Salah al-Obeidi quoted in ICG, *Iraq's Provincial Elections*, 20.

56. "*Lejna Aml Mushtarika Beyn al-Maliki wa al-Teyar al-Sadri*, Joint Working Group Between al-Maliki and the Sadrists," *al-Sabah*, (February 18, 2009), http://www.alsabaah.com/paper.php?source=akbar&mlf=interpage&sid=77659 (accessed March 1, 2009).

57. ICG, *Iraq's Provincial Elections*, 21.
58. ICG, *Iraq's Provincial Elections*, 21. Nirmeen Hamid, "Anbar's Islamic Party and Tribes Vie for Power," (December 12, 2008), http://www.niqash.org/content.php?contentTypeID=75&id=2358&lang=0 (accessed February 8, 2009).
59. Aifan al-Issawi quoted in Steven Lee Myers and Sam Dagher, "Election Results Spur Threats and Infighting in Iraq," *International Herald Tribune*, (February 10, 2009).
60. "The Hadabaa National List," (January 28, 2009), http://www.niqash.org/content.php?contentTypeID=75&id=2368&lang=0 (accessed February 13, 2009).
61. Karim Abd al-Zayir, "*Al-Kashf fi Baghdad An Tazwir 250 Fa'izan fi al-Intikhabat al-Mahalia li-Shihadatihim al-Dirasiya*, Revelation in Baghdad Regarding the Forged Diplomas of 250 Winners in the Local Elections," *Azzaman*, (February 16, 2009), http://www.azzaman.com/index.asp?fname=2009\02\02-16\999.htm&storytitle= (accessed February 17, 2009).
62. Nir Rosen, "The Battle for Sunni Hearts and Minds," *Asia Times*, April 16, 2004, http://www.atimes.com/atimes/Middle_East/FD16Ak02.html (accessed May 23, 2008). Cockburn, *Muqtada*, 149.
63. "The Enigma of Muqtada al-Sadr," *Economist*, February 16, 2008, 53.
64. "*Sadour Kitab Jadeed bi- Anwan 'al-Sahafa al- Araqiya fi Thul al-Ihtilal al-Amreeki*'" [Publication of a New Book Entitled 'The Iraqi Press in the Shadow of the American Occupation'] *Aswat al-Iraq*, May 22, 2008, http://www.aswataliraq.info/look/article.tpl?IdLanguage=17&IdPublication=4&NrArticle=80070&NrIssue=1&NrSection=10 (accessed June 1, 2008).
65. Sabrina Tavernise, "Amid Iraqi Chaos, Schools Fill Up After Long Decline," *New York Times*, (June 26, 2006).
66. Imad Harb, "Higher Education and the Future of Iraq," *USIP Special Report* 195, January 2008, 2–4, http://www.usip.org/pubs/specialreports/sr195.pdf (accessed May 25, 2008).
67. Harb, "Higher Education and the Future of Iraq," 2, 5. John Agresto quoted in Zvika Krieger, "Iraq's Universities Near Collapse," *Chronicle of Higher Education*, 53, no. 37 (May 18, 2007): A35. See also Catharsis weblog, May 22, 2008, http://ejectiraqikkk.blogspot.com/2008/05/universities-in-iraq.html (accessed May 25, 2008).
68. "Karbala Libraries and Bookshops, Mirrors that Reflect Old City Culture," *Aswat al-Iraq*, February 28, 2008, http://www.aswataliraq.info/look/english/article.tpl?IdLanguage=1&IdPublication=4&NrArticle=65991&NrIssue=2&NrSection=4&ALStart=40 (accessed May 23, 2008). "*25 Film*

Sinema'i Tetanawal al-Haya al- Araqiya fi Mahrajan Kuliya al-Finoon bi-Baghdad" [25 Films Dealing with Iraqi Life in College of the Arts' Festival in Baghdad] *Aswat al-Iraq*, May 19, 2008, http://www.aswataliraq.info/look/article.tpl?IdLanguage=17&IdPublication=4&NrArticle=79706&NrIssue=1&NrSection=10 (accessed May 23, 2008).

Chapter Ten: Whither Transition?

1. Robert S. McNamara, *In Retrospect: The Tragedy and Lessons of Vietnam* (New York: Vintage Books, 1995), 330.
2. John Paul Vann quoted in Neil Sheehan, *A Bright and Shining Lie: John Paul Vann and America in Vietnam* (New York: Random House, 1988), 542.
3. General David Petraeus quoted in Thom Shanker and Steven Lee Myers, "Iraq's Military Seen as Lagging," *New York Times*, April 10, 2008.
4. Hanna Batatu, *The Old Social Classes and the Revolutionary Movements of Iraq: A Study of Iraq's Old Landed and Commercial Classes and of Its Communists, Ba'athists, and Free Officers* (Princeton, NJ: Princeton University Press, 1978), 1133–34.
5. Amendment 2997 to House Resolution 1585, "National Defense Authorization Act for Fiscal Year 2008," *Congressional Record*, September 26, 2007, S12093, http://frwebgate.access.gpo.gov/cgibin/getpage.cgi?dbname=2007_record&page=S12093&position=all (accessed June 25, 2008). Reidar Visser, "The U.S. Senate Votes to Partition Iraq. Softly," September 27, 2007, http://www.historiae.org/biden.asp (accessed June 25, 2008).
6. "Iraqi Parties Attack Senate Plan," *CNN*, September 30, 2007, http://edition.cnn.com/2007/WORLD/meast/09/30/iraq.main.ap/index.html (accessed June 25, 2008).
7. For a similar assessment, see "Divisa in Partes Tres," *Economist*, October 14, 2006, 50–52.
8. Carter Johnson, "Partitioning to Peace: Sovereignty, Demography, and Ethnic Civil Wars," *International Security* 32, no. 4 (Spring 2008): 140–70.
9. Samuel Huntington, *Political Order in Changing Societies* (New Haven, CT: Yale University Press, 1968), 31–36.
10. For an interesting look at how France was transformed from a balkanized land of tribes small language groups into a modern nation-state, see Graham Robb, *The Discovery of France: A Historical Geography, from the Revolution to the First World War* (New York: W. W. Norton, 2007). For the landmark essay on the development of nation-states in Europe, see Charles Tilly, "War Making and State Making as Organized Crime," in *Bringing the State Back In*, eds. Peter B. Evans, Dietrich Rueschemeyer, and Theda Skocpol (New

York: Cambridge University Press, 1985), 169–91.
11. Damien Cave, "Nonstop Theft and Bribery Stagger Iraq," *New York Times*, December 2, 2007. Transparency International, *Corrpution Perceptions Index*, 2007, http://www.transparency.org/policy_research/surveys_indices/cpi/2007 (accessed June 6, 2008).
12. Sheehan, *A Bright and Shining Lie,* 518–42. John Paul Vann quoted therein, 542.
13. Anthony Shadid, *Night Draws Near: Iraq's People in the Shadow of America's War* (New York: Henry Holt and Company, 2005), 343.

Index

1920 Revolt, 19, 86, 136, 242
1920 Revolution Brigades, 123, 152, 216

Abbasid Caliphate, 22
Abu Reisha, Abdul Satar, 216–217, 233
Abu Reisha, Ahmad, 216, 233
Afghanistan, 49, 63, 103, 130, 142, 144–145, 147, 215
Aflaq, Michel, 21
Agresto, John, 11, 237
Al Bu Nasir, 43
Ali, 85
Allawi, Ali, 22, 23, 40, 102, 174, 175, 180
Allawi, Ayad, 81, 176–177, 193, 226
Allawi, Hassan, 238
Alliance of Intellectuals and Tribes for Development List, 233
Alliance of the Awakening of Iraq and Iraqi Independents List, 233
Ansar al-Islam, 144–146
Ansar al-Sunna, 145, 149, 153
Arab Afghans, 144–145
Arab nationalism, 16, 22, 28, 99
Arif, Abd al-Salam, 21
arms/weapons, 4, 35, 41, 44, 49, 60-61, 79, 83, 91, 106, 107, 116–118, 123, 125, 129, 147, 151, 153–155, 157, 204, 207
Ashura, 86
Askariyya Shrine/Mosque, bombing of, 84, 149, 199, 205–206
Association of Muslim Scholars, 139, 159, 201
Awakening Movement, 6, 123, 214–219, 222, 229, 233, 235, 242, 244

Aziz, Tariq, 27, 99

Ba'ath Party and de-Ba'athification, 29–30, 118–120, 171, 197, 203
Ba'ath Party and Shi'a membership, 21
Baath Party Revolutionary Command Council, 26, 28, 121
Ba'ath Party, x, 1, 7, 16, 20–52, 54, 56, 59, 60, 64, 72, 73, 76, 87, 93, 99, 101, 105, 114, 118–125, 128, 136–138, 147, 148, 150, 153, 162, 168, 171, 179, 193, 197, 200, 203, 224, 238, 242, 243
Badr Corps/Badr Organization, 42, 89, 100–101, 106, 207–208, 219, 220, 232
Baghdad International Airport, 12, 32
Baghdad, 1, 2, 4–6, 11–15, 17, 22, 24–26, 28, 32, 39–41, 47, 51, 53, 62, 64, 66, 68, 69, 71–74, 77, 79, 81, 82, 89, 90, 109, 117, 119–123, 133, 135, 138, 144, 145, 147, 152, 165, 175, 182, 184, 185, 191, 199, 201, 204–206, 212, 213, 217–219, 227, 230–232, 234, 237, 247, 248, 254
Bakr, Ahmed Hassan, 26–27, 31, 64
Barzani, Masaoud, 115, 193
Barzani, Mustafa, 184
Basra, 17, 35, 82, 88, 106, 185, 195, 196, 219, 220, 221, 222, 226, 228, 231, 247
Basra, 17, 35, 82, 88, 106, 185, 195, 196, 219–222, 226, 228, 231, 245, 247
Batatu, Hanna, 19, 21, 40, 242, 248, 249
Bauer, Eric, 72–73
Biden Amendment (see also partition), 247
Bin Laden, Osama, 145–146, 215

blood money, 46, 126–127
Bremer, L. Paul III, 61, 63, 67, 71, 78, 116–117, 119, 120, 151, 164, 169, 172, 173, 175, 176, 178, 179, 207
British mandatory rule, 17, 19–20, 43, 44, 86

Casey, George, 11, 106, 121
Central Command (CENTCOM), 61, 64, 124
Central Criminal Court, 68–69
Central Intelligence Agency (CIA), 142, 144
Chalabi, Ahmed, 63, 81, 194
civic responsibility, 11, 75–76, 265–266
civil society, 20, 46, 95, 202, 235–239, 246
civil war, 2, 3, 5, 8, 17, 46, 84, 98, 104, 113, 114, 125, 142, 143, 147, 149, 159, 165, 167, 168, 170, 183, 188, 194, 198, 199, 200, 202, 204, 206, 210, 211, 238, 246–248
class divisions, 90–91
clerics, 21, 40, 45, 46, 187, 227
clerics, Shi'a, 4, 13, 19, 63, 81–85, 87–88, 93, 96–104, 162, 173, 181, 207, 244, 246
clerics, Sunni, 47, 48, 85, 139–140, 147, 154, 159, 236
client-patron networks, *See* patronage
Coalition Provisional Authority, 11, 15, 30, 37, 38, 51, 58–61, 64–67, 69, 71, 72, 76, 78, 79, 88, 94, 118–120, 163, 169–174, 176, 178–180, 202, 221
constitution, 1925, 19, 43
constitution, 5, 8, 9, 21, 51, 57, 104, 105, 114, 157, 158, 163, 164, 168–170, 172–177, 181–193, 197, 198, 218, 225
constitution, drafting of, 181–190
constitution, October 2005 referendum, 158, 169, 173, 175, 178, 189, 190
constitutional amendments, 164, 189, 190, 197–198
corruption, x, 3, 31, 38, 46, 59, 73, 76, 77, 122, 138, 140, 155, 163, 169, 202, 235
coup 1963, 21
coup 1968, 25, 26, 43
crime, 3, 38–41, 43–46, 57, 66, 68, 77, 138, 154, 155, 200, 209
crime, black market, 38, 39, 72, 75, 117, 118, 204
crime, organized, 3, 38–39, 110, 154, 156, 200
crime, smuggling, 38, 39, 49, 75, 122, 136, 144, 153, 154, 215
crisis of governance, 3, 4, 7, 16, 50, 51, 53–80, 87, 89, 106, 112, 113, 166, 243

Crocker, Ryan, 212
culture, xi, 9, 11, 24, 34, 55, 56, 69, 76, 77, 127–130, 132, 133, 137, 242, 255

Da'wa Party, 89, 99–101, 103, 181, 192, 194, 195, 221–223, 226, 231
Defense Intelligence Agency (DIA), 120, 142
democracy, ix–xi, 8, 9, 11, 16, 23, 48, 51, 60, 78, 79, 83, 84, 86, 88, 102, 105, 167, 174, 178, 187, 188, 211, 224–225, 235, 239, 241–243, 245–246, 248, 251, 253–254
democratic transition, x, xi, 8, 32, 57, 66, 67, 166–168, 241–244
demographics, 34, 158–159
Department of Defense/Pentagon, 63, 68, 73, 79
Department of Justice, 67
detainees, 12, 41–42, 68, 106, 115, 129, 131, 144, 148, 149, 156, 217, 223
Dhari, Harith, 136, 159, 200, 236
Dhari, Suleiman, 136
Di Rita, Larry, 58
Diamond, Larry, 88, 178, 181, 194
Diamond, Michael, 77
dictatorship, 2, 6, 8, 9, 48, 50, 51, 99, 202, 248
Dujail, 11
Dulaimi tribal confederation, 42, 44, 215–217
Dulaimi, Adnan, 158
Dulaimi, Naziha, 20
Duri, Izzat Ibrahim, 121

economy, ix, x, 7, 9, 17–19, 24, 34, 35–40, 43, 47, 50, 53, 57, 60–62, 72–76, 78, 82, 84, 93, 110, 113, 118, 122, 125, 156, 168, 170, 172, 196, 198, 203, 212, 237, 238, 246, 248, 251, 254
education, 19, 20, 29, 30, 33, 34, 47, 51, 63, 70, 90, 103, 144, 207, 237–238
Egypt, 16, 41, 48, 71, 143, 205
elections, December 2005, 95, 96, 169, 176, 190–194
elections, January 2005, 95, 169, 176–182, 192, 195, 225, 227, 230
elections, January 2009, 227, 230–235
elections, June 1954, 20
electricity, 15, 54, 60, 72–75, 81, 117, 118, 133
Erdmann, Drew, 59, 69–70
Etherington, Mark, 51, 76, 94
Euphrates River, 86, 122, 135
exile politicians, 82, 84
explosively formed penetrators, 106

Facilities Protective Service, 207–208
Fadhila Party, 96, 192, 195–196, 219, 222, 227, 233
Fallujah, 45, 109, 117, 118, 122, 123, 126, 127, 135, 136, 137, 140, 141, 144, 146, 147, 148, 153, 233, 236
Fallujah, battle of, 109–110, 118, 137, 146, 147, 236
fatwa, 93, 103, 171, 208
fedayeen, 41–42, 115, 116–119, 148, 154
federalism, 182–188, 195–197
Feith, Douglas, 63, 65
Feldman, Noah, 202
Fer'aoun, Munqath, 12
Firdaus Square, 1–2, 11, 13–14, 15, 255
foreign fighters, x, 39–42, 49–50, 55, 113, 115, 116, 118, 124, 133, 136, 137, 139, 142–147, 149, 152, 155, 206, 214, 215
former regime elements, 27–33, 115, 116–122, 123–124, 136, 147–148, 151–153, 214, 216
Franks, Tommy, 61, 62
Front de Libération Nationale, 28, 151

Garner, Jay, 61, 64, 116
Governing Council, 99, 121, 172–175, 176, 180
Green Zone, 15, 205
guardianship of the jurist–consult, 102

Hadad, Muneer, 12
Ha'iri, Kadhim, 93, 96
Hakim, Abd al–Aziz, 12, 172,185, 192, 195, 196, 208,
Hakim, Mohammed Baqir, 81, 91, 97, 98–99, 100, 101, 231
Hakim, Mohammed Baqir, murder of, 98–99, 231
Hamas, 42, 141, 144, 152
Hashimi, Tariq, 193, 217
Hawza al-Ilmiyya, 97, 103
Hayis, Hamid Farhan, 217
Hilla, 27
Hizb Allah, 42, 106, 141, 192
Horowitz, Donald, 196–197, 202–203, 208
Huntington, Samuel, 169–170, 249–250, 161
Hussein, Saddam and July 1979 purge, 26–27
Hussein, Saddam and perception of threat, 56, 117
Hussein, Saddam and re-Islamization, 47
Hussein, Saddam and tribes, 43–45
Hussein, Saddam execution of, 11–14, 159, 161–162
Hussein, Saddam rise to power, 25–27
Hussein, Saddam statue of, 1, 2, 11, 13, 14, 51, 53, 255
Hussein, Uday, 39, 99

Ibn Khaldun, 24
identity and conflict, 167–170
identity and politics, 162, 180, 202–203
improvised explosive device (IED), 68, 106
informants, 27, 30, 33, 112, 128
infrastructure, 2, 9, 10, 14–15, 35–36, 50, 56–57, 60, 61, 66, 72–78, 119, 120, 151, 237, 251
in-group solidarity (asabiya), 23–24
insurgency and handlers/facilitators, 143, 148, 151, 152
insurgency and networks, 112, 114–116, 124, 141, 144, 150–153
insurgency and recruitment, 50, 124, 137, 140–143, 146, 149, 152, 155, 156
insurgency, 2, 5–8, 18, 28, 32, 33, 39, 41, 42, 45, 46, 53, 55, 58, 66–71, 73–75, 77–80, 84, 98, 105, 107, 109–159, 161, 165, 169, 171, 185, 199, 200, 201, 208, 209, 212–219, 220, 233, 235, 244, 245, 246, 255
insurgency, funding of, 152–156
Integrity and Construction List, 232
International Committee of the Red Cross, 69, 142
Iran, 3, 12, 17, 21, 22, 35, 36, 37, 83, 84, 88, 91, 93, 97, 100, 101, 102, 103, 106, 107, 117, 122, 125, 145–147, 159, 165, 182, 183, 185, 187, 191, 194, 199, 212, 227
Iraq, Kingdom of, 20
Iraqi Accord Front, 191, 193, 217
Iraqi Awakening Party, 216
Iraqi Communist Party, 28, 194
Iraqi Islamic Party, 189, 193, 209, 217, 230, 233, 234
Iraqi Leadership Council, 170–172
Iraqi military disbanding of, 32, 63–66, 119–120
Iraqi military, 31–33, 63–66, 120, 125, 149, 220–222
Iraqi National List, 191,193
Iraqi National Project Gathering, 233
Iraqi nationalism/identity, 15, 16, 17, 19, 20, 21, 22, 35, 50, 133, 138, 149, 152, 162–163, 193, 200, 201–203

318　Index

Iraqi Nationality Law of 1924, 21
Iraqi Petroleum Company, 26
Iraqi police, 45, 66–68, 79–80
Islam and tribes, 90
Islam, 46–50, 138–150
Islam, political use of, 47–49, 180
Islam, radicalization, 47, 83, 94
Islamic Revolutionary Guard Corps, 101, 106
Islamic State of Iraq/Islamic Republic, 146–148, 214–215
Islamic Supreme Council of Iraq, 89, 101, 105, 219–232, 245–247
Islamism, 47–50, 82, 90–91
Istikhbarat, 12

Jaafari, Ibrahim, 99–100, 179, 194, 226–227, 233
Jazeera, 71
jihad, 39, 41, 47–50, 113, 133, 138, 139, 142, 144, 145, 146, 147, 149, 214, 241
Jordan, 33, 39, 41, 46, 49, 50, 63, 67, 69, 98, 109, 121, 135, 136, 142, 144, 145, 152, 153, 205
Jordanian Embassy, attack on, 69, 142, 145
Juburi, Meshan, 77
justice system/courts, 67–69

Karbala, 86, 195, 219
Karbala, Battle of, 85–86
Kerik, Bernie, 67
KGB, 28
Khalayla, Ahmad Fadhil Nazzal, *See* Zarqawi, Abu Musab
Kho'i, Abd al-Majid murder of, 93, 96-97
Kho'i, Abd al-Majid, 81, 93, 96–97
Khomeini, Ruholla, 88, 100–102
Kilcullen, David, 215
King Faisal of Iraq, 19, 86
Kirkuk, 5, 9, 36, 169, 183–185, 197, 223, 228, 229, 230, 235, 247, 248
Krulak, Victor, 252
Kurdish Democratic Party, 193
Kurdistan Alliance, 191–193
Kurdistan, 8, 145, 146, 181, 191, 192, 193, 201, 223,
Kurds and autonomy/independence, 171–172, 183–184, 191, 193
Kurds, 5, 6, 8, 12, 16, 17, 19, 20, 21, 23, 36, 37, 64, 66, 86, 102, 114, 115, 118, 144, 145, 146, 157, 158, 159, 161, 163, 166, 168, 169, 171, 172, 174, 175, 176, 178, 180, 181, 182, 183, 184, 185, 187, 188, 189, 191, 192, 193, 196, 197, 199, 200, 201, 204, 207, 221, 222, 223, 227, 228, 229, 230, 231, 234, 242, 245, 247

language, 54–55, 130
League of Nations, 19
Liberals' Independent Trend, 232
looting, 40, 45, 54, 59, 60, 61, 64, 72, 74, 75, 89, 92, 117, 237

Mahdi Army, 42, 89, 94, 95, 106, 140, 158, 207, 208 209, 213, 218, 219, 220, 221, 224, 232
Makiya, Kanan, 1, 199
Maliki, Nouri, 12, 194, 195, 208, 211, 221, 222, 226, 231, 232
Mansour, 204
Mansur, Abu Ja'afar, 6
Marine Corps, U.S., xiii, 2, 41, 65, 73, 109, 127, 128, 137, 147, 164–165, 212, 216, 244, 252–254
Martino, Michael, xiii
Martyr of the Mihrab and Independent Force List, 231–232
martyrdom, 86, 91, 98, 139–141, 143, 147, 148
mass graves, 27
Mattis, James, 65, 212
McKiernan, David, 53, 63, 65
McPherson, Peter, 60
media/press, 70–71, 236–237
Medina al-Salam, 6
Mello, Sergio Vieria de, 69
middle class, 40, 82, 205, 209, 219, 233, 244
militia, 2, 4, 7, 26, 40, 41, 42, 44, 47, 50, 57, 61, 78, 79, 80, 82, 88, 89, 91, 92, 94, 95, 105, 106, 107, 114, 127, 130, 147, 163, 184, 196, 200, 201, 203, 204, 206–209, 212, 218, 219, 220, 221, 226, 235–238, 246
modernization, 248–251
Morocco, 144
mosque, 1–3, 32, 46–49, 58, 59, 70, 84, 91, 92, 96, 98, 109, 117, 137, 140–142, 144, 147, 148, 149, 151, 153, 159, 164, 201, 204, 207, 220, 227, 231, 232, 238
mosques and insurgency, 140–142, 207
Mosul, 17, 157, 193, 220, 234, 247
Mukhabarat, 115–117, 151–152
Mutlak, Saleh, 158, 193, 233

Najaf, 82, 89, 90, 96, 97, 98, 103, 162, 173, 175, 195, 219, 227, 231, 232, 236
Nasr, Vali, xiii, 202
National Assembly, 77, 84, 95, 104–105, 158, 169, 174, 176, 177, 179, 183, 187, 189, 191, 193, 194, 229, 235, 238
National Hudaba' List, 233–234
National Reform Current, 233
National Security Council, 65, 164, 174
nation-building, 9–10, 219, 248–249
netwar, 150
Nineveh Brotherly List, 234
November 15th Agreement, 78–79, 174, 176

occupation, 55
Office for Reconstruction and Humanitarian Assistance, 61, 64, 116–117
Office for Special Plans, 63
oil, 9, 14, 25–26, 34, 36, 37, 39, 56, 60, 61, 74–75, 77, 82, 84, 88, 106, 120, 153–156, 167–169, 174, 183–186, 188, 195–196, 212, 219, 242
Oliver, David, 38, 76
Ottoman Empire, 7, 17, 19, 21, 86, 111, 158, 247

Pace, Peter, 164
Pachachi, Adnan, 193
Pakistan, 103, 142, 145, 212, 248
pan-Arabism, 16, 20, 21, 22, 28, 121, 137, 138, 162, 163
partition, 8, 23, 167, 175, 247–248
Patriotic Union of Kurdistan, 193
Petraeus, David, 1, 211–212, 242
political process, 5, 7, 8, 16, 51, 58, 80, 88, 95, 100, 102, 114, 157–159, 161–198, 202, 203, 211, 217, 222–234, 244
primary identity, 18, 202–203
prison and religion, 148–149
propaganda, x, 23, 33–34, 71, 113, 142
Provincial Election Law, 228–229
Provincial Powers Act, 224–226
public good/common good, x, 10, 59, 76, 110, 201
public information campaign, 66, 71
public sector, 29, 37

Qaeda, 48–49, 59, 101, 112, 114, 124, 133, 146–147, 155, 199, 206, 209, 210, 213–220
Qaim, 39, 41

Qusaybah, 39

Ramadi, xiii, 109, 135, 233
reconciliation, 5–6, 8, 33, 50–51, 84, 167, 169, 170, 187, 208, 211, 218, 222, 224, 238, 239, 245
reconstruction, 7, 46, 56, 60–63, 65, 66, 71–72, 74, 76, 78, 94, 114–116, 123, 212, 216, 224, 253
refugee/displaced person, 6, 152, 205–206
rent seekers, 40, 122
Republican Guard, 36–37, 41, 65, 90, 148, 152
Republican Palace, 1, 14–15, 32, 81
revolution 1958, 20
Revolution City (Medina al-Thawra), 81
Rice, Condoleezza, 62, 65, 79
Rubai'e, Mowwafaq, 12, 48, 175
rule of law, 10, 76, 68–69, 126, 251
Rutbah, 39

Saddam City, 1, 72, 81, 91
Sadr City, 70, 72, 81–82
Sadr, Mohamed Sadiq, 13, 81, 90–91, 96
Sadr, Mohammed Baqir, 13, 101, 162
Sadr, Mohammed Sadiq political activism of, 90
Sadr, Mohammed Sadiq, assasination of, 13, 81, 90
Sadr, Muqtada involvement in murder of Abd al-Majid Kho'i, 96–97
Sadr, Muqtada, 4, 6, 12–13, 59, 81, 83–84, 88, 89–97, 99, 102, 103, 105, 106, 137, 162, 171, 192, 195, 200, 210, 212, 213, 219, 220, 221, 226, 232
Sadrists, 89, 94, 95–97, 105, 106, 181, 192, 196, 197, 207, 209, 219, 220, 221, 222–227, 229, 232, 236, 244, 247, 246
Sahwa, *See* Awakening Movement
Salafi, 49, 142, 145–148, 150, 199, 215
Salah al-Din Province, 17, 26, 185, 189, 191
Sanchez, Ricardo, 64
sanctions, x, 3, 36–37, 39, 40, 49, 90, 122, 125–126, 136, 154
Saudi Arabia, 30, 36–37, 49, 86, 116, 135–136, 143–144, 149, 151, 153–154, 206
sect and marriage, 203–204
sect/sectarian, x, xi, 2–9, 16–28, 37, 46–48, 50–51, 59–60, 78, 84–85, 86, 89, 94, 98, 101, 102, 104, 105, 106, 112–115, 119, 130, 138, 142, 149, 158, 162, 163, 165–

182, 184, 187, 188, 190, 191, 193, 194, 196, 197, 198, 199–210, 211, 213, 214, 219, 220–225, 228, 231, 235, 236–239, 243–246, 249, 252, 254
security services, 26–33, 43, 54, 65–67, 120, 121, 136, 197
Shadid, Anthony, 92, 99, 138, 147, 254
Shahristani, Hussein, 104, 231
Shammar, 44
sheikh, 4, 42, 43, 44, 45, 46, 96, 97, 110, 133, 136, 140, 164, 165, 183, 193, 213, 214, 216, 217, 218, 219, 244
sheikh, Taiwan, 44
Shi'a and majoritarian politics, 88, 102, 103, 105, 114, 192, 196–197
Shi'a House, 173, 180–181
Shi'a politics, 23, 82, 88
Shi'a super-region, 183, 185, 195, 222–223
Shi'a uprising, 1991, 36, 60, 87
Shi'a, history of, 85–86
Sinjar, 144
Sistani, Ayatollah Ali and the political process, 104, 171, 175, 177–178, 192
Sistani, Ayatollah Ali, 3, 4, 12, 83–84, 87, 88, 89, 95, 96, 97, 99, 102–105, 115, 157, 169, 171, 173, 175, 177–178, 181, 192, 200, 222, 227, 229, 244, 246
Slocombe, Walter, 64–65
society, ix, 2, 7, 15, 16, 23, 24, 27, 33, 34, 35, 37, 38, 39, 40, 42, 43, 45, 50, 57, 59, 77, 82, 99, 115, 126, 136, 140, 155, 158, 163, 170, 177, 202, 203, 214, 215, 235, 236, 238, 243, 244, 249, 250
Sons of Iraq, *See* Awakening Movement
Special Republican Guard, 32, 44, 149
state collapse, 8, 243, 248
State of Law Alliance, 231, 232
sub-state powers, 17, 50, 58, 61, 62, 63, 70, 78, 79, 94, 155, 177, 182, 183
Sudan, 41, 100, 143, 144
suicide bomber/suicide mission, *See* martyrdom
Suleiman, Ali Hatem Al Ali, 217
Sunni boycott of political process, 114, 157, 171, 177, 181, 191, 225
Supreme Council for the Islamic Revolution in Iraq (SCIRI), *See* Islamic Supreme Council in Iraq (ISCI)
surge, 6, 212–214
Syria, 17, 41, 46, 75, 77, 103, 109, 121, 124, 135, 136, 143, 144, 145, 146, 152, 153, 164, 205, 212

takfiri, 196, 208
Talabani, Jalal, 115, 193
Tigris River, 1, 6, 14, 15, 181, 209
Tikrit, 22, 26, 31, 41, 126, 135
Transitional Administrative Law, 115,169, 174–178, 187–189
Tribal and Criminal Disputes Regulation, 43
tribal identity, 42–43
tribe, 42–46, 82, 110–112, 117
Turkey, 8, 17, 36, 37, 75

U.S. policy and estimates of quick victory, 58, 60–64, 124, 125
unemployment, 9, 36, 37, 38, 61, 89, 111, 119, 122, 133, 147, 152, 156, 182, 203, 218
United Iraqi Alliance, 180–181, 190, 191–192, 193, 194, 195, 196, 219, 222, 225, 226, 227
United Nations, 69, 136, 142, 188, 202–203, 205
United Nations, attack on headquarters, 69–70, 145
urbanization, 25, 43, 82
urban-rural split, 24

Vann, John Paul, 53, 241, 252
Vietnam, 252–255

War, 1991 Gulf, 4, 36, 37, 39, 60, 72, 87, 101, 117, 183, 255
War, Iran-Iraq, 22, 35, 100
Wardi, 23–24, 238
Wasit, 51, 76, 93, 231, 232
weapons of mass destruction, ix, 37, 56, 62, 183
Wolfowitz, Paul, 75
Women, 20, 21, 47, 129, 147, 192, 218, 225–226
World War I, 17, 35, 43, 86, 161

xenophobia, 23, 34–35

Yaqoubi, Muhammad, 96

Zarqawi, Abu Musab, 98, 124, 139, 144–147, 149, 150, 153, 199

About the Author

Peter Munson, a native of Ohio, is a major in the United States Marine Corps with more than eleven years of service. He is a KC-130J aircraft commander and Middle East/North Africa Foreign Area Officer. Since 2001, he has deployed on several operational and combat tours in Afghanistan, the Middle East, the Horn of Africa, and West Africa. He is a distinguished graduate of the Defense Language Institute and the Naval Postgraduate School, where he earned a MA in national security affairs with a concentration on the Middle East and North Africa. Proficient in Arabic, he lived in Muscat, Oman, for a year and traveled the Middle East extensively. In all, he has visited over thirty countries in North America, Europe, Asia, and Africa. His articles have been published in the *Marine Corps Gazette* and the security studies journal *Strategic Insights*. He currently resides in San Diego, California, with his wife, Wendi, and his children, Riley and Lauren.